ECOFEMINIST NATURES

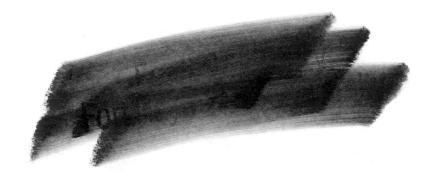

ECOFEMINIST NATURES

RACE, GENDER, FEMINIST THEORY, AND POLITICAL ACTION

Noël Sturgeon

Routledge
New York and London

Published in 1997 by
Routledge
29 West 35th Street
New York, NY 10001

Published in Great Britain by
Routledge
11 New Fetter Lane
London EC4P 4EE

Library of Congress Cataloging-in-Publication Data

Sturgeon, Noël, 1956–
Ecofeminist natures: race, gender, feminist theory, and political action /
Noël Sturgeon
p.   cm.
Includes bibliographic references and index.
ISBN 0-415-91249-0 — ISBN 0-415-91250-4 (pbk.)
1. Ecofeminism. I. Title.
HQ1233.S78   1997
305.42'01 — dc20   96-41479
                                                                          CIP

For Hart and T.V.

Contents

Acknowledgments

At the end of a long project that has taken many more years than I could have imagined to complete, it's hard to thank everyone that has contributed. I'd like to start by thanking all of the activists with whom I have been engaged in the antimilitarist, feminist, and ecofeminist movements. Without a chance to work, sing, do civil disobedience, argue, laugh, and cry with them, this project would never have been conceived, let alone completed. I have been sustained throughout by the promise of such actions, and I hope this book adds something to these and other future activist projects.

Some of the ideas and arguments found in this book were based on my dissertation and were generated from within the intellectual and political community I encountered while attending the History of Consciousness Board of Studies at the University of California, Santa Cruz. For making my graduate experience there so stimulating and rewarding, I thank Don Beggs, Elizabeth Bird, Caren Kaplan, Gregory Calvert, Rennie Cantine Crystal (Chris Hables Gray), Jim Clifford, Giovanna Di Chiro, Barbara Epstein, Ilene Rose Feinman, Ruth Frankenberg, Marge Frantz, Debbie Gordon, Donna Haraway, Jackrabbit (Steven Mentor), Katie King, Hilary Klein, Lisa Lowe, Lata Mani, Helene Moglen, Alvina Quintana, T.V. Reed, Zoë Soufoulis, Chela Sandoval, Jack Schaar, Barry Schwartz, Andrew Walzer, and Hayden White.

As this project has evolved, portions of it have been presented at conferences and read in different stages by generous and critical readers. I thank the audiences at numerous conferences for their comments, and I am deeply appreciative of various readings of my work at various stages by Elizabeth Bird, Elizabeth Carlassare, Greta Gaard, Julie Graham, Donna Haraway, Chaia Heller, Deborah Haynes, Val Jenness, Susan Kilgore, Hilary Klein, Katie King, Ynestra King, T.V. Reed, Virginia Scharff, Frances Jones Sneed, Zoë

Soufoulis, Andrew Stewart, Jude Todd, Anna Tsing, Karen Warren, and Linda Zerrelli.

Two University of California Regent's Fellowships and one University of California Research Fellowship allowed me to lay the groundwork for important parts of this work. Grants I received from the University of California Institute for Global Conflict and Cooperation supported two years of participant-observation in the antimilitarist direct-action movement, most reflected in chapter 2. A Washington State University Research grant supported participant-observation in the ecofeminist movement and interviews conducted during 1993–1994. A Rockefeller Fellowship brought me to the Center for the Critical Analysis of Contemporary Culture at Rutgers University for a year of exciting, challenging, and incredibly productive work. I thank Joan Burbick, Donna Haraway, and Karen Warren for supporting my application to CCACC. For that important experience, I would like to thank John McClure, Bruce Robbins, George Levine, Link Larsen, and all the members of the 1994–95 Colloquium, entitled "Environments in the Public Sphere," especially my fellow "Fellas," Julie Graham, Michael Moon, and Maaría Seppanen. Neil Smith, Cindi Katz, Dorothy Hodgson, and Richard Schroeder were supportive friends, stimulating conversationalists, and knowledgeable resources. I especially thank Neil and Cindy for letting me house-sit when I most needed a space to work (especially since it allowed me to raid their home library!).

Much of my thinking about ecofeminism in transnational politics was formulated during my participation in Joan Scott's feminist theory seminar at the Institute for Advanced Study, Princeton University, January to May 1995, and in the "Transitions, Environments, Translations: The Meaning of Feminism in Contemporary Politics" conference, at the Institute for Research on Women, Rutgers University and the Institute for Advanced Study, Princeton University, New Jersey, April 1995. I thank Joan and Cora Kaplan for making my participation in these events possible. Of my colleagues in the seminar and conference (all of whom were important influences in one way or another), I'd like to single out Anna Tsing and Yaakov Garb for special thanks. They were particularly helpful and influential for me, and I owe them a large debt for shared materials, engaging debates, and insightful critiques. Bina Agarwal was a challenging and gracious interlocutor. Rosi Braidotti was also an inspiration, and her expressions of solidarity with what she saw as my "deconstructive ecofeminist" project meant a great deal to me.

The faculty, students, and staff at the Women's Studies Program at Washington State University have been central to the writing of this book. I thank Sue Armitage, Chris Bergum, Linda Siebert, Patti Gora, Marian Sciachitano, Nancy Keifer, Gail Stearns, Meera Manvi, Judy Meuth, Kendal Broad, Bonnie Frederick, Jennifer Giovi, Wendy Mason, and Reis Pearson for all their help and support. Linda Siebert deserves special thanks for all her hard work in helping this book become a possibility. Ednie Garrison, in her work and in her person, usefully reminded me of the way in which generational tensions affect the history of feminism. Petra Uhrig, Kari Norgaard and Katrine Barber provided excellent research assistance and enlightening conversation about ecofeminism. My tenure review committee (Sue Armitage, Joan Burbick, Bonnie Frederick, Linda Stone, and Gerald Young) was a source of firm support and needed advice. To Jo Hockenhull, my director, I owe endless thanks for her guidance, her example, her protection, and her willingness to fight for me.

I thank Cecelia Cancellaro for having such firm initial faith in this project. At Routledge, Claudia Guerelick, Jeanne Park, Karen Deaver, Laura Ann Robb, Lynette Silva, and Melissa Rosari were patient and supportive. I also thank my anonymous copyeditor for a thorough and immensely helpful editing job; any obscurity remaining in my text is a result of my refusing her excellent advice. Karen Weathermon deserves immense gratitude for putting together such an excellent index under sometimes trying circumstances. I thank the Association for Philosophy Newsletter on Feminism and Philosophy; International Books; Indiana University Press; and Women's Environment and Development Organization for permission to use previously published material.

As I wrote this book, five people played the part of "spirit guides," always in my imagination chiding me and inspiring me even when I disagreed with them. In person, these people also gave me resources; talked to me about movements, feminism, and writing; and in general represented outstanding examples of feminist intellectuals who were also committed to activism. Thanks to Greta Gaard, Marge Frantz, Katie King, Ynestra King, and Donna Haraway for making me believe that my work was worthwhile.

Friends and family have given me the strength, material help, and support that was most essential to writing this book. Paul Williams was dependable and understanding, always ready to pitch in when I needed him. Bob Greene cheerfully ordered books for me, both ones I requested and ones he knew I needed. Don Beggs and Kathy Chetkovich were humorful and dependable friends. I thank Hilary Klein and Larry Dublin for their generosity in always putting me up when I came to New York, and Hilary for applying her considerable intelligence to work on my problems and for her constant love. Deborah Haynes has been my bedrock in Pullman, always there to listen to doubts and spur me on. I owe thanks as well to Val Jenness for feeding me all that junk food, making me laugh, and distracting me when I needed it. Elka Malkis, my lifefriend, always brought me down to earth and made me believe in unconditional love. Ilene Rose Feinman, H.B., challenged me, cheered me on, and was my long-distance writing pal. Joyce Steinlauf helped me to remember what's important in life. My family: Marion Sturgeon, Robin Sturgeon, Tandy Sturgeon, Timothy Sturgeon, Andros Sturgeon, Judith Biewener, Kim Charnovsky, John Wolff, Ben Wolff, Jordan Wolff, Jessamyn Wolff, Alice Reed, Linda Ware,

Michelle Ware, Jim Pizon, Kristel Pizon, Phoenix Pizon, Gabriel Pizon, Petere and Inés Sturgeon, John and Rose McGahan, and Jayne Williams were loving, and patient as I missed visits, and helpful in ways too numerous to detail. To Marion most of all, thanks for your help, your humor, all those phone calls, and your steadfast love. Special thanks to Marion for the cover art and to Timothy for lending it to me. I deeply regret that three members of my family, Grandma Sal (Theresa McGahan), Theodore Sturgeon, and Thomas C. Reed, are not here to see my first book.

My love and gratitude for T.V. Reed are practically inexpressible, but I'll try. As my affinite, colleague, comrade, coparent, partner, and critic, he has contributed immensely to this book. Thanks are due particularly for his assistance with bibliographic materials and his diplomatic editing, useful even when I disagreed with it. I am deeply appreciative of his willingness to put aside his own work while he took over the role of domestic mainstay for such an extended period of time. I thank him for sharing his intellectual excitements with me, especially his love of both practice and theory, and the task of bringing them together. Finally, thanks, T.V., for bringing the most joy into my life (bundled and otherwise). To Hart, my son, thanks for waiting while Mama got her work done. You were a big help, and I love you very much. I hope that if you ever read this book, you will think it was worth all the trouble.

INTRODUCTION

Surrogate Others is an affinity group that has already reached a certain legendary status; perhaps we should start with its story. Affinity groups are small groups organized to create independent actions as part of larger, collective direct actions; they were used in many U.S. antinuclear actions in the middle 1970s to late 1980s. Surrogate Others was a Santa Cruz-based affinity group that came together to join the thousands of people protesting continued U.S. nuclear testing through the Mothers and Others Day Action at the Nevada Nuclear Test Site in May 1987. I was a graduate student at the University of California, writing my dissertation on the antimilitarist direct action movement and acting as the California state contact for the national organizing effort for the Mothers and Others Day Action. It was a women's action, though men were allowed to participate, and many women I knew, from the university and from the town, wanted to attend.

The group that became the Surrogate Others was like many other groups in this action in that the women were of a wide age range, different class locations and sexual orientations, and different political agendas. Yet, as in other affinity groups, we had some commonalities that drew us together. For us, it was a particular, mostly unarticulated and loose agreement of what feminist antimilitarism was or should be. The majority of us knew each other from our work at the university, though two of us were not formally connected to UC. We were all feminists. We were all suspicious of arguments for feminist antimilitarist action that portrayed women as natural pacifists. We were all deeply concerned about militarism. We were not all white, initially. Besides myself, we were Elizabeth Bird, graduate student, author of a now well-known article about the social construction of nature;[1] Barbara Epstein, faculty member, socialist feminist historian, and activist in the New Left, working on a book about nonviolent direct action; Donna Haraway, faculty member, feminist theorist, and historian of science; Marge Frantz, faculty member, feminist historian, and long-time radical activist, starting with the labor movement in the '30s as a Communist Party member and from there active in the civil rights, student, feminist, and gay and lesbian movements; Eleanor Engstrom, Marge's life partner, a community member, and Quaker pacifist activist; Wendy Brown, a feminist political theorist visiting Santa Cruz on a research fellowship; Deena Hurwitz, community member, Jewish feminist, organizer for Middle East issues for the Resource Center for Nonviolence and editor of a book on Israeli and Palestinian peace activism;[2] Sharon Helsel, graduate student working at the time on a study of a group of pagan nuclear physicists; and Rosa Maria Villafañe–Sisolak, undergraduate student, poet, and feminist. When Rosa dropped out early in the planning, we were all white.

We spent several meetings going over the logistics of getting from Santa Cruz to the Nevada Test Site, the legal ramifications of committing civil disobedience there, why we were going and what we wanted to do as an affinity group. We decided on creating a worm, for reasons that can be best explained in Donna Haraway's unique way: "in solidarity with the creatures forced to tunnel in the same ground with the bomb, they (members of the Surrogate Others) enacted a cyborgian emergence from the constructed body of a large, non-heterosexual desert worm."[3]

Sharon and Elizabeth sewed the worm together, as I remember, and it was a colorful, flamboyant object that was quite unwieldy to lift and carry but opened into a graceful, undulating mass of color. We brought the worm to the site, and at the appropriate moment, we hefted it over the fence, and then, stretching it out on the desert floor well inside the fence, each of us moved through it, enacting a symbolic moment of sexuality, birth, digestion—a completely constructed transgressive moment of political passion, mixed together with a lot of nervous laughter. We were arrested by the desert-camouflaged law enforcement personnel as we came out of the other end of our worm. We were taken to a holding site in a bus, led through the formalities of arrest and release, put back in the bus, returned to the gate and disgorged by the side of the road.

Near the fence where we had gone over the first time, we gathered together. I remember I argued for going over again, but by that time the heat had done its work, and as we talked it over, others pointed out to me that we all lay prone on the desert ground, barely able to move from heat and exhaustion. Even so, we were happy. Finally some of us agreed to go over the fence again long enough to plant some seeds someone had brought, and this we did one by one without attracting attention and getting arrested. Our part of the action was over. But I often return to that moment, lying on the ground, surrounded by all of those wonderful women—a chance grouping that in hindsight seems somewhat fantastic—and thinking: What is this really about? Why did these amazing women get together to do this rather bizarre action? What kind of movement is this?

In some ways, the Surrogate Others were the beginnings of this particular book, this particular effort to understand the movement that, in my personal history, was tied historically to a movement now often called U.S. ecofeminism. Were the Surrogate Others "Cyborgs for Earthly Survival!," as the political button invented by Elizabeth Bird proclaimed? Or were we part of an ecofeminist movement that, as Cecile Jackson put it, is "ethnocentric, essentialist, blind to class, ethnicity and other differentiating cleavages, ahistorical and neglects the material sphere"?[4]

How can we understand social movements in ways that capture their contradictions, their deployment of theory-in-practice, their contextual sensibility? What are the processes of creating political subjectivities in oppositional movements? What are the costs and what are the advantages of deploying collective identities? What are the ways in which actions like the Mothers and Others Day Action function as an ecofeminist imaginary? What are the boundaries of ecofeminism and who polices them? What are the consequences of that policing for ecofeminism as a feminist theory and as an activist movement?

ECOFEMINISM: MOVEMENTS, HISTORIES, THEORIES

This book explores ecofeminism from a number of different angles (historical, ethnographic, sociological, political, theoretical), as an oppositional political discourse and set of practices imbedded in particular historical, material, and political contexts. The ecofeminist movement I examine, and in some ways construct throughout this book, is a fractured, contested, discontinuous entity that constitutes itself as a social movement with a particular place in a tradition of U.S. radical social movements. I explore, characterize, and investigate ecofeminism as a social movement in ways not entirely historical or sociological, attending to ecofeminism's development as a movement within particular political locations, tracing both its effect on those locations and its construction by particular structural factors in our late twentieth-century moment. My version of a history of the origins and development of ecofeminism is thus not so much a coherent narrative of the even, dependable growth of an independent political position as it is several snapshots of scattered, uneven, and in many ways disconnected beginnings, retreats, dormancies, and proliferations imbedded within several different political locations. This is a genealogy rather than a history, and as a result I am not following one unitary subject (ecofeminism) through different historical moments. Instead, I am articulating relationships, legacies, simultaneous births of related entities, discontinuities, renamings, mutations, and throwbacks.[5] Readers will notice, and may sometimes be frustrated by, the related necessity to keep the definition of ecofeminism flexible and somewhat amorphous; my refusal to essentialize essentialism as one thing is purposeful and methodological.

In recognizing rather than obscuring its discontinuities and contradictions, I want to analyze this social movement in relation to shifting political and socioeconomic contexts embedded in transnational relations of power. This effort is, in part, a case study, a methodological exercise in understanding social movements as contestants in hegemonic power relations, through which change is produced by numerous kinds of "action," including that of the deployment of symbolic resources, shifts in identity construction, and the production of both popular and scholarly knowledge—as well as direct action, civil disobedience, strikes, boycotts, demonstrations, lobbying, and other more traditionally recognized forms of political action. I stress not only the synchronic aspect of ecofeminist deployment of concepts (of nature, women, and race) within certain specific moments of socioeconomic restructuring, but also the diachronic aspect of ecofeminism as a form of theorizing about social movements themselves in contestation with other social movements that precede and operate alongside it (such as radical environmentalisms, civil rights movements, anticolonialist movements, and women's movements) and in relation to other interposing elements such as academic feminism and policy-oriented discourses on women and development.

Though I will not stress this aspect in the chapters that follow, my characterization of ecofeminism as a social movement in the ways I have elaborated above is meant as an intervention into the arena of social movement theory as well as feminist theory. For instance, in contradistinction to the U.S. social movement theory paradigm called "resource mobilization,"[6] I do not produce, through my narration of ecofeminism's beginnings and development, a story of self-interested individuals mobilizing resources to influence policy formation, though there are individuals in my story (some self-interested, some not), the use of resources (but theoretical, rhetorical, and historical resources as well as material and political ones), and occasions of institutional, governmental, and elite policy change in reaction to political organizing by ecofeminists. Neither—in contradistinction to the predominantly European school of new social movement theory[7]—do I see ecofeminism primarily in terms of the creation of new forms of collective identity. Rather than understand ecofeminism as a new form of identity politics, I want to challenge the notion that movements produce fixed identities. Instead, I want to demonstrate the shifting and strategic qualities of various forms of identity politics.

Pointing to the usefulness and limits of political identities that can mobilize collective action (such as claims that all women are naturally environmentalists) or be used as tools for political analysis (such as claims about different ways of knowing generated from women's, or workers', or people of color's standpoints), I want to also show the way these identities appear and disappear, shift and change, when viewed in movement contexts. I have argued elsewhere that social movements are involved in theorizing both the relations of power existing at particular conjunctures as well as previous traditions of opposition through their forms of action and their particular political rhetorics, and I call this aspect of movements *direct theory*.[8] Though I will not elaborate this concept in what follows, it is this understanding of a social movement that informs my exploration of ecofeminism and my methods of characterizing it as a movement.

The questions that guide me are numerous and intersecting. Why does ecofeminism arise during the late 1980s? What are the processes of exclusion and inclusion that ecofeminism is subject to within movement and academic contexts? What kind of resonance does ecofeminism have with popular notions and global constructions of environmentalism and feminism? To what uses are ecofeminist theory put in various movement, policy, and academic arenas? Finally, and most fundamentally, is ecofeminism a political location productive of radical action, a political position worth struggling over? With these questions as backdrop, my focus in this book is on assessing problems involved with essentialist constructs of nature as well as gender and race identity within ecofeminism as a social movement. By "essentialist constructs," I mean notions of nature, women, or certain racially defined groups, that use biological, universalist, ahistorical, or homogenizing ways of definition; I call these constructs "ecofeminist natures." Ecofeminism seems to be situated in a history of feminism in such a way that it is required to solve the mystery of how to create an anti-essentialist coalition politics while deploying a strategic politics of identity. Why is this so? And can ecofeminism solve this mystery?[9]

Through the lens of ecofeminism it is possible to explore a range of contemporary feminist and radical politics and to offer some tentative answers to these questions. I want to use the problem of essentialism, one that troubles virtually all contemporary movements, as a focus for such an inquiry. This focus on the problems with essentialism calls for some explanation, and I will spend most of the rest of this introduction in this task.

CRITICS OF ESSENTIALISM AND ESSENTIALIST CRITICS

In working on this book, I have often felt torn between contradictory expectations. One is the frequent reluctance of those actively engaged in building ecofeminist theories and movements to openly critique "ecofeminism," to involve themselves explicitly in debates between ecofeminists of various persuasions. The other, opposite phenomenon is the disparagement and rejection of ecofeminism by many of my colleagues in the field of feminist theory because of its purported "essentialism" in arguing that women and nature can be connected in positive ways. Such is the prejudice against ecofeminists among many academic feminist theorists that I was once advised, by a prominent feminist theorist who wanted to support my work, to remove the word "ecofeminism" from the title of one of my papers about the movement, because she said she would never choose to read an article about ecofeminism. I have been advised by a feminist mentor to leave my editorship of *The Ecofeminist Newsletter* off my vita when applying for grants and jobs. I have been challenged by a commentator during a conference presentation to call my position "feminist" rather than "ecofeminist." These are personal anecdotes, but many more examples of feminist distancing from ecofeminism will be reported in these pages. These factors—a reluctance for ecofeminists to criticize each other and a hostility to ecofeminism in certain feminist circles—are, of course, related, for external hostility to ecofeminism will inhibit internal debate within ecofeminism.

Unwilling to completely concur with either of these tendencies toward complete rejection or unconditional support of ecofeminism, I have struggled to maintain the somewhat precarious position of what, in a number of very different contexts, has been called "the outsider within."[10] I am engaged here in a constructive critique of both ecofeminism and feminist theory. This positioning leads me to pay special attention to particular theoretical problems. Thus, a great deal of this book is engaged in one way or another in the theoretical problem of essentialism, exploring strategic essentialism or strategic anti-essentialism in ecofeminist and feminist conceptions of gender, race, and nature.

ESSENTIALISMS IN PRACTICE

While the political implications of essentialist constructs of women or of race are some of the central problems of contemporary feminist theory, they are not often discussed in the context of a particular social movement practice. Movement contexts suggest certain approaches to theoretical problems that we will not find elsewhere. In general, feminist theory is not used as much as I think it should be to illuminate radical activist movement practice. Doing the reverse, looking to oppositional movement practice to clarify theoretical problems, is also a necessary and underutilized analytical method. Focusing on the relation of theory to practice is a very old problem within political theory indeed, but teasing out the theorizing embedded in various political practices is an overlooked procedure crucial to sustaining activist practice within and outside the academy. Thus, I have tried to understand the reasons why feminist theory has created what might be pictured as an invisible moat between its most sophisticated and complex political critiques and various kinds of social movement practices. Debates around essentialism are at the heart of this problem.

One can even see this division as created between feminist theory and the politics of the *practice* of feminist theory. These terms, "theory" and "practice," are centrally contested and immensely slippery. Certainly, "doing" feminist theory in a university context is a political act, particularly as it is embedded in teaching, promotion, and publishing practices that form, critique, and resist unequal arrangements of power. Yet much of the time, the politics of the production of feminist theory are not articulated within the theory itself.[11] Further, and most crucial to the way I will be using the terms "theory" and "practice" throughout the book, certain strands of academic feminist theory are not sufficiently articulated to feminist activist practice outside, as well as within the interstices, of the university. My efforts here grow out of the desire to sustain a critically constructive theoretical practice that supports and furthers feminist movements rather than simply rejects them for their theoretical insufficiencies.

An analysis of ecofeminism that problematizes the divide between theory and practice is particularly interesting because of the way in which ecofeminism itself both recreates and confounds this dualism. As I will show in this book, U.S. ecofeminism's strongest connection with an activist *mass* movement is its relation to feminist antimilitarism. With the ebbing of that movement in the late 1980s, ecofeminism's role in activism (read for the moment as "out-in-the-streets" political action) can be seen in feminist animal liberation actions, U.S. Green politics, Earth First!, and international development politics; ecofeminist theorists also often claim the large numbers of environmental activists who are women, whether they identify as "ecofeminists" or not, as proof of the ecofeminist argument that environmentalism and feminism are profitably merged. Other than this sometimes problematic relation to activism, U.S. ecofeminism is not, at this writing, an activist mass movement.

But if one thinks of political action as including the production of oppositional knowledges, as theories that have popular resonances, then ecofeminism certainly can be described as activist in this sense.[12] Theories of the connections between sexism and environmental problems are enjoying a widespread application, some of which I will be examining in this book. Ecofeminist texts typically take up large areas in many bookstores, usually next to sections on feminist spirituality or radical environmentalism. Ecofeminist theories are influential in several disciplines with a focus on "applied" scholarship, such as development studies and natural resource sciences. Feminist artists creating environmental art are reading ecofeminist theories. And young women, who frequently are deeply concerned about environmental questions, are often introduced to feminist arguments through exposure to ecofeminist theory.

Can academic feminists afford to dismiss ecofeminism because this popular resonance is gained partly through the deployment of arguments that make essentialist connections between women and nature, sometimes claiming, for instance, that women are "naturally" environmentalists or that the feminization of nature contains resources for empowering women in a sexist society? I see the feminist contests over essentialism (and their operation within the construction of various feminist politics of identity) as creating barriers between academic feminism and feminist activist practices of various kinds, including the political practices of academic feminism. My objection is not to the prevalence of a feminist critique of essentialism; on the contrary, both my academic training and my political persuasions have produced a strong anti-essentialist imperative in my work. Indeed, Virginia Scharff once characterized my work as a "Western feminist postmodernist critique of a Western feminist postmodernist critique." Given my historical location, as a second-generation second-wave feminist located in a postmodernist feminist theoretical moment, I encountered the growing dominance of feminist anti-essentialism in specific, formative ways. In particular, I noticed the ways a reductive anti-essentialism distorts the history of second-wave feminism,[13] and the ways in which, more recently within the academy, a reflexive anti-essentialism too often substitutes for the critique of power that motivated earlier anti-essentialist critiques. Since, as I will examine shortly, a number of feminist theorists have made clear that anti-essentialism itself is dependent upon essentialism and cannot be a pure position, my point is that we need to look more carefully at precisely when and where both essentialism and anti-essentialism are useful, and where and to whom they may prove to be disabling.

ANTI-ESSENTIALISMS IN PRACTICE

Feminism has generated a powerful critique of the way in which sexism was upheld by humanism, that is, Enlightenment ideologies that constructed a generically masculine ideal of what it meant to be truly human. Relying on notions of universal qualities of human nature, Enlightenment thinkers consistently identified characteristics associated with masculinity (rationality, the ownership of a soul, objectivity, membership in the polis, etc.) as features of a universal, ahistorical, and naturally constituted "humanity." Feminist thinkers pointed out the way in which these notions were defined against a similarly ahistorical, biologistic, and universalist characterization of femininity (as emotional, soul-less, irrational, domestic, and embodied). Feminists pointed out that humanism was masculinism, and that the language of the generic masculine-as-human obscured the social and political means of women's oppression in sexist societies by a method of naturalizing women's supposed inferiority to men. As Trinh T. Minh-ha says: "What can such a word as 'human' mean when its collaboration with 'man' and 'men' throughout the history of *man*kind has become obvious?"[14] Feminists, as well as other anti-racist, postcolonial, and poststructuralist theorists, have persistently called into question the move toward dominance contained in any attempt to identify universal, ahistorical, cross-cultural human qualities. They have argued that these discourses collude in making invisible not only those coded as "different" but also the complicity of Enlightenment humanism in justifying various modes of oppressing those Others defined as less-than-human, or not-human. Feminists have been particularly critical of ways in which female biology (pregnancy, menstruation, lactation) is used in sexist ideology to justify women's unequal treatment.

A critique of the idea that social roles and personal identities must be and are built on biologically determined, or ahistorical, or naturalized essences is a crucial tool in the dismantling of ideologies of domination. This motivation, however, must always be kept in view. In other words, *unequal power relations* are the subject of an anti-essentialist critique, not essentialism alone. The use of essentialist arguments to uphold inequalities and perpetuate injustices is a historically situated phenomenon, not an essence in itself. Essentialism is not a sin nor a permanent mark of unexamined prejudice nor an enduring implication in domination. Though it certainly can have the effect of maintaining positions of privilege, it can also have the effect of producing an "oppositional consciousness."[15] Thus, one trajectory of this book is to entertain the idea that essentialist rhetorics in the construction of political collectivities, in circumscribed situations, can be a positive tool of liberation. I believe the important question is what conditions serve to undercut the negative aspects of these universalizing rhetorics. This can only be examined if we are willing to analyze contextually the strategic nature of movement rhetorics, emphasizing the political motivations of both the essentializing rhetorics and our critiques of them. This method is crucial in providing theoretical criteria by which to judge political discourses within radical movements.

To do this, as many feminist theorists have noted, we must move away from reductive notions of essentialism as itself an essence. Below, I'll sketch the ways in which feminist theory has reached this conclusion and posited various solutions. To anticipate this argument for a moment, I want to point to one of the crucial ways to de-essentialize our understanding of essentialisms: to differentiate what kinds of essentialism we are objecting to, and pay attention to the consequences. For example, it is important always to foreground the fact that unmasking the essentialism of the sexist conception of women as more nurturing, more natural, more emotional, more passive, and more exploitable than men is a political critique aimed at producing equal and just relations between men and women. This is the heart of the feminist critique of sexist essentialisms that describe "men" and "women" as masculine and feminine (as biologically determined rather than social categories). Similarly, attacking the essentialisms of feminists who think "all women" are confined to suburban domesticity, or "all women" are more concerned with gaining the right to abortion rather than the right to have children, or "all women" are obliged to negotiate better sexual and domestic relationships with men: these arguments are political critiques aimed at producing equal and just relations between women of different class, race, and sexual locations. It complicates a critique of essentialism considerably if we recognize that different political aims may produce different forms of essentialisms *and* anti-essentialisms. Additional complexities appear if we acknowledge that particular strategic essentialisms may have positive oppositional ends, even while they may limit radical results; or if we posit that politically well-intentioned anti-essentialisms may have destructive consequences for a promising radical social movement.

Keeping the political endpoint in view means producing a critically situated feminist theory that deconstructs any universalist version of the category "women" through attention to historical and cultural specificities of race, class, sexuality, religion, nationality, language, and culture. But there is more and more agreement that such a politically motivated feminist theory must also recognize the need for "contingent foundations"[16] (i.e., moments of toleration for certain universalisms and essentialisms) if it is to remain politically useful, if it is to develop tools for the creation of a more just society. This is the "essential difference," as Teresa de Lauretis points out, between feminist theory and any set of theories that deconstruct for the sake of deconstruction.[17]

It makes sense, then, in the present context of feminist theory, that a reductive anti-essentialist position as well as an essentialist feminism can produce politically problematic effects. This is a proposition I will explore through a sympathetic, yet critical, analysis of certain kinds of "ecofeminist natures" throughout this book. In this book, I distinguish between essentialist notions of women and of racial identities, even while I aim to point out their interaction. For example, while particular notions of women as inherently sympathetic with wilderness preservation may operate to exclude women from some racial or class locations, other notions of "indigenous" women may work to confirm patriarchal assumptions about the nature of women. Since essentialist concepts are often ultimately grounded in notions about what is biologically or naturally determined, I think of some ecofeminist notions of gender and race identity as "ecofeminist natures," even when they are not necessarily biologically deterministic. Thus, one important trajectory of this book is to point out the essentialism of some ecofeminist conceptions of "nature" and their relation to gender and racial essentialisms.

In short, identifying problems with some anti-essentialist arguments does not mean that I don't myself find such a critique useful when called for as a critique of power. At many places in this book, I engage in a critique of various essentialisms within ecofeminism. In particular, I argue that the compounding of essentialist notions of gender with essentialist notions of race is deeply problematic for ecofeminism. However, I move beyond just a critique of ecofeminist essentialism by insisting that the frequency of such symbols and language must be *explained* as well as resisted. Essentialist rhetoric and theorizations within oppositional social movements should be recognized as complex deployments within particular social, political, and historical contexts with ambivalent, contradictory outcomes.

Furthermore, the conditions for destabilization of these essentialisms need to be explored. I find these conditions in particular U.S. social movement practices and organizational structures, rather than simply in improved theoretical approaches; more specifically, I use "direct theory" to counter reductive understandings of "essentialism." I show that certain essentialist moments in ecofeminism, given particular historical conditions, are part of creating a shifting and strategic identification of the relation between "women" and "nature" that has political purposes: it creates unity between very different kinds of women; it justifies a feminist critique of environmentalists; and it solidifies connections among feminism(s), participatory democratic structures, and nonviolent direct action. Drawing my examples from ecofeminist theories, organizations, conferences, gatherings, rituals, and direct actions, I argue that radically democratic movement structures—such as alliances, coalitions, networks, affinity groups, and consensus process decision making—that bring together different kinds of women for the purposes of political action have served to destabilize essentialist ecofeminist formulations, even if those formulations enabled these structures in the first place.

In this book, then, I will suggest that one way to understand solutions to what I see as a political stalemate between tropes of essentialism and anti-essentialism within feminism is to carefully theorize feminist activist practice and to see the theory in that practice. This might seem at first an odd place to look for solutions to the problem of finding collective political strategies in the context of anti-essentialist theoretical frameworks. Feminist activists have been criticized frequently for using essentialist formulations to justify political action: arguing that women's difference from men is an inherent mark of superiority to men, and/or assuming that women are in most important ways defined by the same qualities or experiences. Because I have been both an activist in and a scholar of the feminist antimilitarist direct action movement and now the ecofeminist movement, I have been struck by the way in which these activists have frequently appeared as the quintessentialists against whom feminism must be protected. This rhetorical move replicates previous debates within feminism in which first "lesbian separatists," then the "antipornography movement," stood in as the primary representatives of an essentialist position, sometimes codified as "cultural" or "radical" feminism, for many feminist theorists.[18] However useful the critiques generated from them, these rhetorical moves have been costly to feminism as a social movement. Instead, I wish to point to the way in which ecofeminism has sought to make political connections between various radical movements. A closer look at feminist debates about the role of essentialism and anti-essentialism within feminist theory can provide a context for my treatment of these tensions and clarify the political stakes (my own included) of these debates.

CRITIQUING ESSENTIALISM, DEPLOYING DIFFERENCE, RECONSTRUCTING FOUNDATIONS

Essentialism, or the positing of natural and ahistorical essences to define characteristic qualities or behaviors of individuals as members of groups, has been a central object of feminist critiques, because anti-essentialism is the epistemological method for deconstructing sexist notions of what women are supposed to be, as well as racist, classist, and heterosexist notions of what kind of woman counts as woman. Historically, as I have indicated earlier, these critiques of essentialism have been leveled at masculinist ideas of "woman," but more recently anti-essentialist critiques have been directed also at certain *feminist* conceptions of "women."[19] The earliest critiques of feminist essentialism were leveled at a white, middle-class, heterosexual feminism that dominated the representations of the beginning of the "second wave" of U.S. feminism. Important moments in that process occurred within the history of U.S. second-wave feminist activism from its beginnings, but can be represented here by various landmark publications. These writings were often not simply "publications" but came out of particular feminist political contexts, especially conferences. Some of these were Adrienne Rich's essay "Compulsory Heterosexuality and Lesbian Existence," which challenged the prevailing assumption within feminist theory that heterosexual women were the norm; the essay by Angela Davis, "Racism, Birth Control and Reproductive Rights," which challenged the racism and classism of the feminist reproductive rights movement; Audre Lorde's "The Master's Tools Will Never Dismantle the Master's House"; the publication of *This Bridge Called My Back* and the "Combahee River Collective Statement," which challenged the combined racism, classism, and heterosexism apparent in feminism at the time; the publication of Carol Vance's *Pleasure and Danger*, which challenged the "vanilla" sexuality of the antipornography movement as an essentialism dangerous to the expression of a variety of female sexualities as well as to feminist freedom of speech; and the publication of Chandra Mohanty's "Under Western Eyes: Feminist Scholarship and Colonial Discourses," which characterized prevailing U.S. feminist theory as imbedded in Western colonial ethnocentrism.[20]

These critiques came from feminists who were lesbians, U.S. women of color, and nonWestern. That these feminists were often deeply involved in feminist activism makes more curious the common implication that feminist theory is anti-essentialist while feminist activism is essentialist. But these critiques referenced above have been fairly successful, at least within an academic feminist context, at dislodging a homogenizing feminism that kept white, middle-class feminists as the implicit or explicit model for "women."[21] As bell hooks points out: "This effort at revision is perhaps most evident in the current widespread acknowledgment that sexism, racism, and class exploitation constitute interlocking systems of domination—that sex, race, and class, and not sex alone, determine the nature of any female's identity, status, and circumstance, the degree to which she will or will not be dominated, the extent to which she will have the power to dominate."[22]

The critiques of feminists who were marginalized from the standpoint of white, middle-class, heterosexual feminists were strengthened by the influence of poststructuralist and postmodernist theories on the western academy, especially during the past two decades.[23] Indeed, one could argue that the influence of poststructuralism on feminist theory came from its usefulness for constructing theories which avoided essentialisms and centralized difference as their object of study. Joan Scott succinctly summarizes the innovations in poststructuralism that have been particularly useful for feminist theory, identifying three interrelated and illuminating concepts. The first is the idea that language structures meaning rather than referring to things outside of language, an idea that points us toward the historical, political, and institutional contexts in which meanings are constructed. The second is the realization that these contextual "ways of knowing," or epistemological constructions, are irreducibly implicated in power relations, which are produced within discursive fields. The third is the recognition that the power relations imbedded within meanings are constructed through the deployment of differences that are usually expressed as binary, oppositional, hierarchical, and unequally valued (such as culture/nature; white/black; masculine/feminine, theory/practice). Scott calls the analytical method that these poststructuralist ideas embody "deconstruction," which she defines as the procedure that interrogates the operation of power within contextualized discourses, involving an uncovering of the way in which oppositional differences are not naturally separate entities but also require and produce each other.[24]

In the effort to deconstruct essentialist understandings of differences between women and men—as well as between groups of women—which operate to justify and maintain structural inequalities, it has become commonplace for feminist theorists to decry any sort of essentialism and to center their work not on sexism conceived simply as hierarchical relations between women and men, but on the assumption that there are multiple genders, various notions of femininity differentially articulated by race, class, sexual, and national differences and structured by specific historical contexts. Thus, any statement about women must now be modified by specifying what kind of "woman" is under consideration. Additionally, this kind of theoretical prac-

tice often demands a politics of identity, which asks feminist scholars to identify their own location within various fields of power; whether they are white,
working class, lesbian, Third World, Catholic, and so on.

The poststructuralist feminist practice which questions the construction of
universalizing, stable notions of "woman" has been a useful assistant to feminists of color, lesbian feminists, and postcolonial feminists in their efforts to
undermine the foundations of racism, classism, heterosexism, and ethnocentrism within contemporary feminist scholarship. But this attention to difference within the category "woman" has had it own problems. First, inasmuch
as "difference" operates to modify some assumed "sameness," the process of
producing various identities as indices of particular "experiences" can even
reinscribe the dominance of the unmarked category, the white, the middle
class, the Western, the heterosexual. This is Chandra Mohanty's point when
she objects to the "third world difference" produced by white Western feminist scholars; as they mark the particularities of "third world women," they
reinforce problematic notions of Western women. "Universal images of 'the
third world woman' (the veiled woman, chaste virgin, etc.), images constructed from adding the 'third world difference' to 'sexual difference,' are
predicated upon (and hence obviously bring into sharper focus) assumptions
about Western women as secular, liberated, and having control over their own
lives. . . . If this were a material reality, there would be no need for political
movements in the West."[25] Hence, alongside the effort to specify differences
of race, class, nationality, and sexuality, which may produce different kinds of
genders, there must be a vigilance directed at previously "unmarked" categories that are often presumed to be not raced, classed, etc.: categories such as
white, middle class, Western, heterosexual. Differences within these categories as well as the marked categories must be uncovered and explored.

Second, there has been growing impatience with a notion of difference
that, in its effort to avoid essentialism, becomes itself an essentialist notion.
Historical specificity alone does not solve the problem of essentialist constructs; it only defers the problem to another level. Diana Fuss writes: "To insist that essentialism is already and everywhere reactionary is, for the constructionist, to buy into essentialism in the very act of making the charge; *it is
to act as though essentialism has an essence.*"[26] Fuss argues that deploying a
plurality of identities does not escape the problem of essentialism, except to
multiply it:

> The constructionist strategy of specifying more precisely these sub-categories
> of "woman" does not necessarily preclude essentialism. "French bourgeois
> woman" or "Anglo-American lesbian," while crucially emphasizing in their
> very specificity that "woman" is by no means a monolithic category, nonethe-
> less reinscribe an essentialist logic at the very level of historicism. Historicism
> is not always an effective counter to essentialism if it succeeds only in fragment-

ing the subject into multiple identities, each with its own self-contained, self-referential essence.[27]

Indeed, she claims that the difficulty of eradicating essentialism stems from its necessary relation to the concept of constructionism. "[E]ssentialism underwrites theories of constructionism and . . . constructionism operates as a more sophisticated form of essentialism."[28] This is because, she says, the "strength" of constructionism as a theoretical position is "not built on the grounds of essentialism's demise, rather it works its power by strategically deferring the encounter with essence, displacing it, in this case, onto the concept of sociality."[29]

Like Fuss, Cristina Crosby is concerned about the use of historicism to interrogate differences, because this method does not automatically address the problem of the production of knowledge.

> The problem is that differences are taken to be self-evident, concrete, *there*, present in history and therefore the proper ground of theory. . . . It is impossible to ask how 'differences' is constituted as a concept, so 'differences' become substantive, something in themselves—race, class, gender—as though we knew already what this incommensurate triumvirate means![30]

Instead, Crosby suggests, "knowledge, if it is to avoid the circularity of ideology, must read the processes of differentiation, not look for differences."[31] Joan Scott makes a related argument by challenging the way in which the concept of "experience" is used to mask the processes through which experiences are socially structured or semiotically constructed.[32]

Third, the emphasis on anti-essentialism in contemporary scholarship may have produced a methodological trap of sorts. This is the argument Jane Roland Martin makes in pointing out that the anti-essentialist trend in recent feminist theory has often ruled out consideration of certain "general categories like women, gender, mothering, reproduction, and family" unless those categories are thoroughly historicized. Martin argues, however, that even historical treatment of particular categories "masks difference," and that a more effective treatment of the problem of essentialism is to explore the *use* of these categories, to "decide to use ones that uncover the differences we consider most important and that best fit our practical and theoretical purposes."[33] This may mean, she points out, using many kinds of questions and methods without overprivileging historical ones, since historical methods produce only particular (though useful and necessary) kinds of knowledge. Though it is important to recognize how feminist thinkers who are scholars of color, lesbian, and nonWestern have been included as a result of the widespread recognition of the dangers of essentialism, Martin argues that there may also have been costs. The use of an essentialist label as a form of accusation against feminist scholars, and the operation of a double standard of harsher critiques of feminist rather than nonfeminist essentialists, are phenomena that Martin claims lead to a "chilly research climate . . . [that] is far from welcoming to diverse methodologies and divergent thought."[34] With particular relevance to the subject of ecofeminism, Fuss has pointed out that the constructionist position assumes that the category of the "natural" is always already essentialist. This is an assumption that has led some feminists to be hesitant to investigate nature from a feminist perspective. A great contribution to efforts that address the dangers of essentialism, therefore, would be "questioning the *constructionist* assumption that nature and fixity go together (naturally) just as sociality and change go together (naturally)."[35]

Fourth, as I've suggested above, much of the anti-essentialist theory produced in recent years has created a false and deeply problematic division between feminist theory and feminist activism. Some of this stems from the inaccessibility of most feminist poststructuralist theory; as bell hooks has pointed out, "The separation of grass-roots ways of sharing feminist thinking across kitchen tables from the spheres where much of that thinking is generated, the academy, undermines feminist movement."[36] Some of this division has stemmed from the way in which, as Teresa de Lauretis points out, "this word—essentialism—time and again [is] repeated with its reductive ring, its self-righteous tone of superiority, its contempt for 'them'—those guilty of it."[37] This division between feminist theory and feminist activism has been deeply inscribed by certain retellings of the history of second-wave feminism that construct a "radical" (read "activist") feminism that is defined by its essentialism. The critique of essentialisms of various kinds has been a prominent tool in creating various typologies of feminisms, usually to support an "agonistic narrative structure" in which certain feminist theories (usually socialist feminism or poststructuralist feminism) come out to be the winners in the contest for the most politically useful feminist theory.[38] That these winners in the anti-essentialist competition have also been the feminist theories most embedded in academic contexts is suggestive and will be looked at more carefully in chapter 6.

DIFFERENCES IN ACTION

Thus, in recent years, many feminist theorists have been concerned with the problem of difference, that is, how to conceptualize women's differences from men (differences, from a feminist point of view, imbued with the consequences of women's domination by men) and at the same time acknowledge differences among women (also imbued with unequal power relations). The heart of this concern is a political and practical one: How can feminist coalitions be created without assuming (or requiring) that all women are the same in some essential way, relying on some notion of natural or universal female characteristics? The rationale for women acting together politically against sexism contains its own challenge: if feminists argue that "femininity" and women's material inequality in relation to men are not biologically determined but socially constructed, historically specific, and variously shaped by hierarchies of race, class, culture, and sexual orientation, how can feminism work against the oppression of women as a group based on gender? Linda Alcoff puts it this way: "What can we demand in the name of women if 'women' do not exist and demands in their name simply reinforce the myth that they do?"[39] As the trajectory of feminist theory has problematized a unitary conception of gender, it has become unclear how to create collective political strategies for feminists while at the same time avoiding essentialist formulations of the subject category "women." As Rosi Braidotti argues, it is not necessarily the case that "the postmodernist emphasis on the contingency of identity and the decline of metanarratives undermines political agency and feminism with it. . . . [Rather] Postmodern nomadic feminism argues that you do not have to be settled in a substantive vision of the subject in order to be political, or to make willful choice or critical decisions."[40] Still, the question remains how to accomplish the feminist political project without relying on a notion of a stable collective identity.

Most answers, including Braidotti's, to the political questions brought about by the predominance of anti-essentialist theories within feminism have centered on the notion of *strategically* deploying political identities. That is, if subjects are created within processes that are multiple and ongoing, the task for scholarship is to analyze the operation of these processes in producing subjectivities. As Butler has put it, "the task is to interrogate what the theoretical move that establishes foundations authorizes, and what, precisely, it excludes or forecloses."[41] The task for politics, however, is one of producing collective political subjectivities that can be deployed in oppositional ways, while acknowledging that these subject-positions are not universal, natural, or fixed, but positional,[42] situated,[43] strategic,[44] mobile,[45] nomadic,[46] and/or differential.[47]

The popularity of recent anti-essentialist theories of situational political identities notwithstanding, such theories rarely make explicit the *conditions* for the creation of a politically "oppositional consciousness"[48] that is strategic and positional. There is acknowledgment that an oppositional consciousness is created by those movements that engage in "consciousness-raising." bell hooks, among others, points out that consciousness-raising in small groups is a crucial practice for building both a feminist movement and feminist theory.[49] But as I will point out later in this book, simply exploring differences, finding patterns in experiences, and bonding between women in such small groups is not sufficient. What is also called for are specific political projects for such small groups that operate with awareness of multiple and intersecting kinds of difference and under conditions that allow these differences to influence the definition of issues and the choice of strategies. A similar point is made by Val

Plumwood, who notes that "forms of oppression" can be seen "as very close-ly . . . related, and working together to form a single system without losing a degree of distinctness and differentiation."[50] She recommends that such a conception of oppression as both a "single mutual supporting system" and a "differentiated system," requires a "cooperative movement strategy [that] sug-gests a methodological principle for both theory and action, that whenever there is a choice of strategies or of possibilities for theoretical development, then other things being equal those . . . that take account of or promote this wider, connected set of objectives are to be preferred to ones that do not. This should be regarded as a minimum principle of cooperative strategy."[51]

Even more specifically, I argue that radically democratic, participatory, and nonhierarchical movement structures, especially within movements that attempt coalitions, provide the conditions for *destabilizing* the essentialist mo-ments that are perhaps inevitably involved in the construction of a political collectivity or an oppositional consciousness. I intend to explore the uses of various and heterogeneous kinds of essentialist formulations for ecofeminism and at the same time point to the ways in which radically democratic ecofem-inist organizations and theoretical production constantly revise and contest political identities.[52] I will try to mitigate what I see as a prevailing reduction-ist account of the essentialism of ecofeminism by examining contradictions, fractures, and debates within the movement's discursive practices. I also pay particular attention, however, to the moments these essentialisms become barriers to more productive coalitions, especially between ecofeminists and the environmental justice movement, and between U.S. ecofeminists and nonWestern feminist environmentalists.

Ecofeminism seems to me to be an important candidate for the kind of sus-taining theoretical critique I try to develop here. While not presently a coher-ent movement in most senses of the word, ecofeminism nevertheless is a po-litical location that I think has a great potential for supporting progressive social, cultural, and economic change. It is an interesting object of study for a constructionist feminist analysis, because an environmentalist politics is a useful location for interrogating the construction of an "identity politics" (or the deployment of strategic, political, but often *embodied* identities), since it is not a political location solely located around a human body constructed by axes of naturalized hierarchies of value, as in racism, sexism, classism, and heterosexism. "Naturism" is about another kind of body, "Nature's body." Primary among ecofeminism's strengths is a political theory that attempts to deploy at once a number of radical analyses of injustice and exploitation fo-cused on racism, classism, sexism, heterosexism, imperialism, speciesism, and environmental degradation. It may even be that this attempt to connect different radical analyses is one source of ecofeminism's essentialist moments. Where I think ecofeminism underutilizes its most radical potential is in the possibility, and the necessity, of theorizing the connection between these injustices through a critique of the ways in which various raced and gendered concepts of "nature" naturalize social inequalities and ecological crises. In particular, the deconstruction of the category "nature" with a feminist political intent should be extended as a crucial theoretical practice within present political conditions. In several ways, then, ecofeminism is potentially a meeting ground for contemporary radical movements. This is one reason why its popularity as a set of theories continues despite the uneven development of its radical political synthesis and its present lack of a movement infrastructure.

OUTLINE OF THE BOOK

This book, then, tries to do two things at once. On the one hand, I wish to critique ecofeminist theory and practice with the goal of making suggestions for the formation of a more inclusive, more politically engaged ecofeminist movement. On the other hand, I seek to show the ways in which ecofeminist practice provides resources for solutions, or at least instructive concretizations, of central problems in contemporary feminist and political theories.

But the ways in which I go about these tasks are determined largely by the conditions in which I work, the political meanings attached to my life history and construction of self, many of which are internally as well as externally divisive. As an academic feminist theorist, I have found it necessary to argue the political importance of my own location as an "ecofeminist." As a white person who has practiced being a "race-traitor" most of my life, I want to critique particular kinds of antiracist theory and practice within ecofeminism to the end of furthering coalitions between white ecofeminists and women of color in the environmental justice movement. As an activist in the antimilitarist direct action movement of the 1980s, I end up arguing for repeating certain of those movement structures and practices in ecofeminism at the same time as I point out the limitations for ecofeminism engendered by its historical connection with that movement. An atheist by upbringing, whose only comfortable experience of spirituality has been the "public happiness"[53] of collective, oppositional political action, I try to account for the positive aspects of ecofeminist spirituality at the same time that I criticize certain of its effects. An Americanist by training, I explore ecofeminist efforts at creating a global movement, and argue against certain U.S. notions of race, gender, and nature that constrain such efforts.

The framework for these arguments and explorations is roughly historical, though it is an interested, contested, disrupted, and unfinished historical narrative. In significant ways, each chapter in this book can be seen as offering a different inflection on the story of ecofeminism's origins, development, and boundaries. In "Movements of Ecofeminism" (chapter 1), I start by tracing some beginnings, offering some definitions, and mentioning some important moments in the formation of U.S. ecofeminism. I then explore one way of thinking about the origins of U.S. ecofeminism—as a feminist rebellion within male-dominated radical environmentalisms—using as my examples social ecology, deep ecology, and Earth First! I note along the way the different strategic but often essentialist notions of women that ecofeminists deployed in the effort to carve out a place for feminism in radical environmentalism.

A recurring theme throughout the book is ecofeminism's connection to feminist antimiliarism. In "Ecofeminist Antimilitarism and Strategic Essentialisms" (chapter 2), I concentrate on the feminist critique of essentialism that was leveled at the feminist antimilitarist direct action movement in the 1980s (and that continues to be assumed in many arenas as the only acceptable feminist reaction to ecofeminism). I offer some other ways of understanding the essentialist moments of this manifestation of ecofeminism as tactical by closely examining writings by Ynestra King and early ecofeminist direct actions for the existence of debates, contradictions, and analytic fractures.

While chapters 1 and 2 focus on questions concerning essentialist constructs of gender, the two chapters that follow interrogate essentialist constructs of racial difference in ecofeminism. In the latter half of the 1980s, some ecofeminists, like other white feminists of the period, responded to critiques of feminism for its racism by making various efforts to decenter white feminists and to encourage antiracist feminist analyses. Within the context of a general critique by feminists of color of the racism of the dominant version of feminism, some ecofeminists reacted to criticism of the whiteness of antimilitarist ecofeminism by attempting to create an organization, WomanEarth Feminist Peace Institute, which would bring together white women and women of color on an equal basis, a concept they called "racial parity." In "WomanEarth Feminist Peace Institute and the Race for Parity" (chapter 3), I examine some of the problems WomanEarth encountered with the conception of racial equality as racial parity. Reading from a position of hindsight, in which multiple rather than binary notions of race are assumed, I show how racial parity prevented these activists from identifying and processing conflicts stemming from other kinds of difference. Despite these problems, I point out ways the efforts of WomanEarth broadened the concerns of ecofeminists, who, after WomanEarth, could no longer present ecofeminism as a purely white women's concern. In "The Nature of Race: Indigenous Women and White Goddesses" (chapter 4), I show how, in the context of the waning of ecofeminist antimilitarist action, a different ecofeminist antiracist discourse centered on the category of "indigenous women," often resulted in the co-optation of Native American women and Asian Indian women as the "ultimate ecofeminists." Further, I show the manner in which the context of this antiracist discourse produced a logic closely connecting ecofeminism with certain versions of white pagan feminist spirituality. Thus, I argue that this connection, which many feminists see as one of the marks of ecofeminism's inherent essentialism, ironically stems from antiracist desires.

In "Ecofeminist Natures and Transnational Environmental Politics" (chapter 5), I examine a dynamic effort in the early 1990s to construct an international ecofeminist movement in tandem with the growth of the disciplinary area called "women, environment, and development," in the context of a hegemonic process I call "globalizing environmentalisms." Here, I return to the same ecofeminist discourse about "indigenous" women as the "ultimate ecofeminists" that I critique in chapter 4 as well as the notion of women "mothering" Earth that I examined in chapter 2. But in chapter 5, I am interested in the effects of the deployment of these discourses under different organizational, political, and transnational conditions. I center this discussion on the formation of an organization called "Women's Environment and Development Organization," or WEDO, which was instrumental in orchestrating a "women's voice" at the UN Conference on Environment and Development at Rio in 1992. I critically examine WEDO's efforts to form an international movement that can take advantage of more mainstream state and UN organizations, which may see the "women and environment" tag as useful in competing ways (as feminist or nonfeminist, for instance).

In "What's in a Name? Ecofeminisms as/in Feminist Theory" (chapter 6), I bring the narrative up to date through a discussion of certain ecofeminist texts published from 1992 to 1996, tracing the patterns of inclusion and exclusion within an academic feminist context that marked contests over the relationship between feminism and environmentalism. In the early 1990s, U.S. ecofeminist activism of the kind I focus on in chapters 2 and 3 had not given way just to attempts to create international ecofeminist coalitions, but also to the production of ecofeminist criticism and theory. To pay attention to this development, I address the strategies certain texts have used to carve out a place for ecofeminism within feminist theory—especially apparent in the search for the "correct" name for an ecofeminism that contains no trace of essentialism. This chapter has the aim of illuminating and interrogating feminist theory's relation to feminist political action, for academic feminism as well as ecofeminism (including academic ecofeminism!). I close the book by offering some suggestions for ecofeminist theorists and activists.

Overall, the aims of the book are to introduce new material on the history of ecofeminism, to generate different ways to understand social movements, and to interrogate the notion of strategic identities. I hope that my work here goes some way toward furthering feminist and ecofeminist political action and toward laying the groundwork for a wide variety of radical political alliances.

1

MOVEMENTS OF ECOFEMINISM

Ynestra King, one of the founders of U.S. ecofeminism, has called it the "third wave of the women's movement," indicating her sense, at one time, that this most recent manifestation of feminist activity was large and vital enough to parallel the first-wave nineteenth-century women's movement and the second-wave women's liberation movement of the 1960s and 1970s.[1] I agree with this assessment, understood as describing a potentiality rather than an actuality, and this book is an attempt to analyze what prevents the closing of the gap between the vision and the practice. The task here is to seek out guides for radical political action from ecofeminism while at the same time fully recognizing its limitations. But first, I want to attempt some descriptions and definitions of ecofeminism as a movement[2] and as a set of theories.

Most simply put, ecofeminism is a movement that makes connections between environmentalisms and feminisms; more precisely, it articulates the theory that the ideologies that authorize injustices based on gender, race, and class are related to the ideologies that sanction the exploitation and degradation of the environment.[3] In one version of its origins, the one I will privilege throughout the book, ecofeminism in the United States arises from the antimilitarist direct action movement of the late seventies and eighties, and develops its multivalent politics from that movement's analysis of the connections between militarism, racism, classism, sexism, speciesism, and environmental destruction. But, as I will also show, ecofeminism has multiple origins and is reproduced in different inflections and deployed in many different contexts. In particular, in this book I will argue that ecofeminism has roots in both feminism and environmentalism.

Given both its attempt to bridge different radical political positions and its historical location as at least one of many third-wave women's movements, U.S. ecofeminism aims to be a multi-issue, globally oriented movement with a more diverse constituency than either of its environmentalist or feminist predecessors. Ecofeminism is thus a movement with large ambitions and with a significant, if at the moment largely unorganized, constituency. Many people are interested in the scope of ecofeminism, its drawing together of environmentalism and feminism. Environmentalism is one of the most popular and significant locations for radical politics today; it attracts people because of the seemingly apocalyptic nature of our ecological crises and the many ways in which environmental problems affect people's daily lives, as well as the sense of its global relevance. As a feminist movement, ecofeminism reworks a longstanding feminist critique of the naturalization of an inferior social and political status for women so as to include the effects on the environment of feminizing nature. Coupled with environmentalism, this version of feminism gains a political cachet not easily matched by other radical political locations, particularly for young U. S. feminists who already think of themselves as environmentalists, having been more or less socialized as such. Ecofeminism is a significant and complex political phenomenon, a contemporary political movement that has far-reaching goals, a popular following, and a poor reputation among many academic feminists, mainstream environmentalists, and some environmental activists of color. Part of what I want to do in this book is to understand the sources of that poor reputation and to explore the reasons for the failure of ecofeminism to live up to its potential.

ECOFEMINIST GENEALOGIES

A name that can usefully if partially describe the work of Donna Haraway and Mary Daly, Alice Walker and Rachel Carson, Starhawk and Vandana Shiva,[4] ecofeminism is a shifting theoretical and political location that can be defined to serve various intentions. The present chaotic context of the relatively new and diverse political positionings that go under the name of "ecofeminism" allows me to construct within this book a series of definitions and historical trajectories of the movement, ones I recognize as always interested and certainly contestable.[5] In this chapter, I will piece together stories about ecofeminist beginnings and evolution by tracing the use of the word "ecofeminism" as it appears in political actions, organizations, conferences, publications, and university courses. Not a history so much as a genealogy, imbedded in this tracing is an effort to tease out the label's shifting meanings and political investments in order to delineate the construction of ecofeminism as an object of knowledge, as a political identity, and as a set of political strategies within the convergence of local and global environmentalisms, academic and activist feminisms, and anticolonialist and antiracist movements.[6] In this chapter, I will focus on ecofeminism as a manifestation of feminism within environmentalisms; in the last chapter, I will focus on ecofeminism within feminist movement and theory.

Both an activist and an academic movement, ecofeminism has grown rapidly since the early eighties and continues to do so in the nineties. As activists, ecofeminists have been involved in environmental and feminist lobbying efforts, in demonstrations and direct actions, in forming a political platform for a U.S. Green party, and in building various kinds of ecofeminist cultural projects (such as ecofeminist art, literature, and spirituality). They have taken up a wide variety of issues, such as toxic waste, deforestation, military and nuclear weapons policies, reproductive rights and technologies, animal liberation, and domestic and international agricultural development. In academic arenas, scholars who are either identified with or interested in ecofeminism have been active in creating and critiquing ecofeminist theories. A wave of publications in the area, including several special issues of journals, indicates research activity on ecofeminism in religious studies, philosophy, political science, art, geography, women's studies, and many other disciplines.[7]

In this chapter, I concentrate on the way in which ecofeminism can be seen primarily as a feminist rebellion within male-dominated radical environmentalisms, where I have found it popping up in almost every arena, often without communication between these slightly or greatly different versions of ecofeminism. Thus, one can find ecofeminists appearing within the antinuclear movement, social ecology, bioregionalism, Earth First!, the U.S. Greens, animal liberation, sustainable development, and, to a lesser extent, the environmental justice movement. In chapter 4, I take up the issue of why the last, which is an environmental movement primarily of people of color and working-class people, should be a place where ecofeminism has had difficulty making a sustained appearance.

The origins of this varied activity called "ecofeminism" have been described in different ways.[8] Certainly, an ecological critique was an important part of women's movements worldwide from the mid-1970s, particularly those concerned with nuclear technology, neocolonialist development practices, and women's health and reproductive rights. In my reading of these developments, ecofeminism in the U.S. arose in close connection with the nonviolent direct action movement against nuclear power and nuclear weapons. Until the Women's Pentagon Actions in 1980, however, there were numerous events and groups connected with ecofeminism that were concerned with a number of issues, militarism being only one of many.

The earliest event I've seen described as making the connection between women and the environment was in 1974, at the Women and the Environment conference at UC Berkeley organized by Sandra Maburg and Lisa Watson. An ecofeminist newsletter, *W.E.B.: Wimmin of the Earth Bonding*, published four issues from 1981 to 1983, concerned with feminist and lesbian back-to-the-land communities, health, appropriate technology, and political action.[9]

Most influentially, however, U.S. ecofeminism's initiating event was the Women and Life on Earth: Ecofeminism in the 1980s conference at Amherst in 1980, organized by Ynestra King (then of the Institute for Social Ecology), Anna Gyorgy (an organizer in the antinuclear Clamshell Alliance), Grace Paley (a feminist writer and pacifist activist), and other women from the antinuclear, environmental, and lesbian-feminist movements.[10]

The Women and Life on Earth conference organized panels and workshops on the alternative technology movement (staffed by the group Women in Solar Energy, or WISE), organizing, feminist theory, art, health, militarism, racism, urban ecology, theater, as well as other topics: eighty workshops in all. Over 650 women attended, far beyond the expected hundred or so.[11] Speakers included Patricia Hynes of WISE; Lois Gibbs, then of the Love Canal Homeowners Association and later of the Citizen's Clearinghouse for Hazardous Waste (CCHW);[12] and Amy Swerdlow, feminist activist and historian.[13] The conference generated an ongoing Women and Life on Earth (WLOE) group in Northampton, Massachusetts, which published a newsletter entitled *Tidings*, as well as several other WLOE groups in New York, Cape Cod, and other areas in the Northeastern United States.[14]

Several other ecofeminism conferences and organizations were either inspired by Women and Life on Earth or assisted by WLOE organizers. A conference already in the planning stages in 1980, Women and the Environment: The First West Coast Eco-Feminist Conference drew 500 women, who listened to talks by Angela Davis, Anna Gyorgy, China Galland, and Peggy Taylor. Workshops were offered on "alternative energy, global view, planning, health, organizing media, no nukes, and peace."[15] In London, a Women For Life on Earth (WFLOE) group formed, inspired by the Amherst conference, and organized a conference in 1981. Energy from that conference spawned numerous WFLOE groups, twenty-six in the United Kingdom and nine in other countries, including Australia, Canada, France, Japan, and West Germany.[16] WFLOE put out a newsletter at least until Winter 1984, organized a number of gatherings, and supported the Greenham Common peace camp. Organizers of WFLOE, Stephanie Leland and Leonie Caldecott, edited the first ecofeminist anthology, *Reclaim the Earth: Women Speak Out for Life on Earth*, in 1983.

From the Women and Life on Earth conference at Amherst also grew the organizing efforts for the Women's Pentagon Actions (WPA) of 1980 and

1981, in which large numbers of women demonstrated and engaged in civil disobedience. As defined by the Unity Statement of the WPA,[17] the politics behind these early ecofeminist actions were based on making connections between militarism, sexism, racism, classism, and environmental destruction (however unevenly the action may have addressed these issues).[18] Influenced by the writings of Susan Griffin,[19] Charlene Spretnak,[20] Ynestra King,[21] and Starhawk, a set of political positions that began to be called ecofeminism developed among women sympathetic to the politics of the WPA and other antimilitarist and environmental actions. Many women involved in later antimilitarist direct actions thus began to call themselves ecofeminists in the middle eighties as a way of describing their interlocking political concerns.[22] In fact, an article in the 1981 issue of *Tidings*, the newsletter of WLOE and the WPA, states that organizers decided not to get involved with a Mother's Day Coalition for Disarmament March in Washington, DC, because "The Mother's Day action is a single issue action and not explicitly feminist." Furthermore, the march was not organized using a "participatory feminist process."[23] Thus, even after the WPA, "ecofeminism" referred not to antimiliarism alone but to a particular kind of feminist, radically democratic antimilitarism that made connections to other political issues. Rather than arising from "the peace movement," ecofeminists deeply influenced the nature of feminist peace politics in the 1980s.

As the label became more common among feminist antimilitarist activists, a concomitant interest in ecofeminism was emerging in the academy. The two arenas were intertwined at the Ecofeminist Perspectives: Culture, Nature, Theory conference in March 1987 at the University of Southern California (USC), organized by Irene Diamond and Gloria Orenstein. This well attended conference was the beginning of a rapid flowering of ecofeminist art, political action, and theory that continues today.[24] This conference also marked the point where the word ecofeminism began to be used outside the antimilitarist movement to describe a politics that attempted to combine feminism, environmentalism, antiracism, animal liberation, anticolonialism, antimilitarism, and nontraditional spiritualities.

During the years following the USC conference, U.S. ecofeminists became active in the international arena, intervening in the process of the globalization of environmentalism. In 1991, a World Women's Conference for a Healthy Planet in Miami, Florida, was organized by the Women's Environmental Development Organization, or WEDO. For political reasons, which I will discuss later, WEDO did not explicitly identify as "ecofeminist," but its rhetoric and vision were clearly in the ecofeminist tradition. This conference brought together women from all over the world to discuss environmental issues in the context of women's knowledge, women's needs, and women's activism. It served as a springboard for an ecofeminist presence at the UN Conference on Environment and Development at Rio de Janeiro in 1992, which had some influence on the international deliberations about solutions to worldwide environmental problems. Besides this activity in an international arena, there have been other important ecofeminist conferences, such as the Eco-visions: Women, Animals, the Earth, and the Future conference in Alexandria, Virginia, in March 1994 (which emphasized connections between feminism, environmentalism, and animal liberation), and the Ecofeminist Perspectives conference at University of Dayton, Ohio, in March 1994 (which emphasized ecofeminist interventions into environmental philosophy). In all these events, organizers stressed ecofeminism's ability to make connections between various radical politics. Which part of this multivalent politics is emphasized or even included varies widely and remains deeply contested among those that identify as ecofeminists. In particular, until the late eighties, antispeciesist theories were underdeveloped portions of the ecofeminist tool kit. Theories of the connections between heterosexism and naturism remain underdeveloped within ecofeminism as of this writing.[25]

WOMEN AND NATURE, FEMINISM AND ENVIRONMENTALISM

Within this multivoiced and vibrant set of political positions were very different theorizations of the connections between the unequal status of women and the life-threatening destruction of the environment. A constant and ongoing focus of ecofeminist theorizing, as well as critiques of ecofeminism, has been how to conceptualize the "special connection" between women and nature often presumed by the designation *ecofeminism*. Very briefly and generally, I will outline five ways this relationship is described. Though I isolate these analyses as positions, in operation they are often combined and intertwined.

One position involves an argument that patriarchy equates women and nature, so that a feminist analysis is required to understand fully the genesis of environmental problems. In other words, where women are degraded, nature will be degraded, and where women are thought to be eternally giving and nurturing, nature will be thought of as endlessly fertile and exploitable.

Another position, which is really the other side of the position just described, argues that an effective understanding of women's subordination in Western cultures requires an environmentalist analysis. In a culture that is in many ways antinature, which constructs meanings using a hierarchical binarism dependent on assumptions of culture's superiority to nature, understanding women as more "natural" or closer to nature dooms them to an inferior position. Furthermore, in a political economy dependent on the freedom to exploit the environment, a moral and ethical relation to nature is suspect. If women are equated with nature, their struggle for freedom represents a challenge to the idea of a passive, disembodied, and objectified nature.

A third position argues for a special relationship between women and nature using a historical, cross-cultural, and materialist analysis of women's work. By looking at women's predominant role in agricultural production and the managing of household economies worldwide (cooking, cleaning, food production, and purchasing of household goods, health care, and child care), this position maintains that environmental problems are more quickly noticed by women and impact women's work more seriously.[26]

A fourth position argues that women are biologically close to nature, in that their reproductive characteristics (menstrual cycles, lactation, birth) keep them in touch with natural rhythms, seasonal and cyclical, life- and death-giving. Ecofeminists who are comfortable with this position feel that women potentially have greater access than men do to sympathy with nature, and will benefit themselves and the environment by identifying with nature.

A fifth position is taken by feminists who are interested in constructing resources for a feminist spirituality and who have found these resources in nature-based religions: paganism, witchcraft, goddess worship, and Native American spiritual traditions. Because such nature-based religions historically contain strong images of female power and place female deities as at least equal to male deities, many persons who are searching for a feminist spirituality have felt comfortable with the appellation of "ecofeminist."

Before proceeding, I want to point to just one of the most obvious contradictions within ecofeminism: the serious lack of agreement between positions one and two and position four. The first two positions see the equation of women and nature as patriarchal; the fourth position sees this equation as empowering to women and as providing resources for a feminist environmentalism. Some variations of position five, concerned with feminist spirituality, also see the equation of women and nature as empowering. This contradiction is obscured by reductive depictions of ecofeminism as "essentialist" without noting the existence of strong constructionist positions within ecofeminism. That this contradiction—between the critique of the connection between women and nature and the desire for a positive version of that connection—is so deeply embedded illuminates the consistent recurrence to essentialist notions of women and nature that ecofeminism encounters in its attempt to construct a collective subject within a social movement. It is also what prevents me from assigning one or the other of the positions described above to one or another ecofeminist author; in most cases, these different analyses of the connections between women and nature are operating at the same time. One of my contentions here (see chapter 4) is that white ecofeminist discourses about "indigenous" women function to obscure this particular division within ecofeminism. Thus, particular ecofeminist discourses of racial difference side-step the contradictions between particular theorizations of the connection between women and nature. Other political dangers as well as advantages inhering in the essentialism of some ecofeminist formulations of the connection between women and nature are discussed in the next chapter. But to make a more general point about these positions here, there has been a greater effort within ecofeminist theory to make connections between women and nature rather than between feminism and environmentalism as political movements, even though, as I show here, such movement connections are often at stake in the production of these theories. The subtext of movement contexts influences theoretical constructions in which essentialist connections between women and nature are more frequent than they otherwise might be.

To construct these and other variations of the theoretical connections between women and nature, or between environmentalism and feminism, ecofeminists have drawn on a number of feminist theories that, while not necessarily aimed at answering questions about the relationship between feminist and environmental politics, provided crucial analytical tools. Feminist philosophical critiques of forms of abstract rationality that reify divisions between culture and nature, mind and emotion, objectivity and subjectivity; psychoanalytic theories of the ways in which masculinist anxiety about women's reproductive capacities structures male-dominated political and economic institutions; feminist rethinkings of Christian theology; critiques of the patriarchal nature of militarism; feminist anthropological research; feminist critiques of science; feminist analyses of the sexual objectification of women and feminist poststructualist theories of constructed subjectivities and critiques of essentialism: these are only a few of the vital feminist resources for ecofeminist theories.[27] Despite its reliance on central feminist theories, most strongly reflected in position two above, ecofeminist theory remains in a tenuous relation to feminist theory, a problem I'll address more directly in chapter 6.

Feminist antiracist theory was also an important resource for ecofeminists, providing a foundation from which to analyze the ways in which hierarchies were created and maintained as well as a guide to constructing a movement that attempts to be inclusive and antiracist. Antiracism was thus a political position apparent in the very beginnings of ecofeminism as theory and as practice, even though it has been a movement that is predominantly white. At the same time, there are many women of color who are either prominent in the movement or who serve as role models for white ecofeminists. To further complicate the picture, many environmental activists are women of color who do not identify as ecofeminists, given that the genealogy of the label arises from the white feminist antimilitarist movement and that U.S. ecofeminism has continued to be a movement largely of white, middle-class women.[28]

In the sections that follow, I examine some environmental and feminist contexts of ecofeminism's development as a political location. In doing so, I will be tracing the way in which ecofeminism developed as a process of political negotiation within various environmentalist and feminist political spaces.

ECOFEMINISM AS A FEMINIST INTERVENTION INTO
ENVIRONMENTALIST CONTEXTS

Among other things, ecofeminism can be seen as a feminist rebellion within radical environmentalism. Given that feminists had developed a number of theoretical critiques of the ways in which the nature/culture split produced various kinds of dominance that undergird sexism, racism, and classism,[29] it made sense that feminism should especially inform those radical versions of environmentalism that analyzed the exploitation of nature as related to various social injustices, and that feminisim would also be quite useful for critiquing the bases for continued environmental degradation.

But such a logical relation between feminism and radical environmentalism was not enough in itself to overcome sexism within environmentalism. In a number of radical environmentalist contexts, feminists had to challenge both male leadership and patriarchal thinking in order to make room for a feminist analysis and presence. Often, these challenges were not received positively, and, in reaction, feminists carved out their own position: ecofeminism. To do so, essentialist notions of women (and of men) were often deployed. This pattern can be traced in a number of radical environmentalist contexts, as I have said, including the antinuclear movement, social ecology, deep ecology, bioregionalism, Earth First!, the U.S. Greens, animal liberation, and sustainable development. (To some extent, I'll address feminist interventions into the antinuclear movement in chapter 2 and into sustainable development in chapter 5. But in this chapter, I have only the space to trace this pattern in social ecology, deep ecology, and Earth First! Such an analysis, however, could also be made of the U.S. Greens and animal liberation.[30] A similar tracing of the intersection of movement contexts could be done in the reverse, examining ecofeminisms as environmentalist interventions into feminist contexts. I will address this aspect to some extent in chapter 6.)

Before I proceed to a discussion of different environmentalist contexts in which ecofeminism has been a factor, I'd like to stress that these accounts are necessarily brief sketches, general pictures, ones that in some of these cases should be considered preliminary. The kind of genealogy I am attempting here is a political history, a narrative about social and intellectual movements that are complex, contested, and amorphous. There are written histories of various complexity and thoroughness for each of these movements as movements as well as bodies of thought. I am interested here in each environmentalist context only as ecofeminism appears as a point of negotiation, a political location within different radical environmentalisms. I am focused specifically on the appearance and definition of feminism as ecofeminism; this gives an emphasis to each environmentalist context that skews it toward its relationship to feminism rather than providing an explication of each environmentalist context in its entirety. I draw on published material, personal accounts of participants, and my own experience as a participant within or observer of these movements for my narrative to make a tracing of ecofeminism's construction in relation to strategic concerns within these political contexts.

ECOFEMINISM AND SOCIAL ECOLOGY

Murray Bookchin, a socialist-anarchist, is the founder and primary theorist of social ecology. As an anarchist theory, social ecology advocates the elimination of all social hierarchies, including that between humans and nature. As a socialist theory, a critique of capitalism is at the center of its vision of an ecological and free society. Bookchin's influence on U.S. radical environmentalism is enormous, though not often attributed. He was an ecological activist as early as 1952, when he published an article on chemical additives in food; he protested nuclear radiation and nuclear power from 1954 onward. He was also an early advocate of alternative technology.[31] Social ecology, the radical environmentalist theory that Bookchin did so much to promote, analyzes the relationship between environmental problems, capitalist labor relations, and social hierarchies. It is a central and influential radical environmentalist theory that inspired many organizational entities and environmental activists.

The development of Bookchin's thought and of the Institute for Social Ecology (ISE), which he cofounded in Vermont with Dan Chodorkoff, had a close relationship to the thought and activism of second-wave feminists, particularly those who were interested in anarchism, antimilitarism, and environmentalism. Bookchin at one point recognizes this, in an essay published in 1980. There, he said, "Only insofar as a counterculture, an alternate technology or anti-nuke movement rests on the non-hierarchical sensibilities and structures that are most evident in the truly radical tendencies in feminism can the ecology movement realize its rich potential for basic changes in our prevailing anti-ecological society and its values."[32] From 1976 to 1984, the feminist activists in the antinuclear movement came closest to Bookchin's vision of radical social ecology, and many of them were involved in the Northeast communities that formed the basis for the ISE. Most relevant to our subject here, Ynestra King was closely involved with the ISE from its beginnings, as a colleague of Bookchin who deeply influenced and was influenced by him. King's brand of ecofeminism was a social ecofeminism (though she did not often use this label), a form of social ecology that put questions of sexism at the center instead of the periphery. The first classes in ecofeminism in the United States were taught by King at ISE in 1978, and there has been an annual colloquium on ecofeminism held there almost every summer since.

Social ecology had a strong influence on two areas of left environmentalist activism: the U.S. Greens and the antinuclear nonviolent direct action movement. In both cases, ecofeminism was a concurrent influence. The antimilitarist nonviolent direct action movement was in many respects an anarchist movement advocating decentralization, cooperative structures, and the elimination of hierarchies, and as such, was deeply informed by social ecology. The influence of Bookchin on this movement can be seen especially in its use of affinity groups, which Bookchin did a great deal to popularize, though the practice was primarily shaped by Quaker and civil rights protest methods. Bookchin and other members of ISE were involved in the Clamshell Alliance, which was the first antinuclear group formed on the basis of the identifying features of the nonviolent direct action movement, using affinity groups and consensus process and engaging in nonviolent direct action to try to halt the construction of the Seabrook, New Hampshire, nuclear power plant in 1976. These actions and organizational forms were precursors to the first ecofeminist antimilitarist actions, the Women's Pentagon Actions, organized by Ynestra King and others from the Clamshell and from ISE.[33]

Social ecologists from ISE and elsewhere were also important participants in the U.S. Greens, particularly in the Left Green Network, a radical social anarchist wing of the Greens. Again, the stress on decentralization, participatory democracy, and sustainable economic and ecological practices made social ecology a foundation for Green politics, and the Greens' desire for a "postpatriarchal" society made it a logical place for ecofeminist practice. Thus, for both the antimilitarist nonviolent direct action movement and the U.S. Greens, social ecology and ecofeminism were foundational radical political theories.

But the link between ecofeminism and social ecology contained several tensions. Primary among them was the secondary place of feminism within social ecology for Bookchin. Despite his organizational and activist ties to feminists, his theoretical practice tended to elide these connections. A brief foray into Bookchin's written work will demonstrate this point.

An essay by Bookchin entitled "Ecology and Revolutionary Thought" was published in 1971, at the very beginnings of the radical environmentalist movement in the United States. This essay made the central connection between growing ecological devastation, social hierarchies, and capitalist labor relations that defines social ecology. Here, Bookchin argues that

> the notion that man must dominate nature emerges directly from the domination of man by man. The patriarchal family planted the seed of domination in the nuclear relations of humanity; the classical split in the ancient world between spirit and reality—indeed, between mind and labor—nourished it; the anti-naturalist bias of Christianity tended to its growth. But it was not until organic community relations, feudal or peasant in form, dissolved into market relationships that the planet itself was reduced to a resource for exploitation.[34]

Bookchin's work ties together the ecological concepts of balanced ecosystems and unity in diversity with the anarchist values of decentralization and participatory democracy.

As is apparent in the language of the above passage, an analysis of sexism was present but underdeveloped in Bookchin's conception of social ecology at the outset. In this selection, he points to the domination of "man by man," stemming from the "seed of domination" planted in the "patriarchal family." Though he does not spell it out, here Bookchin seems to be following Engels in arguing that the patriarchal family served as originary foundation for exploitative relationships between men (as owner and slave, lord and serf, capitalist and worker) — indeed, as the foundation of property and capital accumulation.[35] The domination of women by men, or the possible relation of that specific form of domination to the exploitation of nature, is not considered explicitly, points that would have been part of an ecofeminist analysis. In an article written ten years later, Bookchin makes a similar statement: "Intertwined with the social crisis is a crisis that has emerged directly from man's exploitation of the planet." But this time he footnotes his use of the generic masculine. In the footnote, he states: "I use the word 'man' here advisedly. The split between humanity and nature has been precisely the work of the male, who, in the memorable lines of Theodor Adorno and Max Horkheimer, 'dreamed of acquiring absolute mastery over nature, of converting the cosmos into one immense hunting ground'."[36] The shift in emphasis between these (representative) moments in the development of Bookchin's thought show that while his early formulations potentially include a feminist perspective, it is unarticulated. Ten years later, he's aware of the need to mention the "male-dominated" characteristics of the social and ideological systems he is criticizing, but only in a footnote, and only with reference to Adorno and Horkheimer, rather than to feminist thinkers (to whom, by 1981, he must have had access).

The essay from which the quotation above, citing Horkheimer and Adorno, is drawn is an excerpt from Bookchin's classic work, *The Ecology of Freedom*.[37] In this book, Bookchin presents a more thoroughly worked-out analysis of the relation between sexism and the origin of hierarchy. Here, again, the possibilities of a feminist analysis within the framework of social ecology are clear but underdeveloped. Bookchin sees the gendered division of labor in what he calls "organic" societies (or tribal, hunting-gathering, non-hierarchical cultures) as a natural one, based on the reproductive characteristics of women. He rejects the notion that women are physically weaker or less intellectually capable than men,[38] but he posits the idea that the gendered division of labor produced different masculine and feminine "temperaments."

> The male, in a hunting community, is a specialist in violence. From the earliest days of his childhood, he identifies with such "masculine" traits as courage,

strength, self-assertiveness, decisiveness and athleticism—traits necessary for the welfare of the community. The community, in turn, will prize the male for these traits and foster them in him. . . . Similarly, the female is a specialist in childrearing and food-gathering. Her responsibilities focus on nurture and sustenance. From childhood she will be taught to identify with such "feminine" traits as caring and tenderness, and she will be trained in comparatively sedentary occupations. The community, in turn, will prize her for these traits and foster them in her.[39]

Bookchin does not argue that these different temperaments must be, or were, valued unequally. He argues that many organic societies saw the two sexes, their temperaments, and their spheres of work as complementary. It is only after hierarchy is introduced by a gerontocracy, especially elders-cum-shamans,[40] that the domination of women and the equation of women with nature is achieved. First, Bookchin argues, the elders begin to "abhor natural necessity," the "dumb 'cruelty' that the natural world inflicts upon them" as they age, lose strength, and become dependent on others.[41] But notably these are not just all elders, but specifically male elders, who begin to equate women with nature because, Bookchin argues, of women's reproductive capacities.[42] Like all origin stories, this one depends upon logic that seems commonsensical to the teller of the tale. Nothing about these causal links—neither an apparent separation between nature and human, nor a greater fear of nature by the aged rather than the young, nor the assumption that the elders whose interpretations would predominate would be the male rather than the female elders, nor the more apparent "naturalness" of women's reproductive capacities rather than other biological capacities—is logically necessary. Even if one accepts that the aged would begin to fear "nature" (rather than death, for instance), it is not clear why women would then be equated with nature, or that nature would be thought to be inferior, producing the social superiority of male rather than female elders. Bookchin assumes that it is women's ability to reproduce that produces this equation. And this reduction of women to their roles as mothers is important to his own thesis. Throughout the book, Bookchin celebrates the mother-infant relationship as the basis of ethics and reason in a social ecological society, the "cradle in which the need for consociation is created."[43] In doing so, even though Bookchin clearly wishes to see women as equals to men, he leaves intact the familiar patriarchal reduction of women to their reproductive role. While he stresses that an ecological society is not the same as the organic societies he treats favorably as nonhierarchical, he nowhere discusses whether gender roles in the future utopian ecological society would be different, or would need to be different, than those "temperamentally" different masculine and feminine roles he described in organic societies.

My point here is not that Bookchin's work is antifeminist, but that he does not use feminist texts (*The Ecology of Freedom* mentions only Simone de Beauvoir's *The Second Sex*, and only in a rather unfavorable and dismissive footnote), he does not employ the feminist concept of gender, he does not explore the implications of seeing the gendered division of labor as socially constructed for his vision of a social ecological society, and he does not examine motherhood as an historical and social institution (which seems particularly lacking, given the emphasis he places on motherhood as social fundamental). In short, he does not engage in a feminist analysis. While several nuances to this conclusion could be added from Bookchin's later work, the choice of an excerpt from *The Ecology of Freedom* to represent the position of social ecology in Merchant's *Key Concepts in Critical Theory: Ecology*, published in 1994, suggests that little of substance has changed in Bookchin's treatment of feminism.

Related to the tension around Bookchin's lukewarm acceptance of feminism is the central place Bookchin has held within social ecology. As its grand old man, Bookchin has maintained a strong sense of ownership of the theory, and this aspect of his influence was an obstacle to the growing independence and popularity of ecofeminism. As ecofeminism found it necessary, in some of its versions, to critique Marxist and Enlightenment rationalism as well as notions of evolutionary development,[44]—both of which were important to Bookchin as a theorist—it became more difficult to contain ecofeminism as a subsidiary theory within social ecology. The organization of the Women's Pentagon Actions as separate, women's-only actions indicates the felt necessity for an independent ecofeminism and a decisive break with the ambivalent treatment of feminism by masculinist radical environmentalists, because of the difficulty of sustaining equal leadership roles for women or a central theoretical place for feminism within social ecology as well as other forms of radical environmentalism. As I will argue in more detail in the next chapter, this imperative for autonomy supported a particular rhetoric centered on justifying both separate (or, in some cases, separatist) women's actions and organizations and a close connection between feminism and nonviolent direct action. It is this particular rhetoric in early ecofeminism that has often been criticized as essentialist by other feminists, but without a recognition of its function as a feminist rebellion within a male-dominated form of radical environmentalism.

Another tension generated between the early formulations of ecofeminism and social ecology came from the complex interrelationship between ecofeminism and feminist spirituality. As I've mentioned above, some of those searching for forms of feminist spirituality turned to nature-based religious practices, such as Native American religions, Goddess worship, Wicca (witchcraft), or, in general, what Barbara Epstein (following Margot Adler) calls "neo-paganism."[45] Practitioners of these forms of feminist spiritualities, as well as feminist and radical Christians and Jews, were very active in the

nonviolent direct action movement. Thus these three sets of interests—
ecofeminism, social ecology, and feminist spirituality—were intertwined in
the antinuclear and antimilitarist movement of the mid-1970s to the mid-
1980s, as well as in the U.S. Greens. But this interrelationship was not a totally harmonious one. Murray Bookchin was particularly disturbed at connections with feminist spirituality, perceiving it to be the worst form of apolitical
mysticism.[46] Ynestra King, while not an adherent to and at times a critic of
these forms of spirituality herself, nevertheless was more tolerant of them, seeing the ritual practices of neopaganism within political groups as helpful in
some cases for producing group cohesion—not unlike the songs, dances, and
other ritual forms used in left movements such as the civil rights and labor
movements. In this she was influenced by Starhawk, a Witch who had developed an intricate theory of group processes to be used for radical political
goals using pagan symbols and rituals. Starhawk clearly operated with a complex awareness of the metaphorical power of these tools, of their instrumen-
tality for political action rather than a naive conversion to neopaganism.[47]
Her influence on antimilitarist nonviolent direct action was especially strong
in the San Francisco Bay Area, where neopagan practices and left political
groupings coexisted with somewhat less tension than on the East Coast. King,
aware of the importance of Starhawk's brand of feminist spirituality to the
nonviolent antimilitarist movement, and appreciative of the effectiveness, in
some cases, of such practices in creating forms of radically democratic, anar-
cha-feminist politics, refused to repudiate feminist spirituality outright. Chaia
Heller, another important social ecofeminist theorist (she coined the term
"social ecofeminism")[48] who taught at ISE from 1983 onward, was similarly
ambivalent about certain forms of feminist spirituality. Critical of the conceptualizations she considered apolitical, she nevertheless saw the practice of
feminist spirituality within the feminist antimilitarist movement and within
particular lesbian-feminist communities as complex and often positive.[49]

In the late 1970s and early 1980s, Bookchin engaged in several acrimonious and often public debates with advocates of feminist spirituality, particularly Charlene Spretnak, the editor of a ground-breaking anthology on feminist spirituality who was active in the U.S. Greens. But since his adherence to
feminism was tenuous in the ways I've outlined above, his critique of feminist
spirituality could be easily dismissed on those grounds. To legitimate this critique, a female feminist who was a social ecologist needed to conduct it.
Since both King and Heller's complex appreciation of the diversity within
feminist spirituality did not lead them to publicly denounce it, another social
ecofeminist and student of Bookchin's, Janet Biehl, came forward to do this
work.

Biehl identified as a social ecofeminist originally, writing two important
ecofeminist essays, "It's Deep, But Is It Broad? An Ecofeminist Looks at Deep
Ecology,"[50] and "What is Social Ecofeminism?"[51] However, in Biehl's 1991

book, *Rethinking Ecofeminist Politics*, she disassociated herself from ecofeminism, saying that "the very word *ecofeminism* has become so tainted by its various irrationalisms that I no longer consider this a promising project."[52] As the book was being written, the conflict between Bookchin and King over the place of feminism and the superficial attention to antiracism within social ecology had increased to acrimony, leading to King's ceasing to teach the summer classes on ecofeminism in 1989 (though she once again participated in the summer colloquia from 1994 onward). By the time Biehl's book was completed, it was more than a critique of feminist spirituality within ecofeminism: it was a denunciation of ecofeminism itself as a form of feminist spirituality.

Biehl's book is a thoroughgoing attack on ecofeminism for what she sees as its incoherence, its rejection of the liberatory potential of the Western philosophical tradition, its reliance on metaphor, its mysticism, and its essentialism. Many of Biehl's critiques are worthwhile and thought provoking. In particular, her warnings about the reactionary possibilities in holistic thinking, her rejection of any kind of biologistic arguments for women's greater sympathy with nature, and her cautions about the idealization of ancient Goddess religions are important contributions to ecofeminist thought.[53]

What remains problematic about the book is its desire to draw a sharp line between ecofeminism and social ecology, its misleading (and some claim unscholarly and dishonest)[54] portrayal of some ecofeminist positions (particularly those of Ynestra King, Charlene Spretnak, and Starhawk), its uncritical valuation of "rationality" and the project of the Western Enlightenment, and its simplistic rendition of complex theoretical problems (such as the use of metaphor in theoretical work, the role of "scientific" thinking in political movements, or the analysis of gender as an historical category). But most blatantly unreliable about Biehl's portrayal of ecofeminism is her willful ignorance of the work of ecofeminists who do not fit her characterizations. Through the twin distortions of unfairly presenting some ecofeminist positions in the book and completely ignoring other ecofeminist work that cannot be twisted to be appropriate targets of her critiques, Biehl achieves a reductive description of ecofeminism, a straw-woman against which she can define "social ecology." Douglas Buege describes in detail the ways in which Biehl's criticisms cannot be leveled at the work of Karen J. Warren, Jim Cheney, and Val Plumwood, for instance, pointing out that their work was available to Biehl at the time of her writing, and therefore their invisibility within her book is inexcusable. However useful or accurate Biehl's criticisms may be in relation to certain kinds of ecofeminism or feminist spirituality, Buege points out that the narrow and misleading nature of Biehl's characterization of ecofeminism "leaves in question both the value of Biehl's criticism against ecofeminism, conceived as one position, and her scholarly integrity."[55]

As I will have occasion to discuss at different points in this book, the creation of an ecofeminist straw-woman by reducing ecofeminism to its most biologistic, essentialist, and apolitical manifestations is a technique used by many critics of ecofeminism (many of whom compound the problem by relying heavily on Biehl's critique). I focus on Biehl's book here because it is so important in the history of the relationship between social ecology and ecofeminism. The publication of Biehl's book marks a moment in which social ecology begins to be thought of as separate from ecofeminism by many people, particularly those unaware of the close relationship between the two in constructing social ecological theory and in building the Institute for Social Ecology. This appearance of separation and intolerance has been particular difficult for social ecofeminists who have remained connected to social ecology. Chaia Heller, for instance, has worked at ISE for over twelve years without encountering personal or theoretical difficulties with the integration of feminism within social ecology. Indeed, her invention and continued use of the label "social ecofeminist" shows that she didn't think the two were incompatible. From this perspective, it's ironic that Biehl's book is seen as representative of social ecology's negative assessment of ecofeminism. Biehl's arguments, however, were prominently featured in Bookchin's 1991 introduction to the revised *The Ecology of Freedom*, where he followed her reduction of ecofeminism to the most essentalist practitioners of feminist spirituality and her misleading representations of many ecofeminist positions. Given Bookchin's adherence to Biehl's critique and his prominence within social ecology, Biehl's book has become the one social ecological critique and definition of ecofeminism that has mattered publicly.[56]

The widespread concern over Biehl's book among ecofeminists made its mark in a continued unwillingness to directly critique the use of feminist spirituality within ecofeminism. Critiques of biological essentialism are frequent among ecofeminist theorists, but since the publication of Biehl's book, a certain agnosticism prevails among those ecofeminists who are not practitioners of feminist spirituality. Rather than be associated with Biehl's critique, many ecofeminists have remained silent on the problems embedded in the relationship between ecofeminism and feminist spirituality. While there have been numerous writings on *connections* that can be made between feminist spirituality and ecofeminism, the possible *conflict* between the two has not been addressed with equal attention. This does not mean that the connection is always made in the essentialist, romanticizing manner criticized by Biehl.[57] Acknowledgment of the stigma attached to ecofeminism through its alliance with certain essentialist, apolitical, and ahistorical forms of feminist spirituality exists as a mumbling around the edges of ecofeminist gatherings, a venting within isolated personal conversations, or negotiations around whether and how to include discussions of spirituality at ecofeminist conferences; but these are anecdotal and subtextual knowledges of the conflict rather than worked-out or published analyses or critiques.[58] This silence has its costs, however, as critics of ecofeminism (or feminist spirituality, for that matter) who are willing to reduce it to its most essentialist practitioners can use Biehl's book as support for their claims unchallenged.

In its critique of all forms of hierarchy, ecofeminism remains close to the anarchist political theory of social ecology. Some ecofeminists have pushed an antihierarchical stance farther than social ecology. Val Plumwood points out that Bookchin's "defence of the supremacy of reason and the western tradition" and his view that politics is "confined to intra-human relationships" means that social ecology "defends assumptions associated with the human colonisation of nature and retains forms of intra-human hierarchy which draw on this." Thus, his theory falls short of "reconciling the various critiques of domination."[59] Though these comments by Plumwood would seem to locate her version of ecofeminism as a stronger version of anarchism, for the most part ecofeminists who are not explicitly social ecofeminists have not developed an anarchist critique of bureaucracy and the state.[60] Another theoretical difference, as I've mentioned above, is that ecofeminism's emphasis on feminism is more central than that found in social ecology. But the fact that some social ecologists, notably Chaia Heller, have brought social ecology and ecofeminism closer together theoretically than has Bookchin suggests that theoretical differences are less important in understanding the distinction between the two than ecofeminism's history of conflict within the organizational formations of social ecology. As long as Bookchin retains a proprietary interest in social ecology, an independent identity for ecofeminism is a requirement for its full development. Social ecology remains a valuable potential ally for ecofeminism, however, given the important place it gives to the relationship between social problems and ecological problems, and its highly developed analyses of the environmental and social costs of hierarchical economic, political, and technological arrangements.

ECOFEMINISM AND DEEP ECOLOGY

One of the most exciting moments of the Ecofeminist Perspectives: Culture, Nature, Theory Conference in March 1987 at the University of Southern California occurred when George Sessions, one of the founders of deep ecology, was challenged on the podium by ecofeminists in the audience. While constituting a relatively friendly challenge, and acknowledging Sessions' courage in even attending the conference, the sight of various ecofeminists standing in the audience to insist that Sessions attend to the inherent sexism of his version of deep ecology was a deeply satisfying experience for those feminists who had chafed under the pronouncements of deep ecologists that their version of environmentalism was sufficient ground for an adequate radical environmentalism. This event was an embodiment of the sharp conflict between theorists of ecofeminism and deep ecology that had preceded the conference and continued after it, as well as of the conflicts over sexism within radical environmentalist groups inspired by deep ecology. Deep ecology is a radical environmentalist philosophy formulated primarily by Arne Naess, Bill Devall, George Sessions, and Warwick Fox. Its central point is that environmental problems stem from anthropocentricity, a human-centered ideological position. Thus, environmental problems can only be solved by taking a biocentric or ecocentric[61] approach, one that puts the needs of nature first, or at least on a parallel with human needs. Though deep ecology has had an abiding influence on a number of activist-oriented movements, it remains primarily an intellectual movement. Though Earth First!, as an activist movement, hews to a similar biocentric line, the two have separate origins; the founders of Earth First! were not carrying out a plan laid down first by philosophers of deep ecology. I will treat them as separate here, while acknowledging their connection and their theoretical similarities.

In challenging deep ecology, ecofeminism was not alone; social ecologists, particularly Murray Bookchin, had sharply critiqued deep ecologists. Some of the ecofeminist and social ecologist objections to deep ecology were shared ones, others diverged. The triangulation of this debate is not always acknowledged, and this has functioned to obscure the close theoretical relationship between social ecologists and ecofeminists as well as to marginalize ecofeminism.[62] What is called the "deep ecology-social ecology debate" is emphasized by many male historians of environmentalism, often without reference to ecofeminist critiques of deep ecology. What is called the "deep ecology-ecofeminist debate" similarly ignores the social ecological critiques of deep ecology.[63] The frequent obfuscation of this strategic alliance between social ecology and ecofeminism by ecofeminists is one consequence of the split between the two discussed above. The obfuscation of this alliance by social ecologists is an indication of both the sexism of some of its practitioners as well as their acceptance of Biehl's reductive portrayal of ecofeminism.

Usually, the reference to the debate between ecofeminism and deep ecology is to a series of disputes that have been carried out primarily in the pages of *Environmental Ethics*, within the parameters of environmental philosophy.[64] At the same time, conflicts over sexist theories and practices have occurred within two radical environmentalist activist areas, Earth First! and bioregionalism, which have been deeply influenced by the theories of deep ecology. I will examine the theoretical debate first, and then discuss the conflict within activist arenas, concentrating on Earth First!. One of my points here is that though in both arenas we have "ecofeminists" critiquing a biocentric perspective, these ecofeminisms (philosophical and activist) are different from each other, and indeed not often in communication in any active sense.

Arne Naess, in his 1973 essay, "The Shallow and the Deep, Long-Range Ecology Movement," first introduced the term "deep ecology" to describe an environmentalist tradition of ecocentrism as opposed to "shallow ecology," characterizing the latter as a "fight against pollution and resource depletion [with the central objective of] the health and affluence of people in developed countries."[65] The position that nature has its own value and should not be seen as principally a resource to satisfy human material needs is traced by deep ecologists through Henry David Thoreau, John Muir, Robinson Jeffers, and Aldo Leopold. Many deep ecologists also claim a spiritual aspect to the position. As one introduction puts it: "Further inspiration for contemporary ecological consciousness and the Deep Ecology movement can be traced to the ecocentric religions and ways of life of primal peoples around the world, and to Taoism, Saint Francis of Assisi, the Romantic Nature-oriented countercultural movement of the nineteenth century with its roots in Spinoza, and the Zen Buddhism of Alan Watts and Gary Snyder."[66] Snyder, in particular, is credited with a major influence on deep ecology, and his essay "Re-Inhabitation," as Drengson and Inoue note, "is a seminal essay"; his writings, they state, deeply influenced the countercultural back-to-the-land movement, "implicitly [conveyed] the shallow-deep continuum for discovering the inherent values of nature . . . [and] crystalized the Eastern influence on the Pacific side of North America."[67] Eastern religions are thus refigured in deep ecology as ecological spiritualities and reflected in deep ecological philosophy as a specific psychology of the self-in-nature. Naess's version of this construction of self is most influential for deep ecology and is explicated in what Naess called "Ecosophy T," the "T" standing for "Tvergastein, the name of Naess' tiny mountain hut in Norway," in which he "developed a deep spiritual kinship with the hut and its surroundings."[68] "Ecosophy T," in Naess's words, has "only one ultimate norm: 'Self-realization!'"[69] Naess distinguishes between "self" and "Self": the lower-case nomenclature indicates an individualistic, egoistic self; the upper-case Self is an expanded Self, "as conceived of in certain Eastern traditions of *atman*. This large comprehensive Self (with a capital 'S') embraces all the life forms on the planet (and elsewhere?) together with their individual forms (jivas)." Such an expanded Self is achieved through identification with others, including nonhuman others, since "the higher the levels of Self-realization attained by any one person, the more any further increase depends upon the Self-realization of others."[70] Fox's word for this ecological self-realization is "transpersonal ecology," and he emphasizes that this "cosmological" or "ontological" identification (in which "I" am seen as part of a "whole"—nature, or the cosmos, or "being"), rather than "personal" identification (in which the whole, or the other, is seen as part of "I"), is central to deep ecology.[71]

Early in the elaboration of deep ecology as a position, ecofeminists critiqued this notion of Self-realization achieved through a process of identification with or incorporation of the Other, whether that Other be human or nonhuman. Before the publication of George Sessions and Bill Devall's landmark book, *Deep Ecology: Living as if Nature Mattered*, Ariel Salleh critiqued deep ecologists for identifying anthropocentrism (human-centeredness) rather than androcentrism (male-centeredness) as the culprit in producing a world view that assumed not only a radical split between culture and nature but also the right of mankind (generic masculine intended) to use nature at man's discretion. Salleh criticized deep ecologists for turning to an abstract, transcendentalist view of becoming one with nature, rather than grounding their arguments on women's lived experience of boundarylessness between themselves and Nature. Further, though Salleh notes deep ecology's concern with "biological egalitarianism," "diversity and symbiosis," and class domination, she asserts that without recognizing, analyzing, and opposing male domination, such a theory will not eradicate domination unless it accounts for the "parallel between the original exploitation of nature as object-and-commodity resource and of nurturant woman as object-and-commodity."[72] Salleh, articulating a point that will be echoed throughout the debate, warns that the focus on reducing population—a central principle of deep ecology—without a feminist politics visits a set of technocratic, oppressive policies on women resulting in what she characterizes as "another [male] grab at women's special potency."[73] Finally, Salleh is deeply suspicious of deep ecologists' reliance on Eastern religious philosophies, which as she points out, cannot simply be assumed to be feminist. The desire to become one with nature that is celebrated by deep ecologists reflects, in Salleh's view, "not just a suppression of real, live, empirical women, but equally the suppression of the feminine aspects of men's own constitution. . . . This is the self-estranged male reaching for the original androgynous natural unity within himself."[74] Thus, without analyzing and eradicating the sexist sources of masculine alienation from nature, solutions to that alienation will in turn replay flawed masculine preferences for abstraction, atomism, and domination.

Written in 1984, Salleh's piece is perhaps one of the best examples of a clearly essentialist version of ecofeminism. She identifies patriarchy as a realm of male dominance, without allowing differences of class, race, or other vectors of hierarchy to modify male responsiblity for the domination of nature. Though she acknowledges a social dimension to women's experience that accounts for the fact that "the traditional feminine role runs counter to the exploitive technical rationality which is the current requisite masculine norm,"[75] she privileges a biological determinism to explain her position that women's identity with nature is a "fact of life": "Women's monthly fertility cycle, the tiring symbiosis of pregnancy, the wrench of childbirth and the pleasure of suckling an infant, these things already ground women's consciousness in the knowledge of being coterminous with Nature."[76] These turns to essentialism occur in her essay precisely where she is trying to establish that women and women's lives should be resources for a new environmentalism aimed to eliminate the domination of nature. In two later essays, however, Salleh rejects an essentialist position explicitly and clarifies her comments in the earlier essay by pointing to "the historical process at work here, namely, that it is patriarchal domination that puts women close to nature. Not only is the feminine pysche constructed differently by this means, but the work roles that women are assigned also revolve around nature."[77] Further, she explains:

> It is nonsense to assume that women are any closer to nature than men. The point is that women's reproductive labor and such patriarchally assigned work roles as cooking and cleaning bridge men and nature in a very obvious way, and one that is denigrated by patriarchal culture. Mining or engineering work similarly is a transaction with nature. The difference is that this work comes to be mediated by a language of domination that ideologically reinforces masculine identity as powerful, aggressive, and separate over and above nature.[78]

Salleh concludes that deep ecology cannot reach its goal of a biocentric egalitarianism without attending to sexism, racism, classism, and the "complex interlocking issues, economic and ideological, that have to be dealt with, [as well as] a sense of the 'labor' involved in bringing about social change."[79] She suggests that ecofeminism has a clearer sense of the integrated nature of these issues and the activist challenges that must be engaged, a sensibility that, unlike deep ecology, does not shy away from human concerns in its struggle for ecological sanity.

Marti Kheel was also an early ecofeminist critic of deep ecology. In "The Liberation of Nature: A Circular Affair," she argues that a feminist version of holism that values individuals as interrelated, dynamic constituents of a whole is preferable to the holism found in deep ecology (her examples are versions proposed by J. Baird Callicott and Aldo Leopold), which allows a unified (biotic) whole to determine the value of individuals.[80] Further, in a paper originally delivered at the 1987 Ecofeminist Perspectives conference at USC, Kheel points out that:

> When deep ecologists write of anthropocentrism and the notion of an "expanded Self," they ostensibly refer to a gender-neutral conception of self. Implicit in the feminist analysis of the androcentric worldview, however, is the understanding that . . . women's identities, unlike men's, have not been established through their elevation over the natural world. On the contrary, under patriarchal society, women have been identified with the devalued natural world, an identification that they have often adopted as well.[81]

Kheel's work, less explicitly than Salleh's early essay, exhibits arguments referring to women's biological attributes as establishing a superior standpoint in relation to nature compared to men's. This tendency in Kheel's work occurs where she feels the need to argue for the usefulness of a feminist analysis of environmental exploitation, and as an explanation for the inadequacy of the deep ecologist position.

Other ecofeminist critiques of deep ecology more firmly reject the biologism of Salleh's 1984 article, taking up some of the same critiques of deep ecology, but through a feminist politics grounded on an analysis of women's experiences as ordered by patriarchy rather than biology. Ynestra King states that "connecting women to nature need not acquiesce to biological determinism . . . if nature is understood as a realm of potential freedom for human beings—both women and men—who act in human history as part of the natural history of the planet, in which human intentionality and potentiality are an affirmed part of nature."[82] She goes on to argue that "deep ecology ignores the structures of entrenched economic and political power within society, concentrating exclusively on self-realization and cultural transformation, taking the side of nature over culture, thereby insisting that human beings conform to the laws of nature as understood by deep ecologists."[83]

Influenced by the debates between ecofeminism and deep ecology, a distinctively philosophical version of ecofeminism arose that, in opposition to the incorporative holism of deep ecology, constructed a contextual ecofeminist ethics oriented toward a relational notion of self and a feminist analysis of the patriarchal socialization of women and men into different ethical practices. Jim Cheney notes that: "The basic claim [of ecofeminism] is that, through linking or identifying women with nature, the need for domination and control of nature becomes charged with the same irrational fury and ambivalence as the need for domination and control of women."[84] Deep ecology's desire to rid society of the need for the "domination and control of nature" would seem to ally it with ecofeminist concerns, but, as Cheney argues, "deep ecological attempts to overcome human (really masculine) alienation from nature fail in the end because they are unable to overcome a masculine sense of self and the kinds of ethical theory that go along with this sense of self."[85] The "oceanic feeling of fusion" with nature promoted by deep ecologists is just the flip side of a dualism that allows only two choices in our relationship with nature (and with other human beings): "either we 'respond to nature as a part of ourselves,' or we treat it 'as a stranger or alien available for exploitation.'. . . We have either atomistically defined selves who are strangers to one another or one gigantic self."[86]

Moving beyond a critique of deep ecology, Cheney offers an account of an ecofeminist ethical perspective that honors both nature and human beings, the whole and various selves. Instead of seeing ourselves either as atomistic or a "community of one," he suggests that we use the feminist idea of the "defining relationship," or that we use how "our relationships with others are central to our understanding of who we are"[87] as a way to understand selfhood and appropriate ways of being in the world. Thus, he argues, moral decisions would be contextual rather than abstract and rule bound. Cheney recognizes that in a patriarchal society, women who define themselves by their relationships to others are often subject to the "pathology of self-sacrifice," but he argues that such pathology only arises when others in the society define themselves atomistically, using a masculinist notion of autonomous self-construction.[88] In Cheney's view, contextual ethics in a society where selves are defined relationally and decisions are based on the most complex, detailed narratives possible is potentially more able to break down Western dualisms between culture and nature than can deep ecology's false "feminization" of environmental attitudes grafted onto masculine ethical sensibilities.

Cheney's argument is closely associated with, and indeed constructed in relation to, the work of Karen Warren. Warren's classic description of ecofeminism, "Feminism and Ecology: Making Connections," appeared in the same 1987 issue of *Environmental Ethics* as another important essay in the ecofeminist/deep ecology debate, Michael Zimmerman's "Feminism, Deep Ecology and Environmental Ethics." Warren's essay outlines the "minimal conditions" of an ecofeminist theory, positions with which, she says, all ecofeminists might agree: "(i) there are important connections between the oppression of women and the oppression of nature, (ii) understanding the nature of these connections is necessary to any adequate understanding of the oppression of women and the oppression of nature, (iii) feminist theory and practice must include an ecological perspective, (iv) solutions to ecological problems must include a feminist perspective."[89] Clearly, Warren's argument is aimed at convincing both feminists and radical environmentalists that ecofeminism is the best theoretical grounding for their arguments. I shall examine Warren's claim about the importance of making "eco-feminism central to feminist theory and practice" in chapter 6. Here I want to underline the second part of Warren's agenda: making ecofeminism central to radical ecology. Though not emphasized in this essay, one part of Warren's project is to argue that deep ecology cannot substitute its own principles of "biospheric diversity" and "holism" for a feminist perspective. If one aspect of the devaluation of nature in our culture is the feminization of nature, then a feminist analysis must be part of a perspective that wishes to revalue nature. Warren is more explicit in a 1990 essay, "The Power and the Promise of Ecological Feminism." Here she takes on Warren Fox's critique of ecofeminism, in which he argues that there is no conflict between deep ecology and ecofeminism, but that a critique of anthropocentrism can easily incorporate a critique of androcentrism.[90] On the face of it, this position might not seem objectionable to ecofeminists, many of whom have noted the similarities between the two positions. But Fox, in arguing that anthropocentrism is the "root cause" of not only ecological destruction but also of human domination of other humans, refuses to deploy the ecofeminist analysis that locates "humanism" as a specifically masculinist construct. Warren says:

Whatever the important parallels between deep ecology and ecofeminism (or, specifically, my version of ecofeminism)—and indeed, there are many—it is precisely my point here that the word *feminist* does add something significant to the conception of environmentalist ethics, and that any environmental ethic (including deep ecology) that fails to make explicit the different kinds of interconnections among the domination of nature and the domination of women will be, from a feminist (and ecofeminist) perspective such as mine, inadequate.[91]

Warren's version of ecofeminism, in which she argues for a "transformative feminism" that moves beyond the inadequacies in—as well as building on the strengths of—liberal, Marxist, socialist, and radical feminism, places analyses of the domination of nature in relation to, rather than superior to, other analyses of domination. A "transformative feminism" would, according to Warren, make the connections between all systems of oppression explicit, including racism, classism, sexism, heterosexism, speciesism, and naturism; it would "provide a central theoretical place for the diversity of women's experiences, even if this means abandoning the project of attempting to formulate one overarching feminist theory or one women's voice"; it would promote values and social processes (such as "care, friendship, reciprocity in relationships, appropriate trust, diversity) underplayed or lost in traditional . . . ethics"; and it would challenge masculinist versions of science and technology.[92]

A similarly complex version of ecofeminism, opposed to essentialism and holism (whether feminist or masculinist versions) can be found in Val Plumwood's work, which, like Warren's, develops in the context of philosophical debates between deep ecologists, social ecologists, and ecofeminists. Plumwood's work centers on the deconstruction of Western versions of the self, humanity, and nature, which she argues are imbedded in a tradition of rationalism that has had damaging consequences for women, people of color, and nature. An Australian theorist, Plumwood brings to her theorizing a particularly sharp understanding of the horrifying uses that rationality and humanism have been put to in colonialist endeavors.[93] Like Warren, Plumwood prefers a relational account of the construction of self, and promotes an "ethic of care" as one contribution ecofeminist theorists make to an adequate environmental ethic. But Plumwood is focused on more than ethics; she is also interested in a critique of ontological and epistemological aspects of the Western attachment to a masculinist and naturist version of rationality. "Mainstream environmental philosophy is problematic not just because of restriction *in* ethics but also because of restriction *to* ethics. . . . [T]his neglects the key further aspects . . . of dualism and the account of the self and of human identity as hyperseparated from nature . . . as well as the broader historical and political aspects of the critique of dualism and instrumentalism."[94] The ways in which Western rationalism and humanism have defined humanity and the self as precisely *not nature* (and the ways in which nature has been defined as those aspects that are seen as particularly feminine) are labeled by Plumwood as the "discontinuity problem," i.e., constructing the essence of (masculinist) humanity as its separateness from nature. Deep ecologists, she says, have been an exception to mainstream environmental ethicists in attempting to address the "discontinuity problem," but they have done so in ways that are inadequate and can be traced to their dismissal of feminist arguments about the self, ethics, difference, and the critique of humanism. Plumwood identifies three ways that deep ecologists have tried to argue for bridging the gulf between humans and nature: the "indistinguishability account," "the expanded self," and the "transcended or transpersonal self."[95] In all cases, Plumwood says, the solutions offered by deep ecology ignore difference and particularity and imagine a "oneness with nature" that leaves no room for the separateness and autonomy of the other. Plumwood points out that feminists have long critiqued the idea of feminine self-sacrifice for the other, and have been suspicious of "the arrogance in failing to respect boundaries and to acknowledge difference which can amount to an imposition of self."[96] Instead, she prefers the feminist idea of the "rationality of the mutual self, the self which can take joy in the flourishing of others, which can acknowledge kinship but also feast on the other's resistance and grow strong on their difference."[97]

The deep ecology/ecofeminism debate, as Deborah Slicer has pointed out, has not been much of a debate. Most of the deep ecologists purporting to answer ecofeminist critiques do not seem to have bothered, as Slicer puts it, "to familiarize themselves with the feminist and ecofeminist literature that has been accumulating in various feminist journals and texts for some three decades now before taking feminists and ecofeminists to task."[98] She notes that Warwick Fox, in his essay "The Deep Ecology-Ecofeminism Debate," takes up ecofeminist arguments primarily in the form of two male authors, Jim Cheney and Michael Zimmerman. While Slicer does not dispute that Cheney, in particular, and Zimmerman, with qualifications, present satisfactory ecofeminist arguments, she notes that this rhetorical strategy of taking men's arguments, even about feminism, more seriously than similar or better ones made by women is a familiar experience for women in a sexist society. The experience of "having men talk through [women] to other men as though they did not exist" is relived by Slicer "each time I read the essay by Fox, who is having a conversation with Zimmerman and Cheney while the women stand gagged in the footnotes."[99] The attempt by deep ecologists to subsume ecofeminism is an attempt to silence them and to avoid learning how to engage in the kind of complex feminist analysis of sexism (or androcentrism) that underlies an ecofeminist critique of anthropocentrism.[100] Instead, deep ecologists like Fox claim that ecofeminism simply adds concerns with gender equality to the foundational positions of deep ecology that construct a radical environmentalist stance beyond "reformist" environmentalism. As Slicer points out, some even go so far as to say that ecofeminism is *derivative* of deep ecology.[101]

In elaborating the variant of ecofeminism found in environmental philosophy, especially environmental ethics, I have not argued that this ecofeminism is born from its debate with deep ecology. Rather, I have tried to show that the debate has pushed ecofeminist philosophy to emphasize certain concepts, particularly the idea of the relational self, a contextual ethics of care, and a respect for difference and particularity over universalism and holism. There is much more to ecofeminist philosophy than these concepts, of course, but my purpose here is not to elaborate the entirety of ecofeminist philosophical positions. Rather, I want to note the historical and political specificity of these debates—which influence the creation of a particular form of ecofeminism—centered on specific concerns that both differ and resonate with other ecofeminisms. In particular, as one would suspect because of the ideological relationship between Earth First! and deep ecology, ecofeminist philosophers come to somewhat the same positions and articulate similar critiques of the sexism of biocentrism as ecofeminist activists in Earth First!. Yet the route taken to these ecofeminist places is separate. It is to the place of ecofeminism in Earth First! to which I will now turn.

ECOFEMINISM AND EARTH FIRST!

Given that deep ecology is often credited with being a major philosophical influence on the radical activist organization Earth First!, it is not surprising that similar ecofeminist critiques have been made of both deep ecology and Earth First!. Like the ecofeminism-deep ecology debate, ecofeminism has had social ecology as an unacknowledged partner in this critique. And, in similar ways, ecofeminists have sometimes been excluded in order to portray the debate as being between men only.

For example, one of the most glaring omissions of ecofeminism as a critic of deep ecology and Earth First! occurs in a book called *Defending the Earth*. This book arose out of a public dialogue set up between Bookchin and Dave Foreman by the Learning Alliance in New York City, which has organized a number of public radical political debates. That no one in the organization saw the need to include an ecofeminist as one of the main contenders (Judi Bari, an Earth First!er critical of Foreman's brand of eco-macho as well as Bookchin's perceived "anthropocentricity" would have been an appropriate and interesting addition) is bad enough. But ecofeminists were not even allowed a secondary role. The format of the dialogue was to have Bookchin and Foreman each stake out their positions. Then they were questioned by various speakers positioned as interrogators from the outside of both social ecology and deep ecology: Paul McIsaac, representing "the left"; Linda Davidoff, representing "reformist environmentalism"; and Jim Haughton, representing "anti-racist environmentalism." That ecofeminism was not considered a worthwhile participant given this structure is indicative of the widespread sexism of radical environmentalisms.[102]

What is interesting, however, in thinking about ecofeminism as a movement that arises out of different movement contexts, is that the ecofeminists who critique deep ecologists are a different group from those that have critiqued Earth First!ers. The latter have generally been Earth First!ers themselves, while the former have been feminist philosophers. That a similar critique should be generated by two groups of feminists in very different class and philosophical locations, without communication between the two, shows the way in which ecofeminism has developed as a feminist rebellion within various radical environmentalisms rather than as a coherent, single-source movement. It also demonstrates the strength of feminism as a widespread and diverse political consciousness.

Earth First! was the brainstorm of five men who were on a camping trip in 1980 in the Southwest: Dave Foreman, Howie Wolke, Mike Roselle, Burt Koehler, and Ron Kezar.[103] Like their fictional counterparts in Edward Abbey's 1975 novel, *The Monkey-Wrench Gang*,[104] the five men turned their camping trip into a prowilderness action. The mythology of this trip is replete with masculinist images: drinking beer, visiting a whorehouse (probably apocryphal), smuggling beer over the border, erecting a sign memorializing an Indian warrior.[105] The motto: "No Compromise in Defense of Mother Earth!" was Earth First!'s war cry: a volatile mix, part male protectionist, part biocentrist, and part determined confrontation. Nevertheless, Earth First! attracted women activists from the start.

Earth First!'s exclamation point signaled the imperative quality of its intention to stop the destruction of wilderness. Defending Mother Earth for Earth First!ers was an activity characterized by direct action, with no hesitation about property destruction, motivated by a passion for protecting wilderness areas and their dependent species. The forms of direct action pioneered or preferred by Earth First!, such as "desurveying" (pulling up stakes marking future roads through wilderness areas), disabling road-building and logging machinery (through sugar or sand in gas tanks, or breaking delicate parts with hammers and wrenches), tree spiking (putting nails into trees chosen to be logged causing damage to logging machinery), and tree sitting (occupying trees which had been marked for logging for days or even weeks), were all tinged with a patina of toughness, risk taking, and military-like stealth that lent itself easily to machismo. A refrain from a popular Earth First! song written by Mike Roselle, one of the founders, and Darryl Cherney, one of the most prolific and well-known of the Earth First! traveling bards, went: "We'll have an Earth Night Action, it's instant satisfaction,"[106] marking the pleasure in taking direct action aimed precisely and often effectively at the agents of wilderness despoliation, and constructed in opposition to both environmentally exploitative corporations as well as mainstream environmentalism. Such delight in radical action attracted both men and women, but remained embedded in a masculinist culture. As "redneck" environmentalists, Earth First!ers constructed an ironic image counterpoised to the image of mainstream environmentalists as middle- to upper-class liberals. A popular portrayal of Earth First!ers, printed in *The Earth First! Journal*, depicted a hairy man outfitted in "size 11 mountain-climbin', woods-hikin', desert-walkin', butt-kickin', rock-n-rollin' waffle stompers," complete with "massive 12 inch knife," "massive 40-inch beer belly," "camouflage bandanna (multi-purpose)," "permanent snarl," and "wrench—fer 'fixin' things." Joni Seager, reprinting this image in her book's section on Earth First! entitled "Deep Machismo," appropriately notes the image's "self-irony."[107] The ironic, humorous, and theatrical element of Earth First!, not generally appreciated by outsiders to the culture, also made it possible for women Earth First!ers to appropriate "deep machismo" for their own purposes of empowerment in rejecting a feminine (and middle-class) stereotype of delicacy and passivity. Yet, given the masculinist basis of the eco-warrior image, this feminist appropriation was severely limited by the requirements of such a sexist culture that women also act as earth mothers and sex objects. Joni Seager notes that "with very few exceptions, the self-styled leaders and spokespeople of Earth First! were all men, as was a considerable proportion of its membership (in contrast with all other environmental groups). . . . It is clear that Earth First! is attractive to women who want to participate in environmental change; it is not clear how feminist women within Earth First! reconcile their involvement with the deeply misogynistic face of the national and international branches of the movement."[108]

One answer to Seager's question is found in the decentralized structure of Earth First!. Organized in small, independent, "affinity groups" (though the term was not always explicitly used within Earth First!) and tolerant of individual, autonomous actions, the anarchistic structure of Earth First! allowed for a great deal of variation along the lines of political beliefs, direct action tactics, and use of cultural symbols. That this variation and this humor does not come across at the "national and international level," as Seager says, is a result of the sexism and conservatism of the press as much as of Earth First!'s own sexism. In his book on radical environmentalism, Rik Scarce quotes Nancy Zirenberg, long-time merchandise manager for *The Earth First! Journal*, as saying: "There's a macho image. There's also a very feminist image that is not portrayed in the media," and she notes that the media insists on male spokepeople at Earth First! actions.[109] Contrary to this public persona, Scarce found that several Earth First! women felt that there was more equality at the grassroots level of the organization. As a result, the adherence to the macho public face of Earth First! was uneven and, within certain areas, actively rejected. Nevertheless, conflicts over sexism within the movement and its cultural symbols was one major bone of contention within Earth First!, adding to a series of internal conflicts from 1987 to 1992 that changed its tenor away from its original conception as a loose affiliation of "butt-kickin'" radical biocentrists identified not as leftists but as wild men of the forest.

One influential region in the often acrimonious debates over the politics and cultural symbols of Earth First! was Northern California, where organizing against the logging of old-growth redwood forests brought Judy Bari to prominence. Bari, a feminist with considerable experience in labor organizing, was pivotal in the creation of ecofeminism as a feminist rebellion within Earth First!, and her story will be the centerpiece of my discussion here.

Bari was deeply influenced by Marxist analysis as an anti-Vietnam war activist in her college days. After several years of radical union organizing, Bari moved in 1988 to Northern California, where she became involved in trying to prevent the logging of old-growth redwood that was planned by the multinational conglomerate Maxxam. Her interest in saving the trees was complemented from the first by her interest in labor and feminist issues. As Scarce writes, "In order to pay off the massive junk bond debt it had incurred in the purchase of Palco [the local family-owned logging company], Maxxam had to 'liquidate' the only real 'capital' Palco owned—the redwoods. That, Bari recognized, spelled doom not only for the forests but for the workers as well. There was forced overtime, meaning less time with family and more accidents, and the faster the trees were cut, the sooner the workers would lose their jobs."[110] Bari's politics were always multileveled; concerned for the environment, she also focused on the mostly male workers' labor conditions as well as on issues important to women and to the families of the loggers. Within Earth First!, she argued for a change in tactics as well as analysis: "By and large, most of the people who had the freedom for [the] kind of travel and risk-taking [characterized by early Earth First! actions] were men."[111] Instead, when Bari organized the massive actions in 1990 against the logging of redwoods in Northern California called "Redwood Summer" (a reference to the civil rights mobilization in Mississippi in 1964 called "Freedom Summer") she promoted an explicit code of nonviolence, renounced tree spiking in order to maintain an alliance with timber workers, and encouraged female leadership within the action.[112] Indeed, the organizing culture of the region was oriented toward a different kind of direct action from that preferred by Earth First! founders. Northern California had been a hotbed of antimilitarist nonviolent direct action in the 1980s, and hundreds of activists had experience in direct actions against nuclear weapons, nuclear power, and anti-U.S. intervention (all of which also contained an environmentalist analysis).[113] Borrowing from the antimilitarist movement organizational methods such as affinity group structures, nonviolent training and nonviolent guidelines for activists, and actions involving hundreds rather than tens of people, Redwood Summer marked a significant departure from earlier Earth First! action styles.

And such new tactics and multilevel politics caused considerable controversy.

Much of the debate over the political shift represented by Redwood Summer can be traced within the *Earth First! Journal*. A lot of these debates also took place within Earth First! regional or national "rendezvous," which were gatherings of Earth First!ers in wilderness area for several days of meetings, music, and partying. The biggest gathering was the annual Round River Rendezvous, which essentially served as a national policymaking entity for the loosely affiliated Earth First! regional groups. In the *Earth First! Journal*, Bari's voice appears consistently as a feminist agitator, marking many women's discomfort with the macho tendencies within Earth First! and promoting Northern California Earth First! as a region in opposition to this aspect of the movement. In a report on the California Rendezvous, for instance, Bari says: "Another significant facet of this rendezvous was the absence of that male machismo with which EF! has become associated. This was partly because California has such a strong feminist contingent, and partly because some of the worst offenders didn't show up."[114] Bari's comments were objected to by a number of letter writers to the *Journal*, including some women.[115] Her insistence on including sexism as an important issue within the movement was forcefully rejected by many Earth First!ers, such as co-founder Howie Wolke, who wrote: "Racial and sexual discrimination, human rights, religion, foreign policy, lifestyle, diet and a host of other issues are important, and do have serious ramifications for the health and survival of diverse life on the Earth. But in the *Journal* and elsewhere in EF!, any discussion or inclusion of issues such as these should be subservient to the real focus of our movement: wilderness, biodiversity, planetary survival."[116]

This debate, defined as a conflict between "biocentrism" and "humanism" by the old guard of Earth First!, raged throughout the movement until 1990, when it came to a head. Though, as in Wolke's statement above, other issues besides sexism were seen as tainting the purity of Earth First!'s commitment to biocentrism, feminism was hotly debated within the movement. Dolores La Chappelle had a short-lived stint as a columnist in the *Journal*, where her essay "No, I'm Not an Eco-Feminist: A Few Words In Defense of Men," generated intense reaction from several feminist Earth First!ers.[117] Much of the argument took place in the Redneck Women's Caucus (convened annually, along with a Men's Caucus, during the Rendezvous): Loose Hip Circles reported in "Riotous Rendezvous Remembered" that the 1989 Women's Caucus "renamed ourselves the Wild Women, [and] decided that we didn't need to talk about male domination anymore."[118] Until 1990, however, feminist voices besides Bari's were mostly restricted to the letters section, which was called "Dear Shit Fer Brains."

In September 1990, in response to criticisms from many Earth First!ers, including a vocal Northern California contingent, that the *Journal*'s emphasis on a purist version of biocentrism and its continued criticism of Redwood

Summer as a "leftist" rather than a "biocentric" action was unrepresentative of the movement, the original *Journal* staff resigned en masse. In addition, stung by internal criticisms of statements he had made that were widely seen as racist, misanthropic, and misogynistic, Dave Foreman resigned from Earth First!. Foreman, the most well-known founder of Earth First!, was seen as a liability at this point by many Earth First!ers, because of his widely reported statement in an interview that famine relief in Ethiopia was contrary to a biocentric perspective opposed to population growth, and because of his refusal to repudiate Edward Abbey's statements that immigration into the United States should be halted for environmental reasons. In addition, articles printed in the *Journal* in 1987 by a pseudonymous author, Miss Ann Thropy, suggested that AIDs may be a natural defense of the Earth against overpopulation.[119] Taken together, these statements tarred the biocentric perspective, opening Earth First! to criticisms of being against people, especially people of color. Though there was also plenty of positive feeling toward Foreman, particularly since he had been recently arrested by the FBI as a co-consipirator in an attempt to cut down power lines (an action promoted by an FBI inflitrator), the extremist biocentric position he represented came more and more under attack. In the September 1990 issue, Foreman and his long-time companion, Nancy Morton, wrote a letter announcing their resignation from Earth First!. A relatively gentle letter, calling the decision a "no-fault divorce," Foreman and Morton cited as their reason

> an effort to transform an ecological group into a Leftist group. We also see a transformation to a more overtly counterculture/anti-establishment style, and the abandonment of biocentrism in favor of humanism. Mind you, we are not opposed to campaigns for social and sconomic justice. We are generally supportive of such causes. But Earth First! has been from the beginning a wilderness preservation group, not a class-struggle group. . . . Moreover, we are conservationists. We are not anarchists or Leftists. We are biocentrists, not humanists.[120]

In the same issue, founder Howie Wolke and deep ecologist Bill Devall also said good-bye to Earth First!. Wolke wrote: "I'm tired of being sidetracked by eco-feminism, sanctuary, anarchy, woo-woo, coalition building, bleeding heart humanists against misanthropy, sexist animal lovers for gay rights, and all of the other egostical fodder for human chauvinistic cause-lovers."[121] And Devall complained that "it seems the rainbow coalition, anarchists, hippies, ecofeminists, anyone who wants to be 'where the action is,' and leftists of all varieties, including so called social ecologists, have infested radical environmentalism because radical ecology seems to be the only game in town in the 1990s."[122]

In the same issue, Judi Bari responded: "The only way to preserve wilderness and the only way to save our planet's life is to find a way to live on the earth that doesn't destroy the earth. In other words, Earth First! is not just a conservation movement, it is also a social change movement." And she argued that an important cause of the dispute within Earth First! was sexism in the movement:

> Another change that goes with our world view is the prominence of women in EF!. Ed Abbey's retrogressive view of women as sex objects doesn't make it [at Redwood Summer], where about 3/4 of the EF! organizers are strong and competent women. And although male dominance is not the only problem with our society or the sole reason for the destruction of nature, it's definitely a factor. Any change toward a non-exploitive culture would have to include a balance between masculine and feminine, and we had better start with our own movement.[123]

Clearly, the tactics and political philosophy of Redwood Summer were seen as one of the major problems for the "old guard" of Earth First! in this debate. The renouncing of tree spiking, the prominence of women, the adherence to explicit nonviolent guidelines, the recruiting of thousands of new activists in mass actions, and the forming of coalitions with non-Earth First!ers such as the Industrial Workers of the World and Seeds of Peace[124] were all seen as threatening to a purist notion of biocentrism embedded in the masculinist culture of early Earth First!. And just as obviously, the more inclusive politics of Redwood Summer were also threatening to timber interests and to the U.S. government, who saw such widening of Earth First!'s concerns and constituency as alarming. On May 24, 1990, at the beginning of Redwood Summer, a car bomb exploded in Judi Bari and Darryl Cherney's car, crippling Bari for life. Despite Bari and Cherney's well-known commitment to nonviolence, and despite a complete lack of evidence linking them to the bombing, the Oakland Police and the FBI charged Bari and Cherney with constructing the pipe bomb themselves. Though they eventually backed down from that charge, little investigation was done to find the actual bomber. A letter from a person self-named "The Lord's Avenger" was sent to a Northern California paper taking credit for the bombing, and specifically pointing to Bari's pro-choice and feminist stance as the cause for the bombing.[125] As of this writing, the FBI and Oakland Police still have not done a satisfactory investigation of the bombing.[126]

Despite the intentions of the bomber and the FBI, Redwood Summer continued without Judi Bari. Thousands of activists engaged in numerous big and small actions throughout the summer of 1990, trying to stop the logging of old-growth redwoods and to bring up the issues of the loss of jobs and the stress on logging families brought on by clear-cutting versus sustainable logging practices. As a result of Redwood Summer, a small portion of the old-growth redwoods that Redwood Summer activists were fighting for, called the Headwater Forest, were preserved.

Bari had self-identified as a feminist for many years prior to her involvement with Earth First!; at some time in the midst of her struggle with sexism in Earth First!, she began to identify as an ecofeminist. In 1992, she published an article called "The Feminization of Earth First!" in a *Ms.* column called "Ecofeminism." In 1995, she was interviewed by Greta Gaard for a video documentary entitled *Ecofeminism Now!*[127] Bari's brand of ecofeminism was activist and materialist, including, as we have seen, an analysis of sexism and classism as well as environmental destruction. Oriented less toward the production of theory and more toward the production of direct action, Bari focused on the daily lives of the women she worked and lived with, and constructed an ecofeminist politics that could enable their empowerment and political engagement. An example of Bari's analytical approach can be seen in a story she tells in "Ecofeminism Now!" about a tactic developed in post-Redwood Summer actions called "the Albion uprising."

[In the Albion Uprising we] developed a tactic explicitly as a women's tactic. We talked about why are there not more women in these demonstrations, well there were plenty of women, but not compared to the population. And we discussed the fact that women can't just show up, because they have to get childcare, and can't risk arrest because they have to be at work the next day to take care of their kids, so we came up with a tactic to answer specifically to those needs, this tactic called "yarning." And what we'd do, is we'd go out at night, so you can get childcare and it's a very low arrest risk, and we'd take yarn and weave it in and out, and in and out of the trees, and it may not sound like much, but it turned out to really slow them [the loggers] down (and all of these tactics only slow them down, they don't stop them) because when they come in and try to cut it with their chainsaw, the yarn wraps around the chainsaw and stalls the chainsaw out, and when they try to whack it with their logging axes, which is always the next thing, the logger's axe bounces off. Actually the most efficient and aggressively nonmacho way to get rid of a web is to cut it with a scissors, but they won't do that, they use their knives instead which takes longer. . . . [Yarning] became the symbol of the Albion Uprising and along with it developed a mythology. We said to the loggers: "This is the web of life and when the web is cut the spell is cast." You know, just little things like that to freak them out.[128]

It is interesting to note the way in which the primary rationale for the tactic of "yarning" is to facilitate women's participation, and the "web of life" imagery is ironically chosen after the fact, contrary to the way in which this "web" imagery is thought to inspire or represent women's actions. Bari's form of ecofeminism is inclusive and pragmatic, activist and analytical.

While all feminist Earth First!ers may not have been as willing as Bari to wear the label, after the 1990 controversy over which many of the Earth First! founders resigned, the *Earth First! Journal* became much more open to feminist expression and analysis, though not without continued controversy. On the cover of the last issue of the *Earth First! Journal* edited by the original journal staff, there was a cartoon of "The Compleet Radical/Woman Environmentalist," a counterpart to the "Compleet Radical Environmentalist" that celebrated earlier Earth First!'s "redneck warrior" image. Obviously meant as a parting shot from the old guard and as an implicit comment on appropriate "feminism" within biocentric Earth First!, the cartoon depicted a blonde, long-haired, big-breasted, and slender-waisted woman who nevertheless modeled "trail-trekkin' tree-climbin' river-runnin' butt-kickers," "bolt-cutters (for bulldozer modification)," "natural body hair" [on her lower legs], and a clenched fist labeled an "attitude adjuster." In a position allowing display of her shapely legs, she has her foot on the back of a prone "timber beast (degeneratus humanoidia)" wearing a hat with the label "Kleercut Logging Co." This image among others was the subject of a feminist analysis of cultural images used by Earth First!ers printed in the new *Earth First! Journal* several months later.[129] Criticitizing images of women as sex objects and as Mother Nature, the author, Simon "De Beaulivar" Zapotes analyzes the feminization of the earth and the naturalization of women in fine ecofeminist terms. Though there were many letters written rejecting the article, the *Journal* under new editorship continued to make much more room for women's voices and feminist analysis than the old *Journal* had ever done. Thus, ecofeminism found a place, albeit under constant attack from sexists, in Earth First!

ECOFEMINISMS REVISITED

In this chapter, I've moved through a constructed history of ecofeminism from 1980 to 1994 by examining the use of the label "ecofeminism" as a point of negotiation against sexism within male-dominated radical environmentalisms. In doing so, I want to make several points. The first is that ecofeminism has multiple origins. The second is that ecofeminism is centrally a part of a history of feminism in the United States, a result of a broad feminist consciousness that provides resources for resisting sexism in numerous locations. The third is the diversity within ecofeminism. As feminist resistance to different kinds of male domination in radical environmentalism appears, it takes a variety of shapes and inflections suitable to a strategic intervention within a particular political context. In the examples I've examined in this chapter, ecofeminism has used separatist arguments for the necessity of women's independent action; biologistic arguments for the value of women's experience; materialist arguments for defining women's experience as socially constructed and internally differentiated; arguments for an "ethic of care" that assumes a universalistic aspect to a female ethics; arguments for a feminist re-working of "holism" that rejects totalizing understandings of human relation-ships to nature and to other humans; arguments that insist on including racism and classism as factors which divide women into different groups and deeply influence the tactics that must be used against a sexist and environ-mentally destructive culture. It is central to my thesis in this book that the the-oretical inconsistency found in these various ecofeminist positions is a result of the strategic and dynamic qualities of the formation of ecofeminism as a po-litical location within specific historical and political contexts.

The environmentalist arenas I have examined in this chapter—social ecol-ogy, deep ecology, and Earth First!—are not the only or the most important arenas in which ecofeminism arises as a political location. Similar stories could be told about others, especially the animal liberation movement and the U.S. Greens. I do not cover these areas in this book, not because they are not important (in particular, animal ecofeminists are an important facet of ecofeminism), but because of space considerations. I am at ease in doing this because I know that others, better equipped than I am, will tell these stories in the near future.[130] In the rest of the book, I will sometimes revisit portions of this history by looking in more detail at particular ecofeminist organizations and texts. In the next chapter, I will look more closely at the connection be-tween ecofeminism and feminist antimilitarist direct action.

ECOFEMINIST ANTIMILITARISM AND STRATEGIC ESSENTIALISMS

In this chapter, I want to present one of ecofeminism's early manifestations, in the antimilitarist movement, in ways that include its being an intervention into radical environmentalisms, but that also explore the development of ecofeminism as a process of coalescing different movements. I suggest that this coalescence is implicated in various essentialist elements of antimilitarist ecofeminisms. I will closely examine the ways in which early ecofeminists constructed and connected "women" and "nature."[1] I assume and refer to a current critique of ecofeminist essentialism and address the political dangers of using such symbols as "Mother Nature," which may reinforce patriarchal assumptions about the more "natural" status of women. I also examine the other danger of essentialist rhetorics: the ways in which essentialist formulations obscure important differences *among* women (of race, of class, of nationality, etc.). However, as I stated in the Introduction, I want to move beyond the usual critique of essentialism by insisting that the frequency of such essentialist symbols and language must be *explained* as well as resisted. In this chapter I argue that these essentialist moments are part of creating a strategic political identification between "women" and "nature."

Antimilitarist ecofeminists in the 1980s were attempting to create unity between very different kinds of women and to connect radical analyses from a number of disparate, though related, social movements. They were also, as discussed in the last chapter, creating a feminist critique of sexism in environmentalism and attempting to fashion new feminist political spaces for an environmentalist activist politics. In addition, they were attempting to solidify connections between feminism(s) and nonviolent direct action. All of these goals are implicated in the production of particular essentialist notions of women as more peaceful, more nurturing, and closer to nature then men.

Drawing my examples from feminist antimilitarist actions that I characterize as early ecofeminism, I argue that radically democratic movement structures, such as coalitions, networks, affinity groups, and consensus process decision making, may have served to destabilize essentialist formulations in early ecofeminism. I hope that this grounded analysis of the uses of "essentialism" in a feminist movement will serve more generally as an example for the theoretical assessment of feminist activism by feminist scholars. As I have already mentioned, because I have been both an activist in and a scholar of the feminist antimilitarist direct action movement, I have always been struck by the way in which women in the peace movement of the 1980s—particularly in those actions organized by and for women—have appeared as the quintessentialists against whom feminism must be protected. I remind the reader that this does not mean that I do not think that the characterization and criticism of feminist antimilitarism as essentialist is unjustified. But here I want to offer a different perspective on the essentialist formulations of antimilitarist feminism, or early ecofeminism.

I intend to explore the uses of essentialist formulations for feminist peace activism and at the same time point to the ways in which radically democratic movements constantly revise and contest political identities. I will try to mitigate what I see as a prevailing reductionist account of the essentialism of feminist peace activism in the 1980s by examining contradictions, fractures, and debates within the movement's discursive practices, using as examples writings by Ynestra King in the early to mid-1980s, as well as several debates concerning the definition of "women" in several feminist peace actions during this time period.

THE ANTIMILITARIST NONVIOLENT DIRECT ACTION MOVEMENT

Let me begin by being specific about what I mean by the "direct action movement," because I do make a distinction between this movement and the "peace movement."[2] This distinction is important to my argument, because my contention here is that the specific political practices of the direct action movement destabilized but did not prevent essentialist formulations of political identities. In my work, the "direct action movement" refers to a series of "actions" engaged in by groups that organize themselves in a decentralized, nonhierarchical manner (frequently in small groups called "affinity groups"), which use a participatory, democratic, decision-making process (usually called "consensus process") and which prefer direct action to institutionalized, electoral, or interest-group politics. Frequently, such groups are involved in civil disobedience, that is, the principled breaking of the law in the process of political protest. Using this definition, I include in the direct action movement the actions organized by and for women that have been often singled out for their essentialism[3] and that have been claimed as early manifestations of ecofeminism, such as: the Women's Pentagon Actions of 1980 and 1981; the Seneca Falls Women's Peace Encampment, the Puget Sound Women's Peace Camp (both begun in 1983); and the Mother's Day Actions at the Nevada Test Site in 1987 and 1988. This form of organization and practice has also been used by lesbian and gay activists, homeless activists, and activists involved in a myriad of other issues.

Whatever an action's particular target, the movement's goals were argued for in terms of a political vision that synthesized different branches of radical politics. The politics, and practice, of the direct action movement aspired to be feminist, participatory democratic, antiracist, anticapitalist, antiheterosexist, environmentalist, and anti-imperialist, as well as opposed to ageism, disability prejudice, and sometimes speciesism.[4] However, the movement's politics and organizational structures were continually contested, and thus explicitly argued for as well as against, in the internal debates that repeatedly took place over the use of affinity groups, consensus process, and nonviolence. Conversely, the use of these structures, which require broad participation, meant that people in the movement were consistently exposed to many different life experiences and political analyses. Thus, participants in the movement who might not totally subscribe to all aspects of the movement's politics were nevertheless significantly exposed to them. I repeatedly observed during my study of this movement that the openness and diversity of the movement's politics existed in tension with the universalist, essentialist formulations of a great deal of the movement's rhetoric. Now I will turn more directly to an examination of this contradiction.

ECOFEMINISM AND ESSENTIALISM IN THE WRITINGS OF YNESTRA KING

As a theoretical and political position intimately linked to the direct action movement, ecofeminism has been most completely formulated by Ynestra King. King was one of the founders of the Conference on Women and Life on Earth, subtitled Eco-feminism in the Eighties, which took place at Amherst, Massachusetts, in March of 1980; she was also a primary organizer of the Women's Pentagon Actions in 1980 and 1981. Besides teaching at several colleges in New England and New York, King has regularly taught ecofeminism and related subjects at the summer Institute for Social Ecology in Vermont. Her writings on ecofeminism have been included in important ecofeminist anthologies and are widely cited as examples of ecofeminist theory. King was a featured speaker and outspoken participant at the Ecofeminist Perspectives: Culture, Nature, Theory conference at USC in March 1987, and she was a cofounder of the WomanEarth Feminist Peace Institute, which I discuss in chapter 3. King has also been involved in a debate between deep ecologists and ecofeminists carried on in the letters sections of *The Nation* and the *UTNE Reader*. Thus King has prominently figured in the promulgation of ecofeminism as a position on the American Left that is deeply rooted in the politics and practice of the direct action movement.[5]

An analysis of King's writings shows the changing complexities of her position on "essentialist ecofeminism," that is, whether women are inherently peaceful and akin to nature, while men are inherently violent and on the side of a destructive culture. One of her first published pieces, a description of the Women's Pentagon Actions, describes what motivated her to begin organizing the conference that preceded these actions:

[As a graduate student] I was trying to work out the thought behind the coming together of feminism and ecology, and my intuition that these are and should be connected. The nuclear power plant at Three Mile Island [in] Pennsylvania melted down as I completed the exam process, alternating between the typewriter and the television, listening to male technocrats talk about slamming rods into the core to stop the reaction, referring to the runaway nuke as a "her" who needed to be "cooled down." I argued with my feminist friends about whether nukes (power and weapons) were really "feminist issues." I knew that it was time for me to become politically active again, as I imagined millions of women all over the planet "taking the toys away from the boys." I decided to begin talking seriously to other feminists in New England who shared my ecological perspective, about getting women together to talk about our fears for our own lives and the life of the Earth and what we could do together. . . . We were from different movements, feminist, lesbian, disarmament, anti-nuclear, ecology, and now after Three Mile Island we were ready to make a major commitment to bring our communities together to resist male violence against the living world.[6]

This quotation demonstrates several elements that enter into King's early understanding of ecofeminism. First, the conversation among feminists that results in the Women and Life on Earth Conference and the WPA actions is stimulated by a fear that the Earth, and life itself, is threatened by nuclear technologies that she represents as "male."[7] Second, she must argue with "other feminists" about whether ecological issues are legitimately feminist issues. Third, the conference is made up of women who come from "different movements," although I think that many people would not have been able to distinguish as neatly as King does between the "feminist, lesbian, disarmament, anti-nuclear, ecology" participants. Finally, she implies that all of these women would characterize the main threat to be countered as "male violence against the living world."

What these elements indicate to me is that King's (and perhaps other feminists') early formulation of an "ecofeminist" position takes place in a historical context of (1) real fear of ecological disaster (the accident at Three Mile Island), (2) disagreement among feminists about what feminism is, (3) a gathering together of women from various movement locations—including movements of mixed gender—who wish to work together as women, and (4) the use of a common rhetoric that depicts "male violence" as a threat to women and the world. That this common rhetoric seeks to overcome the disagreement among feminists over feminism itself and to facilitate and justify the collective action of women from different political locations seems clear; the connection made by this rhetoric to the very concrete dangers of nuclear technologies provides an impelling reason for women to want to act together against them. On the other hand, this rhetoric becomes too easily a dichotomous opposition between "men" (inherently violent) and "women" (inherently on the side of life), quite clear in the language King uses in this article.

The other danger of this rhetoric is that it obscures the complexity of the political analysis developed by the women organizing the WPA actions (which arose out of the Conference on Women and Life on Earth organized after Three Mile Island). Committed to a democratic process because of their backgrounds in various left movements, the women who met to organize the WPA had to begin by a *collective* defining of their goals and politics. As King writes:

> Somehow the Women's Pentagon Action had to reflect our feminist principles and process. And we began to talk about what these principles were. We talked about connections between violence against women and the rape of the earth. We talked about racism and American imperialism. We heard from women about the effect of military spending on the human services upon which women depend. We connected the masculinist mentality and nuclear bombs. Lesbian oppression and reproductive freedom were also issues that concerned us. We reflected on the election of Ronald Reagan and what that would mean to us. And we talked about how we might do our action with ritual politics and theatre and images. . . . We were defining feminist resistance.[8]

That this list of issues greatly widens the definition of feminism as the struggle against sexism is clear and proved to be disturbing to several observers. Writing in June of 1980, while the organizing for the WPA was just beginning, Ellen Willis launched a blistering attack against "ecofeminism" for the "insistence of some antinuclear activists that this issue should be *the* priority for women"—indeed, that this should be an issue around which women should organize as women. For Willis, for women to organize around issues that were not specifically "feminist" meant implicitly that they must organize as cultural feminists, raising immediately the dangers of "essentialism." "From a feminist perspective," Willis states with all the authority of her long association with feminism, "the only good reason for women to organize separately from men is to fight sexism. Otherwise women's political organizations simply reinforce female segregation and further the idea that certain activities and interests are inherently feminine."[9] While these dangers are properly noted, Willis never entertains the notion that perhaps women-organized direct actions were, to some extent, aimed at sexism *within* the environmental and antinuclear movements, as I've argued in chapter 1. Beyond this, she does not consider other reasons women might want to organize separately from men in these movements: for instance, to provide a location for women to engage in feminist consciousness-raising in the context of their other political concerns. Nor does she consider the possibility of expanding the definition of feminism or of using feminist analyses to understand issues not (yet) defined as aspects of sexism.[10]

In fact, the impetus for having women-only actions like the Women's Pentagon Actions, the Seneca Falls Women's Peace Encampment, and the Puget Sound Women's Peace Camp seems to have been partly to more fully mobilize feminists in separatist communities, partly to establish militarism as a feminist issue, and partly to provide, in Donna Warnock's words, a "safe space to explore new possiblities because we didn't have to interpret sexism, or explain or argue over feminist issues. (Though that happened some, of course. But the nature of it was different because we knew everyone was basically supportive.)"[11] In other words, for some at this time, there was a need for feminists to organize autonomously from men, away from the strain of being, as Warnock says, "on the defensive or having to prove ourselves" and at the same time without giving up their political priorities.[12]

Neither does Willis's criticism of ecofeminism take into account the appropriateness of linking feminism to antimilitarism in the historical context of Reaganism, in which the growth of militarism was inextricably linked to an antifeminist backlash, reflected in the masculinism of the Reagan administration's public rhetoric.[13] Thus, as strong as Willis's critique of the essentialism of ecofeminism was, and remains, there is a way in which it pales besides the attempt to link numerous radical political analyses that is evidenced in the "Unity Statement," the manifesto produced for the WPA in 1980 that served as the public statement of the goals of the action.[14] First drafted by Grace Paley, the "Unity Statement" was subject to innumerable revisions and arguments about its contents and language, resulting in a collectively produced document to which hundreds of women from very different class, race, and political backgrounds had contributed.[15] The Statement is incredibly comprehensive, connecting a myriad of issues from nuclear weapons; to cuts in domestic services; to urban decay; to the racism manifested in the draft, South Africa, and the women's movement; to the destruction of Native American lands; to the lack of good and available health care, child care, and education; to violence against women; to the imprisonment of the poor and people of color as criminals; to underemployment as well as unemployment; to comparative worth; to nuclear power; to environmental degradation; to U.S. support of "juntas" in El Salvador and Guatemala; to the growth of the New Right as manifested in the Family Protection Act, the opposition to the ERA, and the Human Life Amendment; to imperialism; to the growth of multinational corporations; to homophobia; to discrimination against the disabled; to ageism; to reproductive rights. And it does this in language that is relatively simple and jargon-free. In its complex weaving of a number of issues into a coherent left political position, it most closely resembles the Port Huron Statement, except for two important differences: It is both a feminist and an environmentalist statement, and it is, amazingly, only four columns of typescript, fitting on one leaflet as opposed to the sixty pages of the Port Huron Statement. This means, of course, that the connection it makes between radical issues is more of a list than an analysis, but as such it also signals its production in an ongoing and unfinished process of collective theorizing rather than as one political thinker's production of a "finished" analysis that presents itself as having figured out all the answers. It is clear that the participatory democratic process used to produce the "Unity Statement" undercut the universalizing, essentializing rhetoric employed by organizers such as King through its close detailing of the numerous axes of power (racism, classism, etc.) that position women in very different material and political locations.

Ynestra King's reaction to criticisms such as Ellen Willis's can be found in her 1981 article published in the special *Heresies* issue on feminism and ecology, the appearance of which was a signal of the growing feminist interest in the connections between sexism and environmental issues. In this article, King distinguishes her position both from that of Willis, whom she places in the camp of "rational-materialist" (or sometimes "socialist") feminism, and from Susan Griffin and Mary Daly, who as "radical cultural feminists" posit a "metaphysical-feminist naturalism." The problem with these positions, King argues, is that "gender identity is neither fully natural nor fully cultural."[16] Women, she argues, are located in a marginal position in relation to the conventional dichotomy between nature and culture, being at once constructed by patriarchal ideology as more "natural" beings than men, and acknowledged as (the lesser) half of a human race that is to be distinguished from nature because of its ability to reason. Speaking from this position of ambiguity between nature and culture, King writes, feminists can place themselves outside of the culture/nature dichotomy, a crucial move for the possibility of critiquing and resisting a patriarchal and capitalist culture built upon the destruction and domination of nature.

Yet, to maintain this position of "critical otherness," women must engage in a cultural and political practice, according to King, that is separate from men and has "roots in traditional women's ways of being in the world." Here King, through her demand that feminism "insist that we remember our origins in nature" seems to forget her earlier claim that ecofeminism must go beyond the dualism of "radical-cultural feminism" or "rational-materialist feminism." "The ecology question," King states,

> weights the historic feminist debate in the direction of traditional female values over the overly rational, combative male way of being in the world. Rationalist feminism is the Trojan horse of the women's movement. Its piece-of-the-action mentality conceals a capitulation to a culture bent on the betrayal of nature. In that sense it is both misogynist and anti-ecological. Denying biology, espousing androgny, and valuing what men have done over what we have done are all forms of self-hatred which threaten to derail the teleology of the feminist challenge to this violent civilization.[17]

Aside from the ironically "combative" tone of this statement, King here retreats from a promising attempt to go beyond the limitations of either an essentialist or constructionist position. In this statement, the terms "traditional female values," "biology," and "nature" are unproblematically opposed to a "combative male way of being," which represents "culture" and a "violent civilization." But note that this slip into essentialism occurs right after her argument for a "separate [from men] cultural and political activity so that we can imagine, theorize or envision from the vantage point of *critical otherness*."[18] The question of whether feminist political practice should be based on women's similarity to or women's difference from men is at issue here; her opponent at this juncture seems to be a liberal feminism that seeks equality with men in terms set by the capitalist political institutional system. King opts for the vantage of women's difference from men for theoretical and strategic reasons and, in doing so, lapses into an "essentialist" position, irrational on her own terms.

It is the need to speak from a standpoint of "critical otherness" or, in other words, claiming the right to constitute meaning from women's location within an oppressive system, that leads King to use essentialist language. Additionally, what kind of political action feminists should involve themselves in is at stake here: extra-institutional, perhaps separatist, actions *or* interest-group lobbying within the framework of the political bureaucracy. But a contradiction repeatedly appears between the essentialism that arises in the context of justifying separatist feminist direct actions and the wide-ranging, integrative political analysis promulgated through the process of these actions.

King's later published work reflects a more consistent approach to the problem of the dualism of culture/nature (and related constructionist/essentialist positions), but her emphasis on *direct action* as a description of ecofeminist political practice retains a tension between feminist separatism and a synthetic radical politics that ranges beyond "strictly feminist" concerns. In her 1983 article,[19] King more carefully locates ecofeminism as a "third direction," not severing the connection between woman and nature (like socialist feminists) nor reinforcing it (a position she acknowledges is taken by "many feminists [who] call themselves ecofeminists").[20] Instead, ecofeminism should

> recognize that although the nature/culture opposition is a product of culture, we can, nonetheless, *consciously choose* not to sever the woman/nature connections by joining male culture. Rather, we can use it as a vantage point for creating a different kind of culture and politics that would integrate intuitive/spiritual and rational forms of knowledge, embracing both science and magic insofar as they enable us to transform the nature/culture distinction itself and to envision and create a free, ecological society.[21]

In this article, King outlines four ecofeminist principles: (1) the subjugation of women and the subjugation of nature are dialectically related; (2) hierarchy justifies domination and must be resisted on all levels, including within ecofeminist political practice; (3) diversity must be maintained, for ecological and political reasons, thus domination based on class, race, nationality, sexuality, and various forms of privilege as well as the destruction of whole species and ecosystems must be resisted; and (4) dualistic thinking, particularly distinctions between culture and nature, supports all kinds of domination. The deconstructive and oppositional practice that supports these principles is "anti-militarist direct action." This assertion is supported by an analysis of militarism, which constructs it as the repository of the structures of domination that produce and perpetuate sexism, racism, imperialism, environmental destruction, and classism. Similarly to the politics of the "Unity Statement," ecofeminism here is described as a politics that can make "connections" between various radical positions and analyses. In particular, the principles of radical democracy and diversity require a constant re-evaluation of any attempt at a fixed definition of women.

At the heart of this politics, for King, is direct action, but of a particular kind: actions organized by and for women. "The politics being created by these actions draw on *women's culture*: embodying what is best in women's life-oriented *socialization*, building on *women's differences*, organizing anti-hierarchically in small groups in visually and emotionally imaginative ways, and seeking an integration of issues. These actions exemplify ecofeminism."[22]

If "these actions" (here King is referring to the WPA, the women's action at the Bohemian Grove in 1981, and Greenham Common in 1982) "exemplify ecofeminism," this does not mean that ecofeminism as King presents it is an uncontested political position, or even widely understood as an appropriate label within the direct action movement. That King knows this is clear in her acknowledgement of the other ecofeminists in her footnote cited above, but also in her consistent attempt to define ecofeminism in such a way that it could possibly appeal to both "cultural feminists" and "socialist feminists." At the same time, she wants to justify to other antimilitarist activists the appropriateness of women organizing separately from men and the importance of a feminist analysis to a integrative left politics.

What happens in her argument at this point is that she sometimes conflates ecofeminism and the participatory democratic politics of the direct action movement, which has been a mixed-gender movement while claiming feminism as one of its political positions. Thus, the reader is left with the impression that she is arguing that feminists, or women, are inherently nonviolent, antihierarchical, and always prefer a decentralized politics of direct action; or that antimilitarist direct action is the special provenance of feminist separatists.

These motivations and complexities occur again in King's response to Kirkpatrick Sale's article on "Ecofeminism" in *The Nation*. Here King specifically attacks Sale for characterizing ecofeminism in such a way that essentialist elements predominate, specifically Sale's emphasis on "goddess cultures" and "earth-based spirituality" as "hallmarks" of ecofeminism.[23] King complains that this creates the "impression of [ecofeminism as] a sentimentalizing religion of earth mothers."[24] On the other hand, King distances herself from a totally "constructivist" position by criticizing "ex-Marxist academic postmodernists [who] reject subject, history, and human agency." Instead, King offers ecofeminism as a position that "shares the project of other feminisms, which seek to draw on women's unarticulated (up until now) life experience to reconstitute the subject, and history, and a nondomineering agency rather than totally discard these modern (and problematic) concepts."[25] In addition, King uses her critique of Sale's article to point up the sexism inherent in left environmentalism, specifically "bioregionalism" and "deep ecology." Finally, King maintains that the true "hallmarks" of ecofeminism are a multivalent left politics based on a critique of domination (which includes both the domination of people and of nature) and the practice of direct action.[26]

Throughout her writings, King's formulation of ecofeminism is a political intervention with several complexly intertwined goals. First, she wants to overcome oppositions between feminists who identify with constructivist positions and essentialist positions. Second, she attempts to destabilize easy essentialist assumptions within the direct action movement by insisting that women are a part of culture and can construct their own definition through collective political action. Third, she provides a standpoint from which to criticize sexist environmentalists and practitioners of direct action, and an argument that justifies women organizing separately from men if they wish. And finally, she argues for the "decentralized," "antihierarchical" practice of direct action as the praxis of a politics able to synthesize various radical political positions, though she frequently conflates this practice with "feminism." It is in the third and fourth areas that "essentialist" formulations most often characterize King's arguments; otherwise, she is often consciously anti-essentialist. In sum, King's essentialism is tactical and unstable, one could even say "positional," employed when arguing for the need for women to organize on their own terms and for the importance of a feminist analysis within antimilitarist and environmentalist politics.

FEMINIST DIRECT ACTIONS AND THE "MORAL MOTHER"

In 1983, in the context of an antimilitarist movement that claimed feminism as one of its elements, and international resistance to the intention of the United States to deploy the Cruise and Pershing missiles in Europe, many women all over the world organized as "women" to fight militarism. Much of this antimilitarist feminist organizing employed essentialist rhetoric, evidenced by what Micaela di Leonardo has called the "Moral Mother" position: "nurturant, compassionate, and politically correct—the sovereign, instinctive spokeswoman for all that is living and vulnerable . . . [the] Moral Mother represents the vision of women as innately pacifist, and men as innately warmongering."[27] While I do not directly dispute di Leonardo's characterization, in every feminist antimilitarist action I have studied (from 1976 to 1988), I have found evidence of significant internal debate around essentialist definitions of "women." I will try to give some examples of these debates here.

Certainly it is the case that recurrent features of the direct action movement have been symbols and language that make uncritical connections between women, nature, and mothering: the use of Mother's Day for women's antimilitarist actions, an analysis of militarism that connects it with male violence against women and the "rape" of the earth; the prominence of feminist pagans, the witches that weave webs; and, within the movement, the frequent parallels, or even equations, made between feminism and nonviolence, feminism and antihierarchical politics, and feminism and environmentalism.

Di Leonardo's critique is directed at this visible manifestation of a feminism that argues against war because it is a male construction, and argues for peace because it is seen as a woman's way. She suggests, rightly I think, that any short-term benefits of the extensive use of the Moral Mother argument don't by themselves outweigh the dangers of this rhetoric potentially reinscribing women into a sexist stereotype of feminine virtue and passivity. Still, I think that her account (which I use here as representative of other accounts) is problematic.

First, the Moral Mother imagery, though "popular and ubiquitous," was not as central to the movement as the multivalent radical politics I have already described. In fact, accounts like di Leonardo's tend to use a definition of antimilitarist feminism limited to the maternalism they critique. Besides the symbolic discourse concerning women as natural peacemakers, the feminism of the nonviolent direct action movement was manifested in other ways as well: for instance, women and men participated equally, in most cases, in decision making, organizing, and support tasks. In addition, feminist antimilitarism is one key historical link between the second-wave feminism of the 1960s and '70s and contemporary feminist activism. A majority of direct actionists have been women, comprised of many different kinds of feminists and many women who would not identify themselves as feminists. Many of the feminists in the movement tended to be young and had been affected by the struggles of older feminists in the universities, in women's centers and crisis shelters, in the secondary schools, and in the work place. The direct action movement may well have been their first experience of working collectively with other women apart from men, and perhaps apart from the dominance of older feminists. The experience of acting politically with other women, using techniques in decision making and political analyses developed from the early second-wave feminist movement, made the direct action movement an important arena for feminist consciousness-raising and, during the 1980s, one of the few existing outside of universities.

Second, women's actions were frequently the focus of much debate over the meaning of "feminism," and the participatory democratic practice of these actions consistently destabilized any one definition of "women" or "mothers." An example of such a debate, or the nature of feminist discourse in the movement, is recounted in "Agreeing to Disagree" from We Are Ordinary Women, a book about the Puget Sound Women's Peace Camp. Formed in solidarity with the women's peace camps in Europe (such as Greenham Common) and other American camps (such as the one at Seneca Falls in upstate New York), the Puget Sound Peace Camp lasted for a full year (1983–1984) outside the Boeing Corporation's weapons plant in western Washington.[28]

In this one incident, similar to thousands of others in women's actions of the time, the Puget Sound Peace Camp women decided to leaflet the pornography district in Seattle as part of an attempt to link militarism and violence against women. In preparing for this action, two leaflets were independently produced, each analyzing pornography in different ways: one prominently featured an exhortation to "stop violence" and asserted that "pornography is violence." The graphics on this leaflet were of flowers and plants. The other leaflet argued that a military build-up that deprived women of needed social services could only occur in a society in which violence against women was tolerated and women's worth was cheapened. This leaflet argued that violent pornography contributed to the societal devaluation of women. There were no graphics on this leaflet; on the bottom-right corner it said "labor donated." Thus the first pamphlet could be read as promulgating an essentialist analysis of pornography as an expression of innate male violence directed at women as victims; while the second pamphlet could be read as a materialist analysis of a historically situated relationship between pornography and sexism. Because the presumption in the camp was that consensus must be reached on actions engaged in by affinity groups, the differences in style and content between the two leaflets caused a heated conflict over which one should represent the Camp. After a prolonged discussion, which ranged over all of the ways to conceptualize the connections between sexism and militarism, the peace campers decided to distribute both leaflets. According to the narrators of this incident, "It became clear that many women felt their individual expression was being masked by the 'correct' political line that the Camp wanted to put out."[29] The book does not say, however, which leaflet represented that "correct" line.

Incidents that occurred during the early organizing for the Mother's Day Action at the Nevada Test Site in 1987 can serve as further examples of the way in which the structures of the movement led to debates over the meaning of feminism and the subject categories "women" or "mothers." Although the Mother's Day Action was to be a "women's action," some of the women who originally conceived of it did not want to, as they put it, "exclude" men. So their compromise was that the action was to be *organized* by women, but men would be "welcome to participate." Quite reasonably, given the decentralized nature of the affinity group structure and the requirements of consensus process for participatory decision making, this language was interpreted very differently in different parts of the country and among different communities of women. In many parts of Northern California, this compromise wording was interpreted (after some debate) to mean that only women would organize and make decisions prior to the actual action; once affinity groups were formed, of course, men would participate in decisions within affinity groups of mixed gender. In other areas, this compromise was interpreted to mean that men could make initial organizing decisions *equally* with women. In a very few areas, men were actually the sole organizers for this "women's action" until affinity groups were formed. Thus, the notion of a "women's action" meant different things to different participants, despite the overarching rhetoric of maternalism embedded in the notion of a Mother's Day action.

In another example from the early organizing period, women organizers in Santa Cruz (including myself at the time) became concerned that the emphasis on Mother's Day would be construed to exclude women who *weren't* mothers. So the Santa Cruz organizing group (most of whom were nonmothers) proposed that the action be called "the Mothers and Others Action." This was very enthusiastically received at the national organizing level in Las Vegas; but it wasn't until weeks later that the Santa Cruz group realized that the women in Las Vegas understood "Mothers and Others" to mean "women and *men*" rather than women who were and weren't mothers.[30] Even though this understanding conflated women and mothers, a number of men who participated in the action were interested in claiming their status as "mothers": one affinity group, half of which were men, arrived at the site all wearing pillows under large T-shirts, pregnant with meaning; and many men enthusiastically volunteered for child-care duties during the action.

I recount these examples to show that a closer look at the discursive practices of the early ecofeminist actions reveals that the organizational structures of the nonviolent direct action movement, which allowed for a great deal of autonomy within collective actions and required a lot of (perhaps too much!) discussion and participation, constantly destabilized any fixed notions of feminism or of what women should be. This means that it was very difficult for that movement to sustain a particular analysis, or to control the meanings produced in actions, or to strategize over a long campaign of actions. But its other result is that political meanings and identities were constructed in an open and flexible way, available to the interpretation of diverse participants.

OPPOSITIONAL CONSCIOUSNESS AND ESSENTIALIST DISCOURSE

There are several difficulties with the prevailing (but, I contend, reductive) description of feminist antimilitarism, or early ecofeminism, as "radical" or "cultural" feminism as long as this is a code for "essentialist." As I hope I have shown, such a description obscures the contested nature of the movement's feminism. It also does not give an accurate picture of the diversity of women and feminisms within the movement. In practice, the movement managed, in both mixed-gender and women-only actions, to have as participants people diverse in almost every respect, with the reservations about racial diversity noted above (see especially n.4, this chapter). Reductive descriptions of the feminism of the direct action movement, and by extension any other political movement, are unintentionally damaging to these movements, because they obscure their politics for those people who might be their most helpful critics, powerful allies, or potential participants. Such reductive characterizations may discourage feminists of anti-essentialist persuasions from participating in a movement and thereby further destabilize essentialist discourse.

Further, in rightly pointing out the dangers of symbolic codes that uncritically bring together women and nature, mothering and peace, a critique of the dangers of essentialism too easily substitutes for an analysis of antimilitarist ecofeminism as a discourse of resistance specific to its historical and ideological context. For instance, when di Leonardo characterizes the feminism of the peace movement as "radical feminist," she conflates it with the "social feminism" of the nineteenth century. As a result, she cannot adequately analyze the material and historical basis for the symbolic codes used by feminists in the contemporary movement. As she herself realizes, she leaves unexplained the persistence of such imagery, even though she several times asks the question.

I can only indicate the outlines of a historical analysis of antimilitarist ecofeminism here. The early ecofeminist analysis of the direct action movement, which connected violence against women, militarism, and ecological destruction, begins to be widely articulated in 1980. At this time, partly through a backlash against feminism, a New Right administration was installed that used patriarchal ideology to justify a huge military build-up and an economic restructuring from which women, particularly single mothers and women of color, suffered a great deal. In this context, early ecofeminism can be seen as an "oppositional consciousness" or a "positional feminism," a tactical politics of identity that provides a way of knowing and naming the existing complex relations between oppression, resistance, and identity.

Moral Mother rhetoric and imagery in the antimiliarist direct action movement frequently stemmed from the participation of women who joined the movement because they were concerned for their children and their children's children in a nuclear age, or they were women who easily thought of themselves as one day becoming mothers, accepting the burdens of the reproductive function in a patriarchal society. Having joined the movement on these terms, they found themselves working collectively (though not necessarily without considerable debate) with women who were witches, lesbians, radicals, socialists, and (generally white) women who spoke out against racism (many of whom were also mothers). Thus the language of motherhood provided a kind of salve to the divisions among women (and feminists) in the movement, or, seen another way, a glue that resulted in the adhesion of different kinds of women to each other. Beyond this, mothering itself is an "ideological seam"[31] in contemporary society; the oppositional consciousness of the movement deployed various images of "mothers" (men as mothers, grandmothers, lesbian mothers, Mother Earth, etc.) in an attempt to replace the Reaganesque image of the militarized white mother of two who willingly supports the sacrifice of "her" men and children in war and in nuclear industries.

In this case, early ecofeminism struggled to move women from being a fulcrum of militarist ideology to a position of resistance to militarism, to which women are particularly vulnerable in a patriarchal society (though they are not exempt from complicity in militarism).[32] The symbolic discourse of webs, witches, and rituals of exorcism outside the gates of military facilities can be understood, as Donna Haraway has pointed out, as a specific critique of the fatal intertwining of postindustrial technology, capitalism, militarism, and commodity culture.[33] The magic of witches in the direct action movement opposes the "magical" characteristics of a nuclear technology that maintains the balance between life and death through arcane, secret operations known only to the initiated. The rituals of paganism that celebrate nature, life, and sexuality take place in the wastes of irradiated lands and in the face of technologies of death justified by a New Right ideology of patriarchal "family values," including chastity, obedience, monogamous heterosexuality, and unquestioning patriotism. Early ecofeminism was specifically constructed to challenge the articulations supporting the hegemonic bloc we now call the "Reagan-Bush years." In other words, I am suggesting that many of the elements of the Moral Mother rhetoric rejected by anti-essentialist feminists can be analyzed as useful parts of a theory of resistance. In addition, this constructed identity serves as a method of deconstructing specific formulations of power in the 1980s. The theory embedded in the practice of antimilitarist feminism is thus akin to poststructuralist feminist theories, which are portrayed as antithetical to "essentialist" antimilitarist feminism. In chapter 5, I will similarly posit that essentialist ecofeminist rhetoric aimed at constructing an international movement is engaged in a similar deconstruction of a new hegemonic bloc, which I call "globalizing environmentalisms."

Earlier, I've referred to the two dangers of essentialist formulations of feminist discourse: that positing universal female characteristics obscures differences among women, and that essentialist discourse reinscribes women into patriarchal ideology. I have tried to show so far that while the dangers of essentialism that arise out of use of Moral Mother imagery and some other ecofeminist arguments are real and should be addressed, within and without the movement, the democratic practices of the movement tended to deconstruct universal descriptions of women, feminism, or mothers. Ultimately, the identity constructed by women in the antimilitarist direct action movement was not simply an essentialist one (i.e., based on beliefs about women's innate natures) but a result of negotiation and agreements necessary for collective action, a political identity that was not singular but the "we" of a movement. As an expression of solidarity based on common beliefs and goals worked out through an ongoing process of discussion and debate, such an identity was also a tool of analysis for an antimilitarist theory of resistance. Differences between women were not simply obscured, but reconstructed as a flexible analysis of the different kinds of oppression women were subjected to. Despite these promising aspects, these actions remained predominantly white women's actions; while antiracist in theory, they remained segregated in practice. In the next chapter, I will examine an attempt by some of these feminist antimilitarist activists to overcome this segregation, and in chapter 4, I analyze reasons for the persistence of such racial segregation.

But what about the danger of women becoming reinscribed into patriarchal discourse? Again, this was a serious risk of much of the movement's rhetoric and practice. But I think it is important to point out that the mainstream press and the people who lived in the communities in which these actions have taken place rarely perceived women in the movement as "traditional" wives, daughters, and mothers. Frequently it was the women-only actions, or the women's groups within mixed actions, that received the worst press, as the media was faced with women behaving in an aggressive and outrageous fashion, staining the walls of military and corporate buildings with their blood, living together happily without men, and going to jail. Gay-baiting, in particular, was and still is a common reaction to women's actions. It is ironic that where feminist observers see dangerous essentialists, patriarchal observers see dangerous lesbians.[34] During actions at the Diablo nuclear power plant and the Livermore Laboratories, the Feminist Cluster (a grouping of women-only affinity groups) had the reputation of being the most militant in their actions, consistently stretching the definition of nonviolence beyond the comfort of other participants. Even at the Mother's Day Action in 1987, which was one of the milder manifestations of feminist antimilitarism, the local headline the next day read: "'Mothers' Protest," with quotation marks around "Mothers," as if the reporter had great doubts that there were any real Mothers there.

3

WOMANEARTH FEMINIST PEACE INSTITUTE AND THE RACE FOR PARITY

The story of WomanEarth Feminist Peace Institute illustrates both the serious antiracist efforts of some ecofeminists as well as particular problems with a U.S. discourse on race that is prevalent inside and outside of the movement. As noted in the previous chapters, ecofeminism has been primarily a white women's political location, and yet it is a movement that thinks of itself as antiracist. As I will discuss at greater length in the next chapter, many environmental activists who are women of color don't want to identify as "ecofeminist," as they see ecofeminism as not concerned in important ways with racism or with the issues central to environmental activists of color. In this chapter, I wish to explore a serious attempt to overcome barriers between white women and women of color within an ecofeminist organization during the period when ecofeminism was becoming an identifiable political location. My analysis here locates some of these barriers in the history of U.S. social movements and the antiracist discourses they have generated, some of the barriers within the particular form of ecofeminism constructed in the late 1980s, and some of the barriers in structural U.S. racism.

As I have said, despite the racialized divide between those who would or would not identify as an ecofeminist, antiracist analyses consistently appear in ecofeminist literature, and racism almost always counts as a factor in ecofeminist assessments of the causes and consequences of environmental problems. These antiracist analyses display the qualities of their origins. Political discourses in opposition to U.S. racism have followed particular histories constructed in the context of particular "racial formations."[1] Thus, it is no surprise to find U.S. ecofeminism using discourses of racial difference embedded in its historical context, especially the contexts of the social movements that have influenced it.

Ecofeminism moves beyond early second-wave radical feminist discourse, which presented racism and sexism as analogous, speaking of "women" and "blacks" in ways that made women of color invisible and that prevented the analysis of the "double jeopardy" of racism and sexism.[2] Indeed, beginning in 1979, early ecofeminism was most interested in establishing the interconnections between various forms of discrimination and oppression rather than ranking them or seeing them as separate forces affecting distinct kinds of individuals. Despite this greater complexity, early ecofeminist discourses of racial difference follow a course of development patterned on the broader context of U.S. feminist and antiracist oppositional culture. Perhaps stemming directly from the personal evolution of white feminist civil rights activists into feminist antimilitarists,[3] race appears in early ecofeminist analyses defined primarily as a dichotomy: white and black. During the mid-1980s, when women from a variety of racial/ethnic backgrounds finally were able to make visible a thoroughgoing critique of the racism of white feminists, the binary conception of race shifted to white and nonwhite, or white women and women of color. It is in this context that the organization called WomanEarth was formed. However, I am examining it from of a very different political context, one in which there are widespread critiques of binary notions of racial difference and a preference for the deployment of multiple notions of racial difference. Thus, my analysis is informed by an antiracist discourse not available in the same way for the organizers of WomanEarth. I want to keep sight of the fact that the same shift in anti-racist discourses that produces my analysis will also have affected the members of WomanEarth, and thus their positions today may well be very different from their positions as I characterize them here.

THE STORY OF WOMANEARTH

Begun in 1985, WomanEarth Feminist Peace Institute was founded with the intention to establish an ecofeminist educational center, at first in the form of a summer institute, that would produce theory, conduct research, teach classes, publish an ecofeminist newsletter or journal, and support political activities of various kinds. Another conception of the project involved the creation of ecofeminist "locals," each with their own community project, connected in a national network by WomanEarth. At the heart of WomanEarth was the idea that it would confront racism head-on—that antiracism would be central to its definition, unlike previous versions of ecofeminist political action. Following the advice of African American feminist Barbara Smith, WomanEarth was founded on the principle of racial parity: that is, there would always be an equal number of white women and women of color within the organization, particularly within its decision-making structures. The core members of WomanEarth, sometimes called "Circle One," were eight women. Four of them were women of color: Rachel Bagby (African American), Papusa Molina (Mexicana), Rachel Sierra (Chicana), and Luisah Teish (African American). Four were white women: Gwyn Kirk, Ynestra King, Margie Mayman, and Starhawk.[4]

WomanEarth organized a successful ecofeminist conference based on racial parity in 1986 at Hampshire College, but it disbanded after a period of disorganization and false starts from 1987 to 1989. Despite this short and conflicted history, WomanEarth influenced the formation of U.S. ecofeminism by broadening the notion of ecofeminist politics at a crucial time and by publicizing ecofeminism as an antiracist political location. In this chapter, I will tell the story of WomanEarth's efforts, concentrating on the way in which racial parity operated to shape the organization's goals, practice, and understanding of racism within an ecofeminist context. While this history is interesting in itself as a piece of the development of ecofeminism that has until now remained largely unknown, I am most interested in analyzing the organization in terms of what it can tell us about the practice of feminist antiracist social movements, particularly those that are predominantly white. I begin by tracing the history of the organization in some detail and then analyze specific areas in order to explore the political lessons of the experience: the implications of racial parity as a principle of operation, and the effects of WomanEarth's identification as an *ecofeminist* organization.

Before I begin tell the story of WomanEarth, however, I would like to reflect briefly on the problems involved in reconstructing the history of a movement organization. This story is indebted to the women involved in WomanEarth, who have been very generous with their time and trusting of my good intentions in gathering this information. Though I will use the information I have gathered to attribute positions, intentions, actions, and opinions to different people involved, I want to caution that this is my story, my interpretation, constructed out of weaving together the words of separate testimonies about events that in some cases are almost ten years distant from the time of the interviews. I did attempt to give my interviewees some control over what I could attribute to them personally, but ultimately they had no control over the context in which I place their words and the rhetorical methods by which I give them the specific meaning they will have here.[5]

I think it is important to understand the achievements, struggles, and debates that made up the experience called WomanEarth, but I worry over the inevitable decontextualization of my account from the personal relationships, the day-to-day contexts of collective work, the hopes and fears that went into the experience. Recovering the histories of feminist organizations is crucial to putting together strategies for feminist futures, and I remain convinced that WomanEarth is a very important part of feminist and ecofeminist history, which, if lost or unexamined, would impoverish us. Yet I am acutely cognizant that the analysis I engage in here is both advantaged and disadvantaged by hindsight. In addition, my account is influenced by my outsider status, my ability to take a disinvested position in relation to the very personal and individual attempts required to make a particular political organization work and survive. I am very much aware that should another analyst turn her attention to organizing efforts I have been involved in, particularly in the same time period, she would find similar flaws to those I find here. None of the problems encountered by WomanEarth are unusual for radical, grassroots organizations. Finally, my interest in specific aspects of the organization over others inevitably skews the narrative. In particular, my interest in the construction of difference puts a spotlight on conflict within the organization, emphasizing it over agreement, friendship, political solidarity, and play. In some recognition of these problems, I will try to note uncertainties and the possibilities of multiple interpretations as I proceed. Though my account, organized as it is toward object lessons for the future, is inevitably long on critique and short on approbation, I came away from my research with a great respect for each one of the participants. I recognize that their aspirations were so high that the disappointments encountered were particularly sharp. My purpose here is not to increase or to revive that past pain (though I think I cannot avoid doing so) but to honor each woman's effort by offering the experience as an important place to learn about constructing better and more effective feminist politics. I raise these issues not just for the sake of the members of WomanEarth, but as a methodological caveat for the study of movements generally. A greater degree of reflexivity on the part of researchers should lead to greater understanding of the choices and intentions of activists.

A FEMINIST PEACE INSTITUTE

The impetus for WomanEarth came from Ynestra King and Starhawk. King reports being motivated by two main desires. First, she wanted to create an institution that sustained the kind of decentralized, action-oriented feminist antimilitarist politics she had been engaged in. The challenge was to develop some stable means of movement building and at the same time not undermine the democratic, participatory nature of the politics. She wanted to "grapple with some of the questions of insitutionalizing a kind of politics which were so anti-institutional."[6] She felt it was important to continue to do political work based on the interconnections identified by activists in these actions between patriarchy, militarism, social justice, and ecology—the position that, beginning in the early 1980s, began to be called "ecofeminism." By 1984, with the reelection of Reagan, the feeling in progressive circles was one of retrenchment, of the need to solidify oppositional efforts for the long haul. Having taught in the Institute for Social Ecology's summer program for several years, King thought that what was needed was an ecofeminist educational institution that could provide resources for ecofeminist action, engage in networking, and support research on relevant issues. This vision was shared in important ways by Starhawk, who had taught in several alternative educational institutions and wanted to create one that was focused on the connections between feminist politics and spirituality.

King and Starhawk's second aim was to create an ecofeminist institution that was antiracist as a central part of its definition. King, in particular, took seriously the critiques of the Women and Life on Earth conference and the Women's Pentagon Actions as being too much about white women and white women's issues, focusing on the critique of the essentialism of these actions that pointed out the racist effects of their rhetorics. The argument that these essentialist rhetorics reinscribed women into patriarchal stereotypes apparently had less importance for her. From her perspective, the network of Women and Life on Earth, which had been the basis for the organization of the Women's Pentagon Actions, had later "come apart because of racism."[7] Despite good intentions, the network had not dealt with the problem of its appeal to white women over women of color, a characteristic evident from its inception in the Women and Life on Earth: Ecofeminism in the 1980s conference held at Amherst. As a result, all of the actions organized by the network had been primarily white women's actions, even though racism had been identified as a problem all along in the movement's analyses of militarism.

To overcome this problem, King recognized, "somehow we had to address from the beginning the problem of racism." King argued that there were two responses to the criticism of early ecofeminist politics as racist. One was to say that "people organized politics and actions to their own communities, and this is a racially segregated society, and . . . coalitions were the appropriate response to racism. But the other alternative was . . . to have a multi-racial organization." To do this, King realized, the organization would have to have the input of people of color from its inception. The effort would need to avoid at all costs "anything that could be called 'outreach' . . . [which is] really in a way a whole racist construction. It still has the white elitist center, and you have the periphery, and we're going to reach out to the 'others'." Instead, King wanted the ideas and issues central to the new organization to be formed by women of color from the outset. As we will see, these two goals of King's— forming an ecofeminist educational institute and making antiracism central to ecofeminism—turned out to be in considerable conflict: not because they are logically or necessarily incompatible, but because of the specific history of

WomanEarth. It turned out to be not so easy to "start from the beginning" and at the same time construct an organization with a particular place within a developing social movement history.

King's antiracist strategy was deeply influenced by Barbara Deming, a lesbian-feminist, antiracist activist, and pacifist who was a strong role model for feminist antimilitarists of the time. During Deming's last illness, she and King discussed the importance of forming interracial organizations. Deming suggested that King talk with Barbara Smith, an African American lesbian-feminist, writer, publisher, and pacifist activist, about how to do this. In fact, according to King, Deming "gave me something to take to [Smith], which I had to take, so that was a way to make sure that we connected." In early 1986, King talked to Smith about wanting to form an interracial organization that would bring together feminist, social justice, spiritual, antimilitarist and ecological concerns. Smith then suggested to King the principle of racial parity upon which WomanEarth was based, and indeed made racial parity the condition of her involvement in the early stages of such an organization. Smith agreed to contact other women of color who might be interested in the project, and was responsible for the initial participation of Papusa Molina, a Mexican feminist attending graduate school in the United States; Luisah Teish, an African American feminist and Oshun priestess; and Chandra Mohanty, an Asian Indian feminist theorist (who participated only in one or two meetings). Teish and Molina went on to become core members of WomanEarth. Though Smith was involved only in two or three early meetings of the organization, her influence in the form of the principle of racial parity was crucial to the shape of WomanEarth.

King was sensitive to the dangers of asking women of color to come into a project that had been initiated by white women, but her conversations with Smith came after a considerable amount of planning, discussion and fundraising had gone into the creation of a "Feminist Peace Institute." Ynestra King and Starhawk had discussed the idea of a new ecofeminist organization with an educational focus on several occasions from 1984 to 1985. During this period of time, they had worked together on drafting a proposal for an institute that would begin in 1986 with a summer program of courses on ecology, feminist peace politics, and feminist spiritualty, and they used this proposal to seek funding for their idea.

In preparation for the UN Conference on Women in Nairobi in 1985, Starhawk worked with a white U.S. woman (whom I will call by the pseudonym "Camille Daney") who was very interested in international feminism and antimilitarism; Daney was the primary organizer and financial supporter of the Nairobi Peace Tent, a place where women at the UN conference gathered for workshops and discussions about the relation between women's issues and peace issues. King had also participated in the Peace Tent, and was impressed with Daney's commitment to both personal involvement in and financial support of the political issues she cared about. After discussions with Starhawk and King, Daney became the primary funder of the Feminist Peace Institute, and contributed a large amount of money for the start-up of the organization. She continued these large contributions up until the Hampshire conference, after which she ceased to fund WomanEarth, for reasons which I will discuss later.[8] By December of 1985, Daney's money enabled King to start an office (in space provided by the War Resisters League) in New York, and to pay Gwyn Kirk (a white British feminist who had been active in Greenham Common) some money to work on the Institute. During the last months of 1985 and the first of 1986, King and Kirk looked over a number of possibilities for summer venues for the academic program, sought possible faculty, investigated the mechanics of nonprofit incorporation, applied for fiscal sponsorship from the A. J. Muste Memorial Institute (under whose auspices the War Resisters League operated), and acquired letterhead and an address stamp.[9] Several meetings had also been held in New York during this time involving Grace Paley (a white feminist writer and activist), Ann Snitow (a white feminist activist and scholar), and several other white feminists.

Meanwhile, as a representative of the Feminist Peace Institute, Starhawk was engaged in what were to be successful negotiations with Antioch West to obtain college credit for student participation in the program planned for the summer of 1986.[10] Sometime in the middle of February, the work had increased to the point that Margie Mayman, a white New Zealander who knew King from feminist antimilitarist actions, was hired part-time as an office manager. During this period, Starhawk and King met a number of times with Daney, whose support was enthusiastic.

According to many of my interviewees, Daney was most interested in an organization that promoted an international feminist focus on spirituality, the environment, and antimilitarism. For her, the question of U.S. racism was secondary, or at the very least equal, to the problem of creating international diversity within an ecofeminist organization. This tension between the desire for a focus on international diversity and the requirement of racial parity defined in terms of U.S. racial categories was most apparent in the early stages of the organization's existence. In what I think of as the "preracial parity phase," from 1984 to the first meeting with Barbara Smith in March of 1986, the idea of a Feminist Peace Institute was focused on the formation of an educational "think-tank," and the creation of a diverse constituency for the institute was thought of more often in terms of international diversity than of racial diversity. In what has been called by the participants "WomanEarth I," the period of time from the first meetings with Barbara Smith to the gathering of fifty women at Hampshire College in August of 1986, resolving this tension between definitions of diversity and implementing the principle of racial parity was the primary work. The remaining life of the organization, from September 1986 until August 1989, when the office was moved to the Bay Area and efforts were focused on publicizing WomanEarth as a model of antiracist ecofeminism, was called "WomanEarth II." As it turned out, the process of working through the implications of operating on racial parity that consumed the efforts of both WomanEarth I and II also radically changed the original conception of the organization as an ecofeminist educational institute.

WOMANEARTH I

As King began to work with Barbara Smith to build in the participation of women of color, the previous history of her and Starhawk's efforts to start a Feminist Peace Institute began to recede into the background.[11] The initial discussions about forming WomanEarth as a feminist organization based on racial parity, were held in New York in early 1986 and were attended by several women, including Barbara Smith, Chandra Mohanty,[12] Marta Benavides[13], Luisah Teish, Papusa Molina, Margie Mayman, Ynestra King, Gwyn Kirk, and the funder, Camille Daney.[14] At these meetings, the discussion ranged across several issues: the need for a revitalization of feminist politics, differing visions of feminist education, the necessity of local work on global issues, the complexity of racial and personal identities, and the importance of racial parity.[15] After these meetings, both Smith and Mohanty ceased to be actively involved (though Smith apparently consulted with King occasionally in the months before the conference).

The reasons given by others for Smith's lack of continued participation vary. (I found no similar interest in the lack of continued participation by Chandra Mohanty or Marta Benavides; clearly, this has to do with the symbolic importance of Smith as the initiator of racial parity.) King attributed Smith's leaving primarily to her busy schedule as the publisher of Kitchen Table: Women of Color Press, whose activity increased greatly during this period. Both King and Mayman also indicated that the emphasis on pagan feminist spirituality in the early meetings (which habitually began and concluded with rituals from non-Christian traditions, usually led by Starhawk or Teish) was not to Smith's liking. King felt that Smith's becoming a nonparticipant was a defining moment within the organization in terms of the definition of feminist spirituality. She says, "There was some question, I think, about how spirituality was going to be constructed . . . and rather than have those differences out within WomanEarth, certain people just sort of pulled back and left, [so that] what might be called earth-based spirituality people really defined the thing." Molina, on the other hand, recounted a moment of conscious discussion among the women of color about their participation. "After the meeting, the four of us (Smith, Mohanty, Teish, and Molina)[16] got together and discussed it and we decided not to be involved, that the white women weren't serious about wanting to include our analysis of the issues, but that they just wanted to be politically correct."[17] At the same time, Molina continued, the operative critique of white feminist organizations by women of color at that historical moment stressed the lack of effort of these organizations to be inclusive. Here women of color were specifically being asked to participate and on terms that they had set. It would have seemed strange not to agree. As Molina put it: "We had asked for that. We decided that I should stay because I had the most experience in coalitions with white women, and Teish should stay because she had experience [Molina doesn't identify what kind: with white women? with nontraditional spirituality?]."

Two things are interesting to note here. First, although King portrays the issue of spirituality as settled in this moment, in fact, as we will see, differences about spirituality had just gone underground. Second, according to Molina's account, the operative problem here was the racism of the white women. For Molina, this is partially evidenced by the use of particular kinds of spirituality: "I had some problems with the way [spirituality] was constructed, for instance with the way Native American spirituality was used by the white women." Yet one of the most committed practitioners of "unconventional" spirituality was the African American Teish, and the other two women of color who became part of the core group, Bagby and Rachel Sierra, were both interested and involved with similar traditions of alternative feminist spiritualities. I will return to the complexities of this conflation of differences about spirituality with differences of racialized perspectives later in this chapter.

The next meeting was on April 17–20, at Daney's home in the Southwest, where a group of women met and began to discuss the interconnection of the issues that WomanEarth would address. At this meeting Luisah Teish came up with the name "WomanEarth" through a chant used in a ritual. From then on, the name of the organization was "WomanEarth Feminist Peace Institute," most often referred to simply as "WomanEarth." Almost all of the women who made up the core group of WomanEarth, or what came to be called "Circle One," were present, except Starhawk: King, Kirk, Mayman, Bagby, Teish, Molina, and Daney had been in previous meetings, and Teish had invited Rachel Sierra, a Chicana feminist with a history of Saul Alinsky-style grassroots activism in poor people's movements. The meeting began with presentations on issue areas that were felt to be connected by the politics of the participants: "ecology, spirituality, global feminism, women of color, and strategies for confronting state power." The next day it was decided that these would be the five organizing themes for the August gathering being planned, with two small but significant changes. The area called "women of color" was called "isms" (to indicate a greater scope of examining several kinds of inequalities besides those based on race) and the area "strategies for confronting state power" became "activism."[18] These five themes stayed relatively constant for the August gathering, with some interesting reformulations that I will discuss later. Racial parity does not appear here as an issue area;

rather, it was thought of as an operating principle. Notably, these issue areas were not much different from those King and Starhawk had outlined in the original proposal for the Feminist Peace Institute in 1984, which shows the organization's continuity with the political tradition of feminist antimilitarism that inspired that proposal.

Over the next two days of the April meeting, the group laid some important foundations. They discussed "lesbian visibility" and "unconventional spirituality," and decided "the core group would be limited to lesbians and non-homophobic straight women. In the wider meetings there should be a commitment to education and to making all women comfortable." They also agreed that "the same understanding applies to the issue of unconventional spirituality. A majority opinion asserted that it would not be possible for women who were anti-ritual to participate in the core group." The language here is interesting, and connotates neither an entirely unanimous nor an openly challenged decision ("a majority opinion asserted"). Perhaps this language is an unconscious reflection of the feelings of the writer of the minutes, Margie Mayman, who on the one hand was not, as hired help, entirely an equal participant in her view, and who on the other hand was somewhat skeptical about the particular form of "unconventional spirituality" in use.[19]

The group agreed to meet again in May to make final plans, but went on to discuss the general shape of the August meeting: that it would be a "peer conference—no teachers, no students"; that money for childcare would be provided and not just limited to on-site child care; that disability access should be available; that each woman would invite five other women; and that participation would be by invitation only to ensure parity.[20] In this meeting, parity was described as "a mix of race, class, age, and geographical location within the U.S. and internationally."[21] This is very different from the assumptions operative after this meeting, in which racial parity for the August gathering was discussed only in terms of an equal balance between women of color and white women. Similarly, the issue area called "isms" in the April meeting, which addressed numerous kinds of inequalities, was called "Race, Class and Ethnicity" at the August gathering, even though the paragraph describing it referred to "racism, classism, sexism, heterosexism, and other forms of discrimination."[22]

This shifting in the meaning of parity demonstrates the tension in the April meeting between a conception of parity as being primarily about racial diversity (defined in terms of U.S. racial categories), and a conception of diversity defined more broadly, with a special emphasis on "international" diversity. Interestingly, it was possible to define the identities of the participants in both ways. As Gywn Kirk pointed out to me, they could be seen either as a group of white women and women of color, or as a group of women divided in different ways by national background. Kirk was British, Mayman was a New Zealander, and Molina was Mexican.[23] But even previous to this April meeting, these "international" (the term as used in WomanEarth meant "non-U.S.") women had been identified as either "white" or "of color." This identification was felt to be somewhat externally imposed but accepted for Mayman and Kirk, both of whom expressed a willingness to be responsible for their white privilege within a U.S. context, a willingness that partially arose out of their experience of a specific form of white racism existing in their home countries. At the same time, they both felt some inauthenticity in their placement as "white" defined by the particularities of a U.S. historical context they did not share. Mayman's experience was formed by the central racial opposition in New Zealand between European colonizers and indigenous people. Kirk felt that there were nuances in the way different women of color related to her as a British white woman; she indicated that this left some room for her, particularly in her relations with the African American women, that King, as a U.S. southern white woman, did not have. Teish mentioned this difference too in relation to Kirk, but downplayed it as only as a difference in that "her [Kirk's] experience is Caribbean blacks in England rather than American blacks in America." King, on the other hand, felt that her experience growing up in Selma, Alabama, during the civil rights movement gave her a particular connection to antiracist work in the U.S. not shared by the other "white" women.

These nuances in the "white" women's racialized identities were not openly articulated at the time, but surfaced in the interviews as I asked WomanEarth members to consider the question of how they came to define "diversity" as "racial" rather than "international." Nuances in the racialized identities of the "women of color" were also an undercurrent. These nuances had to do with the conflation of race and class in U.S. culture. Molina seemed to feel no ambivalence about her identity as a "woman of color" even as she portrayed it as fully externally imposed. As she explains in another context, despite her upbringing as a member of a privileged, wealthy, liberal Mexican elite, when she came to the United States, "I suddenly became a 'woman of color'. . . . Suddenly I was a second-class citizen."[24] However, Rachel Sierra, at least, did not perceive Molina's status as a "woman of color" with the same felicity, feeling that her upper-class status made such an identity questionable. Seeing Molina as "international" may have eased this ambivalence for Sierra, had the definition of parity as being about international diversity prevailed over the definition of parity as being about U.S. racial diversity.

As the contradictions between these two understandings of "parity" became apparent, a confrontation occurred between Rachel Sierra and the funder, Camille Daney. Sierra knew both Teish and Molina and had responded enthusiastically to the invitation to the April meeting. She was drawn primarily by the commitment to racial parity (understood by her in terms of U.S. racial categories) and secondarily by the idea of exploring the connection between her spirituality and her political action. Unaware up to this point in the

April meeting that the white woman to whom everyone listened so respect-fully was the sole funding source for the incipient organization, Sierra found her frustration growing. "She was talking about Nairobi and her involvement with the Peace Tent, and then she was talking about global poverty. And what was frustrating to me was that she was talking as though this kind of poverty could never exist in this country."[25] When Daney, coming back from a break in the meeting, announced that she had, on her own, invited a woman she knew to join them, a woman she described as an upper-class, fair-skinned, and blue-eyed South American, Sierra immediately objected. She pointed out that the balance of white women to women of color was already less than parity (assuming the ongoing participation of Starhawk, who had been unable to come to this meeting), and she said that she felt that the collective process promised to the group had been violated by such individual action. Note that though Sierra voices her concern about Daney's involvement in terms of her avoidance of class issues in the U.S., it is her deployment of the category of racial difference within the context of racial parity that is used to object to Daney's participation.

In the course of this argument, a second confrontation occurred between Daney and Luisah Teish. Teish was sensitive to the inequality within Circle One engendered by the group's dependence on one participant's money. At one point, she remembers "dramatizing how I felt about it, sort of 'I thought we were equals here, but Miz Ann you want me to,' just to let it be known . . . that I felt at that point that the idea of equality among the steering committee [she means Circle One] had broken down."[26] Her reference to Daney as "Miz Ann" recalled the legacy of slave-holding for U.S. white women, histori-cizing the unacceptable nature of racialized power imbalances for Teish. Molina also remembers Daney's participation as an issue, because her pres-ence imbalanced racial parity within Circle One. At the same time, just adding another woman of color to balance Daney's participation wouldn't have eased the situation, because, according to Molina, "we would have needed a woman of color who had the kind of money [Daney] had. She would have had to have ownership of the project in the same way." Note here that the sense of parity imbalance voiced here by Molina is not about race, but class inequality. Stung by these confrontations, Daney left the meeting in anger (only then was Sierra informed of her role in the group).

These confrontations had important repercussions for WomanEarth. First, the resolution of the conflict had the effect of resolving the tension between the conception of the group as having a focus on international diversity and it being focused on the problems of U.S. racism. From then on, the latter con-ception of racial parity between U.S. white women and U.S. women of color prevailed. It was also the first test of the seriousness of racial parity as an un-derlying principle. While Daney had less insistence on this principle, it was crucial for the participation of the women of color; Teish, Molina, Bagby, and

Sierra all emphasized to me that the idea of racial parity was the primary reason they had agreed to participate. Though they were all interested in the combination of ecology, feminism, and spirituality, racial parity was a basic condition for their commitment to WomanEarth. Thus, Daney's more flexible notion of parity, one that decentered race, needed to be challenged. After these confrontations, according to King, "the women of color said that if she [Daney] was going to continue to participate in the group then they weren't going to participate." Under these circumstances, King, Kirk, and Starhawk all clearly took the position that racial parity was more important than international diversity, and that the collective process was only properly supported by sticking to racial parity as strictly as possible (which meant that the existing make-up of Circle One, which included Daney, would be in imbalance). The risk of alienating their funder over this issue must have been felt particularly strongly by these three women, who at this point had put in years of work on the idea of a Feminist Peace Institute and who had considerable political and personal investment (especially King and Starhawk) in the notion of continuing and shaping ecofeminism as a political location. But since the amount of previous work had been somewhat downplayed to give the women of color the sense that they were in on the ground floor of the project, the amount of risk and change in the original conception of the project that existed at this moment went unacknowledged by all involved.

To King, this moment of ultimatum concerning Daney's direct participation was important, because it allayed remaining suspicions on the part of the women of color about the strength of King's antiracist politics. She says, "That was a sort of baptism by fire for the women of color, that I was really just willing, because I was, [to] just quit the project or have it not go on rather than take [Daney's] side against them, even though that was where the bread was buttered. You know, I had no problem with really seeing that the integrity of the project [required this], because she just kept trying to say to me that it was just these particular women that were problematic and that was why we're having all these difficulties, why don't we get some other women. . . . And I said, well people are who they are." But, as I have pointed out above in discussing the different possibilities of naming people's identities, people are also who they need to be at a particular moment. Thus, the resolution of the debate with the funder solidified the racial identities of the Circle One members as well as the notion of the importance of racial parity.

The other important effect of these confrontations was that Daney ceased to actively participate in WomanEarth meetings, and her financial support became uncertain. This was not a surprising outcome. After all, Daney was paying for WomanEarth to become a viable organization, and her vision was being discounted. According to Mayman, "She had done the Peace Tent at Nairobi, and I think she saw it as more like that . . . and yet here were these uppity women of color who were shaping the agenda. . . . She was upset by confrontations about race issues." In King's estimation, Daney, who had just returned from many years living outside of the United States, had no experience with the ongoing critiques by feminists of color of the racism of white feminists. King notes, "She had given substantial amounts of money to Chicana and poor organizing in Texas and other places . . . so it's not to say that she was without knowledge or concern totally, but she had not really been embedded in the political context . . . out of which I felt, and other people as well, that somehow taking on the issues of racism . . . was really the next stage of feminism in general and ecofeminism in particular. . . . She really didn't know a lot of what had been going on with U.S. white movements and women of color movements and the critiques of feminism." King's statement here indicates the way in which the notion of racial parity belongs to a particular moment in the history of U.S. feminism.

After these confrontations, Daney's commitment to supporting the organization was relatively tenuous. She decided not to participate in future meetings, but to continue funding WomanEarth up to the Hampshire conference. Daney made it clear, however, that after the conference future funding was unlikely. Despite her disappointment in the definition of diversity within WomanEarth, she kept to her promise, and indeed supported the group generously throughout the time of organizing for and conducting the conference. Mayman, however, remembers that her financial support required constant negotiation by King, and generated considerable uncertainty about when and whether the group would have the money to accomplish the activities that were being planned.

At the same time, the large amount of money that was provided determined crucial aspects of WomanEarth. Wanting to be an organization based on racial parity, it achieved its particular version of this through being able to bring together a racially diverse group that was also geographically far-flung. Teish, Sierra, Mayman, King, and Kirk all remarked on the unusual circumstance of having enough money to provide air fare to Circle One members to enable them to meet together, although even with this support, meetings were hard to arrange for members with very busy schedules. The money also supported a central office in New York, initially staffed by King, who hired first Kirk and then Mayman and then, two months away from the August conference, Molina. Thus an organization that intended to operate democratically under the principle of racial parity, in fact, given its geographically distant membership, operated for most of the preconference time period with a central office staffed entirely by white women.

At a meeting of Circle One in Connecticut held May 26–30, 1986, attended by Bagby, Kirk, King, Mayman, Molina, Sierra, Starhawk, and Teish, this situation was discussed. It was understood to be quite problematic, because the agenda of the organization was to a great extent controlled by the day-to-day decisions in the office. The decision was made at the Connecticut

meeting to ease the parity imbalance somewhat by hiring Molina for the summer preceding the conference. More than that could not be done, because
the other members of the group had responsibilities that prevented them
from participating in the office any more than by occasional long-distance
consulting. From Mayman's perspective, Molina's hire did not entirely resolve the problem, because what was needed was "somebody to have the same
level of power Ynestra had, in terms of shaping the agenda." While relations
with Daney were more generally understood to be problematic because of the
group's dependence on her funding, a less openly articulated perception existed that since King made the decisions about the spending of the money
once it had arrived, she could be seen as exercising undue financial influence. After Molina's arrival, additional friction in the office was caused by inequalities in pay: King (who carried the title of director from the earlier, preracial, parity phase, and which only had meaning in terms of the need for
legal incorporation), as someone who was giving most of her time to the organization, was paid the most; Kirk and Molina less than King but the same as
each other; and Mayman the least. Note that these differences in pay were not
racially distributed, but related to the kind and amount of work done by each
staff member.

The meeting of Circle One in Connecticut in May 1986 was otherwise focused on getting geared up for the conference. Whatever criticism may exist
of WomanEarth's process and achievements, it should be recognized that the
time frame of this effort was quite challenging. From the time that the date for
the gathering was finally set at the April meeting in the Southwest to the time
of the conference in August was a mere four months. Primarily because of the
geographical distance between the participants, the real nitty-gritty work planning the conference did not occur until after the May meeting in Connecticut. Adding to the tensions, it was unclear at the May meeting whether the
funder would come through with all of the money she had promised, thus
leaving the group uncertain even at that late date about crucial aspects of the
upcoming conference: for example, size, availability of scholarships, or number of days that could be afforded. That WomanEarth managed to put together any conference at all under these circumstances speaks to the commitment and hard work of the participants. At this May meeting, feeling the
pressure of such a short preparation time, financial uncertainties, and the
number of differences between group members that were yet to be worked
out, Rachel Sierra expressed doubts about having the conference so soon and
suggested postponement.

A number of conflicts erupted during this meeting, one of which concerned the use of "unconventional" spiritual ritual in the group. Sierra reported that when Molina questioned whether ritual practices were always
appropriate, Starhawk perceived this as an attack on witches in general.
Mayman, for her part, challenged the way in which Starhawk and Teish were

perceived as the spiritual leaders within the group. Her understanding of feminist spirituality involved a deep critique of hierarchy within patriarchal, traditional religions. On the other hand, Teish's practice of feminist African-centered spirituality involved respect and recognition of the greater knowledge and spiritual power of elders and priestesses. These controversies were resolved with a determination to respect different spiritual traditions within the group, but at the same time affirming that "Starhawk and Teish have been asked into Circle One as ritual leaders among other things."[27] Sierra, however, did not feel that the problem had been solved. Though perhaps more comfortable with pagan spirituality than Molina or Mayman, she felt the use of spiritual ritual within the group stifled criticism. "One of the things it did is it kept us from being honest with each other, because I feel as though in the guise of wanting to respect all the different traditions, and wanting to share each other's traditions, that some part of us was also shut down, because it wasn't nice. Here we're doing something communing with the earth and then we're going to yell at each other? So I think that really was a stunting thing." One result of this conflict can be seen in the invitational letter for the conference, which carries a paragraph warning that "rituals from women- and earth-centered traditions (Native American, African, and European) will be part of the meeting. We ask that women come in a spirit of openness, willing to enter into some experiences which may be unfamiliar, so that together we may push back the boundaries of our knowledge and power towards a vital, peaceful world."[28]

Another conflict centered on the decision-making process used by the group. Though many members had been trying to work together for at least five months, the only specific discussion of process I found in my research was found in the papers. It was a discussion recalled by none of my interviewees, which shows the lack of stress on the question of decision-making process.[29] Coming from similar backgrounds in the feminist antimilitarist direct action movements, Starhawk, King, Kirk, and Mayman perhaps needed little discussion of the assumption that consensus-process decision making would be used or the reasons why it was preferred over other forms. Yet none of these more experienced practitioners of consensus process (and, in Starhawk's case, a teacher and theorist of the practice) felt it necessary to use the formal version of consensus developed within the antimilitarist movement to produce a consciously egalitarian operation of decision-making power. While the invitational letter to the April 17–20 meeting contained a description of some of the formal roles for a consensus decision-making process (facilitator, time-keeper, and "vibes-watcher") as well as some of the procedures (opening exercise, agenda formation, rotation of roles), these were not identified as part of a specific decision-making practice, with a specific history within U.S. antimilitarist politics. Nor did other meetings continue the use of these formal consensus decision-making structures, as far as I could discern.

Thus, by the time of the May meeting, the participants were used to the assumption that decisions were collective as much as possible, and that they took place after a great deal of discussion, but there was no apparent consciousness of these procedures as a choice of decision-making possibilities, or that there could be a more formal, thought-out method of proceeding that was being elided by informality. Some participants were in fact uncomfortable with the informal consensus process already in use. Teish, for instance, says that "tediously and fastidiously we discussed everything. Within the steering committee we were really reaching for absolute consensus, to the point that after WomanEarth I remember putting a lot of space between me and other people when they would talk about consensus. I would say it left me in a funny space because my response to it was actually to give up power, which is not like me. Usually I'm the one who's saying if you've got power use it and use it wisely, don't never give it up." She also remarks that "it made me feel that there really were things that I didn't mind not voting on."

Despite the informal assumption of a collective and egalitarian decision-making process, there were inequalities in decision-making power, mostly stemming from King and Starhawk's previous work on the project, their relation to the funder, and King's day-to-day financial responsibility. For example, the decision-making issue at the May meeting was brought up by the announcement that Starhawk had managed to secure Antioch West credit not just for a "summer program" put on by WomanEarth, but for a "year-long program" as well, the details of which seemed to be fairly worked out. To be affiliated with Antioch's Women's Studies Program, courses would follow the five thematic areas of the August conference and would take place in the day and evening over three quarters at both the B.A. and M.A. level. Community as well as student participation would be encouraged. A half-time faculty position would be available for the first year, and it was agreed by the group that this be taken by Starhawk, who already was teaching at Antioch West.[30]

Since much of this plan had begun in the preracial parity phase of the Feminist Peace Institute, the amount of decisions that had been made already came as a surprise to some members of WomanEarth. Questions about Starhawk's ability to make individual decisions about the relationship between Antioch and WomanEarth were raised. Finally, it was made clear that "Starhawk had gone ahead . . . at the request of the Institute at the January meeting," in other words, that she had been authorized at a time before most of the present participants had joined. This led to a general discussion of decision making, who could decide whether WomanEarth would make political endorsements, and when and where an individual asked to speak publicly as a representative of WomanEarth needed to give the organization a portion of her speaking fees.

Another difference aired during this meeting was the participants' varied understandings of the importance of accreditation for educational experience, and indeed of the goal of a radical educational institution at all. Molina, deploying an Althusserian analysis of education as an apparatus of the production of state ideology, expressed doubts about the aim of any formal educational aspect within WomanEarth. Teish was concerned that life experience be given as much weight as academic experience. King, in response to some of these concerns, identified three foci that WomanEarth presently displayed, all of which were "educational" in different ways: the institute (either the summer program for the future or the Antioch year-long program, which allowed credit for life experience); a peer think-tank (for which the August gathering would be a model); and resourcing and networking the movement (a process envisioned to assist political activism directly).[31] This summary seemed to resolve the differences around the issue of forming an organization focused on education.

Despite these conflicts and Sierra's doubts, the group agreed to continue working toward the conference in August. Considerable work had already been done and the money that had been promised, though not yet in their hands, had been earmarked for the conference, not any other projects. They each agreed to invite at least four or five women from their own "communities of reference" (Bagby's term), keeping the goal of racial parity for the conference in mind. The five thematic areas for the conference, already identified at the April meeting, were developed, and presentations were done again at this meeting on every area except "global feminism." In the absence of Daney, none of the participants had prepared for this section.

Some time was spent on discussing the need for fund-raising to ease their dependence on one source. They also discussed the need for scholarship money. To achieve racial parity at the conference, it was not enough to simply state it as a purpose of the gathering or as an important principle of operation. The group agreed to provide economic compensation for the loss of working days and the costs of child care for women who needed these things in order to attend the conference. Of the women who were being thought of as conference participants, there was considerable overlap between the categories of working-class or poor women, mothers, and women of color. But economic compensation for attending the conference was provided mostly to women of color, even though many of the white participants were activists or members of low-paying professions, because the white women, already interested in the subject of the August gathering, did not require as much convincing to attend. As Rachel Bagby wrote: "it took many calls . . . much coaxing . . . to convince the few women-of-color on the list to agree to come to Amherst that summer. Over and over came the questions. Why should we go there? Take a whole week off from work? What's the purpose?"[32] Economic compensation, as well as the emphasis on racial parity, was required to have the participation of women of color. As Teish said: "If you are inviting this woman to come spend X number of days discussing this and these are days when she would ordinarily be at work earning money to support her family, she can't just jump up and do that unless you are going to support her, and that is one of the things we talked about and that is one of the things we did. For women with children we had to be sure that child care was provided and those that had to bring their kids with them would be able to do that and that's always a class and race issue. . . . It was more difficult to [get women of color to participate] and required more than just saying, 'Oh, come on, let's have a feminist chat.' . . . It's got to be more concrete." The concreteness of WomanEarth's approach to racial parity was thus made possible by the large amount of money that had been provided for the conference. It is clear as well that there was significant conflation between thinking about racial parity and thinking about class parity.

After the Connecticut meeting, organizing for the conference intensified. On June 27, an invitational letter describing the conference went out to selected possible participants. This letter, written primarily by King, was the first place where the name, goals, and politics of the organization were concretely specified for public viewing. In some important ways, this letter drew on the original proposal for the Feminist Peace Institute written by King and Starhawk. Most reminiscent of that earlier proposal, in this mailing the conference was named "Reconstituting Feminist Peace Politics." This location of WomanEarth's political position and aims was quite accurate, considering its genesis in the feminist antimilitarist movement. But it came as a surprise to Sierra, in particular. In response to the mailing, she wrote a long letter to Circle One expressing her doubts about the mailing and various organizational dynamics she had witnessed at a staff meeting just after the Connecticut meeting. A number of issues were raised by Sierra about this mailing. One was an issue of process: because of the pressures of time, the letter had not been passed out to the group as a whole before it was made public. The other was the locating the purpose of WomanEarth as "reconstituting feminist peace politics."

Sierra explained her surprise by recounting a revelation she had experienced during the time the group was together in Connecticut. The passage, because it points up the difficulty of overcoming past movement segregation, is worth quoting at length.

> It was the evening most of us (Teish and Rachel B. weren't around, as I recall) were sitting outside in the screened-in porch. Star, Ynestra, and Gwyn were talking about various peace conferences/gatherings and some of the women they all seemed to know. It "hit me" for the first time, that the Feminist Peace Institute had its roots in the peace movement. I remember thinking, "Aha! Us colored girls are really just guests at the white girls' tea party." Call me slow, naive, or stupid, but I really hadn't understood the foundation of the Institute until then. Please understand that at the time the observation was just that: an observation. By the end of the week, I was confident that we were committed to

facilitating the creation of a "new" reality, understanding that WomanEarth
would have to be radically different from our parent movements.

Then I got the mailing. Now I feel the need to say to all of you very clearly: I
am not in the market for a movement. My commitment to the struggles of poor
people, especially people of color, cannot and *will not* take a "back seat" to another movement. My own quandary for the last 2–3 years has been because my
soul longs for a way to expand the scope, meaning, and effort of that work, as
well as the results. For the most part, poor people aren't winning the kinds of
victories that add up to meaningful systemic change, but then, neither are workers, women, third world countries/peoples, environmentalists, peace groups,
etc. To me, that means we must define and do our work differently—ALL of us.
To characterize the August gathering as a time to "re-evaluate and reconstitute
the feminist peace movement" is so limited. It also presumes that all of us are
prepared to forsake our respective movements in favor of jumping on this particular bandwagon. I, for one, am not.

Sierra, as a scholar of social movements and a long-term activist, had a sophisticated understanding of the need to move from separate movements to
an integrated analysis of oppression and exploitation. To do this, she argued, it
was necessary not just to work through personal differences, but to reconstruct
a new movement based on a "new reality." In the letter, she went on to say:

> I have no interest in reconstituting *any* of the traditional movements. As long as
> we think of things in isolation from one another (i.e., peace movement, work-
> ers' movement, poor people's movement, feminist peace movements) we are
> actively contributing to the view of the world (white, male reality) that requires
> winners and losers, oppression, racism, and exploitation. I believe . . . that the
> "we" of all those movements can create a new reality. That's what I thought
> WomanEarth was exploring. And so, my friends, while a potential funding
> source may need to think we are merely trying to "provide resources and create
> educational settings where women from all racial and socio-economic back-
> grounds can meet to broaden their understanding of peace politics" [here
> Sierra is quoting from the mailing], the women we're inviting to the August
> gathering deserved a lot more.[33]

Sierra was particularly concerned that this language was not going to appeal to some of the women she wanted to invite. Her letter generated a number of phone calls and letters among the group, and King took responsibility
for the error of sending the letter out without proper consultation under the
press of time and difficulty of long-distance consultation (a situation that,
with our present-day use of email and faxes, might not occur). Sierra agreed
to continue on to August, if Molina could be delegated to make phone calls
directly to the women of color receiving this letter in order to mitigate the

appearance that this event was only about "reconstituting peace politics." Though King realized her mistake in characterizing the August event this way, at the same time it was imperative for her to establish WomanEarth as a continuation of feminist antimilitarism. To understand this, it is important to recall that this was before ecofeminism has its own identity, separate from feminist antimilitarism (a separate identity that continues to be important to those ecofeminists who see the origins of their politics in other movements, such as animal liberation or sustainable development). Later in this chapter, I will discuss in more detail the conflict within the group around the naming of their politics as "feminist peace politics."

During this period of preparation, the pitfalls of the isolation of the office and the daily work from the rest of the group became clear. Personality clashes within the office hampered the work. Besides the differences in the way people were paid, there were also differences in the kind of work people in Circle One did. In the summer before the conference, the burden of the "workie-work" (in King's words) was accomplished by the four paid staff in the office. Just before the conference and during the conference, this unequal division of labor shifted, with the "go-fer" work (in Sierra's words) falling on Sierra, Kirk, and Mayman. The latter took this with a certain equanimity; since she was the only one of the group hired specifically to do "secretarial" work, the menial nature of her labor was accepted by her (and the others) as appropriate. As she said in her interview, "I felt hired as a sympathetic sort of person, but clearly . . . most of these people were known for what they were doing, and I wasn't." None of the members of WomanEarth, including Mayman, seemed to recognize the disparity between treating Mayman as "hired help," on the one hand, and seeing her as an equal participant when it came to assessing racial parity, on the other.

Even given the existing cleavages and debates within Circle One, the group by this time had developed some strong internal ties and a gutsy, intimate, and open style of relating to each other. In the interviews, Teish, Sierra, Bagby, and King all mention the way in which they felt comfortable airing differences within the group, even though there were different senses of whether these differences achieved proper resolution. Only Molina seemed to feel, at least retrospectively, that the group wasn't willing to openly deal with clashes and disagreements. King and Teish both talk about the pleasure of jokes, the discussions of food, and the personal stories that were told; King mentions that within the core group "culturally in some ways we were sort of hippiesh, really . . . I mean we'd have all these fights and then we'd have these funny conversations and it would turn out that all of our mothers disapproved of us, and we would talk in these different ethnic vernaculars about what pejorative things they said — 'why don't you get married and have proper lives' — because we were all sort of counter-cultural in that way . . . and [we all] sort of appreciated the aesthetic flair of food and clothes and things."

The gathering at Hampshire from August 17 to 23, 1986, was the culmination of months of hard work and a lot of careful thinking. The participants were varied in a number of unusual ways for a women's event in the U.S. in 1986. Between seventy and eighty women were invited, and fifty-five ended up attending. Importantly for WomanEarth, racial parity was clearly achieved, with twenty-two of the participants falling into the category "white women," and twenty-three falling into the category "women of color." According to a roster of the participants, the great majority of the latter were African American women; there were two Chicanas and two Latinas, four Native Americans, and one Asian woman. A few of these self-named identities crossed categories: one listed her racial/ethnic status as "Black/Cherokee," another as "Black/Panama." Eight women were listed as "Jewish," though in assessing racial parity they were counted as white.[34] The roster also recorded the theme areas of interest to each participant. "Action" (that is, political action) appeared for twenty-two, "spirituality" for twelve, "isms" for fifteen, "ecology" for five, and "global feminism" for four.[35] The participants included teachers (some listed as "teachers," others as "professors"—sometimes with disciplinary identifications such as history, sociology, feminist ethics, religion), dancers, writers, midwives, lawyers, artists, singers, gardeners, carpenters, organizers, day-care and social workers, mediators, therapists, rape-crisis shelter workers, one Democratic Party politician, one witch, one priestess, one masseuse, two graduate students, and one philanthropist.[36]

The deliberate manner of creating racial parity went against the usual free and open practice of oppositional events of the period, and WomanEarth came in for some criticism by some members of the feminist antimilitarist community for its methods. In fact, to achieve racial parity, several white antimilitarist activists had to be "disinvited," in some cases resulting in their long-term resentment of King in particular, who had originally invited some of them. Bagby, in her article on the conference, refers to this problem in a particularly challenging way: "Story has it that responses to the controlled access to WomanEarth I by some white women active in the peace and ecology movements was fiery. 'We don't *do* things that way,' some said. Or, 'that's a good idea, but, *of course I'll be able to come no matter what*, right?' The women catching that fire, also white, also active in those movements, were both shocked and equal to the responses. Why this fear and anger in response to an experiment? What are you feeling as you read this paragraph?"[37]

Despite the complaints from those not allowed to participate, those that did attend were appreciative of the framework of the gathering. By all accounts, it was a lively and politically engaged group, and the event was "overfull," in Mayman's words. The five days of the conference had been organized around the five theme areas of "Global Feminism and Militarism: the World at War," "Spirituality, Healing and Sexuality: the Power of the Whole Person," "Race, Class and Ethnicity: Crossing the Barriers," "Ecology: Making Living

Connections," and "Frontiers of Public Action: Strategies for a Feminist Peace Politics." The plan was that each day would begin with a roundtable for the entire conference, involving a presentation and discussion on that day's theme area. A lunch break would be followed by workshops on both the theme areas and topics organized by participants. Since this was to be a meeting of peers, some effort was made to generate workshops by participants sharing their own interests and skills. Dinner was to be followed by a general assembly, and the evening would end with various music, performances, and rituals provided by the participants.

Participants were also gathered into small groups, each including one member of Circle One and identified by a particular color (red, silver, indigo, orange, purple, and yellow). These small groups were called "color clans," but also "discussion groups" and "affinity groups." The color clans were structured by racial parity and met for an hour each day, discussing general visions for the organization and issues that arose during the conference. At the end of the conference they reported back to the gathering as a whole.

The conference, by all accounts, was infused with excitement about the chance to work under the rare condition of racial parity and the approach of interconnecting various political agendas in those circumstances. The decision to make the conference a peer experience was also unusual and enthusiastically supported by the participants. This egalitarian approach led to the carefully imagined agenda quickly being altered by the empowered participants, who decided a number of times to proceed in different directions than had been planned. A round of personal introductions, for instance, took up much of the first day's program. It was clearly important to the participants to know each other and to appreciate different skills and political interests. Another important time the agenda was derailed is recounted by Rachel Bagby in her article, "A Power of Numbers."[38] Despite, or because of, racial parity, tensions between some white women and some women of color were apparent, and the suggestion was made to address them by running the Wednesday session on "Race, Class, and Ethnicity" as an "antiracism" workshop for the whole group. Mary Arnold, an African American woman who was part of the Women Against Racism group in Iowa City, began the workshop by dividing the participants into white women and women of color. Each group faced the other. Then each woman made two statements: about what she loved about herself, and about what she never wanted to hear again from women in the other category. Strict confidentiality governed what was said during this process, but by all accounts it was both painful and joyful, and altogether a very powerful experience. Another independent undertaking of the participants was the formation of a lesbian caucus, who met alongside the color clans and like them made a report to the conference as a whole on the last day.

In general, the conference was unusual in its deliberate achievement of racial parity. This did not mean that conflicts around racial difference did not break out, but unlike other women's gatherings during the 1980s, this conflict neither went underground nor disrupted the entire work of the gathering.[39] Still, other kinds of conflict rocked the gathering at different points: an argument about whether two of the participants were "real" Native Americans; a row between a Jewish American woman and a Palestinian woman over the Israeli-Palestinian struggle; the rejection of the vegetarian menu of the conference by some African American women, who went into town to get meat to eat; debates about the use of ritual and what could be properly called feminist spirituality; conflict between lesbians and homophobic women; and differences in ideas about appropriate and effective radical political strategies.

Despite all this, the conference participants, in their reports on the last day, indicated the importance of addressing the interconnections of the five theme areas in the context of an organization based on racial parity. They seemed to agree with Teish's statement to me that the effort of WomanEarth was powerful and visionary, an effort perhaps made before its time. The color clans and the lesbian caucus made many suggestions for ways to continue and expand WomanEarth's work. Offers were made to take on tasks and responsibilities, even to replace core group members who were clearly showing signs of exhaustion. But it wasn't possible to take this energy and turn it into concrete results. Kirk, speaking during this last day, stated that the core group had "quite a lot of unfinished business . . . if it sounds like we are kind of holding back [and] don't have a clear way of proceeding to the next moment it is because there are a number of things we need to evaluate among ourselves."[40] What is apparent as well is that in the rush to plan the conference, and in the desire to leave the participants room to join or influence WomanEarth, no future structure had been imagined into which new participants could be integrated. And, of course, all of the Circle One participants knew that future funding at the rate they had previously enjoyed was coming to an end.

For the core group, the ending of the conference was chaotic. Originally the plan was that Circle One participants would stay several days after the conference to evaluate it and lay plans for the future. However, they were exhausted and relations were strained from the numerous confrontations that had occurred during the conference. In addition, Sierra had to leave with one of her invitees whose husband had died of a heart attack on the way to the airport to pick her up, and Bagby was dealing with the death of her grandmother the week before. They were not able to meet again until the end of September, when they gathered at Rachel Sierra's house in Oakland, CA. At this meeting seven members of Circle One (minus Mayman, whose employment had officially ended after the conference) aired their personal resentments stemming from arguments and actions during the conference, and evaluated their effort. Two members of Circle One ended their participation here: Teish, relatively amiably with support from the others, and Molina, less amiably. It was also felt to be important by all concerned, including King, to decenter King's role in the organization in the future. The decision was made to move the office to the West Coast in order to shift the immediate support network and daily work away from New York. The group also agreed to try a more collective form of directorship, one that followed the principle of racial parity. Rachel Bagby and Gwyn Kirk agreed to "co-hub" the organization, with Kirk moving to the Bay Area, where Bagby lived, for the following summer. This manifestation of WomanEarth, to symbolize the break with some of the previous problems encountered, was called WomanEarth II.

WOMANEARTH II

WomanEarth II was marked by two opposing tendencies. One was the growing interest in ecofeminism across the country during this period. The product of a number of forces, that interest became focused on WomanEarth to some extent because of reports of the August gathering, and because of public appearances by high-profile members like Starhawk, King, and Teish. This momentum was intensified by the presence of King, Starhawk, Kirk, and Bagby as members of WomanEarth at the March 1987 Ecofeminist Perspectives: Culture, Nature, Theory conference held at the University of Southern California. Armed with their fresh understandings of the importance of analyzing racism and of including women of color on their own terms, both King and Starhawk rose at different times to intervene in moments of white arrogance and presumption during this conference. The name of WomanEarth was invoked a number of times as an ecofeminist organization centered on antiracism, and flyers inviting membership in the organization were available to conference participants.

The USC conference brought ecofeminism wide publicity and confirmed its place as a oppositional political location in the United States. Articles on the USC conference appeared in numerous places, and WomanEarth was sometimes mentioned in them.[41] The results of this publicity were "close to 2,000 requests for more information" from WomanEarth in the year following the USC conference, often containing "news of actions, letter campaigns, conferences, and educational programs on a variety of ecology and peace-related issues" felt by the submitters to be related to "ecofeminism."[42] According to Bagby, "so many women were interested, it was astounding." Two other results were Bagby's article on the August 1986 gathering, which appeared in the first important anthology explicitly designated "ecofeminist," Judith Plant's *Healing the Wounds: The Promise of Ecofeminism*; and Lindsy Van Gelder's article on "ecofeminism" in *Ms.*, in which WomanEarth was prominently featured. Both were published in 1989.

The other momentum apparent in WomanEarth II was in an opposite direction from this outpouring of interest, publicity, and support. Bagby, though working hard on a number of aspects of WomanEarth, was terrifically over-burdened with responsibilities during this period of her life. At the meeting in September 1986, when she offered to take on the position of "hubbing" the organization with Kirk, she remembers someone saying, "But Rachel, you've got three jobs!" In hindsight, she said, taking on "co-hubbing" at this time was a "archetypical super-colored woman thing to do." She began the project chronically overextended, and matters only worsened as time went on. She and Kirk worked well together, according to both of their accounts. But around September, after the USC conference, Kirk returned to work in Boston, and there wasn't enough money to bring them together on a regular basis, let alone hire a full-time staff person. This situation continued for two years, from the spring of 1987 to the spring of 1989, at the same time that tremendous growth in ecofeminism was taking place. During these two years, Kirk and Bagby put together at least one issue of a newsletter (called *WomanEarth Review*; it was never sent out), a bibiliography, and a grant pro-posal, entitled "From the Earth to the World: Voices of Ecofeminism." But they were unable to get enough money to reconvene a new group of women to work as a core group. At the same time, a number of women, primarily white women who were active in constructing the politics of ecofeminism, were very interested in participating in a new Circle One: Irene Diamond (white coorganizer of the USC conference), Susan Griffin (white author of *Women and Nature*, at this point widely seen as a founding ecofeminist text), Marti Kheel (white writer and cofounder of Feminists for Animal Rights), and Charlene Spretnak (white activist in the U.S. Greens and author of *The Politics of Women's Spirituality*, also now seen as a founding ecofeminist text). With the help of some of these women's connections, a grant proposal finally did garner enough money to bring elements of the old and new Circle One together on May 5–8, 1989, at Starhawk's house in San Francisco.[43]

Though taking place with great optimism about a revitalization of WomanEarth, this meeting turned out to be almost its last event, though the organization struggled on until August 1989. Of the original members of Circle One, Starhawk, King, Bagby, Kirk, and Sierra were present. Also in at-tendance were new people, including Irene Diamond, Susan Griffin, Marti Kheel, Margo Adair (a white grassroots activist based in the Bay Area), Sharon (or Shea) Howell (a white grassroots activist and scholar based in Michigan), Victoria Bomberry (a Native American feminist based in Northern Califor-nia), Tia Wagner (an African American activist), and Deeanne Davis (a com-munity organizer, Davis was identified by Sierra as "biracial" but in a flyer describing the San Francisco meeting as "African American"). Comparing the accounts of this meeting, it is apparent that another African American woman was also present, but I have been unable to identify her.

The meeting began with a potluck dinner on Friday night and was ex-pected to continue into Saturday. However, the problem of racial imbalance occupied the whole of Friday night's meeting. At first Shea Howell and Margo Adair and then Marti Kheel and Susan Griffin volunteered to leave to help restore the racial balance. With their absences, the meeting on Saturday thus proceeded on the basis of racial parity. The Friday night discussion was variously described. Rachel Bagby commented: "I had an appreciation for struggle after that meeting." The writer of a flyer describing the meeting characterized this process as "unrushed, unpressured, inclusive, and revealing of deep feelings about the dynamics of power relations and tokenism and about personal commitment."[44]

On Saturday, the participants made up a three-year plan for WomanEarth, and decided to turn over the "co-hubbing" responsibilities to Margo Adair and Rachel Sierra; a few weeks later, they received the computer, files, and other WomanEarth materials from Rachel Bagby at a meeting also attended by Victoria Bomberry and Charlene Spretnak. A long letter written by Sierra summarizing the two meetings and detailing the plans for the future was sent to all participants. Though enthusiasm for the project appeared high at both of these meetings and in Sierra's letter, a series of personal crises in Sierra's life derailed the momentum gained through these meetings. The last WomanEarth document I have seen is dated August 10, 1989. It is a letter from Ynestra King to the participants of a meeting Sierra was planning to hold, detailing some of the history of the organization and the challenges facing it at that time. She mentions four pressing needs: a clear definition of parity in broader terms that would allow, for instance, decisions about which white women were included; an agreed-upon political analysis and statement of purpose; a consensus on organizational structure and decision-making procedures; and stable and unconditional sources of money. Near the end of the letter, her writing is interrupted by a telephone call from Rachel Sierra, who called to tell her that she could no longer "co-hub" WomanEarth. King ends the letter with great sadness, emphasizing the need for secure financial support for feminist organizations, and with a "fervent wish . . . that you find it in you and among you to continue." Despite King's hope, this did not happen. With Sierra unable to continue, two possibilities remained: Margo Adair stood ready to take on WomanEarth,[45] and it also would have been possible to return the responsibility to King, who still had a large personal investment in the project. Neither of these possibilities could be seriously considered, however. Under the requirements of racial parity (and given the past history of WomanEarth), it was unthinkable to have the organization facilitated solely by a white woman. Ironically, in the middle of a historical moment in which ecofeminism was flourishing, WomanEarth Feminist Peace Institute was ending.

In the remainder of this chapter I will explore some conclusions garnered from this complex history of an organization identified as ecofeminist and focused on antiracism as its principal work. I hope that this analysis will enable others to respect and continue the work of the WomanEarth members by taking seriously the political possibilities it represented. I want to focus on a couple of areas. First, I will draw some conclusions about the notion of racial parity and the peculiar effects of the binary conception of racial difference that undergird that notion. Second, I will explore the definition of Woman-Earth as "ecofeminist," and its ties to feminist antimilitarism.

THE RACE FOR PARITY

In the interviews I've conducted with WomanEarth members, it was emphasized that there were many reasons why the organization didn't continue besides difficulties with questions of race. Lack of funding after the conference, the geographical dispersal of the members, the amount of resources and energy depleted by organizing the Hampshire conference, and poor delegation of responsibility were probably the most important factors in WomanEarth's demise. But there were indeed problems in accomplishing the goal of racial equality within the organization that racial parity was supposed to achieve. Meetings were difficult enough to arrange on a limited budget with a far-flung membership; but when they did occur, a great deal of time was occupied with sorting out issues stemming from racial difference. Some of the members I talked to expressed the sense that the agenda of WomanEarth was constantly shifting because of the attempt to construct an organization based on racial parity.[46] This did not at all mean, for them, that antiracist work was not properly *on* the political agenda, but that the need to constantly address racial differences within the group meant that organizing efforts, in the words of Kirk, "unraveled at the same time (they) were put together . . . nothing could be assumed." For all members, there was clearly a great deal of pain associated with the memory of these discussions, as well as a sense of having learned a great deal.

The women in WomanEarth were on the whole powerful, experienced feminists with long histories of activism and antiracist work. Why did they run into so much difficulty operating under the requirement of racial parity? One answer is that working in coalition, as Bernice Johnson Reagon has pointed out,[47] is difficult, painful work and cannot be expected to be otherwise. Taking this to heart means understanding that the difficulties experienced in WomanEarth were a sign that its members were practicing serious antiracist politics.

But I would like to suggest that another factor increasing the difficulty could be the way in which racial difference was defined by WomanEarth: in terms of white women and women of color. This dualistic conception of race gave the women involved only two choices of racial subjectivity, and thus impoverished the conversations among the members, continually returning them to only one axis (white and nonwhite) along which to conceive of the social construction of race and the operations of racism. In addition, it ob-

scured the clear consideration of other extant differences operative in different ways of working, different political investments, and different personal expectations. The focus on difference, and on difference of one kind, pointed
continually to identities, not structural processes.

When binary rather than multiple subject positions are emphasized,
racialized identities appear to inhere only in the nonwhite women. Emphasizing multiple and overlapping subject categories, in contrast, points to the
creation of subjectivities in part by the *intersection* of broad social structural
factors such as racism, classism, sexism, and heterosexism. Such a theoretical
approach, more understood as necessary today than it was for the members of
WomanEarth, allows people to complicate their identities beyond simple
racial categories. This process points to the way in which it is *racism* that insists on the binary conceptualization of "white" and "nonwhite."

Antiracist work, according to a dualistic way of thinking, can only be done
with those who are "raced." Thus, antiracist practice appears to be appropriately conducted between differently raced individuals, rather than a practice
that targets the consequences of U.S. racism. In this way, a dualistic conception of race leads white people to believe that the best way to work against
racism is to find some way to get people of color to join white organizations. It
does not lead white people to examine the way in which they are "raced"
themselves, that is, the way in which they are carriers of racial identities constructed by structural racism. It does not present these structures as problems
for their own lives, but for the lives of others.

Additionally, this dualistic conception of race does not encourage discussions of the different ways in which U.S. racism affects various "women of
color." A nuanced, historical analysis of how racism is reproduced and maintained is thus difficult to achieve. "Women of color," as Chela Sandoval,
among others, has argued, must be seen as a "tactical subjectivity," an "oppositional consciousness" of a social movement formed from the ongoing political and strategic negotiations for and against power carried on within feminist
and antiracist circles.[48] As an oppositional category, it is useful inasmuch as it
is understood not to be an essential category. That is, "women of color" are
not in some biological or unchangeable way alike. They share a struggle
against racism because U.S. racism allows only two racial categories of importance: "white" and "nonwhite."

To fully understand and resist U.S. racism, however, dualistic conceptualizations must be resisted and the flexibility and historical variation of racism
must be fully confronted. For example, I've mentioned at the beginning of this
chapter that it is possible to trace a historical transition from racial discourses
within social movements that emphasized a division between "white and black"
to racial discourses focusing on "white people and people of color." One of the
problems of the earlier discourse was the emphasis on African American experience over the experience of other racialized U.S. groups. But the retention

of a dualistic frame allows the dominance of African American experience to slide back in. Especially in the late 1980s, the use of the category "women of color" does not preclude the metonymical dynamic in which African American women stand in for the whole of "women of color," as, for instance, in their predominance in the make-up of WomanEarth's August 1986 gathering.

It is certainly the case that because U.S. racism operates through the construction of dualistic categories, people who are able to occupy the category "white" are significantly privileged over people who occupy the category "nonwhite." It is a truism nowadays to say that this situation is what antiracist politics must address. But what is not often seen is the danger of allowing that analysis to justify the importation of these categories, unchallenged, into antiracist work.

To understand my point here, let's look at the way in which racial parity as a dualistic operating principle designed to resist racism ends up replicating its structures. What Sandoval does not emphasize, although it is implied by her work, is the way in which the political construction of the category "women of color" reflects and maintains the processes of the construction of the category "white women." As the marked category in a binary antiracist discourse, white is defined as "not of color," as lacking, from the point of view of "women of color"; yet the category "white" nevertheless continues to operate within a context of racial privilege and power. While "women of color" is a political coalition masquerading as an identity, "white women" retains its shape as a monolithic "personal" identity. This accounts for the ease with which Molina appropriated the identity of "woman of color," consciously seeing it as both imposed by the structures of U.S. racism and as chosen for the purposes of political alliance and placement within the U.S. women's movement. Kirk and Mayman, on the other hand, were more uneasily placed within the category "white women," made to account personally for a U.S. racist history they did not share. Though, like Molina, both of them accepted this identity for political reasons (in their case, through a political analysis of the need to take responsibility for the personal privileges they gained through their placement within structural power relations), such an analysis could not be openly articulated within the framework of racial parity as an antiracist discourse. Critiques they may have generated of the particular, specific nature of "whiteness" in a U.S. context stemming from their experience as "international" women were unavailable as long as the binary nature of racial parity constructed their status as "white women" to be of a personal, fixed nature.

Ironically for the members of WomanEarth, trying to achieve racial parity using a dualistic conception of race insured that white women, as one-half of the oppositional pairing, retained a dominant position within the organization. Simply from a numerical point of view, giving an entire half of Woman-Earth to white women increased their numbers (assuming they occupy one political position on a racial continuum) relative to different racial categories within "women of color" (i.e., African American, Chicana, Native American, Asian American, and all the racial pluralities subsumed under these categories). Further, since they are defined by the concept of "white" as unproblematically unified, bereft of history and cultural complexity, a "given" racial location, white women can more easily occupy this position without the kind of historical and critical analysis that would uncover its instability.[49] What is lost to ecofeminism by the unproblematic use of a dualistic conception of racial difference is the kind of nuanced, complex analysis of power found in theories of simultaneous oppressions, which present racial identity as a problem, as both an achieved and compulsory political location.[50] My earlier point about the binary form of the antiracist discourse in WomanEarth preventing the possibility of Kirk and Mayman articulating their "white" identity as an achieved and compulsory identity, which may have enriched the analysis of racism within the organization, is an example of the way in which white identity becomes presented as immutable. Also fixed by a dualistic conception of racial parity, "women of color" were located on the other side of the racial divide together, forced to minimize their differences and ironically solidify the racist category "nonwhite" as an antiracist political strategy. For example, the need to present themselves as one category prevented the women of color in WomanEarth from presenting an analysis of class differences that divided them or from articulating differences in extant kinds of feminist spirituality.

Finally, the conceptualization of racial parity as a dualism precluded an analysis of power that identifies the intersections of multiple forms of domination, discrimination, oppression, and privilege. My interviews with Woman-Earth members showed clearly that the emphasis on racial parity served to obscure or trivialize many other differences that turned out to have almost equal force in the meetings and at the conference: differences in religious or spiritual orientation, sexual orientation, economic privilege, national backgrounds, and go forth. One reason for the detail of my narrative about the history of WomanEarth is to show that these nonracial differences would often arise with great force, unanticipated because of the focus on racial differences. Or, just as problematically, these differences would be retranslated into "racial" differences, and thus left unanalyzed.

There are a number of means by which a variety of differences were conflated into racial differences. One was the assumption that the white women and the women of color were interchangeable representatives of their groups, thus obscuring differences between members of each group. An example of this is the idea that Molina's presence in the New York office would solve the problem of the lack of broad participation in decision-making because Molina could "represent" the women of color. The problem of not seeing dissimilarities among the women of color or the white women was exacerbated by the frequency of understanding a particular difference (i.e., sexual orientation or political analysis) as a racial difference. A relatively trivial example can be given here: there was concern expressed by some of the African American women at the August gathering that there were cats allowed around the food. Several interviewees saw this as a racial difference, as something that African American women (in this case standing in for all of the "women of color") minded while white women did not. Another case of "mistaken identity" was the previously mentioned perception on the part of some women of color that "unconventional" spiritual practice was a "white thing," when in fact many of the women of color within Circle One and at the August gathering were practitioners of or sympathizers with alternative feminist spiritualities. Even more seriously, perhaps, sexual orientation was perceived by some participants in the August conference, as well as some members of Circle One, as a racial difference. Despite the presence of several lesbians of color, many of the women of color and white women presumed that the only lesbians at the August gathering were white.

Similarly, a class analysis wasn't articulated in the group except insofar as class and race were conflated. This led to questions of inauthenticity around racial identification, e.g., Molina's upper-class background undermining her legitimacy as a representative of U.S. women of color. Comments by Margo Adair made in discussing whether Rachel Bagby, whose activism Adair saw as centered primarily in white university communities, had the equivalent organizing experience as Rachel Sierra, who Adair saw as being involved in "all people of color contexts," also point up the need to analyze the conflation of race and class. To Adair, organizing in a university context meant organizing in a white context (because the university was by definition middle class) whether or not Bagby was African American. While race and class *are* conflated by the intersections of racism and classism in this country, there is still a need in oppositional discourses to analyze their separate effects in order to disentangle the knot created by unequal power relations. The lack of a class analysis as a separate mode of understanding inequalities made the effects of Mayman's position as a "wage laborer" invisible to the members of WomanEarth.

Examining the history of WomanEarth, it is obvious that the structure of racial parity provided a way to talk about conflict between women of color and white women. This is most clearly evidenced by the speak-out on racial identity at the August gathering, which ended up being a very positive experience. But the structure of racial parity did not allow for conflict stemming from other differences. In particular, it could not frame how to resolve conflict within, rather than between the two racialized groups nor within categories that confused these racialized boundaries. Examples of these abound. For instance, Sierra ruefully remarked about the August gathering that the "colored girls get together and they fight," a comment that references what

Teish called the "great Native American debate," that is, the argument over which of the Native Americans present were "real" Indians. Another example was the argument at the August gathering within the lesbian caucus between lesbians who were out and lesbians who were not. Among the reasons for these struggles was the effort behind WomanEarth to combine a number of social movement approaches, to produce a multivalent politics, and to do so not in the form of a coalition but in a single movement. The emphasis on racial parity took precedence over the other difficulties inherent in the admirable attempt to create a movement location that combined a number of internally contested political positions. This meant that the conflicts between and within these positions could not be resolved.

DEFINING ECOFEMINISM

The history of WomanEarth shows clearly the close link for many between feminist antimilitarism of the late 1970s and early 1980s to ecofeminism in the late 1980s and early 1990s. What's interesting to look at in this history, however, are its different meanings for white women and women of color. WomanEarth was an attempt to overcome previous racial segregation between white feminist antimilitarists and feminists of color who also saw the threads running through militarism, sexism, racism, classism, heterosexism, and environmental destruction. In addition, the women of color drawn to WomanEarth tended on the whole to be interested in bridges between feminist politics and feminist spirituality as well. The analysis was shared; the nuances and emphases may have differed. But the past movement experience was not shared. This is why the members of the organization who were women of color were excited about the political project of WomanEarth, but uniformly rejected the label "ecofeminist."[51] For them, "ecofeminism" meant a white movement.

The sense that "ecofeminism," or "feminist peace politics," meant a white movement was accurate not only because historically this has been true of feminist antimilitarism but also because it described the specific genesis of WomanEarth as a project initiated by King and Starhawk, supported in its beginnings by a white funder who emphasized not racial diversity but rather international diversity. Despite King's sensitivity to the dangers of "adding on" women of color to a white project, and the considerable risks she and Starhawk took to recast the conceptualization of the project in order to "bring the women of color in on the ground floor," the organization was never able to avoid the consequences of this history. And indeed, given the importance of King and Starhawk to the development of ecofeminism as a political location in the United States, this difficulty is not surprising. The irony here is that WomanEarth was an important effort to derail the "white-only" development of ecofeminism. It served as a consequential example to other ecofeminists of the possibility and need for interracial ecofeminist organizations. Establishing WomanEarth as *outside* ecofeminism in a serious way would have prevented it from serving an antiracist function *within* ecofeminism. King, in particular, became torn between the desire to locate WomanEarth within a developing tradition called "ecofeminism," and the need to present it to the women of color as a "new" effort. One can view this as self-aggrandizing, or one can view it as a useful intervention into the "white-only" environment of ecofeminism. The importance of this can be seen particularly in the effect of the existence of WomanEarth on the 1987 USC ecofeminist conference. Here, WomanEarth served to broaden the notion of what constituted the purview of ecofeminism, stressing the need for active inclusion of women of color and of analyzing internal racism within the movement. The fact that WomanEarth did not have any concrete antiracist ecofeminist political projects made this intervention almost entirely a symbolic one and one that benefited white ecofeminists far more than the women of color who were their potential allies.

Ultimately, the focus on racial parity became a goal for the organization rather than just an operating principle, obscuring other possibilities, like concrete, localized political actions. Racial parity resulted in antiracist work taking place between individuals (not entirely a useless practice) to the detriment of a focus on environmental and feminist problems caused or exacerbated by structural racism. Both a historical perspective of the variable ways in which racism has operated, and a focus on the consequences of racism rather than raced individuals, would put white ecofeminists in a position to form coalitions with the movement against environmental racism, which grounds its analysis on both of these elements, but which does not often include an analysis of sexism along with its analysis of the intersections of racism and environmental exploitation.[52]

WomanEarth's effort to work on the principle of racial parity was based on a binary antiracist discourse common to the feminist movement in the 1980s. Thus, the racial essentialism of its presuppositions (conceiving of women of color and white women as two essentially different and homogenous groups), was part of a strategic antiracist feminist intervention into early ecofeminism. It was one attempt to undermine the gender essentialism of claiming universal status for a maternalist conception of women, a notion that was prevalent (though unstable) in the feminist antimilitarist movement that was one important origin of U.S. ecofeminism. In the previous chapter, I argued that judging the gender essentialism in early ecofeminism without taking into account its strategic purposes prevents us from adequately analyzing feminist antimilitarism as an oppositional discourse and practice. Similarly, evaluating the racial essentialism imbedded in WomanEarth's notion of racial parity must also involve taking into account its strategic attempt to counter racism in early ecofeminism, racism partially produced by feminist antimilitarism's reliance on certain gender essentialisms that erased difference within the category "women." These moments of essentialism, these ecofeminist natures, are historically contingent, contradictory and contested. They remain politically important even when they have particular political costs.

THE NATURE
OF RACE

INDIGENOUS
WOMEN AND WHITE
GODDESSES

4

While WomanEarth Feminist Peace Institute was focused on U.S. racism in binary terms that tend to emphasize white and African American relations, there is
another set of ecofeminist discourses about racial difference operative in the same time period (the latter half of
the 1980s) that center on the idealization of "indigenous" women as symbolic representatives of ecofeminism. By putting indigenous in quotes here, I am pointing to the conflation of three ecofeminist discourses on
racial difference that partake of the same form and function: that of creating an image of "the ultimate ecofeminists" as idealized tribal peoples. These three discourses
of racial difference are those about Native American
women, about Third World women (in which certain
Asian Indian women tend to stand in as generalized
Third World women), and about pre-Christian European pagan women. I will argue that the conflation of
these three categories into a symbolic indigeneity is ironically a form of antiracist discourse that, like the binary
discourse in WomanEarth of white women and women
of color, ends up, despite good intentions, reconstituting
white privilege. One way this occurs is through the racial
essentialism of the idea of the indigenous, which erases
all difference between and within the categories "Native
American" and "Third World" and constitutes them as
racialized Others to a white Self that is Western, modern, and industrialized. Though these first two cate-

gories contain within them many different kinds of women, white ecofeminism in the late 1980s and early 1990s has been most concerned with those women in these categories that are involved in cultural and economic practices, usually that of subsistence agriculture or hunting and gathering, that are seen as "sustainable" and "ecological." These practices are often defined as ecological for ecofeminists (and other U.S. radical environmentalists) simply by contrasting them to industrialized, commodity-based economic practices (which are, through this move, also essentialized as always already anti-ecological as well as "white").

The logic of this preference for indigenous cultures is deeply implanted in ecofeminist theory. The ecofeminist critique of the hierarchical dualism of culture/nature at the heart of Western science and ideology therefore privileges those cultural and economic arrangements that are seen not to divide culture from nature, and that do not think of culture as superior to a degraded, inferior nature. This pervasive, and in many respects persuasive, critique of Western Enlightenment rationalism directs ecofeminists to non-Western cultures for examples of ecofeminist politics, culture, and economy. Further, in line with ecofeminist analyses of the interdependent relation between Western culture/nature dualism and sexism, such "indigenous" cultures are seen as possible examples of more feminist societies. The term "indigenous" thus primarily signals for many white U.S. ecofeminists the extent that these cultures are nonindustrialized and therefore, from this perspective, more ecological; secondarily, it symbolizes the extent to which these cultures may be more egalitarian in their gender relations.[1]

I am critical of this logic on a number of grounds. The cultural imperialism embedded in this discourse of racial difference has been criticized by others besides myself, including other white ecofeminists. While the connection between Western culture/nature dualism and Western sexism is convincing, the mutual support of these two ideological systems is not, as Huey-li Li points out, universal or necessary. Li argues that several cultures, notably Chinese culture, have seen the coexistence of sexism and nondualistic understandings of the relation between culture and nature for centuries.[2] Furthermore, as Donna Haraway has pointed out, nondualistic philosophies of the relationship between culture and nature can still construct hierarchies of status and merit that may include the debasing of animals and other entities in "nature" in relation to humans. In arguments that prefer the organic, the nondualistic, she says, "there is little or no analysis of the historical and textual forms of power and violence built into 'holist,' 'non-western' frameworks."[3] Similarly, the ecofeminist reliance on the idea that nature-based spirituality reflects more ecological societies leads to the debatable assumption that certain "indigenous" spiritualities (Native American, Hindu, ancient European Goddess religions, paganism, and witchcraft) also promote feminist social and economic relationships.[4] Besides these critiques of the valorization of indigenous women, I am also interested in the ways in which this ecofeminist discourse maintains certain notions of white identity, the kinds of ecological solutions this discourse offers and obscures, and the relation of this discourse to an ebbing of distinctively white ecofeminist activism. Once again, I am not interested in critiquing ecofeminist racial and gender essentialisms simply as theoretical problems, but in seeing their strategic effects in particular historical circumstances.

HEALING AND REWEAVING ECOFEMINISMS

I begin this chapter with a focus on two ecofeminist stereotypical formulations: those of Native American culture and those of Asian Indian women's activism. In both cases, I argue that white ecofeminist discourses of racial difference implicitly attempt to resolve three contradictions. One is the apparent contradiction of being an antiracist movement that is predominantly white, stemming from the segregated history of social movements from which ecofeminism arises and the binary antiracist discourses it inherits, which, as we saw in the last chapter, tend to result in a focus on racial identities rather than racist social structures. The second contradiction is the coexistence of an ecofeminist critique of the patriarchal connection between women and nature with the deep desire for a nonpatriarchal version of that connection. This contradiction was mentioned in chapter 1, where I discussed it as one source of repeated gender essentialism within ecofeminism (by "gender essentialism," I mean arguments that unproblematically connect "women" with "nature," assuming a universal, essential feminine identity constructed out of biological femaleness that exists cross-culturally and across racial and class structures), such as arguing that women are "naturally" environmentalists. Here, I argue (as I did in relation to the binary discourse of racial parity employed by WomanEarth) that certain discourses about idealized Native American and Asian Indian women are racial essentialisms that attempt to avoid the problem of gender essentialism (by "racial essentialism," I mean conceptions of group difference based on generalized "racial" or "cultural" attributes that produce notions of universalized, ahistorical, innate group characteristics). The third contradiction, ever more apparent in the early 1990s, is the continued orientation of ecofeminism toward radical politics while experiencing a growing separation from localized, issue-oriented direct action. I argue that part of the reason for this is the prevalence of the ecofeminist discourse of indigenous women as the "ultimate ecofeminists," a discourse that, ironically, means to point in one metaphorical turn to the antiracist, nonessentialist, and activist imperatives of ecofeminist theory.

To give a few examples of this discourse, I will use as representative artifacts of U.S. ecofeminism two anthologies, *Healing the Wounds: The Promise of Ecofeminism*, edited by Judith Plant and published by New Society Publishers in 1989 (hereafter *Healing*); and *Reweaving the World: The Emergence of Ecofeminism*, edited by Irene Diamond and Gloria Orenstein, published by Sierra Club Books in 1990 (hereafter *Reweaving*). I chose these books because they illustrate, in different ways, the problems I want to examine, and because they are a significant part of the historical narrative I construct throughout this book. While there are many other important ecofeminist books published after 1990, including four other important ecofeminist anthologies,[5] *Healing* and *Reweaving* play a crucial role in the development of U.S. ecofeminism as a political position. They have been criticized, I think often unfairly, for their gender essentialism, but here I am most concerned with certain kinds of racial essentialisms, tropes that are less apparent but still present in the later three anthologies. The two anthologies under examination here establish ecofeminism as a political location independent of the feminist antimilitarist movement with which early ecofeminism was so closely identified. They grow out of the same historical and cultural context as WomanEarth (the late 1980s, the ebbing of antimilitarist direct action with the ending of the Cold War, and widespread critiques of feminist racism and feminist essentialism) and with a similar sense of the necessity of antiracism to an ecofeminist project. These books, however, in contrast to WomanEarth, are aimed at producing a theoretical base for ecofeminist activism rather than an ecofeminist activist organization itself. At the time of their publication, these books were the most prominent representatives of the diversity within ecofeminism, the many voices constructing the position.

They are not identical, however. *Healing* is a collection of articles put together by one author, an attempt to stake out the territory of ecofeminism as a new radical environmentalism. Published in 1989, it represents a white ecofeminism beginning to grapple with the problems of how to articulate a white ecofeminist antiracism. *Reweaving*, on the other hand, is the product of the Ecofeminist Perspectives: Culture, Nature, Theory conference held at USC in 1987, and is edited by the two conference organizers. Given the multiplicity of perspectives represented at this lively and contentious event, *Reweaving* has much less of a single voice, more divergent analyses and subjects, and more attention to multiple axes of difference than *Healing*. This distinction is represented on the back covers of the volumes; where *Healing* has a picture of its editor, Judith Plant, *Reweaving* features two lists of its contributors, advertising its multiple voices. The slightly different historical locations of the two anthologies can be read in their subtitles: *Healing*, put together at the outset of the construction of ecofeminism as a location independent of feminist antimilitarism, is subtitled "The *Promise* of Ecofeminism"; *Reweaving*, located more firmly in a sense of an already existing "ecofeminist movement," is subtitled "The *Emergence* of Ecofeminism." Both anthologies, however, focus on antiracism as a crucial aspect of ecofeminist theorizing, and aim to represent ecofeminism as a political location both containing and promoting racial diversity.[6]

However, this diversity is articulated in some problematic ways. Unlike WomanEarth, these anthologies are not explicitly organized around a binary notion of racial difference; rather, they rely on a notion of ecological diversity as an analogy for cultural diversity. Contained as it is within an image of a system-in-balance (the ecosystem), racial and cultural difference is represented in this kind of antiracist discourse as nondisruptive, complementary, and ultimately, in a nonracist world, meaningless *as* difference. For example, Judith Plant's introduction to *Healing* states that "giving up patriarchy with all its deadly privileges . . . means valuing diversity above all else." Yet, a few lines later, she imagines that in the context of local communities organizing for global change, "Differences—if not useful in the defense of the local community—fall off as unimportant. Thus, on the front lines are people of different cultures, colors, ages, sexes, and political persuasions. Here is power-from-within expressing itself—the power to find unity in diversity."[7] I am sympathetic to the political vision behind this rhetoric of difference as healthy diversity, but it too easily ignores the power relations that in many cases are productive of *unequal* differences or even difference itself. For example, should class difference be a valued part of a utopian society based on respecting differences? However much a notion of cultural diversity might be preferable to our present system of racial segregation and inequality, a binary division between possible racial identifications operates underneath this notion of cultural diversity in U.S. ecofeminism. This is the division between "indigenous" and "Western." The maintenance of this binary conception is in fact an exercise of racial privilege in defining difference.

The categories of indigenous versus Western are continually (re)-constructed by the repetition of references to three forms of "indigenous" women: Native American women, Asian Indian women, and prehistoric European pagan women. All three categories are always counterposed to the Western industrial system, which destroys nature and oppresses women. African American women also make appearances within these volumes, as authors and as referents, but they don't carry the symbolic charge of the "indigenous," and thus references to them are rare. This distinguishes the discourse of the indigenous versus Western from the binary discourse of white women versus women of color used by WomanEarth, in which African American women's voices predominated. It is important to note that there are essays in both books that do not contain references to these three kinds of "tribal" women, and those that do sometimes complicate them in ways that confound the duality of "indigenous/Western." But the overall effect is one in which this binary, racialized division defines the ecofeminist approach articulated by these anthologies.

In the continual appearance of this binarism, we can see a reappearance of the tension experienced by WomanEarth between definitions of diversity that stress U.S. racial divisions and those that stress "Western" versus "non-Western," or "international," difference. This tension is resolved by these anthologies through deploying a notion of the indigenous that is "nonWestern" *and* also subject to U.S. racism, an ecofeminist imaginary which conflates the situation of Native American women *and* Third World women and thus can be used, in Plant's words, "to define a truly international movement."[8] The binary sense of this racialized difference is particularly apparent insofar as the economic, cultural, and spiritual practices of indigenous women are presented as available for use by white, Western, urbanized, and industrialized women.

NATURALIZING THE NATIVES

I want to look first at the representation in these two anthologies of the relation of Native American women to an ecofeminist movement that so far had had predominantly white participants.[9] This is not to make invisible all of the feminist environmental activists who are Native Americans. On the contrary, my point is precisely that "ecofeminism" is not a designation automatically accepted by environmentalist activists who are women, nor by feminists who are concerned about the environment.[10] A few Native American women have been willing to be identified with ecofeminist activism and theory.[11] It is important to note, however, that my interrogation of the relation between white ecofeminism and Native American women environmentalists is not intended to argue that such an incorporation within ecofeminism would be an advantage to Native American women; rather, I stage this dialogue in order to examine the barriers white ecofeminists have constructed between their movement and the movement for environmental justice and against environmental racism, of which Native American women have been an important part.[12]

Healing has twenty-seven articles, whose authors' racial identifications are as follows: two Native American, one African American, four Asian Indian, twenty European American/Canadian. *Reweaving* contains twenty-six authors: one Native American, three African American, one Asian Indian, and twenty-one European American/Canadian.[13] Again, the fact that European American/Canadian women are the most represented authors is not necessarily problematic in itself. Ecofeminism has been primarily a white women's political identification and, as I've said throughout this book, it does not necessarily follow that the movement cannot be antiracist because it has mostly white participants. But Native American cultures, their rituals, beliefs, and practices (but not, as one would expect, their specific activist struggles), are frequently referenced so that their voices are silenced even while they are idealized.

This is much more the case with the earlier book, *Healing*, whose cover art, a piece called "Captive Maiden" by Susan Point, features a female figure in a near-fetal position, enclosed with the moon in a circle surrounded by traditional Haida (Northwest Coast Indian) motifs. It is interesting that the cover of *Reweaving* repeats this figure of the woman with the moon, in a form very like the "captive maiden." In the picture on the cover of *Reweaving*, however, this woman, her head upturned to gaze at the moon, her arms clasped around her knees, is in a tree, in contrast to being surrounded with Haida totem figures as she is in *Healing*. The Native American referent in the cover art of *Reweaving* is thus more indirect, contextually referring to the essay within by Paula Gunn Allen (a Native American writer), "The Woman I Love is a Planet, the Planet I Love is a Tree." Allen's essay is the most direct deployment of a Native American perspective for ecofeminist use within *Reweaving*, which has far fewer examples of this rhetorical move than *Healing*. Thus the more indirect reference to Native American cultures symbolizes the lessening of the reliance on this connection in the later book. But why should Native American cultures be such an influential referent for ecofeminism at this historical juncture?

Native American cultures appear so often in these ecofeminist writings because they represent ecological societies that in some instances can also make claims to relative equality between men and women.[14] The combination seems to be ecofeminist by definition. Further, imagining that Native American women embody the "special relation" between women and nature at the same time that they are portrayed as representing nonpatriarchal cultures achieves an apparent resolution to one of the major contradictions within ecofeminism, which I identified at the start of the book. It is not necessary to make essentialist, biologically determinist arguments about the connection between women and nature in the case of Native American women; rather, their cultural traditions and their economic practices can be seen as making positive connections between nature and the feminine, as well as nature and the masculine. For the most part, Native American tribes have practiced a nonexploitative use of natural resources, and Native American women are often equal partners with men in the construction and maintenance of harmonious relationships between people, soil, animals, trees, wind, water, fire and plants. The figure of the Native American woman as the "ultimate ecofeminist" mediates, for white ecofeminists, the conflict between the critique of the patriarchal connection between women and nature and the desire for a nonpatriarchal version of that very connection by representing a living, materially grounded example of such a relationship with nature.[15] Thus, a form of racial essentialism is used in part to avoid the appearance of a form of gender essentialism.

But, as for other environmental activists who are women, there has been some resistance among Native American women to the identification of "ecofeminist." This resistance, for Native American women in particular, stems from three factors: a critical stance toward white separatist feminism, a critique of New Age spirituality's use of Native American religious practices, and a suspicion of white environmentalism's reification of wilderness. To the extent that U.S. ecofeminism has imported into its political location problematic aspects of all three of these related movements (separatist white feminism, New Age spirituality, and white environmentalism), Native American women are understandably reluctant to accede to an ecofeminist desire to incorporate them.

One perception among Native American women is that the emphasis on the masculinism of the social and ideological systems involved in environmental destruction implies an essentialist division between women and men, which is problematic for those resisting racism as well as sexism. When I asked Winona LaDuke, Anishinaabeg feminist and environmental activist, if she called herself an ecofeminist, she said that while she was glad there was an ecofeminist movement developing, she thought of her activism as stemming from her acculturation as a member of her people.[16] Marie Wilson, a Gitksan woman who is interviewed in *Healing*, expresses a similar distance from ecofeminism: "When I read about ecofeminism I find that the attitudes towards women and the feelings inside myself are quite different. It's difficult to explain, but it's as if women are separate. Though I agree with the analysis, the differences must be because of where I come from. In my mind, when I speak about women, I speak about humanity because there is equality in the Gitksan belief: the human is one species broken into two necessary parts, and they are equal."[17] Such articulations point to different racialized histories of sexism and of feminism. White ecofeminism's legacy of a racist and classist feminism—which could unproblematically argue for the "maleness" of oppressive structures without analyzing the negative consequences for poor men or men of color—bears strange fruit in the unwillingness of some Native American women (or for that matter, some working-class white women) to identify as a "feminist" of any kind. To the extent that ecofeminist theory identifies the intersection of sexism and environmental degradation as a result of "male" thinking rather than a particularity of white, Western, patriarchal capitalist social structures, ecofeminists participate in a kind of separatist feminism that has, since the late 1960s, been identified as a form of racism.[18] Though this kind of gender essentialism is not often apparent in the two anthologies under consideration, it has been one strand within ecofeminism.[19]

Another uneasiness expressed by Native American women concerns the use of their spirituality within ecofeminism, which results from the intersection of ecofeminism with New Age feminist spirituality. Though this is only one strand within ecofeminism, the use of Native American rituals and the symbolic positioning of Native American women as white ecofeminists's spiritual teachers comes close to what Andy Smith, a Cherokee woman, has characterized as "spiritual abuse."[20] Smith has argued that the use of Native American spirituality in the New Age movement, without a concomitant willingness to get to know Native American communities and become allies of Native American political struggles, constitutes an appropriative silencing of Native Americans. Furthermore, generalizing Native American spirituality to apply it to white ecofeminist concerns violates the very embeddedness in land and tribe that attracts white ecofeminists. As Smith says: "Indian religions are community-based, not proselytizing religions. For this reason, there is no *one* Indian religion."[21] As we saw in the chapter on WomanEarth, ecofeminism's connection with "alternative," nature-based feminist spiritualities can be construed as a problem, and acts in some instances as a barrier to forming alliances with Native American women in particular.

Ecofeminists in these two anthologies are not unaware of this. In *Healing*, Judith Plant, in particular, warns against the problem of "stealing" Native American rituals. Her essay, "The Circle is Gathering," goes out of its way to honor the embeddedness in a particular landscape and the cultural particularity of the Native American tribe that is her intentional community's neighbor, demonstrating that friendship, respect for cultural difference, and lived, daily alliance is the only basis for nonexploitative political relationships between white people and Native Americans. Her approach is a model for a productive political alliance. Yet, despite her concern and her sophistication, her book is particularly reliant on Native American religious rituals as examples of ecofeminist practice.[22]

Given that there are these problems in claiming Native American women as ecofeminists, does this mean that ecofeminism cannot learn from the Native American concept of nature, and perhaps in some cases from its examples of more equal relationships between women and men? Why shouldn't ecofeminists, as long as they participate in Native American movements and treat Native American culture with respect, continue to point to the more ecological cosmology, economic practices, and equal social relationships developed by some Native Americans? Can ecofeminists use Native American philosophy and practice as resources for constructing theory and creating strategies for action?

The problem here lies in the characterization of indigenous people as the "ultimate ecologists," to use Calvin Martin's phrase.[23] This is a common feature of European American environmentalism,[24] and one of the legacies of that movement to ecofeminists. Certainly, many Native American conceptions of nature seem to lend themselves to environmentalism, in that they generally don't make adversarial distinctions between humans and animals, or humans and nature. The sense that life involves constant change within a balanced system and that the interdependence of all living and nonliving beings constitutes the environment seems to be, especially in comparison to Western beliefs, to be not only more ecological, but (at least potentially) more feminist. But there are several problems with the valorization of Native American conceptualizations of nature, with conceiving them as, in Dolores LaChapelle's phrase, "ecosystem cultures."[25]

First, the idea that it is possible to borrow from Native American culture without practicing a Native American way of life once again does not respect the way in which Native American concepts of nature are embedded in Native American cultural practice. Greta Gaard gives three examples of how borrowing seemingly "ecological" practices from Native Americans not only is a form of cultural imperialism but also may backfire when placed within the white Western cultural context: a justification for eating meat based on Native American hunting practices, the use of the image of Mother Earth, and copying Native American religious practices.[26]

Second, seeing Native Americans as "ultimate ecologists" conceptualizes them as closer to nature similar to ways some ecofeminists analyze as being negative for women. To me, these problems are amusingly brought home by a remark made by an unnamed Native American man to Judith Plant: "You and us, we're different, but we're sort of the same, too. You want to learn to live off this place, we can already do this. You value the salmon, we value the salmon. You don't trust the government, neither do we. Not all Indian people are like us. Not all white people are like you. We're the natives and you're the naturals." At which point, according to Plant, "He roared with laughter."[27] This distinction between "natives" and "naturals" is very telling. A "native" is primarily identified with a very specific and fixed area of land; a "natural" must have a pre-existing distinction between culture and nature, and perhaps civilization and primitivism, in order to "return" to "nature." As Plant observes, "There's a strong attraction that 'civilized' people often experience toward tribal people. Sometimes it even feels like a longing to belong—even though we were brought up to believe that these peoples are inferior to civilized society. Yet to be civilized means to control and regulate all that is natural."[28] As long as ecofeminists rely on notions of Native Americans as more naturally ecological, they will find access to Native American cultural practices only through a logic of rejecting culture for nature, in which Native Americans *are* nature. Ironically, this theoretical move contains within it notions of separation between the two concepts, which are radically different from much Native American philosophy. In presenting Native Americans as more "natural," ecofeminists simply invert the Western valuation of nature in relation to culture without undermining the dualism.

A third problem lies in the dehistoricizing and stereotypical results of the ecofeminist idealization of Native American culture. As the man in Plant's article says: "Not all Indians are like us. Not all white people are like you." Discussions of Native Americans as the "ultimate ecologists" tend to generalize across tribal cultures and obscure the specific problems and varied solutions that occupy Indian struggles for cultural survival.

Valorization of the ecological and feminist elements of Native American culture reinvigorates a "noble savage" stereotype, which, as the flip side of the "bad Indian" stereotype, has a dangerous history in this country. And, what happens when Native Americans choose strategies that go against ecofeminist political theory and practice? Will they then become "bad Indians" instead of "noble savages"? Marie Wilson expresses this fear when she says: "I have had the awful feeling that when we are finished dealing with the courts and our land claims, we will then have to battle the environmentalists and they will not understand why. I feel quite sick at this prospect because the environmentalists want these beautiful places kept in a state of perfection. . . . In a way this is like denying that life is happening constantly in these wild places, that change is always occurring. Human life must be there too. Humans have requirements and they are going to have to use some of the life in these places."[29] The idealization of the "indigenous" as more ecological creates conditions in which, once again, dominant U.S. white cultural values (this time, ecological ones) can be imposed on Native Americans. In this case the sanctity of the "wilderness" could serve as a justification for restrictions on Native Americans based on U.S. environmentalism.

Fourth, the return of the "noble savage" creates a conceptual paradox in which ecological and feminist solutions are seen to reside *only* in tribal and hunting and gathering societies, in which attempts are made to use Native American culture as a natural resource for ecofeminism, or, indeed, for radical environmentalism. The stereotyping of Indian culture prevents knowledge and analysis of the changes in Native American tribal cultures, of how they have been both resistant and accommodating to the dominant European American culture. Plus, the "noble savage" stereotype brings with it the myth of the "vanished Indian." In other words, without allowing for change, for agency in conditions of cultural transformation, Native American cultures will only be seen as either pure or extinct, as either premodern or assimilated. The "ecological" tribal cultures held up for imitation are thus either characterized as disappearing or as preserved in some ideal state. Such an idealization prevents white ecofeminists from really hearing what Native American women think are serious issues in their communities, what changes they are trying to resist or to have control over.

Finally, a stumbling block is created for ecofeminists trying to imagine solutions to the complexity of contemporary ecological problems. If the only way we can live as ecofeminists is to "return" to a hunting and gathering culture, we cannot begin to inspire people to take action now not only in "indigenous" locations but also in the middle of their urban, industrialized, global—that is, "civilized"—environments. Seeing Native Americans as a part of "culture," indeed, as a part of a contested and fractured U.S. culture, allows white ecofeminists to honor Native American practices and rhetoric in terms of being their own strategies for cultural survival, involving a series of

choices within particularized contexts, rather than an eternal fount of resources on the other side of a divide between culture and nature. Refusing to
essentialize nature as only the wild, the place where "civilization" is not
found, would allow for white ecofeminist action in their own material locations which are likely to include urban Native Americans as well as those living in more traditional contexts.

INDIANS OF THE EAST

Similar problems exist in white ecofeminist discourses that promote subsistence agricultural practices and selected activist politics by Third World
women as examples of ecofeminism at work. Both anthologies position themselves to include "women in the Third World" as exemplars of ecofeminist activism, in an essentializing move similar to what Chandra Mohanty calls
"constructing the Third World difference."[30] The discourse about Third
World women in these books reduces all women in this category to rural village women engaged in subsistence farming or food gathering. In both texts,
however, it is Asian Indian women (particularly village Indian women of the
Chipko, "tree-hugging," movement in Uttar Pradesh, northern India) who
stand in for Third World women as a whole. The breakdown of the authors in
these two anthologies demonstrates this particular problem; remember that
Asian Indian authors were represented in equal or greater numbers to Native
American or African American authors, and they are the only Third World
authors. The presence of Asian Indian authors as equivalent to the presence
of U.S. women of color does two things: (1) the Asian Indian authors are implicitly relied upon to construct racial diversity within the volumes, and (2)
they represent all Third World women.[31] This is especially true for *Healing*.
Once again, as we saw in the chapter on WomanEarth Feminist Peace
Institute, a tension exists between dealing with U.S. racism and with Western
neocolonialism.

But why do Asian Indian women serve as the models of Third World
women at this particular juncture? For one thing, the combination of developed feminist and environmentalist Indian movements has meant a high pro-
file for women's resistance to a number of environmental problems in India.
Thus, *Healing* contains several articles by Asian Indian authors dealing
specifically with Asian Indian women's environmental struggles. Of these
struggles, the most frequently referred to is the Chipko movement (the effort
by villagers in the Gharwal hills to save village forests from logging for com-
mercial, rather than subsistence, use), though other women's activism is also
covered. Besides Vandana Shiva's piece, which I'll discuss shortly, Pamela
Philipose writes about the Chipko movement as well as Indian women's victimization and resistance to the toxic gas release at Bhopal and women's part
in struggles against industrialized fishing in Southern India.[32] And in addition

to a brief mention of Chipko at the end of her article, Rhada Bhatt writes of women's activism against the selling of alcohol in several villages, women's protection of village forests in numerous locations, and women's participation in the land-gift movement.[33] Corrine Kumar D'Souza's article does not examine specific activist examples; rather, it offers the metaphor of "the South" as a method of breaking up the dualistic, linear models of "the East" and "the West." For D'Souza, "the South" is the equivalence of activism, feminism, and anticolonialism: "The South as movements for change in the Third Worlds; the South as the women's movements, wherever the movements exist; the South as the development of new frameworks, seeking a new language to describe what it perceives, rupturing the existing theoretical categories, breaking the mind constructs, challenging the one, real, objective, reality."[34] With such broad claims, D'Souza wants to point to a wide canvas of Third World activism as sources of inspiration for ecofeminism.

But it is the Chipko movement rather than other possible examples of Indian women's activism which quickly attains talismanic status in ecofeminist writings of this period,[35] and references to it are threaded throughout the two anthologies. It is not that other kinds of activism are not examined; the two books, especially *Reweaving*, are rich with various kinds of "ecofeminist" activism, such as Wangari Maathai's Green Belt Movement in Kenya, in which rural women are involved in a program of tree-planting to resist desertification and malnutrition.[36] But the story of the Green Belt movement is not elaborated in these anthologies as Chipko is, and the image of women planting trees is not made to carry the same symbolic force as the image of women "hugging" trees. Chipko reappears consistently, often as the only "Third World" example in an article. For instance, Joanna Macy, in her article in *Healing*, says she sees an "ecological self" in "her sisters of the Chipko" as well as members of Greenpeace.[37] Petra Kelly, in her Preface to *Healing*, identifies as "global sisters" the women of Greenham Common, the Western Shoshone women resisting nuclear testing in Nevada, the Pacific Islander women who suffer from nuclear testing fallout, women in the Krim region in then-Soviet Russia who protested a new nuclear power plant, and the Chipko.[38] Irene Diamond and Gloria Orenstein, in their introduction to *Reweaving*, note that there were many inspirations for Western ecofeminists (including ancient European Goddess worship and Native American philosophy) that led to a "diverse array of innovative practices" and "new forms of political resistance" including, oddly, Chipko along with "women's peace camps." Here, perhaps through a grammatical slip, Chipko is claimed as a *Western* political practice.[39] Carolyn Merchant, in her essay in *Reweaving*, claims that support for "Chipco" (*sic*) is a hallmark of "socialist feminists" (with whom Merchant identifies) rather than "radical ecofeminists." And Ynestra King, in her essay in *Reweaving*, uses Chipko to support her statement that "women have been at the forefront of every historical, political movement to reclaim the Earth."[40] To explain this frequent use of Chipko in ecofeminist writings of this time period, we need to look at the writings of Vandana Shiva.

In 1988, a year before the publication of *Healing*, Vandana Shiva, an Indian theoretical physicist turned environmentalist researcher, published her book, *Staying Alive: Women, Ecology, and Survival in India*. This book analyzed the failure of the Green Revolution in the Third World, particularly its negative effects on rural women, as a symptom of the patriarchal capitalist project of development, which she calls "maldevelopment." Shiva's analysis was extremely influential for U.S. ecofeminists. She combined the environmentalist and feminist analysis of Westernized development policies persuasively and passionately. She also connected her analysis to elements of feminist spirituality and the valorization of "indigeneity." For Shiva, the "death of the feminine principle," which was seen to keep Indian culture in balance with nature, was a necessary part of the project of "maldevelopment." By "death of the feminine principle," Shiva means not some notion of matriarchy nor even Goddess worship, but the idea of gender complementarity in sexual divisions of labor and equality-in-difference she claims existed in precolonial Indian subsistence cultures that were more ecological than those of Western patriarchal capitalism. In crucial ways, then, her argument parallels those of U.S. ecofeminists who look to a prehistoric European past or Native American tribal cultures for the existence of "ultimate ecofeminists." The importance of this inflection of Shiva's argument for ecofeminism in this period is demonstrated by the reprinting of almost exactly the same article she wrote for *Healing* in *Reweaving*; in the latter book she is the only representative of "Third World" women's environmental struggles.[41] Shiva thus holds an important place in the development of U.S. ecofeminism at this particular juncture, at a time when it is just beginning to address Western colonialism's relation to sexism and environmental problems. This historical progression can be seen in the narration of ecofeminism's beginnings and development created in Judith Plant's bibliographic history at the end of *Healing*, where Plant traces the beginnings of ecofeminism in the feminist antimilitarist movement, notes its early theoretical development in Merchant's *The Death of Nature* and Griffin's *Woman and Nature*, mentions the impact of feminist spirituality (much in evidence during this period, as I will discuss more fully below), and finally ends with Vandana Shiva's *Staying Alive*, which, for Plant, "confirms that this movement for life on earth is not limited to the western world, to the privileged."[42]

Shiva offers the story of the Chipko movement as an example of women reclaiming the "feminine principle" in resistance to patriarchal capitalist development. Thus, she authorizes the use of this movement as an exemplar for U.S. ecofeminists eager to add to their parallel analyses her theory of the relationship of Western colonialism to both environmental degradation and sexism in the Third World. The Chipko become a symbolic center of a discourse about Third World women that paints them as "natural environmentalists" or "ultimate ecofeminists," reducing them to an idealized peasant woman who is integrated into "nature" through her daily, lived activities of food gathering and preparation, child rearing, and support of village communities. Once again, the stress on the material, lived, grounded, cultural, and social character of the Third World woman's integration into and care of "nature" is a racial essentialism designed to avoid the gender essentialism of claiming all women to be biologically in sympathy with nature.

Vandana Shiva's influence on U. S. ecofeminism and her problematic shoring up of this particular story of the relation between "indigenous" women and environmental struggles has been criticized on several fronts. In particular, the racial essentialism of U.S. ecofeminism's celebration of the "indigenous" Third World woman and Vandana Shiva's support of this position were addressed in 1991 by Brinda Rao, in 1992 by Bina Agarwal, and in 1993 by Cecile Jackson.[43] In each case, these critics identify problems with the circulation of a particular interpretation of the Chipko as an "ecofeminist" movement, showing that it can be variously interpreted as a peasant or populist movement, or as an environmental movement that is not necessarily feminist.

In their critiques of the ecofeminist use of the "Third World woman" or the Asian Indian subsistence farmer as an "ultimate ecofeminist," none of these critics deny the growing burden on peasant women stemming from the intersection of various environmental problems with gendered divisions of labor and inequalities of power. "Since women in rural societies," writes Rao, "are primarily responsible for providing fuel, fodder and water for their households, lack of access to these resources increases both their already heavy workloads as well as their impoverishment."[44] All three reject the idea that this means either that these women are naturally environmentalists or feminists. They all urge consideration of the historically variable, gendered, classed, and socially complex relationships between household forms, property relations, technology, marital customs, and environmental specificities. Without such careful examination, no positive correlation can be assumed between women's strategies for survival and empowerment and environmentally sound practices. As Cecile Jackson points out: "There is a need, then, to unpack the idea that women's 'responsibilities' make them environmentally friendly. The responsibility to provide firewood for cooking a meal may lead a woman, when faced with a firewood shortage, to plant a tree but it may also lead her to pull up a wooden fence and burn it, to argue for the purchase of a fuel efficient stove, to insist on the purchase of charcoal, to delegate fuelwood collection to a younger woman in the household or any number of alternative responses."[45] The result of the kind of romanticized, reductive, colonialist and essentialized view of "Third World" women in some ecofeminist dis-

courses may very well, in Jackson's view, have negative implications for those
women, including support for the "widespread view that women should be
encouraged to remain in degraded rural environments, 'participating' in conservation projects for the benefit of the community, posterity and nature."[46]
Agarwal concludes that in its emphasis on "Third World" women as an essentialist category, ecofeminist discourse does not take into account questions of
class differentiation, which would lead to more concrete, transformative policies within development practice. "It is in its failure to explicitly confront
these political economy issues that the ecofeminist analysis remains a critique
without threat to the established order."[47]

Thus we can see that the ecofeminist discourse of "Third World" women
as the "ultimate ecofeminists" encounters the same problems found in
ecofeminist discourses about Native American women. Third World women
are used as natural resources for white ecofeminists without respecting the
particularity of their lives and choices; they are reduced to a symbolic general-
ity; and they are seen as "closer to nature." In addition, similar to the effect of
the use of Native American women in this discourse, ecological and feminist
solutions are seen to inhere in an idealized "indigeneity," thus raising the
specter of the *imposition* of "ecological" imperatives on Third World cultures
by Western neocolonialist projects. In the next chapter, I will take up the
question of the effect of these ecofeminist discourses within an international
arena and explore the possibility of their strategic nature in the context of
globalizing environmentalisms.

Besides the same kinds of idealization operative in ecofeminist discourses
about Native American women, painting "indigenous" Third World women
as another version of "ultimate ecofeminists" carries its own specific consequences for U.S. ecofeminism, where the use of non-U.S. ecofeminists to represent "racial diversity" tends to side-step questions of the specific interaction
between U.S. racism and environmental problems. Looking to nonWestern
"indigenous" peoples for examples of feminist environmental resistance obscures the environmental activism of U.S. people of color, many of whom are
women. Additionally, discourses of international "indigeneity" obscure class
relations within the U.S., which operate to identify and disparage "racialized"
groups like Native Americans. Their poverty is implicitly seen as part of their
"sustainable" ecological practices, equal to the "ecosystem" cultures of rural
women in the Third World, rather than the result of the specific interaction
between racism and classism in the U.S.

WHITE INDIANS, CELTIC GODDESSES, AND WHITE IDENTITY

There is a third category of "indigenous women" that operates alongside
Native American women and Asian Indian women: the category of European

tribal women, the prehistoric pagan cultures, the "white Indians" of an imagined (and researched!) European past.[48] In this category, as in that of Third
World women, a particular culture dominates these representations:
European (including Celtic and Greek) pagan or nature-based spiritual practices. The appearances of these traditions as referents for an ecofeminist imaginary is pervasive in the two ecofeminist anthologies I examine here. I describe these referents here not to present all of these articles as equally
problematic, but to show the pervasiveness of the use of these traditions in
ecofeminist work. In *Healing*, we find a Celtic origin myth referencing Native
American origin myths;[49] a guide for worship of the Goddess-as-tree, which
derives from Greek, Hebrew, Celtic, and Druidic practices;[50] a discussion of
the holism of "ancient prepatriarchal myths and religions" such as those
found in pre-Minoan Crete;[51] an essay on Neopaganism that claims as its
practitioners diverse groups such as "feminist goddess worshipers, Celtic re-
vivalist witches, creators of Greek, Egyptian, Norse and Druid revivals, various forms of Shamanism, and assorted other Pagan religious experiments;"[52]
a piece on a number of earth-based spiritualities but particularly the usefulness to ecofeminism of the "pre-Christian Goddess-worshipping religions of
Europe" called Witchcraft;[53] and an essay working from Buddhist ideas toward ecofeminist spirituality.[54] In *Reweaving*, we have writing on ecofeminism's beginnings that identifies the "Goddess in her many guises" as one
"path into ecofeminism;"[55] an essay exploring the "prehistoric," "Paleolithic"
worship of the "Great Goddess" as the "beginnings of Western culture;"[56] a
treatment of the myth of Demeter and Persephone as an ecofeminist para-
ble;[57] a reflection on what a Wiccan perspective, from the "old pre-Christian
Goddess religion of Europe," can add to our understanding of activist politics;[58] a juxtaposition of deep ecology and ecofeminism that describes the latter as analyzing the source of environmental problems and sexism as the defeat of prehistoric European Goddess-worshipping cultures;[59] an ecofeminist
analysis of birth that refers to the reverence for birth in Paleolithic cultures;[60]
and celebration of the "ugliness" of poverty and homelessness as a sign of
"Hecate/Kali."[61]

Coexisting with these essays we have of discussions of feminist spirituality's
relation to ecofeminism that do not reference a tradition of "tribalism" for
white ecofeminism[62] and two pieces that critique forms of white earth-based
spirituality that draw on "tribalism" as resources.[63] The frequency of the references to the European Goddess-worshipping tradition is a primary source of
repeated criticism of ecofeminism as essentialist by critics as diverse as Janet
Biehl and Donna Haraway. I will not expand on those critiques here, but
rather ask: what is the strategic effect of the deployment of Celtic goddesses
and European paganism in the context of ecofeminism at the end of the
1980s?

Explorations into oppositional forms of spirituality that reject the patriarchal heritage of Judeo-Christianity are long-standing feminist projects, and are extremely diverse, ranging from a feminist revisioning of mainstream religions to the creation of new forms of spiritual practice. Ecofeminists, like feminists, take numerous and conflicting positions in relation to the role of spirituality in feminist politics. As Carol Adams writes in her introduction to *Ecofeminism and the Sacred*:

> As women protest, analyze, reform, and envision, there has been no one perspective on the place of spirituality in ecofeminism. Some ecofeminists act from specific religious traditions; others have seen themselves as rebelling against these traditions. For some, the spiritual aspect of ecofeminism is integrally a part of their ecofeminism. For others, spirituality is thought to derail the ecofeminist engagement with social conditions and political decisions that tolerate environmental exploitation, encourage unbridled consumerism, and fail to rein in military spending.[64]

Despite this diversity, it makes a great deal of sense, given their concern with refusing the culture/nature split that informs dominant religions, that ecofeminists would be especially interested in pagan traditions, which do not recognize such a split. For those ecofeminists for whom religious life is important, these traditions would be the most fruitful sources of inspiration. The spiritual practice of these feminist reworkings of pagan traditions has been an important source of personal strength, community cohesion, and oppositional modes of political action.

However, to explain the frequency of the references to European pagan traditions at the particular historical moment of the two anthologies under consideration, it is important to recognize the effects of the critique of the cultural imperialism of some white feminist uses of "Tribal" traditions.[65] It is clear that an initial motive of white ecofeminists (besides the rejection of patriarchal religion and the culture/nature split it relies upon) for their interest in tribal traditions is an antiracist desire to honor those who have been traditionally degraded and exploited. As Catherine Keller puts it, "Perhaps we — White women — can only begin to regain the wisdom and power of relation as we move into contact with non-White, nonpatriarchal, and nonmodern modes of connection with the physical world."[66] But the stance of this form of antiracism ironically still maintains white privilege insofar as it sees women of color, and "nonmodern" women, as natural resources for the betterment of white people. The critique of such attitudes leveled by Native Americans against New Age and feminist spirituality was heard with more and more force by the late 1980s.[67] In response, some white ecofeminists searching to reconcile the usefulness of nature-based spirituality as an analysis and a practice with their desire to combat racism sought a solution in turning to their "own" (that is, European) nature-based religious traditions. This, in fact, is a solution often recommended by Native Americans to white people who wish to learn from tribal cultures that eschew nature/culture dualism and employ nature-based spiritualities. When Judith Plant asks her what white people who wanted to learn from Native American traditions should do, Marie Wilson says: "Each of us springs from some original beginning. It would be uncomfortable for me to attempt to go to Africa and take up their tribal practices, though I could understand the purpose. . . . You will have to go back to your own history, as many Gitksan have had to do."[68] The shift in antiracist discourses that creates an imperative for white women to look to their own cultures for spiritual resources is one explanation, perhaps, for the lessening of references to Native American women in the later *Reweaving* compared to the earlier *Healing*, while the emphasis on the Celtic goddess increases.

This antiracist justification for the development of a white "tribal" spirituality appears in Margot Adler's article in *Healing* and in both of Starhawk's articles in these anthologies. What's more, both of these authors implicitly recognize a connection between the antiracist motives of deploying European pagan traditions and the *construction* of the pagan tradition rather than simply the *recovery* of a tradition. Adler says, for instance, "Since most Neopagans are white, they often look toward Europe, just as Alex Haley looked to Africa. Neopagans are searching among these traditions and creating new religions—in the same way that members of the Society of Creative Anachronism are re-creating the Middle Ages—not as they were, but as they would like them to be."[69] Starhawk writes: "Of course, I cannot speak for all earth-based traditions or for any except my own—and even there I speak *out of* a tradition, not *for* it. . . . Today's Witches are mostly urban people living in the mobile, fragmented, technological modern world. . . . Rather than using our skills, such as they are, to preserve a traditional community, we are faced with the task of reshaping western culture."[70]

The deployment of Celtic Goddesses in ecofeminist discourse, especially when done with some sense of the *constructedness* of the pagan "tradition," is thus partly intended as an antiracist discourse. But it is also one that tries to retain the connection between "indigenous women" and the "ultimate ecofeminists" by seeing as the only appropriate resource for ecofeminism that part of the European American tradition that is "tribal." But is this really U.S. white women's "tradition"? What other kinds of political, ecological, feminist traditions might they look to, ones that would not retain the effect of maintaining white identity as "industrialized" and women of color as "tribal," or which sees ecofeminist resources only in the past? There are a number of examples of U.S. white women's resistance, construction of communities, and ecological efforts which could be suggested; for instance, white women's activism in civil rights movements or the tradition of women's nature writing, illustrating, landscape design, and natural science traced complexly by Vera Norwood.[71] But what is also sought by ecofeminism are traditions that are spiritual and "holistic," i.e. avoid nature/culture and rational/spiritual dualism. However, as ecofeminist critics of deep ecologists point out, there are many pitfalls in holism. Here we can see that ecofeminist deployment of the privileging of the "holistic " and the "indigenous" in the texts we've examined is strategic. When arguing against a dualistic, patriarchal, exploitative, Western concept of nature and of woman, some ecofeminists may argue for holistic, nondualistic conceptions, which may lead them to the valorization of the "indigenous." When arguing against a holistic, abstract, nondualistic, and masculinist deep ecological conception of the relation between Self and Nature, some ecofeminists may argue for contextual, fractured, nonuniversalistic, and pluralistic ideas of self-in-relation. How can we sort out this contradiction?

If white ecofeminists were to stop ideologically separating nature from culture, they wouldn't become tribal peoples—rather, they would be challenged to creatively deal with the politics of their daily technologies, their cyborg natures.[72] White ecofeminists would have to start imagining nature as including the urban and constructed landscapes in which many people live (including Native American and Third World women). Both Rao and Jackson suggest that ecofeminist racial essentialisms that construct "indigenous" women as the "ultimate ecofeminists" include a concomitant essentializing of nature. As Rao notes: "Lurking behind most of these otherwise well-informed studies is a static conception of marginal people, on the one hand, and an equally unchanging conception of their environment, on the other. Peasants are therefore seen as inextricably tied to the land, rural women to their families or households, and tribals to their forests."[73] Jackson, in a more reductive but still useful fashion, states: "Ecofeminists do not see nature and environment as culturally constructed but as biological facts. Yet nature is a product of culture. . . . The meaning of nature is dependent on historically and culturally specific understandings, which reflect gender differences as well as other social divisions."[74] Elly Haney, in an interesting essay entitled "Towards a White Feminist Ecological Ethic," has argued that the legacy of the dominant notion of "nature" employed in American culture is not just gendered, or dualistic, but raced as well. Haney points out that the ecological imagination that thinks of wilderness as a resource for spirituality and purity is "rooted in the same racist legacy" that saw nature, Native Americans, and African American slaves as resources for "civilization."[75] She urges ecofeminists to critically examine their identification of "an ecological approach as similar to Native American attitudes to nature," since such an approach may be "much more indebted to the white experience on this continent then the indigenous one. It may have value for us today, and it is certainly an eloquent heritage, but we should carefully examine it for what it can and can not offer."[76] These comments point to the advantages for ecofeminism of rejecting essentialist notions of "nature" as well as of "women" and "racial difference," and thus producing incisive analyses of the way in which "nature" provides a mutable cultural substance for the rearranging of social and economic power relations. Yet an ecofeminist analysis need not concur with the radical social constructionism of Jackson's position, where in seeing "nature as the *product* of culture," the elements that make up our commonsense notion of "nature" (plants, animals, weather, soil, etc.) lose their material and historical specificity. Instead, we can follow an analyis such as Donna Haraway's or Elizabeth Bird's, in which "nature" is seen as an only imperfectly knowable actor in a complex, constantly negotiated relationship with human beings and technologies.[77] Solutions to environmental problems must be able to be imagined into the future rather than relegated to some idealized past. Ironically, an excellent resource for this kind of imagining of new relationships, which eschews both the divide of "culture" and "nature" and an idealized "indigeneity," is the Pagan imagination deployed by Starhawk in her science fiction utopian/dystopian novel *The Fifth Sacred Thing*.[78] Respecting the integrity of subordinated cultures, articulated away from the search for a utopian past, rejecting essentialist notions of nature, and grounded in political action, a new form of feminist paganism, given its popular appeal, may well serve a radical political alliance.

Whether or not an analysis locates itself within feminist paganism, such a de-essentializing of nature as well as race and women, generating new analyses of the ideological uses of nature as at once raced and gendered as well as materialist investigations of various human/environment interactions, may put ecofeminists in a better position to ally themselves with antiracist environmental movements that are concentrated on urban problems. At present, the problem with the preference for "indigeneity" in ecofeminist discourse and its concomitant stress on nonindustrialized ecological solutions is a barrier between white ecofeminists and environmental justice activists. Women in the environmental justice movement are in a multitude of class and race locations that cut across the "industrial" and the "tribal," concerned about the effects of structural racism on the material conditions of postindustrial society, not just those effects that construct racial identities. Definitions of environmental problems by this movement include a conception of "environment" that does not depend on a notion of unchanging, "original" nature.[79] These movements are also locations with connections to "white" traditions of resistance in the United States—indeed, to multiracial and antiracist traditions of struggle and resistance.[80] Ecofeminists could join in an envisioning of activist strategies that could provide the basis for an effective coalition politics, not just between white ecofeminists and Native American and Third World women environmentalists, but also across a multitude of differences that divide women. As this book argues throughout, this may mean generating new "essentialisms,"[81] new "ecofeminist natures," based on the creation of new collective identities within social movement contexts. But, if my argument here has any merit, these new essentialisms could also be destabilized by political action within a context of coalition politics and ongoing democratic alliances.

Given the problems with the discourse of "indigeniety," of Native American women, Chipko activists and Celtic goddesses as the "ultimate ecofeminists," attempts to construct an antiracist ecofeminist position in the late 1980s foundered within a U.S. context in which there are few extant political arenas for multiracial, cross-class alliances. In the internationalist arena of development politics, however, the institutionalized space of the U.N. provided opportunities for an ecofeminist discourse that promoted the environmental expertise of Third World women. It is to this arena that I will now turn.

ECOFEMINIST NATURES AND TRANSNATIONAL ENVIRONMENTAL POLITICS

5

In previous chapters, I have argued that a tension exists between ecofeminist definitions of diversity that privilege differences based on U.S. racial categories, and notions of diversity based on "international" difference. In this chapter, I will decenter the U.S. context in order to consider the deployment of ecofeminist conceptions of race and gender within a transnational context. I want to ask about their political results within a particular historical, disciplinary, and political context in the early 1990s in order to explore the conditions under which "strategic essentialisms" operate, and to generate ways of assessing their effects. I will start by sketching two interrelated contexts. One is the field of development studies, which, from 1970 to 1990, had experienced shifts from "development" to "women in development" to "women, environment, and development." The second context is a phenomenon I will call the "globalization of environmentalism," or the hegemonic contests over the meaning and use of "environmentalism" within a post-Cold War transnational political arena. Finally, I will look at a specific example of the deployment of an implicitly ecofeminist discourse as a mobilizing tool by an organization called WEDO, or Women's Environment and Development Organization, which was founded in 1990 to orchestrate a "women's voice" within UN deliberations over the intersection between environment and development. What I want to show here is the way in which "ecofeminism," rather than being a fixed group of movement actors or organizations, or even a set of circumscribed theories or analyses, is a political intervention into dominant development discourses that, by the end of the 1980s, were tied to a hegemonic environmental discourse. What ecofeminism allows in this context is a feminist intervention into changing development discourses as well as a location within which coalitions between southern and northern feminists can take place.

Let's begin by briefly outlining some of the more local as opposed to global problems with a U.S. ecofeminist discourse of racial and cultural diversity that privileges "international" difference instead of U.S. racial categories of difference. Within U.S. ecofeminist organizations, conferences, and writings, because the non-U.S. women who are used to construct "international" diversity within ecofeminism are often either of a privileged class in their home countries or are reductively constituted as "indigenous" women, "internationalism," as a U.S.-based discourse of cultural diversity, often elides important differences of class, caste, education, language, or culture that may be very pertinent within the home countries of non-U.S. women. Approaches that focus on questions of the specific interaction between U.S. racism and environmental problems are consistently displaced by the use of non-U.S. women to represent "diversity." And in conflating U.S. racism with U.S. neo-colonialism, U.S. ecofeminists are impeded in offering a politically relevant, materially grounded analysis of the interaction between the two in the creation of environmental problems, whether they are seen as "local" or "global." In the U.S. context, critiques of ecofeminist essentialisms of race and gender that posit "indigenous" women as having a privileged standpoint in relation to environmentalism can be problematic. Nevertheless, as I argue in this chapter, under specific historical conditions, ecofeminism has been an important *international* political location at the intersection of environmentalism and feminism, which has become a globalized space for political demands by women in many countries who might not otherwise have had a voice or an opportunity to create coalitions.

ESSENTIALIZING ECOFEMINISTS

As we saw in the last chapter, critics such as Bina Agarwal, Cecile Jackson, and Brinda Rao have pointed out problems with the production of an "internationalist" ecofeminist movement. Primarily, their critique is focused on an essentialist discourse (which, contrary to their portrayal, is not singularly of ecofeminist origin) that sees symbolic "indigenous" women as the primary victims of the interaction between environmental problems and sexism as well as the inspirational sources of activist resistance to these problems.[1] It is important to note that although this is a discourse that can be found within ecofeminism—perhaps especially within a certain time period, as detailed in the last chapter—it is neither solely ecofeminist nor unchallenged within ecofeminism.

These latter points are not widely understood. Instead, ecofeminism often serves as a straw-woman for a critique of a broader Western environmentalist discourse (in which, as we have seen, some ecofeminists are complicit through a complicated effort intended to construct an antiracist, anti-essentialist ecofeminism) about indigenous peoples as the "ultimate ecologists." However, given its status as a straw-woman in these debates, ecofeminism is clearly not the singular object of this critique; indeed, for Jackson and Agarwal, ecofeminism is a synecdochic figure for a discourse within development studies called "women, environment, and development," or WED. That is, these critics see a growing relationship between essentialist theories of women's stake in environmentalism (which they call "ecofeminism") and contemporary analyses within development studies of environmental problems and their solutions. For Jackson in particular, the main target is development discourses about women and the environment, even though most of her theoretical critique is directed against ecofeminism. This rhetorical move unfairly reduces ecofeminism entirely to an essentialist discourse and abstracts it from its historical and political context. For instance, Jackson writes: "How are ecofeminist ideas reflected in development literature and practice? . . . [I]t is taken as self-evident that harm to nature equals harm to women because of the pervasive perception that women are closer to nature. . . . The linkage of 'women' and environment is either simply assumed or asserted and used to prescribe actions to mobilise women for conservation."[2] This portrayal of ecofeminism as positing women as "closer" to nature is contradicted by many ecofeminist writers, as we have seen. For instance, Ynestra King, Karen Warren, Carolyn Merchant, and others, posit women's relation to the environment as socially constructed and/or arising out of historical, materialist conditions; further, these writers see women's environmental mobilization as arising out of women's political agency rather than their essential similarity to nature. Rao, writing a little earlier than either Jackson or Agarwal, similarly locates problems of essentialism in what she sees, from her historical position, as an "emergent" set of studies (she does not immediately identify ecofeminist work in this category) concerned with the effects of a process she calls "capitalization of nature": i.e., "colonial and capitalist practices, and the so-called development schemes sponsored by international organizations like the World Bank."[3] These studies, Rao claims, whether they are dealing with women as victims of the capitalization of nature or as heroic environmental activists, ". . . are based on almost identical conceptions of. . . the proximity of women to nature."[4] Note that Rao identifies specifically political conceptions of indigenous women-as-victims and therefore women-as-activists as the mo-

ment when essentialist notions are constructed.[5] Whether the close relationship between women and nature is seen as biologically based or produced
from women's material location in socially produced divisions of labor, Rao
argues that these conceptions "perpetuate an essentialist construction of
women and tribals based on nostalgic presuppositions of how they might have
existed in some distant past."[6] Having sculpted this approach from "emergent" development discourses, Rao then identifies it with "eco-feminism" by
using Shiva's work as representative of this position.[7] Here again, a reduction-
ist move results in tagging all ecofeminism with the label "essentialist."

A much fairer rendition of the relationship between ecofeminism and
development discourse—one that includes the internal contests within
ecofeminism over essentialist notions of the relationship between women and
nature—is given by Melissa Leach. Leach notes three strands within development discourse dealing with women and the environment: an ahistorical emphasis on women as the sole managers of natural resources; an ecofeminist argument about the negative consequences of western conceptions of women
and nature (conceptions that conflate and devalue them); and "feminist
analyses of the effects of capitalist accumulation on women and the environment" that, unlike the first approach, are both materialist *and* historical.[8]
What is an improvement over some of the other accounts is Leach's attention
to the debate *within* ecofeminism over how to characterize the relationship
between "women" and "nature." Unlike Jackson and Rao, she notes that there
are "two rather different strands of ecofeminism which must be distinguished": one makes essentialist (sometimes biological) arguments, and the
other analyzes various ideological constructs of women and nature as historically and culturally located.[9] The second she finds potentially very useful for
understanding the processes of "development." Agarwal also notes that there
are both essentialist and anti-essentialist versions of ecofeminism, but she
then goes on to insist that ecofeminism posits "'woman' as a unitary category
and fails to differentiate among women by class, race, ethnicity, and so on. It
thus ignores forms of domination other than gender which also impinge critically on women's position."[10] Though she allows in a footnote that Ynestra
King, in her later work, does not do this, she leaves out numerous ecofeminist
arguments that argue for attention to racism, classism, and other forms of
domination, as we have seen in previous chapters.

A common aspect, then, of these straw-woman accounts of ecofeminism in
development discourse is that they rarely deal with the full diversity of
ecofeminist positions and writers. Oddities of attribution and labeling thus
occur frequently, and, interestingly for the discussion in this chapter, they are
often centered on Vandana Shiva's work. For instance, Leach relies heavily
on Sherry Ortner's classic essay, "Is Female to Male as Nature is to Culture?"
as an example of an essentialist ecofeminist position. This is peculiar, since
ecofeminism postdates Ortner's 1974 essay by a good deal; while some

ecofeminist theorists have used Ortner's arguments, many do not, including many with "essentialist" positions.[11] Leach also counts Shiva in both the "ecofeminist" strand of discourse within development studies and in the "feminist analyses of the effects of capitalist accumulation on women and the environment" strand, which she counterposes to "ecofeminism." Rao, as we have seen, uses Shiva's self-labeling as an ecofeminist to tag "emergent discourses" about the "capitalization of nature" as essentialist. As I will argue throughout this chapter, I think this difficulty in fixing a definition of essentialist ecofeminism, or of ecofeminism as a whole, or of Shiva's work in particular, lies in the fact that ecofeminism in development discourse is not so much an immutable set of theoretical positions as it is a political intervention that continually shifts its discourse in relation to its negotiation with dominant forces in development politics.

What none of these accounts captures is the various political positioning within development studies and international political structures allowed by the ambiguity of the "ecofeminist" position. I do not want to ignore or dispute the dangers of essentialist notions of women, indigenous peoples, cultures, or nature, which critics like those I've discussed above have analyzed so well. Rather, I wish to point to the positive potential for ecofeminism as a strategic discourse within a particular historical moment in international politics. The "discourse of indigeneity"—when coupled with claims about women's stake in environmentalism, which I have identified as a problematic element in U.S. ecofeminism in the late 1980s and early '90s—as an *international political discourse* rather than a *theoretical tool*,[12] opens up some possibilities. First, it creates a space within which southern women are authorized as experts. Second, as discussed in the last chapter, the feminist and antiracist intentions of most ecofeminists exist in tension with their desire to positively revalue nature, women, and indigenous peoples. This contradiction produces opportunities not just to concur with but also debate those essentialist notions of women and nature that already may be circulating within masculinist development discourse, particularly if southern feminist environmentalists are included in coalitions. Finally, ecofeminism inserts feminist demands and analyses within a hegemonic discourse of globalizing environmentalisms at an important historical moment and to do so, it must at least momentarily posit a political collectivity called "women." This is a level of analysis not available in the criticisms of Agarwal, Jackson, and Rao. Leach, though not situated at this level, does note that "when policy-oriented discussions incorporate ecofeminist ideas they often mix [essentialist and anti-essentialist variants] uncritically,"[13] but she does not identify that mix as an opportunity for a strategic notion of ecofeminism that can be inserted into dominant political discourses and that contains the seeds of destablization of its own (and the dominant discourse's) essentialism.

ECOFEMINISM IN DEVELOPMENT

A less reductive story is told of the interweaving of ecofeminism and development discourse approaches by several books on women and development.[14] From this angle, we can see another origin story for ecofeminism: as an international movement rather than a U.S. movement. In her review of the literature on "gender, environment, and development" (note the use of gender instead of women; I will return to this linguistic shift in a moment), Heleen van den Hombergh offers a chronology of the construction of the field, entitled "List of Important Events." I reproduce it here as Figure 1, as it provides a sketch locating some of the texts and events that I will examine in this chapter. I read van den Hombergh's list as a mapping of intersections between feminism and development that produces an intermingling of "ecofeminism" and "women in development," which in turn produces, variously, the disciplinary, policy-oriented locations "women, environment, and development" or "gender, environment, and development."

This map of the connections between the issues of women, development, and the environment makes linear a history in which discourses concerning these three issues were brought together in an uneven, contradictory, and contested process of negotiation over the production of knowledge, the distribution of resources, and the moral underpinnings of various policies and practices within an international political arena. To make this point, one could imagine van den Hombergh's "List of Important Events" as two tables, one tracing the development of international feminism, the other focused on environmental landmarks.

Such an alternative mapping, however, would not adequately capture the complex, ongoing intertwining of these two areas of concern. Sorting out U.S. ecofeminism's part in this complicated process is a difficult task, but it is clear to me that the kind of antiracist desire that produces the discourse of "indigenous ecofeminists" that I've critiqued in the last chapter has its counterpart internationally in environmental feminist efforts to refigure "development" as "sustainable development," and then "sustainable livelihood," within a process in which the categories of "indigenous peoples" and "women" come to have a good deal of discursive, political, and moral weight.

To unravel this history, we need to start acronymically, with a tale of WID in conflict with GAD, WED becoming GED, UNEP organizing SWAGSD which influences the FLS, which begats WEDO which intervenes in UNCED; a story that interweaves international and internally contested movements of environmentalism and feminism with the machinery of UN bureaucracies, state structures and multinational corporate interests.[15]

WID, or "women in development," is the name for a shift in development studies and policies in the early 1970s from women being invisible or appearing only as housewives and mothers, relegated to a privatized notion of repro-

FIGURE I **van den Hombergh's "List of Important Events"**

1962   • Rachel Carson's book *Silent Spring*

1970   • Ester Boserup's book *Women's Role in Economic Development*

1972   • Meadows et al. release "The Limits to Growth"[1]

1972   • UN Conference on the Human Environment (Stockholm)

1975   • International Women's Year; start of the UN Decade for Women

1980   • World Conservation Strategy (IUCN/WWF/UNEP)[2]

1985   • UN Conference to Review and Appraise the Decade for Women
       (Nairobi) Nairobi Parallel Conference: Forum '85

1987   • "Our Common Future" (Brundtland report, WCED)[3]

1987   • Conference on Women and the World Conservation Strategy (IUCN,
       Gland)

1990   • Regional and Follow-up conferences "Action to Our Common Future"
       • NGO Parallel Women's Forum in Bergen[4]

1991   • "Caring for the Earth," Second World Conservation Strategy
       (IUCN/WWF/UNEP)
       • Preparatory Committee Meetings for United Nations Conference on
       Environment and Development [UNCED]

1991   • NGO conference to prepare for UNCED "Roots of the Future" (Paris)

1991   • UNEP's Global Assembly on Women and the Environment "Partners in
       Life" (Miami)
       • NGO Conference "World Women's Conference for a Healthy Planet"
       (Miami)

1992   • United Nations Conference on Environment and Development [Rio]
       • NGO Parallel Conference, "Global Forum"

Source: Heleen van den Hombergh, *Gender, Environment, and Development: A Guide to the Literature* (Utrecht: International Books, 1993), p. 11.

1. As Peter Taylor and Frederick Buttel explain, "The [Limits to Growth] study was funded by the Club of Rome, an elite group of Western businessmen, government leaders, and scientists, and was conducted by system dynamics (SD) modelers at MIT. The predictions from World 3, a SD model of the world's population, industry and resources were for population and economic collapse unless universal (coordinated, global-level) no-growth or steady-state policies were immediately established." Peter J. Taylor and Frederick H. Buttel, "How Do We Know We Have Global Environmental Problems? Science and the Globalization of Environmental Discourse," *Geoforum* 23(3) (1992): 405-16, 407.

2. IUCN stands for International Union for the Conservation of Natural Resources (based in Gland); UNEP for United Nations Environmental Programme (based in Nairobi, but a UN agency for environmental protection); and WWF for World Wildlife Fund (based in Geneva).

3. WCED stands for World Commission on Environment and Development and is also known as the "Brundtland Commission" because it was chaired by Gro Harlem Brundtland, Prime Minister of Norway.

4. NGO stands for "Non-Governmental Organizations" and includes any group or organization not formally representing a government which has membership in the UN. NGOs vary from formalized, government sanctioned entities to alternative, oppositional, and grassroots organizations.

duction, to seeing them as producers and economic actors, especially in the area of agriculture. This shift was brought on by the publication of Ester Boserup's 1970 book, *Women's Role in Economic Development*, which argued, influentially, that women were crucial to agricultural and commodity production in peasant Third World societies, and thus that development policies that failed to include them or to study their roles were doomed to failure. Boserup's goal was to use development efforts to increase gender equity in Third World societies, as part and parcel of the process of modernization.[16] Her approach, which did not challenge the foundational ideas of development itself (that modernization, Western-style, was a good and inevitable thing, and that Western experts should be the leaders in constructing development policy and Third World people the recipients), was crucial in producing new studies of Third World women's productive roles. However, the resulting policy programs did not often stress the need for gender equity. Rather, women were subjects for research which was aimed at creating more "efficient" and "effective" development policies, and their work was seen as an important resource for the success of development projects, even when those policies benefited men far more than women.[17] Indeed, as Leach points out, essentialist notions of nature and women, especially poor and rural Third World women, were common in WID discourse before "ecofeminism" became a player within development politics.[18] Nevertheless, WID was an important location for an internal contest between feminist notions of equality and empowerment and the desire of First World development agencies to craft policies that would successfully export Western products and practices to Third World countries. In practice, WID policies often provided poor women in the Third World with substantial opportunities compared to the previous male-oriented development paradigm.[19]

Indeed, the WID paradigm was intimately intertwined with the growth of an international feminist movement, thus bringing international feminism into close contest and negotiation with Western multinational and state powers. The WID approach became initially institutionalized in the "development bureaucracy" in the North.[20] In 1975, the first UN conference on Women and Development was held in Mexico City. Though the growing legitimacy of WID was not the only impetus behind this conference, it certainly was an important factor in convincing the UN's international policymakers that a conference on women was needed; this is reflected in the title of the conference. By this time, in Sabine Häusler's words, WID "was a more or less respected area of study; the number of publications on women and development topics has increased steadily ever since. Women and men sociologists and anthropologists, as well as a slowly increasing number of women development professionals in technical fields. . . from both North and South, moved into the field of development work."[21]

Coinciding with the Mexico City conference on women, southern women began to be heard more effectively, often as researchers themselves within the field of WID, at the same time as the approach became increasingly influential in development studies. During the Decade for Women, which was initiated by the 1975 conference, both northern and southern feminists began the process of constructing an international feminist movement, in which development policies—especially those that exploited the South by the North—were bones of contention for southern feminists, who accused northern feminists of ethnocentrism and of being tools of Western neocolonialism. In the 1980s, during a period of worsening conditions for women worldwide caused by the "debt crisis,"[22] southern feminists were organizing to influence the international political processes surrounding the UN apparatus that had grown up around women as political and economic subjects. In 1984, an organization called "Development with Women for a New Era," or DAWN, was created. DAWN critiqued the WID approach for its acceptance of the "Western development model" and its failure to focus on the empowerment of women as a primary goal.[23] In Nairobi in 1985, during the Second UN Conference on Women, which culminated the Decade for Women, the parallel Non-Governmental Organization (NGO) Forum involved numerous lively discussions of the need for approaches such as DAWN's.[24]

Many other southern analysts urged WID scholars to alter their approach from one in which women were simply "added on" to existing analyses to one in which gender relations, rather than women as essentialized objects of study, were the focus. This outlook, which aimed to contextualize cultural specificities through—and illuminate power inequities within—gendered relationships as manifested in household forms, marital customs, and gendered patterns of land ownership and use was called GAD, or gender and development. Thus the shift from "women" to "gender" was meant to de-essentialize theoretical understandings of women's roles in their various societies and to reintroduce the feminist imperative of changing unequal gender relations along with promoting "development."[25]

Concurrent with the rise of WID was a growing interest in environmental questions as part of development studies which also included a focus on women—in part because of the new stress on women's management of natural resources through their productive roles, and in part because of an early link made between environmental problems and population growth. Häusler notes, for example, that the "oil crisis" of the 1970s spurred development experts to look closely at the use of firewood by peasant Third World societies for energy. Since, within the WID paradigm, it was clear that women were the primary fuel gatherers and consumers of firewood, a link was quickly made between women, environmental degradation, southern population growth (a major obsession of the "Limits to Growth" report) and poverty. As Häusler comments: "A powerful image emerged of poor people in the South, with too many children, using too much fuel; the poor were seen to have no choice but to destroy their own environment."[26] As a result, as Western consciousness of environmental questions such as resource use, energy production, desertification, and pollution increased during the 1970s, Third World rural women became scapegoats within development planning. The responsibility for population growth and environmental problems was thus placed on poor Third World women rather than on Western industrialized nations that consume most of the world's resources. These assumptions about Third World women's responsibility for dangerous levels of population growth and misguided environmental resource use, widespread in influential reports such as "Limits to Growth," have been a major target of attacks both by southern and northern feminists.

Several events, including those found on van den Hombergh's timeline in Figure 1, served to embed the relation between environment, women, and development both within development politics and within international feminism as they interacted during the late 1970s to early '90s. One could offer many examples of how the two streams of research, policy formation, and movement struggle focused on women and on the environment are not separate but rather interactive from the start. In van den Hombergh's list of events, important environmental paradigms are referenced by the "Limits to Growth" report (the problem of possible scarcity brought on by population growth coupled with resource use) and the Brundtland Commission's "Our Common Future" (which sketches the need for "sustainable development"). Both of these paradigms were challenged by feminist demands to reconceptualize women as having agency and needing power in environmental decisions. The feminist agenda became not only to make women's stake in these issues visible but also to promote women's economic and political empowerment. At the first major international conference on the environment, in 1972 at Stockholm, during the parallel NGO meeting, Sunderlal Bahuguna, a male Indian activist, presented Chipko women as exemplars of community-based, sustainable environmental practices. Because, as Häusler writes, "women had emerged as the main actors in this movement it was concluded that rural women understood that it was in their own interests to protect the environment."[27] The Chipko movement was inserted into the international political context at a moment when the environment became a major agenda item, and in Bahuguna's version, Chipko represented a southern challenge to the notion that Third World women are problematic environmentally; instead, he presented them as natural environmentalists. It is this opening that was later seized by ecofeminists such as Shiva, who pushed the Chipko to represent women not just as natural environmentalists, but women as active, political agents with expert knowledge about the environment. Thus, "ecofeminism," in the late 1980s, entered the international context by attaching earlier feminist efforts to transform WID to a newer environmentalist paradigm, which, as I will discuss shortly, was becoming at the time a hegemonic global formation. In this context, "ecofeminism" *means* this feminist intervention into environmentalism more than it represents a set of new, independent theoretical arguments.

While this "ecofeminist" position thus has political relevance and effectiveness within a political context at a particular time, it also runs the risk of dovetailing with older WID assumptions about women as "natural resources." There was concern that ecofeminist arguments (such as Shiva's) defining women as environmental managers and activists would be translated into development policies that required women to be the primary laborers in conservation schemes that may or may not have benefited them directly. Many progressive development scholars critiqued these arguments as essentialist, though such essentialism had existed as well in older WID discourse.[28] In a pattern similar to the move from WID to GAD, a focus on women, environment, and development, or WED (which could also be seen as the "ecofeminist" moment), has been recently been challenged by GED, or gender, environment and development, a position that pays attention to the nuances of gender relations in households, property rights, labor relations, and kinship systems, all of which determine a differential relationship between women and their environments dependent on age, marital status, and many other factors. GED scholars argue that these nuances must be taken into account in policy planning, and that assumptions of women's natural tendency to protect the environment are deeply misguided. It is this debate with which our critics, Agarwal, Jackson, Leach and Rao, are concerned. But rather than see the recurrence of essentialist moments in development discourses on women being part of an ongoing process of political struggle stimulated by feminist interventions, these scholars critique "ecofeminism" instead.

Nevertheless, it is clear that the insertion of feminist demands into development policy in the period when it became concerned with the environment (in other words, the "ecofeminist" moment) provided particular political and working links between Western feminists and southern feminists. In this political context, "the environment" served feminists as a medium for the connection of critiques of militarism, capitalism, and neocolonialism—similar to the way "militarism" functioned in the 1970s and '80s. Positioning women as environmental activists was one moment in a dialectical process of negotiation between dominant interests in development policies and feminist efforts to insert women's concerns into an international arena. While it is important to critique the limits of such ecofeminist interventions, it is equally important to see the way in which these analytic linkages can operate as "two-way streets" between southern and northern feminist activists.[29] This is particularly the case when ecofeminist arguments, as Leach pointed out, contain a tension between essentialist and anti-essentialist analyses, giving an opening for debates around operative definitions of "women" and "nature" that open the door for more nuanced analyses.

The argument that women have a stake in environmentalist politics became an especially important strategic position within an international context of what I call "globalizing environmentalisms." I will give a more specific example of such "ecofeminist" positioning when I examine WEDO. But first I want to make a few points about the status of environmentalism within global political discourses at the end of the Cold War.

How do we explain the apparent convergence between the approaches of women, environment, and development discourse within development studies and certain strands of ecofeminist discourse? As another example of a feminist intervention into a masculinist environmentalist discourse, but in this case, one embedded in ongoing contests within a process I will call the "globalization of environmentalism."

ECOFEMINISM AND GLOBALIZING ENVIRONMENTALISMS

Without disputing the accuracy of those critiques (especially when it comes to the need to produce feminist scholarship as a basis for effective, empowering policies) that identify the essentialism of the "ecofeminist" discourses deployed in the women, environment, and development arena, I want to take a brief look at the wider context of this deployment. An examination of the context of "globalizing environmentalisms" during the end of the 1980s and beginning of the '90s sheds light on the importance of a deployment of ecofeminist rhetoric for the construction of an international feminist movement.

Environmental problems, it has been pointed out frequently, do not honor fixed spatial areas, whether they be defined as national areas or spaces of private property.[30] This characteristic of environmental problems has been, at different moments, the source of environmentalist claims for the need for a new global cooperation as well as a deep pessimism about the possibilities of solving environmental crises. The optimism of the global environmentalists has a negative side, however, and that is the use that can be made of the "universalizing" momentum of environmentalism by forces of technocratic, exploitative, neocolonialist, neocapitalist political economies. Southern environmentalists, like Guha, have thus critiqued the ways in which consciousness of these environmental problems are "global" in another sense, that is, tools for colonialist projects of northern exploitation of southern peoples and lands.[31]

In a perceptive article, entitled "How Do We Know We Have Global Environmental Problems?" Peter Taylor and Frederick Buttel sketch the growing influence of the characterization of environmental problems as "global." They identify two ways of talking about environmental problems as global that they call the "technocratic" and the "moral." Though in some ways these discourses may seem opposed, since the "moral," or Green, discourse is putatively ranged against the scientistic, economically driven discourse of the "technocratic," Taylor and Buttel claim that there is a convergence between the two in that they propose a unitary human concern that avoids consideration of the varied material and political sources of environmental problems. They thus point out the possibility that the two discourses may operate together, imposing a dominant discourse which assumes the "sameness" of people, in order to achieve particularistic goals (i.e., those of multinational corporations, or Western elites). The idea that environmental problems are global and require global solutions, then, supports "either a moral response—everyone must change to avert catastrophe!—or a technocratic response—only a superintending agency able to analyze the system as a whole can direct the changes needed. There is no paradox here—moral and technocratic responses are alike in attempting to bypass the political terrain in which different groups experience problems differently and act accordingly."[32] Note that this objection to the "globalization of environmentalisms" parallels the ecofeminist objections to the philosophical "holism" of deep ecologists discussed in chapter 1.

Taylor and Buttel locate the origin of the trend toward describing environmental problems as global as a specifically U.S. convergence between the scientific understanding of environmental problems and the environmentalist ("moral") response to them; indeed, at one point they cite the "long hot summer of 1988 in the United States" as one stimulus to the use of "global climate models."[33] But they also suggest another impetus to the globalization of environmentalism:

The rise of global-change-led international environmentalism occurred during a significant shift of the political center of gravity of the industrial world toward neo-conservative regimes. Modern environmentalism has accommodated itself surprisingly readily to the free-market resurgence. While international environmental groups yet reserve the right to criticize the World Bank and related institutions about the environmental destruction that results *from particular projects or types of projects* . . . environmental groups have generally worked with the Bank/IMF in a surprisingly harmonious manner in implementing conservation/preservation policies and programs in the Third World. There is a key coincidence of interest. . . the Bank and IMF gain legitimacy in the eyes of the citizens and political officialdoms of the advanced (increasingly "green"-oriented) countries by helping to implement environmental and conservation policies, while the implied threat of Bank or IMF termination of bridging, adjustment and project loans is useful in securing developing country compliance with environmental initiatives. Given this relationship, most environmental organizations have been disinclined to take on the world debt crisis, the net South-

North capital drain, and the international monetary order as being fundamental contributors to environmental degradation.[34]

Whatever the exceptions that could be taken to Taylor and Buttel's depiction of environmental organizations here, it is important to note that they are not positing a conspiracy but rather a convergence of particularly enunciated concerns that illuminate the contours of a specific conjuncture (one I am calling here "globalizing environmentalisms") within a hegemonic struggle for dominance. And we could enumerate the political struggles engaged in this conjuncture and identify them in multiple ways: between North and South, between class formations, between racial/ethnic groups, between genders, and so forth. Instead of this multiplicity, these struggles take place within internationalized versions of "environmentalism." What strikes me in Taylor and Buttel's historicizing of this hegemonic shift is something they don't mention: the relation of the "ending" of the Cold War in the late 1980s to the appearance of global environmentalisms as a discursive tool within these political struggles. Like the discourse of democracy as a worldwide good, environmentalism similarly turns out to be a two-edged sword.

I will expand on the implications of this point briefly. The modern U.S. rhetoric promoting democracy within an internationalist political arena can be seen first as an antifascist and then as an anticommunist rhetoric, generated during World War II as a justification for U.S. military involvement and then refined after the war as a bulwark against the critique of capitalism. Democracy moves from being an oppositional labor-movement goal to being a statist rhetorical tool in the anticommunist repertoire, with the deployment of the rhetoric of "saving the world for democracy" used to further capitalist, imperialist projects. Like this discourse of global democracy, dominant environmentalist discourse makes similar claims about "universal human conditions," similarly reduced to individualist solutions (for instance, individual recycling, which, like voting as a solution to social inequality, is a form of liberal rather than radical discourse), similarly eviscerated of a critique of corporate agency in either the production of inequalities or environmental problems. As Gaile McGregor comments: "The globalization process is inherent simply in the fact that we all speak the same 'language' of capitalism," and environmentalism is particularly deployed in this context.[35] Anna Tsing makes a similar point when she writes about environmentalism in the 1990s becoming a "leading edge of global civil society. In contrast to social ecologists working for social and economic equity, civil society environmentalists build their message on political *equality*. Since political equality in the 1990s is understood as a concomitant to the spread of markets, it becomes identified with the acceptance of social and economic inequity in the name of democracy."[36] Tsing goes on to describe the way environmentalism as a "strategic universalism" came to "seem a defining feature of the new transnational Europe."

Since it could be argued that environmental activism on both sides of the Berlin Wall was partly responsible for its fall, "one could look to environmentalism for the coming together of the message of science, as universal principles, and the message of universal human rights in the necessity of democracy to preserve the world's health. Furthermore, environmentalism was advanced by the kinds of transnational and global organizations that could make ignorant and uncooperative states, with their entrenched local cultures of power, see the truth of these universals."[37]

Further evidence of the way in which globalizing environmentalism is being used to replace Cold War rhetoric about global democracy is the way in which environmentalism is being grafted onto the "lost" project of militarism, which was centrally supported by "global democracy" discourse during the Cold War period. For example, two recent *New York Times* articles specifically describe the way in which environmental problems have become the focus of new U.S. military endeavors. One article describes the growing U.S. military identification of environmental problems as the new threats to "national security" because of the way they result in "political instability."[38] The other describes the new use of spy satellites for identifying environmental problems, thus justifying the defense appropriation of money for these technologies.[39] The popularity of Fred Kaplan's construction of a connection between environmental disasters and the threatening "chaos" within African nations displays the way in which older Cold War forms of U.S. racist and Western colonialist fears about the "barbarity" of the Third World are transformed into a concern with environmental disaster that unleashes new forms of "savagery."[40] Kaplan makes clear that, like the hegemonic discourse about democracy, the hegemonic discourse of global environmentalism can also be used to impose unjust conditions on the poor and the colonized, who are often represented in this discourse as part of the environmental threat. In some ways, the development of southern environmentalism is a strategy precisely to resist these uses of global environmentalism, in recognition that the environment is now an important terrain of transnational political struggle.[41]

Besides and within southern environmentalism, there have been feminist analyses that have critiqued this kind of hegemonic discourse. Like the feminist discourses which renamed "anticommunism" "militarism," these newer and related oppositional discourses identify "global environmentalism" as another project of "patriarchal capitalist maldevelopment."[42] In both discursive moves, the oppositional accomplishment is to point out the sexism of the appeal to a generic mankind and humanity and to uncover, instead of universality, the connections between sexism, racism, imperialism, classism, and, in both discourses, environmental exploitation. One example of this kind of deconstruction is the feminist analysis of Joni Seager, where she identifies the patriarchal characteristics of governments, militaries, and corporations as one of the main factors in their continuing responsibility for environmental destruction.[43] Another example of a feminist challenge to hegemonic discourses about development, democracy, and the environment is WEDO, which we will examine in a moment. It is important to note the continuity in these projects between a feminist critique of militarism and a feminist critique of environmental problems; both oppositional discourses are aimed at deconstructing the universalism of hegemonic discourses of either the Cold War or of global environmentalism, and at showing their interconnections. In the process of this deconstructiong, these oppositional feminist and ecofeminist discourses often construct their own "strategic universalisms," particularly through claims to be representing "women" as a unity. As Tsing says: "What is global essentialism good for? It is good, it seems, for arguing with other global essentialisms."[44] I will now give a more specific example of this process of constructing "strategic universalisms": the organization WEDO, which, in the middle of this transition from the Cold War to globalizing environmentalisms, constructs a recognizably ecofeminist intervention with a universalist bent.

WOMEN MOTHERING EARTH: WOMEN'S ENVIRONMENT AND DEVELOPMENT ORGANIZATION

In some ways, WEDO is an ironic figure in this book; I use it to illuminate ecofeminism despite its refusal of the term. Like many of the grassroots women's activists who reject the label ecofeminist, WEDO avoids the name (but for different reasons) even while arguing for women's environmental action in "ecofeminist" terms. WEDO makes close connections between feminism, women's movements, and environmental activism and has several prominent ecofeminists in leadership positions. As was true for WomanEarth Feminist Peace Institute, the cofounders of WEDO came from a background of feminist antimilitarism. Yet, unlike WomanEarth, WEDO embraces political action other than direct action, directed toward traditional kinds of institutional change, in this case primarily within the UN. In particular, WEDO shies away from any connection between feminist spirituality and environmental politics. Further, unlike WomanEarth's focus on U.S. racism, WEDO's attempt to create an organization that models diversity defined that diversity as primarily, though not exclusively, international.

WEDO was founded by two white U.S. women, Mim Kelber (activist and writer) and Bella Abzug (a former Democratic Congresswoman from New York). Both had been founders of Women Strike for Peace and active in the second-wave women's movement.[45] After Bella Abzug left the U.S. Congress, Kelber and Abzug formed the Women's USA Fund, Inc.,[46] which supported various subgroups, including one called the Women's Foreign Policy Council, "which was aimed specifically at getting equal participation of women in decision-making, related to women's rights, peace, and security."[47] Basically, the organization performed a networking function, printing a directory of U.S. women involved in foreign policy issues and international affairs in 1987. In 1988, Kelber and Abzug became more centered on the environment, moving easily from their previous concerns with nuclear disarmament to a more generalized concern with environmentalism. As Kelber puts it: "We began to realize in talking about the security of the earth, you're really talking about literally saving the earth from these man-made threats to the health of the planet." Inspired by the Gro Brundtland Report, "Our Common Future," and concerned about the lack of women in policymaking positions in the national and international institutions concerned with the global environment, Abzug and Kelber organized a briefing on the state of environmental problems worldwide for prominent women in the U.S. Congress and women's political organizations.

The organizing for this briefing brought Abzug and Kelber in touch with a number of women environmentalists from the Third World, as well as women working on environmental issues within UN agencies. During this process, Kelber met Joan Martin Brown, a staff member of the United Nations Environmental Program (UNEP) and head of a women's environmental network called WorldWIDE, which had published an international directory of women environmentalists and researchers. Kelber says that at this point (around 1989), "I began to realize the link between environmental protection, development issues, poverty, and property issues," and she and Abzug became committed to engaging these issues as interconnected. Brown told Kelber about a conference UNEP was organizing, in connection with the preparations for the upcoming United Nations Conference on Environment and Development, called The Global Assembly of Women and the Environment, in which women from all over the world were going to be brought together to illustrate environmental "success stories." In line with the image of women as resources for environmental programs, which was prominent in the WID development discourse at that time, the success stories were meant to demonstrate various alternative technologies and environmental practices developed by women in their communities, but not necessarily to generate influence on UNCED at the governmental, policymaking level. Brown suggested to Kelber that the Women's Foreign Policy Council might organize another conference at the same time, which would be more confrontational, more politically challenging, and more policy oriented; one that would deal, as Kelber put it, "with the larger issues."

Kelber and Abzug took up this project, which became the World Women's Congress for a Healthy Planet, held in Miami in 1991. In 1990, to prepare for this effort, Abzug and Keller brought together a fifty-member committee, called the International Policy Action Committee (IPAC), which decided on the name Women's Environment and Development Organization for the entity organizing the conference and chose ten cochairs to direct WEDO. A serious effort was made to create international diversity in both IPAC and WEDO; the cochairs were Bella Abzug (United States), Peggy Antrobus (Barbados), Thais Corral (Brazil), María Eugenia de Cotter (Costa Rica), Elin Enge (Norway), Farkhonda Hassan (Egypt), Wangari Maathai (Kenya), Chief Bisi Ogounleye (Nigeria), Vandana Shiva (India), and Marilyn Waring (New Zealand). These women were already active in development politics, promoting the perspectives of southern women (Peggy Antrobus, one of the founders of DAWN; Thais Corral, information officer for DAWN; and Chief Bisi Ogunleye, a vice president of the Forum of African Voluntary Development Organizations); environmental sustainability (Elin Enge, director of the Norwegian Forum for Environment and Development; and Wangari Maathai, founder of the Kenyan Green Belt Movement); and international feminism (Marilyn Waring, who had been the Executive Director of the Sisterhood is Global Institute; and Farkhonda Hassan, chair of the Executive Committee of the Gender, Science, and Development Program at the Institutes for Advanced Study in Toronto). All, therefore, demonstrated long-term commitments to the intersections of the issues of development, environment, and feminism. Some were also connected with an explicit ecofeminist perspective (especially Shiva, through her inclusion in and authorship of ecofeminist publications; and Thais Corral, who is an editor of *Eco-Femina*, a radio program broadcast throughout Brazil and sponsored by UNIFEM).[48]

The World Women's Congress For a Healthy Planet brought together "1,500 women from 83 countries, with about one-third coming from developing nations."[49] An important feature of the conference was that it took the form of a tribunal: in front of five judges (Justices Desiree Bernard of Guyana, Elizabeth Evatt of Australia, Sujata V. Manahar of India, Effie Owuor of Kenya, and Margareta Wadstein of Sweden), "witnesses" gave testimony over three days. The topics of each day were "Towards Earth Charter '92: Developing a Code of Ethics with a Women's Dimension"; "Saving Natural Systems: Environment and Positive Development"; and "Science, Technology and Population." The witnesses, experts on their topics from a wide variety of countries, gave their testimony before the assembly of 1,500 women, many of whom were women brought as part of the "success stories" conference organized earlier by UNEP, and thus often part of grassroots efforts in their communities.[50] Other attendees at the conference were women who were part of environmentalist and feminist movements and organizations from around the world.

The format of a tribunal created a powerful experience. As each speaker gave evidence of the costs of development policies and environmental degradation for women in her country, the sense of injustice and outrage mounted. One reporter summarized some of the "horror stories":

In a Malaysian village, where a Japanese consortium sold radioactive waste as "fertilizer" for home gardens and window-boxes, children are now dying of leukemia.

In the Marshall Islands, women whose bodies are poisoned with radioactive fallout are giving birth to "jellyfish babies—living blobs of flesh with no limbs, eyes or brains."

From famine-stricken Ethopia came news that the country, once 60 per cent covered with forests, has only 3 per cent left.

In the snow of the Himalyan mountain peaks, scientists have found soot from Kuwait's burning oil wells.

From Tibet came an urgent plea for help in stopping the suspected Chinese dumping of nuclear waste into Tibet headwaters, "threatening the seven great rivers of Asia."

From the Argentine Andes, an indigenous woman whose soft, musical voice riveted the audience, said: "Sisters, as I speak to you, the blasts from oil exploration are rocking my mountain. . . ."

From Bhopal to Chernobyl to the "Triangle of Death" in heavily polluted Eastern Europe, women report birth abnormalities and high levels of sickness among children.

On a coral atoll in the Pacific, where, according to Marilyn Waring, "the French still insist that their nuclear testing has no effect on the food chain," women hang fresh fish like laundry on a line. They eat only those that flies land on; the others are discarded as too contaminated even for flies."[51]

The testimony during the conference covered topics such as "Poverty, Maldevelopment, and the Misallocation of Resources"; "Consumer Power"; "Food Security"; "Interdependence or Dependency: Trade, Debt, and Aid Relations Between Nations and Regions"; "Earth's Refugees: The Causes of Uprootedness and Global Homelessness"; "Ethical Considerations of Nuclear Power and Weapons, and Other Threats to Public Health and the Environment"; "The Appropriation of Tribal Lands by the U.S. Government"; "Biotechnology and Biogenetics"; "Cooking to Climate Change: Energy Needs, Sources, and Alternatives"; "Population Policies, Family Planning, and Sexual Politics"; and "People's Rights, Participation and Resources, Decisions and Actions for Sustainable Development with Justice and Equity."[52]

In organizing the conference, as I have said before, WEDO wanted to generate a diversity defined by international, rather than U.S. racial difference. As a result, most of the U.S. women attending were white women,[53] and representation was distributed by world region rather than by racial difference within the United States. Though the conference opened with a "Traditional Call of Welcome" from "Indigenous Women of Florida," the only other featured speakers who were U.S. women of color were Faye Wattleton (president of Planned Parenthood at the time) and Winona LaDuke, Anishinaabeg feminist activist. LaDuke, as we saw in chapter 4, has expressed ambivalence about seeing herself as part of ecofeminist—or white U.S. feminist environmentalist—movements.[54] After LaDuke's name in the initial program it says "Invited," as though marking her ambivalence.

Asked about the relative invisibility of U.S. women of color in the conference, Mim Kelber explained that WEDO had raised money specifically to bring women from the Third World, including in their number the women brought to the earlier UNEP conference. This combination of funding accounted for the high number of Third World women participants, one-third of the conference attendees. However, a specific effort to bring Asian American, Latino American, and African American women to the conference did not result in significant funding. Kelber says:

> We tried, but we couldn't get enough funding for it. . . funders like to fund activities in other countries, but not so much in this country. And I think it's a constant issue for us in the international environment and development movement. They [funders] tend to count it [diversity] in North/South terms and I don't think there's enough emphasis on class differences. I think it's very important for us to recognize that we have a lot of poor people in this country and a lot of illiterate people and a lot of people in great need who are being exploited by the same global economic forces that are exploiting these other countries . . . our Third World within our borders. . . . [W]e really ought to organize a reverse solidarity campaign, that women in other nations should be expressing solidarity with women in the U.S. who are under such severe attack right now by the right wing.[55]

Though U.S. women of color were more or less invisible within the World Women's Congress for a Healthy Planet in terms of featured speakers or the overall number of participants, there was a caucus of Women of Color of North America at the conference. This caucus made efforts in particular ways analytically separate from some of the other problems discussed by the conference to raise the visibility of the effects of U.S. racism, and, more specifically "environmental racism." This caucus's statement was published in the conference proceedings along with those of other caucuses, which otherwise were organized by geographic region with two specific exceptions, Women of the South and the International Indigenous Women's Caucus.[56] In this way the geographic categories that WEDO used to organize the conference were disrupted by three interventions: one centered on U.S. racism, one on Western colonialism, and one challenging the first two by identifying indigeniety as an independent identity, occupied by members of the "Fourth World." Thus, U.S. racism and Western colonialism were tagged as structuring inequalities and promoting suffering along the lines of three notions of difference separate from geographic regional difference: "nonwhite," "underdeveloped," and "indigenous." The formation of these caucuses created a situation in which each process of identity formation within the conference—by gender, by nationality, by relation to colonialism, by race—was thereby destabilized.

Interestingly, given our discussion in chapter 4 of the deployment of the "indigenous ecofeminist" in close relation to feminist pagan spirituality, the statement of the International Indigenous Women's Caucus is entirely devoted to promoting a spiritual relation to the earth that promotes the well-being of human and of non-human nature. "As indigenous people our lives are intertwined with the natural world," the statement begins, and adds: "Today we face the destruction of the human spirit and the consequent destruction of the natural world. . . . The true challenge of human beings is to place our full attention upon ways in which we can live upon Mother Earth in a manner consistent with natural law and in peace, harmony, and balance with all living things."[57]

Clearly, the politics of the World Women's Congress for a Healthy Planet intertwined feminist and environmentalist positions with a number of radical analyses. This could be called an "ecofeminist" politics, similar to the ecofeminism developed by such writers as Karen Warren, Val Plumwood, and Ynestra King, but one grounded in an exploration of women's daily problems and material constraints and presented within a framework of international diversity. Two things created coherence for the bringing together of such different issues as women's struggles with nuclear contamination, the effects of imposition of debt dependence on poor nations, and coercive population policies: an analysis of the interconnection of multinational capitalism, sexism, colonialism, racism and environmental exploitation and a rhetoric locating women as the primary victims of these forces as well as the most effective political agents against them.

WEDO's published materials construct a unity for women based on their exclusion from male-dominated policymaking institutions worldwide, as well as on their social roles as caretakers. At the beginning of the creation of WEDO, in 1989, the organizers published a statement entitled "A Declaration of Interdependence" (see Figure 2).

Referencing the original Declaration of Independence, in a protest tradition of reworking that document that goes back to the 1848 "Declaration of Sentiments" of the nineteenth-century women's movement, the Declaration displays a perspective recognizably ecofeminist. Using one of the favorite metaphors of antimilitarist feminism and ecofeminism—the web—the Declaration argues that sexism and environmental degradation are ideologically and materially linked: "It is our belief that man's dominion over nature parallels the subjugation of women in many societies, denying them sovereignty over their lives and bodies. Until all societies truly value women and the environment, their joint degradation will continue." Further, the Declaration insists that joining feminist and environmentalist perspectives demands

FIGURE 2

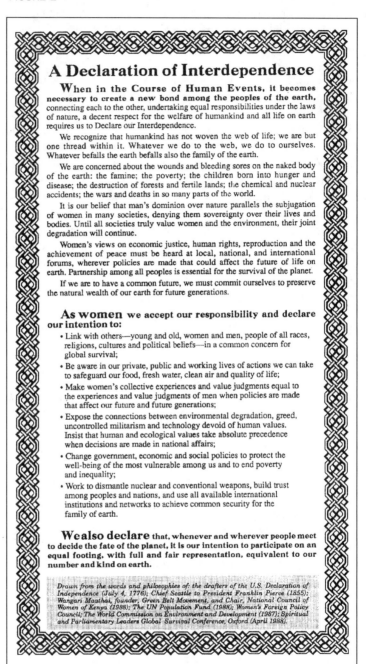

A Declaration of Interdependence

When in the Course of Human Events, it becomes necessary to create a new bond among the peoples of the earth, connecting each to the other, undertaking equal responsibilities under the laws of nature, a decent respect for the welfare of humankind and all life on earth requires us to Declare our Interdependence.

We recognize that humankind has not woven the web of life; we are but one thread within it. Whatever we do to the web, we do to ourselves. Whatever befalls the earth befalls also the family of the earth.

We are concerned about the wounds and bleeding sores on the naked body of the earth: the famine; the poverty; the children born into hunger and disease; the destruction of forests and fertile lands; the chemical and nuclear accidents; the wars and deaths in so many parts of the world.

It is our belief that man's dominion over nature parallels the subjugation of women in many societies, denying them sovereignty over their lives and bodies. Until all societies truly value women and the environment, their joint degradation will continue.

Women's views on economic justice, human rights, reproduction and the achievement of peace must be heard at local, national, and international forums, wherever policies are made that could affect the future of life on earth. Partnership among all peoples is essential for the survival of the planet.

If we are to have a common future, we must commit ourselves to preserve the natural wealth of our earth for future generations.

As women we accept our responsibility and declare our intention to:

- Link with others—young and old, women and men, people of all races, religions, cultures and political beliefs—in a common concern for global survival;

- Be aware in our private, public and working lives of actions we can take to safeguard our food, fresh water, clean air and quality of life;

- Make women's collective experiences and value judgments equal to the experiences and value judgments of men when policies are made that affect our future and future generations;

- Expose the connections between environmental degradation, greed, uncontrolled militarism and technology devoid of human values. Insist that human and ecological values take absolute precedence when decisions are made in national affairs;

- Change government, economic and social policies to protect the well-being of the most vulnerable among us and to end poverty and inequality;

- Work to dismantle nuclear and conventional weapons, build trust among peoples and nations, and use all available international institutions and networks to achieve common security for the family of earth.

We also declare that, whenever and wherever people meet to decide the fate of the planet, it is our intention to participate on an equal footing, with full and fair representation, equivalent to our number and kind on earth.

Drawn from the words and philosophies of: the drafters of the U.S. Declaration of Independence (July 4, 1776); Chief Seattle to President Franklin Pierce (1855); Wangari Maathai, founder, Green Belt Movement, and Chair, National Council of Women of Kenya (1988); The UN Population Fund (1988); Women's Foreign Policy Council; The World Commission on Environment and Development (1987); Spiritual and Parliamentary Leaders Global Survival Conference, Oxford (April 1988).

Source: Women's Environment and Development Organization. Reprinted with permission.

attention to diversity along several axes, as well as to militarism, poverty, and political equality.

WEDO's closeness to an ecofeminist perspective also can be seen in the language of "Women's Action Agenda 21," which was the culmination of the World Women's Congress for a Healthy Planet in November 1991. The document was used as a manifesto for a feminist intervention into the process of UNCED, held in Rio in June 1992. Its title referenced *Agenda 21*, which was the document to be produced by the governmental bodies in Rio. Before and during the period that women met at the Congress for a Healthy Planet in Miami, other preparatory meetings to shape *Agenda 21* were taking place around the world under UN auspices. Bella Abzug had attended many of these meetings, and, alarmed at the lack of participation or power of women in these meetings, had in each case brought those women present together in a "women's caucus," designed to articulate the collective needs of women in relation to the environment and development issues being discussed. This strategy, or "methodology," as Abzug called it, helped to provide WEDO with the personal contacts and sense of the issues that became the basis for the Congress for a Healthy Planet.[58]

The "Women's Action Agenda 21" contained a list of specific demands aimed at the governments participating in UNCED, organized around the topics "Democratic Rights, Diversity and Solidarity"; "Code of Environmental Ethics and Accountability"; "Women, Militarism and the Environment"; "Foreign Debt and Trade"; "Women, Poverty, Land Rights, Food Security and Credit"; "Women's Rights, Population Policies and Health"; "Biodiversity and Biotechnology"; "Nuclear Power and Alternative Energy"; "Science and Technology Transfer"; "Women's Consumer Power"; and "Information and Education."[59] It also issued deliberate challenges calculated to address the lack of women's power within the UN itself as well as the UNCED. The document required that a "permanent gender-balanced UN Commission on Environment and Development" be created; that the imbalance of gender ratios in the UN staff, especially in agencies like UNEP, be redressed; that donor countries increase their funding of UNIFEM (a UN fund for providing resources for and research on women's issues); and that member nations send to UNCED gender-balanced delegations, which would also include representatives of indigenous peoples and grassroots organizations. The creation of a *women's* "Agenda 21" at the Congress required debate and agreement among the 1,500 women present (a process managed through workshops on various issues, in which participants agreed on language to be presented to the larger group). Thus, it is a statement carrying a lot of weight, representing the strong coalitions built among women from very different political and cultural locations, across national borders.

Consolidated by a similar process of debate and agreement among diverse women from around the world at Planeta Fêmea, or the Women's Tent at the

Global Forum, the NGO alternative gathering at the UNCED meeting in Rio in 1992 reworked the document for presentation to the official governmental bodies.[60] In this context, the "Women's Action Agenda 21" was used to lobby for "women's issues" to be included in the formal *Agenda 21*. Indeed, this lobbying effort succeeded in getting specific mention of women's issues in terms of the political perspective of "Planeta Fêmea" in 33 of the 40-plus chapters of "Agenda 21," not counting the inclusion of a chapter specifically addressing the importance of considering women as agents of environmental change as well as the relation between sexism and environmental degradation. This chapter, entitled "Global Action for Women Towards Sustainable and Equitable Development," incorporated the political perspective fostered by WEDO organizers into the heart of the formal government agreements and represented a significant feminist intervention into development politics and the sphere of globalizing environmentalism.[61]

The Preamble of the "Women's Action Agenda 21" couches the diverse issues discussed in the Congress for a Healthy Planet in language that constructs women as activists on behalf of the environment through their commitment to justice, equality, and nurturing. With a recognizably ecofeminist voice, the Preamble argues for interconnections between various political struggles, stating that "a healthy and sustainable environment is contingent upon world peace, respect for human rights, participatory democracy, the self-determination of peoples, respect for indigenous peoples and their lands, cultures, and traditions, and the protection of all species." These things are connected for the writers of the Preamble, because "as long as Nature and women are abused by a so-called 'free-market' ideology and wrong concepts of 'economic growth,' there can be no environmental security."[62] The correspondence is exact between WEDO's arguments here, representing all of the women at the conference, and ecofeminist explorations of the consequences for the environment and for women of how, in Western ideology, women have been equated with nature and both have been devalued.

Despite the similiarity between the analysis and rhetoric of WEDO and ecofeminist writing of the time, WEDO organizers gently shied away from the label "ecofeminism." Exploring this aspect through interviews with Mim Kelber and Bella Abzug, I found that reluctance embedded in the the notion of ecofeminism as a countercultural politics, or a politics based on feminist spirituality, a politics less concerned with institutional politics and more with philosophical argument or direct action. In addition, Kelber and Abzug both expressed that ecofeminism, as they understood it, was about connections between women and nature and was too much a single-issue movement, unable to address the structural processes that produced women's inequality and environmental degradation. However, Kelber and Abzug did not display a thorough knowledge of the complexity of some ecofeminist arguments. For instance, when I pointed out to Kelber that, while WEDO did not use the term "ecofeminist" to describe itself, still many people perceived the "World Women's Congress for a Healthy Planet" as an ecofeminist conference, she replied:

> As you said, I'm not quite sure what the definition of ecofeminism is. The women's movement, including the feminist movement, has a lot of diversity and a lot of different interpretations. There's the whole spiritual group and the cultural group and then there are those of us who come into it via the political project. So we tend to work in a different way. Because there are two approaches, that is, that you create a counterculture, and that's what you do. And then there are others of us who feel that you have to try to make the system work for all of us. It's a reformist approach. I appreciate a lot of what women ecologists are doing and writing [about], talking about alternate ways of living and alternate systems and so on, but unless the global economy self-destructs, and that very well might happen, we have to deal with how the global economy is operating. . . . But I would say that Bella's and my approach has been that you try to work with what's real and change it. But we also understand that women have all different kinds of feelings, different interpretations. And whatever they want to do, it's okay. They can all feed into this so that we can have a common meeting ground on many issues. Our work styles may be different, but I think we all have this common goal of a healthy planet. And the core of it, and I guess Bella and I are very strong on this, is equality for women in decision-making.

Kelber's emphasis on a strategy of reform within existing political and economic institutions is what led Greta Gaard to remark, after her attendance to the Congress for a Healthy Planet, that WEDO was a "liberal ecofeminist" organization (which, to her, "sounds like an oxymoron").[63] Yet what interests me here is that Kelber, while constructing ecofeminism as a countercultural politics *not* interested in "reform," nevertheless sees the rhetoric WEDO employs as creating an umbrella under which many different kinds of women and feminists can create a coalition. The idea that "women all have the common goal of a healthy planet" reverberates within much of WEDO's literature, which relies upon the notion that women's equal participation in political decisions about policy will produce more environmentally sound practices. As Abzug notes: "We do regard . . . a clean environment, a healthy society, the preservation of the earth as being a very fundamental thing for any society, and we feel that women particularly have a very essential role to play."[64]

When asked about the manner in which this connection is made between women's empowerment and environmentalism, Abzug and Kelber articulated two notions: first, that women's particular social and material labor means that environmental issues are important to them (through their roles as mothers, health workers, and food producers); and second, that women have a different sense of connection to nature than men (ironically, the belief that they articulate as belonging to "single-issue" ecofeminism). Often these notions come through in the course of their insistence that giving women an equal say in governmental policymaking would make a difference. On this point, Kelber remarks:

> We keep saying we're not romanticizing women and demonizing men, but I think growing up female and growing up male is just different. It is different. I'm not talking about ability or brain size, or the right side of the brain or the left side of the brain. It's different, it's just an absolutely different experience. Some women may be able to totally separate themselves from the whole weight of tradition and social roles and so on, but for the majority of women in the world certainly, they still bear the weight of the past.

And when asked about her reaction to some feminist criticism of the connection ecofeminists have made between women and nature, for instance in the Women's Pentagon Actions, Abzug responds:

> Some people think that the emphasis on ecofeminism, by ecofeminists, on the natural bond between women and the earth is unacceptable to them. . . . I am basically not an ecofeminist but the point is, I see, there is something that springs from the earth, there is a life, there is a nurturing, there is a symbiotic sense of preserving, and I've often said that as long as discrimination and degradation continue, [as long as] we continue degrading the earth, that we are at the same time creating a discrimination against women. So I think there is a symbiotic relationship.

Whatever the source of the connection made between women's issues and environmentalism, WEDO organizers clearly feel that an appeal to women as a collectivity, to their similarities despite their differences, is an effective organizing practice. Nevertheless, the politics underlying that appeal is one that privileges the southern critique of Western versions of development, as well as an interconnection between radical environmental, feminist, antiracist, and anticapitalist analyses. For example, when asked why she thought of environmental issues as women's issues, Abzug replied: "I always think every issue is a women's issue. I come from that school of thought . . . in fact, [when we had] a congress which we called a World Congress for a Healthy Planet . . . we put together not only our views on earth, air, soil and water, but our views of the total environment, the environment of health, of human rights, of equal rights, of political rights, of economic justice." And again, in explaining why she does not want to restrict herself to being defined as an "ecofeminist," she says: "I am not *just* an ecofeminist. Although we use some language which . . . brings us closer to that posture than most people . . . if you read the Preamble of our 'Women's Action Agenda 21,' we do think there is a bond between the earth and women. But we go much further than [ecofeminism], a much larger definition . . . we are trying to include all kinds of people in our platforms of action and in our activities."

The rhetoric of WEDO thus moves between what might be called an essentialist ecofeminism, calling upon women in their roles as mothers and healers to take on environmentalist causes, and what might be called an anti-essentialist ecofeminism, paying attention to difference within a framework of analyzing the operations of political, economic, and social power. A poster (Figure 3) that WEDO used in the early 1990s demonstrates some of the tensions within its political rhetoric. Under a stunning image of the earth seen from space are the words "It's Time for Women to Mother Earth."[65] The text of the poster says: "With every day that passes, a little more of our world dies at the hands of pollution and neglect. But, *as women*, we can help do something about it" [my emphasis]. The text goes on to mention examples of women environmentalists active across the globe, such as Linda Wallace Campbell, active in the African-American struggle against toxic waste in Alabama; Wangari Maathai, of the Kenyan Green Belt Movement; and Janet Gibson, who worked against the destruction of a barrier reef in Belize. The emphasis in the rest of the poster's text is on the need to bring women into the policymaking institutions that make decisions on the environment, rather than to take environmental action themselves. The assumption is that women will make more environmentalist decisions. And the assertion that "It's Time for Women to Mother Earth," while counting on women's maternalism, moves women from a symbolic, passive identity with Mother Earth to a position as active, political agents.[66]

Notions of WEDO as a maternalist version of ecofeminism that sees women only in essentialist ways are disturbed by watching WEDO's "methodology" in action. The strategy of forming Women's Caucuses within the UN preparatory meetings assumed that women have something in common politically. But the emphasis within the Caucuses on women's unity was most often constructed on the idea of women's exclusion from decision making and power, rather than on essentialist notions of maternalism. The practice of the Caucuses insured that many women heard about other women's political struggles in an atmosphere of coalition-forming and respect. The chair of the Caucus for each meeting was rotated, giving each region a chance to chair a meeting. During the Caucus, agreement was sought on language that teams from the Caucus (formed mostly by members of NGOs) would lobby to be included in the government documents agreed upon at the UN meetings. WEDO provided members of the Caucus with the government document previously produced, and participants in the Caucus would try to agree upon language to amend these documents in directions favoring women and other unrepresented peoples as well as other political positions. If the Women's

FIGURE 3

Caucus's lobbying efforts were successful, this new language would become part of the policy document agreed upon by all the member nations represented at the UN meetings. This "methodology" was so successful at Rio that WEDO continued it beyond the 1992 UNCED meeting that prompted its initial creation. WEDO was responsible for organizing Women's Caucuses before and during UN conferences on population in Cairo, 1993; and on social development in Copenhagen, 1994. Finally, WEDO also organized a caucus to provide a similar space for NGO coalitions for the Fourth World Women's Conference in Beijing, 1995; but since this conference was about women, it didn't make sense to call it a "Women's Caucus." Instead, it was called a "Linkage Caucus," a name that more accurately described, to my mind, what happened in all the preceding Women's Caucuses: the linkage of *issues* rather than *women*.

In these ways, WEDO's organizational format (not a binary construction of difference but choosing multiply-located subjects for their involvement in the issues WEDO has identified as important) destabilizes its essentialist rhetoric about "Now It's Time for Women to Mother Earth." Despite the admirable construction of a politics of connection between important vectors of exploitation and injustice, and its success in influencing UN processes, WEDO's choice of the UN as its main focus of political action has obvious limitations. While an important international political arena, the UN itself has little or no enforcement capabilities to ensure that agreements made by governments during various global summits will be carried out. Though struggles over particular language in official transnational UN agreements are fierce and involve serious political issues, they end up as textual referents, often with their radical force significantly compromised by pragmatic realities of successful lobbying, rather than concrete political or economic practices.

Well aware of these limitations, though still committed to the practice of lobbying within the UN, WEDO has concentrated its energies after the Beijing conference on mobilizing women in their own countries to insist that their governments comply with the international agreements on women, environment, development and population. "We've had all these words on equality," Abzug says, "and now we want the music. Music is the action. . . .So we have been emphasizing the issue of implementation." WEDO plans to continue to create Women's Caucuses in future UN summit meetings (such as the Habitat Summit in Istanbul), but is also looking for ways to assist local organizing around the issues of health, environment, feminist population policies, and sustainable livelihood. One of the tools to further local organizing that WEDO developed early in its existence was the "Women for a Healthy Planet Community Report Card," which provides a framework and resources for community investigation and for publicizing local environmental and health problems. The "Report Card" contains guidelines on how to organize community organizations to create an "action agenda" around the suggested areas of "Natural Environment," "Political Systems," "Social Priorities," and "Human Development."[67]

WEDO has also been asked and has considered setting up local chapters of the organization, but when I talked to her in 1995, Abzug expressed doubt that they had the resources to do this. Still, all of these varied efforts are attempts by the organization to bring their political agenda into local arenas, and national arenas, in which implementation of the U.N.-oriented efforts can take place.

Another aspect to assessing the effects of international strategies appears when attention is paid to the local and regional effects of the organizing initiated by international environmental and feminist groups. An interesting example of this process is reported by María Fernanda Espinosa, who as part of her work with the Indigenous Organization of the Ecuadorian Amazon (CONFENIAE) was asked to organize a Regional Workshop of Indigenous Women in preparation for the World Women's Conference in Beijing.[68] Noting that the "modified version of *Agenda 21*, considering specific recommendations for women, was an attempt to reconcile the sustainable development plan of action with the role and claims of women . . . to serve as a general framework for the deliberations on women and environment," Espinoza points out that "instead of building conceptual, political and operational connections between women, environment and development, the document has [only] superficial addendums." Indeed, Espinosa says, it could be called "a gender addendum not a gender agenda."[69]

Whereas at the international level, women's issues were superficially attended to, at the midlevel of the continental meeting called Encounter of Indigenous Women of the Americas, Espinosa found that women's issues were subsumed to the "struggle of indigenous peoples, about indigenous territorial and cultural rights, self-determination and bilingual education."[70] While this articulation of indigenous politics would seem to include indigeneous women's issues, in fact, according to Espinosa, the statements made by the participants at the Encounter revealed "the predominance of the ethnic emphasis over gender and environmental concerns as well as an implicit critique [of] western feminisms."[71]

Opposed to the international, continental, and national levels of organizing, Espinosa offers the story of the small, localized gathering of indigenous Amazonian women she was asked to organize by CONFENIAE. This effort was very new; CONFANIAE, in its thirty years of existence, had only paid attention to women as a special group when it was prompted to by the organizing efforts for Beijing.[72] Her experience with the Regional Workshop of Indigenous Women ran counter to these tendencies to subsume women's self-perception of their needs and issues. Espinosa arrived at the gathering of forty-five Amazonian indigenous women, who were "local leaders with scarce political experience and often very little formal education,"[73] armed with paperwork to help the women construct their input into the continental group and therefore to the Beijing conference, only to have the women tell her they weren't interested in the UN preparatory process. They had never before been able to get together with others like themselves without elites (even their own elites) present, and they wanted to use the time to talk about how to help each other, to share information, and to strategize about local issues.[74] The document they produced to carry up to the international level was "based on personal testimonies and has a narrative form." Espinosa argues that

> This initial experience, in spite of coming more from external initiatives than from self-generated political needs, is encouraging indigenous women to estab-

lish an intercultural and intergenerational communication; to reflect about their needs and struggles; and think about the skills and alternatives they have to develop in order to face the changes and aggressive demands of the post-industrial world. Furthermore, this process may also contribute to the democratization of indigenous organizations themselves.[75]

Espinosa concludes from this experience,

> Looking to the three conferences [Beijing, the continental Encounter for Indigenous Women, and the local Regional Workshop], there is a disjuncture between the globalized discourse about indigenous women generated in Beijing and local initiatives. . . . What Beijing objectively did was to open spaces and opportunities for dialogue and communication at different scales. The incorporation of indigenous women's perspectives and political leadership in global agendas can be seen as one of the effects of the internationalization of the ethnic and gender debates."[76]

In his essay on the globalization of grassroots politics, Michael Peter Smith points out that in social theory, the local is usually equated with "stasis" and "personal identity," while the global is characterized as the "site of dynamic change, the decentering of meaning, and the fragmentation and homogenization of culture — that is, the *space* of global caplitalism."[77] In contrast, he argues that a transnational grassroots politics has appeared, which confuses these older notions of separate local and global spaces, and which operates within particular transnational arenas. One example he offers is a hearing of "Bay Area migrant women" to give testimony to the UN Summit on Human Rights held in Vienna in 1993. Like the conference organized by WEDO in Miami and other gatherings like it, these activities create new transnational political subjects, brought together as women, or as members of other politically constructed subjectivities. They also create new opportunities for dialogue and coalitions.

These political collectivities very well may be constructed by essentialist discourses, but they are also collectivities built on hard-won unity across radical differences. And they may serve the less powerful groups as well as the powerful within the new collectivity. For instance, as I have argued in the case of WEDO, "ecofeminist" discourses about women's nurturing relation to nature intervene within hegemonic processes in a context of globalizing environmentalisms, and, through an organizational structure that emphasizes equal participation among very differently located political actors, serve to destabilize the essentialism of the rhetoric and produce valuable political effects. Just the construction of these arenas creates new opportunities for the less powerful to gain political leverage. Jane Jacob, in an essay critiquing essentialist Western notions about Aboriginal women's relationship to environmental activism, makes a similar point: "In particular, there are specific problems arising from the essentialized notions of Aboriginality and woman that underpin radical environmentalisms and feminisms. Yet to read these alliances only in terms of the reiteration of a politics of Western, masculinist supremacy neglects the positive engagement indigenous women may make with such 'sympathizers' in their efforts to verify and amplify their struggles for land rights."[78] The ecofeminist intervention into UN processes creates a network, a space for debate, a mechanism not just for the intervention of feminism, environmentalism, and anticolonial scholarship into policymaking; but also for strategic coalitions to take place among disempowered people and between privileged and underprivileged people in one political collectivity. The practices and rhetoric of WEDO do not deal sufficiently with questions of the relationship of U.S. racism to environmental problems and to sexism. We still need organizational frameworks that can deal with this intersection. And we need more ways to intervene in globalizing environmentalisms besides the UN. But we also need to keep in mind that, as in the contribution of the international feminist antimilitarist movement to the end of the Cold War, we may need to tolerate "essentialist" rhetoric that calls women from different locations to act together against power.

WHAT'S IN A NAME?

ECOFEMINISMS AS/IN FEMINIST THEORY

6

Some ecofeminists have argued that there is an "establishment feminist backlash" against ecofeminism, resulting in a lack of ecofeminist writing in prominent feminist journals such as *SIGNS*, as well as the invisibility of ecofeminist theory in important academic feminist conferences and anthologies.[1] In making this charge, Greta Gaard describes the role feminist taxonomies take in what she sees as "establishment" feminism's exclusion of ecofeminism:

> Certainly there are branches of thought within ecofeminism: the branch that has received the most attention to date is cultural ecofeminism. . . . What's curious is that while liberal and cultural feminism are popularly [that is, in the eyes of powerful academic feminists] thought to be wrong (clearly, an assessment made from the standpoint of socialist feminism, which is the current equivalent of establishment feminism), their proponents at least gain access to the [feminist] press. Within ecofeminism, these two wrong branches are the ones that receive the most press, and are then innocently or willfully taken to represent the whole tree, thereby allowing establishment feminism to dismiss ecofeminism entirely.[2]

Gaard goes on to tell a story about the rejection by *SIGNS* of a commissioned piece on ecofeminism, which was then rejected in turn by the *NWSA Journal*. Though I don't know enough about the details of these rejections to judge Gaard's story on its own, I certainly can attest to numerous occasions when, in presenting my work in academic feminist contexts, I was assumed to be making "essentialist" and therefore useless arguments just because I was writing about "ecofeminism." But it has also happened that the anti-essentialist aspects of my work have been objected to by feminist audiences who expected and desired essentialist ways of connecting women and nature. Dealing with my own objections to the essentialism of some ecofeminist arguments, and the effects on my work of a widespread assumption among my academic feminist peers that such essentialisms permanently and thoroughly tarnish ecofeminism as a political position, I have struggled with the question of whether I would want to identify myself and my work as ecofeminist.

Why not ecofeminism? Why shouldn't feminist theorists welcome a political discourse that interrogates the equation of women with nature and examines the political consequences of that equation not just for women but for nature as well? Why don't the many feminists exploring the gendered representations of nature and the naturalized representations of women in various cultural contexts call themselves "ecofeminists"? Why not extend the long-standing feminist interest in patriarchal equations between "women" and "nature" to a feminist consideration of their effects on the environment as well as on women? What has the ecofeminist movement done or not done to deserve its exclusion from certain feminist circles? I trust that, by this point, readers of this book understand some of the problems with certain kinds of ecofeminist discourses that essentialize women, people of color, and nature, thereby making some ecofeminist arguments suspect. But by now, I hope that readers are also convinced that such essentalist rhetoric is not devoid of political usefulness nor the only kind of ecofeminist discourse; and, in any case, is constantly and fairly easily destabilized, though not eradicated.

But this still leaves the question: Why ecofeminism? Why not just call the feminist analysis of the interaction between sexism and enviromental problems "feminism"? I believe that "ecofeminism," as a term, indicates a double political intervention; of environmentalism into feminism and feminism into environmentalism, that is as politically important as the designations "socialist feminism" and "Black feminism" were previously. Perhaps it is a name that will only be transiently useful within our history; but the stakes in such a politics of naming are deeply embedded in a long tradition within the development of U.S. feminism, and can be understood better through an examination of the practice of typologizing feminisms.[3]

In this chapter, a brief look at the genesis of diverse typologies of feminism will bring us to an investigation of assorted efforts to typologize ecofeminisms. I will examine various attempts to rename "ecofeminism" in order to divest it of its essentialist connotations, and to carve out a theoretical apparatus for a feminist critique of environmental problems that does not make the essential-ist move. In embarking on this investigation of naming, renaming, and typol-ogizing, I want to interrogate the anti-essentialist tangent within feminist the-ory (and, by extension, ecofeminist theory) that creates a division between feminist theory and feminist activist practice, one that has demonized "cul-tural feminism." Finally, I will end with a set of suggestions for ecofeminist theory and ecofeminist practice.

TYPOLOGIZING FEMINISMS

In a number of places in this book, I have noted that feminist critics have cre-ated an ecofeminist straw-woman, rejecting it for constructing an essentialism of race, gender, class, and/or nature. At the same time, I have detailed the oc-currence of ecofeminist essentialisms, ecofeminist natures, in nearly every moment of ecofeminism's history as a movement. I have argued that these moments of essentialism are almost always strategic, unstable, and con-tested—as long as the ecofeminist politics in question were aimed toward in-clusion of a variety of radical issues, and/or the organizational practice was oriented toward bringing together women whose political subjectivities were variously located, within a participatory democratic context in which different voices could be heard. I have portrayed the process of radical political move-ments as one in which the creation of collective political subjects always al-ready contains within it the germs of "essentialism" (meaning here, the no-tion that subjectivities are seen as containing some similar, universal, and/or inherent commonality) and hence the danger of exclusionary practices. But I have also contended that as long as our political organizations are radically democratic, and as long as we see political opposition as a contested, histori-cal, dynamic process, these "essentialisms" of strategically created political identities will be constantly destabilized.[4]

In this section, I want to suggest that the same inconstant process is true for the political practice known as "feminist theorizing" within the academy. To show this, I will briefly examine efforts to fix categories of feminism artifi-cially, to lift them out of the dynamic, conflicted, political process, for (impor-tant, and perhaps necessary) analytic purposes. The main tool for producing these fixed "objects of knowledge" (as Katie King calls them) known as "femi-nist theory" is the practice of typologizing. As King argues, the "object of knowledge" produced by typologies is a particular category of feminist theory that is seen as the "best," one that subsumes other categories of feminist theory as well as the political, historically specific, process of contestation in which feminist theorizing is embedded. The "best" feminist theory is the "telos of this machine [the typology] producing identities and processing literatures."[5] King's method of reading the political stakes in typologizing practices is cru-cial to my analysis here.

My examination is prompted by ecofeminism being too easily, in these typologies, relegated to the category "cultural feminism," which, through an earlier process of typologizing, was tagged with the essentialist label and determined to be one of the "losers" of the competing kinds of feminist theories. Since the "winner" of the typologizing process is most often a brand of feminist theory closely associated with white academic feminist theories, and the "losers" with certain kinds of activist, or popular, feminisms, I am concerned with how this practice creates an artificial divide between feminist theory and feminist practices.[6] I also argue that feminisms of women of color are often made invisible by this process. Overall, I think this practice is not attentive enough to historical complexities in the formation and deployment of feminist analyses and theoretical practices. So while it is useful for analyzing different feminist approaches theoretically, it is a poor guide to understanding feminism as a social movement.

Typologizing feminism has a long history in the U.S. feminist movement.[7] Let me tell a story about this history, one that shifts our attention away from the fine theoretical and analytical distinctions that are the useful products of typologizing practices, to focus on the practice of taking various feminist positionings out of their historical contexts and obscuring the minute political contests that generate them. I wish I could tell a story about the appearance of various feminisms with the same amount of detail as the story I've just told about the appearance of various ecofeminisms: a story that would emphasize the construction of political positions out of their engagement with particular political contexts and conjunctures. However, this is not the place, at the end of this book, to commence the history of U.S. feminisms.[8] So I ask for indulgence at this point, to allow me to sketch the outlines of such a story about U.S. feminisms, without filling in all of the details but relying optimistically at numerous points on a reader's own knowledge of the history of U.S. feminism.

The task of analytically separating different kinds of feminisms was, in the second-wave women's movement in this country, embedded in political struggles involving not just different feminist groups but also the relationship of feminism to the existing nonfeminist left. Arising out of the sixties' movements, especially civil rights, student, and antiwar movements, the women's liberation movement contained within it ongoing debates over radical political analyses, strategies, and tactics that made sense in wider movement contexts. Thus, the early differences between groups of feminists are often clarified in terms of their relationships with male New Left groups, or in terms of specific political debates that had at the time special resonance. Referencing them thus generates these difference out of movement contexts themselves.

The earliest analytical division in the women's liberation movement was made between "radical" feminism (committed to structural change and revolution) and "liberal" feminism (committed to reform within existing political structures). But variants were quickly teased out of "radical" feminism as well;

for instance the categories "feminist" and "politico." As Jo Freeman describes it: "The original issue was whether the fledging women's liberation movement should remain a branch of the radical left movement or become an independent women's movement. Proponents of the two positions became known as 'politicos' and 'feminists,' respectively, and traded arguments about whether the enemy was 'capitalism' or male-dominated social institutions."[9] Note that the "feminist" grouping (which later becomes tagged as essentialist) "cultural feminism," is constructed around the felt need to separate itself from the male-dominated white left, similar to some of the ecofeminisms examined in chapter 1 that were aimed at carving out an independent feminist position from male-dominated white environmentalisms.

In the more academic typologizing that developed by distancing itself from movement contexts and is first evident in Alison Jaggar's ground-breaking 1983 book, *Feminist Politics and Human Nature*, the "politicos" evolve into two groups, "Marxist feminists" and "socialist feminists." An interesting aspect to the categories "radical," "liberal," and "socialist," (also found in Josephine Donovan's 1985 *Feminist Theory: The Intellectual Traditions of American Feminism*)[10] that dominate descriptions of second-wave feminism, is the Cold War flavor of the discourse. I am sympathetic to the difficulties of manageably describing contemporary feminism, but "radical feminism" too often seemed to serve early typologizers of the feminist movement as a catch-all category, like "Third World," in which they could safely stow away feminisms that did not fall under the superpower category of "liberal" or "socialist." Thus, some accounts of "radical feminism" put together feminisms of women of color, lesbian separatists, anarchists, and Shulamith Firestone, who often got top billing. For feminists of color in particular, this categorical move made invisible their unique, and varying, contributions to feminist practice and theorizing.

In these academic typologies, the two nonliberal feminist positions—radical and socialist—are often distinguished in terms of divergent analyses of the "root" cause of sexism (that is, early socialist feminism identified a dual system of sex and class oppression; while radical feminism claimed sex oppression). Many feminist typologizers include Marxist feminism, a variant privileging class oppression as the root cause of other forms of domination. But with what might be called, with a certain poignant humor, the world-historical defeat of Marxism during the 1980s, the position seems particularly anachronistic, though it retains a ghostly appearance in later typologies built on Jaggar's and Donovan's.

Another new category generated out of these typologies is "cultural feminism," indicating a supposed preference for cultural strategies for radical change (particularly in the formation of separatist "women's culture") rather than institutional politics (the provenance of liberal feminists) or theoretical understandings of the structural and economic frameworks underpinning domination (the specialty of socialist feminism). Jaggar's 1983 typology does not use the label "cultural feminism," but her description of "radical feminism" incorporates many features of what later is called "cultural feminism." Donovan's 1985 typology includes the categories "cultural feminism" and "radical feminism," but by "cultural feminism" she means feminism of the nineteenth century, which distinguished itself from liberal Enlightenment feminism by aiming for a "broader cultural transformation."[11] Her description of "radical feminism" tallies with Jaggar's.

In 1983, Alice Echols's essay "The New Feminism of Yin and Yang" identified a variant of feminism, for her most clearly exemplified by the feminist antipornography movement, which, like Jaggar and Donovan's "radical feminism," revalued "female" qualities through biologistic arguments.[12] In 1984, Ellen Willis's essay, "Radical Feminism and Feminist Radicalism," first used the term "cultural feminism" to describe the variant identified by Echols, a feminism that "seized on the idea of women's oppression as the primary oppression."[13] In later typologies, "cultural feminism" and "radical feminism" often become conflated.[14]

In this way, "cultural feminism" is the category that most firmly gets tagged with the label "essentialist," because its analysis tends to identify "men" as the problem and "women" as the solution; in doing so, it elides inequalities of race and class among the category "women" as well as idealizes "feminine" qualities and values (note the similarity with essentialist versions of ecofeminism, which turn up in places similarly motivated as the "feminist" version of radical feminism to gain independence from male-dominated left positions). In contrast, socialist feminism (notably, the grouping that becomes most embedded in the academy), with its initial attempt at dual systems theory (paying attention to gender and class simultaneously) and becoming a complex analytic apparatus, slowly and unevenly makes space for poststructuralist feminism, which, giving up the idea of finding a "root cause" along the way, identifies the shared processes (in language, in philosophy, in disciplinary practices of various kinds) of multiple forms of domination, ultimately including (under pressure by lesbian feminists and feminists of color) racism, classism, heterosexism, and sexism as the most important forms of domination. By this description of the relationship between socialist and poststructuralist feminism, I don't mean to imply that all socialist feminists are now poststructuralist feminists, but that socialist feminism, with its emphasis on the social construction of gender and the necessity to see multiple systems of domination in operation, provided the foundation for a turn to poststructuralism. Thus, in more recent efforts at typologizing, it is often poststructuralist feminism that wins the categorical contest, over cultural, liberal, and socialist feminism.[15]

Jo Freeman's *The Politics of Women's Liberation* (as well as her various articles on the women's movement), Ellen Willis's essay mentioned above, and

Alice Echols' book, *Daring to Be Bad*, are rare examples of accounts that generate different feminist categories out of a movement history rather than through textual analysis of feminist writings. Echols's book is particularly important in the process of cementing the label "essentialist" onto cultural feminism. Her interest is in divesting early radical feminism of the essentialist label by generating a separation between "cultural" and "radical" feminists through a rearticulation of the old "feminist" versus "politico" split. As Echols says about the genesis of her book:

> A study of this sort seems to me especially important because radical feminism is so poorly understood and so frequently conflated with cultural feminism. This conceptual confusion arises in part because radical feminism was not monolithic and aspects of radical feminism did anticipate cultural feminism.... But while cultural feminism did evolve from radical feminism it nonetheless deviated from it in crucial respects. Most fundamentally, radical feminism was a political movement dedicated to eliminating the sex-class system, whereas cultural feminism was a countercultural movement aimed at reversing the cultural valuation of the male and the devaluation of the female. In the terminology of today, radical feminists were typically social constructionists who wanted to render gender irrelevant, while cultural feminists were generally essentialists who sought to celebrate femaleness.[16]

Reading this in the very early period of conceiving the project that became this book, I felt a shock of recognition. Here, a political movement that is complex and contradictory (radical feminism for Echols, ecofeminism for me) has been rejected as essentialist ("in the terminology of today") because of reductive, ahistorical portrayals of the movement that conflate its social constructionists with its essentialists.[17] And Echols' solution is similar to mine: to give an account that portrays the movement's divisions, its strategic calculations, its historical specificity, the fluidity of its members' politics and self-identifications. Nevertheless, according to the argument I make here— that all movements contain both essentialist and anti-essentialist moments within a process of political struggle in democratic organizational forms— Echols's distinction would also constitute a reductive characterization of "cultural" feminism, thereby eliminating her differentiation between "cultural" and "radical" feminism. This does not vitiate her fine analysis of the problems encountered by early women's liberation groups, but it points to the difficulty of making typological distinctions stick once you look at the actual complexities of movements.

Before I leave the subject of typologizing feminisms, I want to note two common results of the practice: the invisibility of feminists of color, and the creation of a divide between feminist theory and feminist activism. As I have said above, many of these early typologies either leave feminists of color out or subsume them under the category "radical feminist." Only slowly, after much criticism by feminists of color, do typologists begin to provide accounts of the unique analysis, let alone the varieties of theories, produced by feminists of color, who had from the beginning of the second-wave women's movement generated theories of multiple, simultaneous oppressions of racism, classism, sexism, and, often, heterosexism.[18] An illustration of this slow process is the changing categories in Alison Jaggar and Paula Rothenberg's textbook, *Feminist Frameworks*, which has had three editions, in 1978, 1984, and 1993.[19] In the first edition, Jaggar and Rothenberg identify four forms of feminist theory: liberal, Marxist, radical, and socialist. Very few women of color are included in the book, and none are used to illustrate a particular form of feminist theory. In the 1984 edition, there are the same four kinds of feminist theory, with the addition of "women of color." In the 1993 edition, the original four forms of feminist theory are joined by "multicultural feminism" and "global feminism," enacting categories that finally bring theories constructed by feminists of color and Third World feminists fully into view, though still excluding them from the supposedly "earlier" more entrenched forms: liberal, radical/cultural, and socialist.

Katie King suggests that this pattern of white feminists' omission, subsumption, and dilatory recognition of theories by feminists of color is part of the process of producing theory out of feminist "conversations," or the layering of debates between feminists situated in specific (and often limited) cohorts, networks, and spaces (such as classrooms, conferences, movement groups). Because these early typologies have been produced by white academic feminists, she shows the manner in which their networks and self-understandings construct the categories they use in particular ways that organize out the intellectual production of feminists of color: "The categories for inclusion [in the typology] skew, at the very least, the race and class composition of their writers/theorists." And this is not simply a matter of intention, but the way in which feminist "'theory' and 'theory-makers' are disciplinarily determined objects."[20] The accusation of racism thus made against these typologies has an ironic ring, since it is the charge of racism that is produced as the motivation for the rejection of liberal feminism and the characterization of cultural feminism as "essentialist" by socialist feminists and poststructuralist feminists. Like the antiracist imperative (which ironically is part of the construction of the 1980s ecofeminist discourse of "indigenous women" that we examined in chapter 4), an antiracist impulse (in response to critiques by feminists of color) similarly generates an exclusionary practice by white academic feminist typologists. These complaints by feminists of color about their exclusion from "hegemonic feminism" have an echo in Gaard's complaint about the exclusion of ecofeminists from "establishment feminism."

The label "hegemonic feminism" for what might be called the power elite of academic feminist theorists is Chela Sandoval's term, whose 1991 typology is explicitly a response to the standard categories of liberal, radical, and social-ist feminism organizing the theorizing of feminists of color out. Sandoval ex-amines the "four-phase history of consciousness consisting of 'liberal,' 'Marxist,' 'radical/cultural,' and 'socialist' feminisms, [which Sandoval schematizes] as 'women are the same as men,' 'women are different from men,' 'women are superior' and the fourth catchall category, 'women are a racially divided class.'" She argues that feminists of color have been systemati-cally excluded from these categories, even when their theorizing was the cause of the shifts from one feminism to the other: "I contend that this com-prehension of feminist consciousness is hegemonically unified, framed, and buttressed with the result that the expression of a unique form of U.S. third world feminism, active over the last thirty years, has become invisible outside of its all-knowing logic."[21]

Instead of the standard feminist typology, Sandoval offers another map, a "topography" rather than a "typology," which is not necessarily about feminist theories alone, but about forms of oppositional consciousness possible not only in "struggles against gender domination, but [in] the struggles against race, class, and cultural hierarchies which mark the twentieth century in the United States."[22] This schema replaces the four-part traditional feminist typol-ogy with four categories of oppositional consciousness: "equal rights" (in which a "subordinated group might argue that their differences—for which they have been assigned inferior status—are only in appearance, not reality" and members of that group aim for integration with those in power); "revolu-tionary" (in which "the subordinated group claim their *differences* from those in power and call for a social transformation that will accommodate and legit-imate those differences"); "supremacism" (in which "not only do the op-pressed claim their differences, but they also assert that those very differences have provided them access to a superior evolutionary level than those cur-rently in power" and thus justify their leadership over the powerful); and "sep-aratism" (in which the oppressed claim their differences, but do not aim for integration, transformation or leadership, but rather a "form of political resis-tance . . . organized to protect and nurture the differences that define it through complete separation from the dominant social order").[23] To these four categories, which roughly recapitulate the categories of liberal, Marxist/socialist, radical, and cultural feminism, Sandoval adds a fifth cate-gory: "differential consciousness." This category is unlike the others. It "oper-ates like the clutch of an automobile: the mechanism that permits the driver to select, engage, and disengage gears in a system for the transmission of power."[24] Though she places it in her "topography" as a fifth category, she sees it as operating *through* the other categories, embodied by the struggles of fem-inists of color within and outside of the white U.S. feminist movement, changing each category's emphasis from a fixed set of positions, ideas, and analyses to a fluid set of tools, tactics, and approaches to be used when the situation calls for them—in forming coalitions, resisting power, and generating theories. In Sandoval's words: "For analytic purposes I place this mode of differential consciousness in the fifth position, even though it functions as the medium through which the 'equal rights,' 'revolutionary,' 'supremacist,' and 'separatist' modes of oppositional consciousness became effectively transformed out of their hegemonic versions. Each is now ideological and *tactical* weaponry for confronting the shifting currents of power."[25]

"Differential consciousness," as Sandoval describes it, is a form of mobile political subjectivity, which she is well aware parallels postmodernist and poststrucuralist theories of constructed, fluid subjectivities. But she claims that the differential consciousness generated by "U.S. third world feminists" predates that postmodernist turn, and additionally contains within it an optimism and an experience with the form that allows it to operate more effectively and always in opposition (rather than in possible complicity with) postmodern forms of power.[26] Differential consciousness, in constantly honing in on resistance to power relations rather than on constructing theoretical purity, concentrates on the process of political action and theory making, exploding categorical loyalties, and seeking coalitions, affinities, and allies.

> Differential consciousness requires grace, flexibility, and strength: enough strength to confidently commit to a well-defined structure of identity for one hour, day, week, month, year; enough flexibility to self-consciously transform that identity according to the requisites of another oppositional ideological tactic if readings of power's formation require it; enough grace to recognize alliances with others committed to egalitarian social relations and race, gender, and class justice, when their readings of power call for alternative oppositional stands. Within the realm of differential consciousness, oppositional ideological positions, unlike their incarnations under hegemonic feminist comprehension, are tactics—not strategies. Self-conscious agents of differential consciousness recognize one another as allies, country-women and men of the same psychic terrain. As the clutch of a car provides the driver the ability to shift gears, differential consciousness permits the practitioner to choose tactical positions, that is, to self-consciously break and reform ties to ideology, activities which are imperative for the pyschological and political practices that permit the achievement of coalition across differences. Differential consciousness occurs within the only possible space where, in the words of third world feminist philosopher Maria Lugones, "cross-cultural and cross-racial loving" can take place, through the ability of the self to shift its identities in an activity she calls "world-travelling."[27]

As Sandoval indicates in the above quote, "hegemonic feminist" taxonomies do more than contruct racially exclusive categories of feminism; they also, through their creation of "inferior" and "superior" kinds of feminism, make activist alliances and coalitions difficult. Here we have come to the second (and related) problem with dominant feminist taxonomies of liberal, radical/cultural, socialist and now poststructuralist feminism: they create a division between feminist activism and feminist academic practice. This is mainly achieved by relegating most feminist activism to the (putatively inferior) category of radical/cultural feminism or liberal feminism and either rejecting it as essentialist or locating it in a feminist past. Early feminist "zap" actions, lesbian separatist creations of women's businesses and women's self-help institutions, coalition politics engaged in by feminists of color, anti-pornography demonstrations, and feminist antimilitarist direct actions, have all been placed by white academic feminists into the (essentialist) category of radical/cultural feminism. Organizing for the ERA, lobbying for pro-choice legislation, gaining entrance into male-dominated professional schools and businesses, and arguing for equal social security and pension benefits for women, are all put under the category "liberal feminism."[28] In order to depict "socialist feminism" as a separate category from radical or liberal feminism in 1983, Jaggar strips "politicos" from their engagement with radical feminist activism: she quotes a 1978 statement by Margaret Page: "[Socialist feminism] is a commitment to the *development* of an analysis and political practice, rather than to one that already exists."[29] We can also see the exclusion of women of color and of activists in Ferree and Hess's 1985 book, *Controversy and Coalition*. Ferree and Hess characterize socialist feminist political issues as "the feminization of poverty," "comparable worth," "wages for housework," and "international perspectives," but give examples of socialist feminist engagement with these issues almost entirely in terms of their scholarship.[30] By contrast, political actions and organizations concerned with working-class women and women of color are examined in the section entitled "Sympathizers and Activists: Problems of Mobilization," which effectively segregates activism, women of color, and working-class women from "socialist feminism." The existence of feminist activism is thus kept separate from the feminist theory with the most promise in the authors's eyes. As Ferree and Hess put it in a section called "Realizing the Promise of Diversity": "Despite many barriers [they do not specify precisely the nature of these barriers] to the participation of minority and working-class women, the New Feminist Movement today embraces over two dozen organizations devoted to their concerns. Minority and working-class women are active in all facets of the movement, but only recently has an effort been made to integrate their needs and concerns into the movement's overall goals and strategies."[31] Finally, Chris Weedon, for whom "poststructuralist feminism" is the "winner" of the categorical contest, barely mentions activism at all. In her chapter on "Feminist Critical Practice," she argues that poststructuralism's contribution to feminism is a feminist deconstructive and critical *literary* practice. She quite clearly locates poststructuralist feminism in the academy, separate from other kinds of feminist activism: "For women active in the literary and educational institutions the task of transformation may seem overwhelming. It is important that we continue to be involved in and maintain supportive strategic links with the wider feminist movement, claiming and using the institutional power available to us but always with a view to subverting it and making resistant discourses and subject positions much more widely available."[32] Though her discussion in this section pays rare attention to the political effects of academic critical practice, since Weedon has begun her book pointing out the limits of liberal feminism, the essentialism of radical feminism, and the strengths of poststructuralist feminism, the resulting effect is an impression that poststructuralist feminism is only of use in the academy, and, further, that this political practice of academic poststructuralist feminist literary criticism is the most useful to feminism.

TYPOLOGIZING ECOFEMINISMS

Ecofeminists have been just as sensitive as Alice Echols or Chela Sandoval to the dangers of feminist critics reducing their movement to its essentialist practitioners or its essentialist moments; or to being organized out of typologies of feminist theory. They have reacted in the tradition of feminist scholarship by creating typologies of ecofeminism. These typologies have as their common goal the production of a nonessentializing ecofeminist theory as the "best" ecofeminism.[33] In this section, I will look at various efforts to generate a nonessentializing ecofeminist theory by the creation of a new name for such a position. I will look at the theoretical arguments used to purify these new ecofeminism positions from essentialism and show that none of them succeed in eliminating essentialism (especially particular universalisms generated through the construction of unitary, coherent categories) completely. I will also ask the question of ecofeminist typologizers that I have asked of feminist typologizers above: Do their typologies make ecofeminists of color invisible, and/or separate ecofeminist theory from ecofeminist action?

The various ecofeminisms produced by ecofeminist typologies can be mapped as follows. In Figure 4, under the column "Constructionist versus Essentialist," each author's preferred theory is on the left, while the rejected "essentialist" theory is on the right.

All these ecofeminist typologies locate feminism as the birthplace of ecofeminism, both explicitly in their origin stories and through their overlay of hegemonic feminist typologies onto ecofeminism. Also note the many efforts made to try to create a constructionist position for ecofeminism, giving the lie to those who would create a straw-woman of essentialism to characterize every ecofeminist theory. The last three categories, by Agarwal, Seager, Alaimo, and Rocheleau, et al., are by authors who explicitly locate themselves

FIGURE 4 Ecofeminist Typologies

Constructionist versus Essentialist	Authors
social ecofeminism/cultural ecofeminism	early Biehl[34]
socialist ecofeminism/cultural or radical ecofeminism	Merchant[35]
transformational (ecological) feminism/nature feminism	Warren[36]
critical ecological ecofeminism/papal ecofeminism	Plumwood[37]
conceptualist ecofeminism/radical ecofeminism	King, R.[38]
ecofeminist/ecofeminine	Davion[39]
ecofeminism/nature feminism	Roach[40]
social ecofeminism/nature feminism	Heller[41]
feminist green socialism/cultural ecofeminism	Mellors[42]
feminist environmentalism/ecofeminism	Agarwal, Seager[43]
environmental feminism/ecofeminism	Alaimo[44]
feminist political ecology/ecofeminism	Rocheleau, et al.[45]

outside of ecofeminism; I have included them here as a provocation, one I will discuss somewhat later in this chapter.

But before I examine these typologies more closely, I would like to introduce Kathy Ferguson's analysis of the different kinds of theoretical moves that make up "essentialisms" of various sorts: a typology of essentialism. Ferguson points out that the charge of "essentialism" is often thrown about without specifying what is particularly being objected to. She distinguishes three kinds of "essentialism." The first she calls "essentialism per se": arguments attributing "women's pyschological and social experiences to fixed and unchanging traits resident in women's physiology or in some larger order of things."[46] The second form she calls "universalism," which "takes the patterns visible in one's own time and place to be accurate for all." The third kind she calls "the constitution of unified categories," which "entails any constitution of a unified set of categories around the terms *woman* and *man*."[47]

Ferguson argues that the first kind, "essentialism per se," while it exists in a number of feminist theories and political positions, is rare and always contested from within the given position that generates it.[48] "In fact," she writes, "[feminist theorists] have been so determined not to participate in this [biologistic] discourse that we have difficulty talking coherently about bodies at all." Thus, she argues: "Within current debates in feminist theory, accusations of this form of essentialism do battle with an argument made largely out of straw."[49]

Ferguson finds more frequent examples of "universalism" in contemporary feminist theories. The third kind, "the constitution of unified categories," she finds to be problematic as a charge. "Any analysis requires the naming of such coherencies; it is fundamental to the use of language to employ some set of categories about which generalizations can be made. There are ways to assert one's categories that contain periodic reminders of their partiality, and ways that do not, but the need to operate with some set of unified categories is unavoidable. Feminists who deplore this as essentialist or universalist are overlooking their own necessary participation in this linguistic practice."[50]

The problem that Ferguson identifies with charges of essentialism is that they commonly confuse the three kinds of essentialism. There is a "slippage among different meanings of essentialism":[51] a critique of unified categories often claims that they produce universalism, and then universalism is characterized as essentialism per se; or, the criticism starts with the last term and conflates it with the first. Ferguson identifies this process as the culprit in a constant contest to identify "bad" feminist theories versus "good" feminist theories.

> Beginning with the easy target of essentialism per se, the argument slides through a criticism of universalism into an untenable rejection of unified coherencies themselves. In the process, a comforting but overly simple distinction emerges between virtuous theories that do not employ unified categories of analysis and offensive theories that do. I do not mean to say that there are no offensive theories. . . . My point is that important critics of universalizing weaken their case by neglecting their own participation in the linguistic/political practices they deplore.[52]

I would add to Ferguson's point that if unified categories are a necessary, if sometimes unfortunate, part of an analysis, it may also be true that unified categories, and possibly universalism, are a necessary part of mobilization for political action and strategic positioning within hegemonic political processes. This would explain why feminist activists are so often relegated to the "essentialist" categories of feminist theory. And, as I have tried to demonstrate throughout this book, such "essentialist" rhetorics, seen from *within* movements rather than from an outsider's point of view, are often understood as a political strategy rather than a statement of "fact."[53]

Further, given Sandoval's description of the way in which Third World women of color are willing to strategically occupy politically useful unified categories out of which to construct tactical subjectivities, it would also indicate the (unconscious) logic behind placing "women of color" in these "essentialist" categories of feminism. Thus, in examining ecofeminist typologies, we should not be surprised to find similar patterns of exclusion and rejection of activists, as well as patterns of making ecofeminists of color invisible as theorists. I will turn now to such an examination of ecofeminist typologies.

Carolyn Merchant has used Jaggar's typology of liberal, radical, Marxist, and socialist feminisms, and generated out of it categories of liberal, radical, and socialist ecofeminism. For Merchant, socialist ecofeminism is the "winner" of the categorical contest, because radical ecofeminism, "in emphasizing the female, body and nature components of the dualities male/female,

mind/body, and culture/nature . . . runs the risk of perpetuating the very hier-
achies it seeks to overthrow."[54] In contrast, a socialist ecofeminism "views
both nature and human nature as socially constructed."[55] These quotes come
from an early version of Merchant's typology, and the newness of ecofeminism as a position is signaled by a constant slippage between "feminism" and
"ecofeminism" in Merchant's language. In a later version of this typology,
Merchant's categories are liberal, cultural, social, and socialist ecofeminism,
marking both the successful instatiation of "cultural" over "radical" for the
"essentialist" version of feminism, as well as acknowledgment of the specific
ecofeminist arguments arising out of the social ecological position, which dif-
ferentiates itself from socialism.[56] In this version, "cultural ecofeminism" is
once again marred by essentialism (and Merchant, focused here specifically
on what Ferguson calls "essentialism per se," connects it with "spirituality")
while social ecofeminism "distinguishes itself from spirituality-oriented cultural ecofeminists . . . [by beginning with] the materialist, social feminist
analysis of early radical feminism that sought to restructure the oppressions
imposed on women by marriage, the nuclear family, romantic love, the capitalist state, and patriarchal religion."[57] (Note the resuscitation of the "feminists" versus "politicos" split, here produced as "cultural ecofeminist" versus
"social ecofeminist.") Socialist ecofeminism, on the other hand, "offers a
standpoint from which to analyze social and ecological transformations, and
to suggest social actions that will lead to the sustainability of life and a just
society."[58]

Here socialist ecofeminism takes the role of "suggesting" political action to
others, rather than generating it from within its own location. Merchant's typology consistently places ecofeminist activists in either the "cultural ecofeminist" category or as examples of action "explained" by socialist ecofeminism.
Notably, the activists in the first category are primarily white U.S. ecofeminists or multiraced women environmental activists, while the activists that
conduct actions "suggested" by socialist feminism are from the Third World
and the Second World. This ambiguity around whether these latter activists
are socialist ecofeminists or are simply *explained* by socialist ecofeminism
arises from Merchant's implicit understanding that to claim certain women
environmental activists as ecofeminists, particularly when they are Third
World women or U.S. women of color who do not identify as ecofeminists, is
a form of appropriation. After all (like Jaggar's understanding of socialist feminism), Merchant is aware that socialist ecofeminism is a theoretical position
located primarily in academia, which has been to a great extent generated out
of her own scholarship (work that has made immense contributions to
ecofeminism, whatever the critique I make here of her typology).[59] As she says
in 1992, "Socialist ecofeminism is not yet a movement, but rather a feminist
transformation of socialist ecology that makes the category of reproduction,
rather than production, central to the concept of a just, sustainable world."[60]

Interestingly, Merchant characterizes ecofeminist activists in the two arenas of "cultural ecofeminism" and "socialist ecofeminism" as having distanced, but not equally distanced, relations to "theory." (Even more interesting and amazing, she lists *no* forms of activism under social ecology,
completely eviscerating their considerable activism from "social ecologists"
like Ynestra King, Ariel Salleh, and Chaia Heller.) Before listing protests
against nuclear radiation, pesticides, herbicides, hazardous wastes, household
chemicals, nuclear power plants, and nuclear weapons, Merchant says:
"Much populist ecological activism by women, while perhaps not explicitly
ecofeminist, implicitly draws on and is motivated by the connection between
women's reproductive biology (nature) and male-designed technology (culture)."[61] Discussing Native American women's organizing against uranium
mining and resulting birth abnormalities, she provides this implicit explanation for placing Native American feminist environmentalists in the category
"cultural feminism": "Native American women . . . recognized their responsibilities as stewards of the land and expressed respect for 'our Mother Earth
who is a source of our physical nourishment and our spiritual strength.'"[62]
Thus, "cultural ecofeminist" activists have either an implict, or "spiritual,"
grasp of "theory."

The Third World and Second World activists she cites as examples of "socialist ecofeminism," on the other hand, are characterized as conducting actions based either on critiques of development and industrial capitalism or on
Marxist theory, respectively. Yet the quotes Merchant uses to demonstrate
these theoretical positions differ little from the position she has characterized
as "cultural ecofeminism." Here are a few examples. She quotes Vandana
Shiva as saying: "The life-enhancing paradigm [of forestry] stems from the forest and the feminine principle; the life-destroying one from the factory and
the market."[63] From Isabelle Letelier: "Women give life. We have the capacity
to give life and light. We can take up our brooms and sweep the earth."
Gizelda Castro says: "Men have separated themselves from the ecosystem."[64]
And as for women environmentalists in the Second World, Merchant quotes
Eugenia Afanasieva as saying: "It seems to me that women are more active in
environmental programs than men. We give birth to our children, we teach
them to take their first steps. We are excited about their future."[65] These examples create significant confusion between positions putatively ascribed to
"cultural ecofeminism" and "socialist ecofeminism," making the latter position, once it attempts to indicate examples of appropriate forms of activism,
sound as "essentialist" as the first. The (anti-essentialist and therefore "superior") *theory* of socialist ecofeminism is thus portrayed as *outside* the activist
practice of Third and Second World women, while the (essentialist and therefore "inferior") *theory* of cultural ecofeminism is allowed to directly motivate
the efforts of almost all of the activists she uses as examples.

What I think is going on here is that "essentialisms" of universalisms and unified categories are embedded in activist practice and rhetoric; indeed, these are often indicators of the *theorizing* going on *within* and *through* activist practice, a notion I call "direct theory."[66] That is, the unified categories of "women" are constructed by environmentalist activists to signal and analyze the complicity of masculinism with projects of environmental destruction. Used as a tool to mobilize people on the basis of a collective subjectivity to take action *now* (wherever that particular "now" is historically located), these unified categories slide into a universalism, an argument that the present conditions under which they struggle are applicable over a wide range of cultural differences and historical specificities. To separate oneself from this form of "direct theory" is to separate oneself from the activist component of ecofeminism—or of feminism, for that matter. This is precisely the effect of Merchant's typology, in which "socialist ecofeminism" gains the high ground by distancing itself, especially in its guise as a "theory," from ecofeminist and environmental activism by women (a move that produces the troubling impression that white socialist feminism is the theory, and the environmental justice movement is the practice[67]).

Many of the other typologies generated by ecofeminist theorists in order to identify a nonessentialist ecofeminism make moves similar to Merchant's, especially in placing ecofeminist activism under the rubric of "cultural ecofeminism." This is especially true when they rely upon Merchant's typology for their own distinctions between an essentialist and a nonessentialist ecofeminism. Roger J.H. King, for example, characterizes "essentialist" or "radical" ecofeminism as having "a logic that can link a woman's relation to her reproductive nature to a relation to the environment more generally. Articulating this logic, many ecofeminists have focused on those aspects of environmental destruction that impinge directly or indirectly on women's reproductive nature, that is, on the consequences of the environmental crisis for individual and local community health and the conditions necessary for nurturing the life and growth of future generations of human beings."[68] Relying on Merchant's typology, King goes on to put a variety of ecofeminist actions within the category of "essentialist ecofeminism." "The link between women and biological reproduction," he states, "leads ecofeminists to address the consequences of nuclear radiation, toxic wastes, household chemicals, pesticides, and herbicides for women's reproductive organs, for pregnant women, and for children. But, as [Merchant] also notes, 'A politics grounded in women's culture, experience, and values can be seen as reactionary.'"[69] On the other hand, in describing "conceptualist ecofeminism" (King's nonessentialist version of ecofeminism), he does not refer to any activist component; instead, Karen Warren's work stands in for the "conceptualist" position.

Interestingly, King's depiction of an "essentialist" logic found in "women's reproductive capabilities" that motivates ecofeminist actions is usefully reformulated by Giovanna di Chiro, who describes the impetus for the activism of women of color and working-class women in the environmental justice movement: "Although most of the women in the environmental justice movement will, to some degree, assert that they are acting on behalf of the well-being of their children, their identity as simply 'mothers' is by no means always the central focus of their activism."[70] Rather, she argues, women in the environmental justice movement see their activism as a defense of *community* survival, not just the survival of their own individual children, and in the course of their activism, "they break down traditional constructions of gender, race, and class and construct new empowered identities and political agencies."[71] Once again, a characterization of environmental activism by women as stemming from a "maternalist" and therefore "essentialist" politics (in this case King's) misses the element of the tactical construction of collective identities and the use of such identities to "read" configurations of power that Sandoval claims is the provenance of the "differential consciousness" deployed especially by women of color, such as the environmental justice activists di Chiro has studied, who are deeply engaged in the projects of activism King lists above. It is interesting that theories of activism stemming from collective identities located in community and family are generated out of the environmental justice movement, the majority of whose activists are women of color and working-class women of all races.

Not all of the ecofeminist typologies I've placed in my chart above end up placing "activists" in the essentialist category and "theorists" in the anti-essentialist category, and not all of them make women of color invisible as feminist theorists. Still, these typologies often create oddities of attribution in the course of their effort to demonstrate that not all ecofeminism can be characterized as "essentialist."

One of the most charming and useful typological presentations of ecofeminism, one which I cannot by its nature adequately depict here, is Greta Gaard's illustration of the relation of different ecofeminisms to different feminisms in her video, *Ecofeminism Now!*[72] As the camera zooms in on the words "labor, environmentalism, peace/antinuclear, animal rights," the narrator says: "While people have come to ecofeminism from different paths of activism and spirituality [note that they do not come from academia, necessarily], feminism has provided the defining contours." The camera then pans a range of mountains (appropriately, the Grand Tetons), while the narrator says: "Imagine the several varieties of feminism as if they were mapped onto the land itself." Then we are shown a picture of a mountain range, with each mountain labeled with a variety of feminism: liberal, radical, womanism, socialism, anarchism. The narration resumes: "From these mountains of feminist thought, various streams have contributed to the lake of ideas that is ecofeminism." From the stream of "radical feminism," we get the tributaries "animal ecofeminism," "radical ecofeminism," and "spiritual ecofeminism (goddess worship)"; the three areas are represented by Josephine Donovan,

Marti Kheel, and Carol Adams, all firmly located in the area "animal ecofeminism" by their comments. We are left to wonder about "radical ecofeminism" and "spiritual ecofeminism," or to assume that "animal ecofeminism" incorporates them both. From the stream "anarcha-feminism," we get "social ecofeminism," eloquently articulated by Chaia Heller. From the stream "socialist feminism," we get "socialist ecofeminism," represented here by Vandana Shiva and Karen Warren. Unlike the early academic feminist typologies, Gaard acknowledges the special contribution of women of color to feminist theory by including the category "womanism, " but its legacy for ecofeminism is treated in a unusual way. From the stream "womanism," we get two tributaries: one, unremarked upon, leads to "socialist ecofeminism" (perhaps accounting for Shiva's presence there?); the other leads to a rock labeled "spirituality/politics." Thence ensues some comments on the unfortunate and unnecessary divide created by the opposition of spirituality and politics (from Deane Curtin and Karen Warren), closing with a comment from Winona LaDuke (whose ambivalent relation to ecofeminism I have had occasion to note a number of times previously) about the importance of spirituality to the environmental activism of Native American peoples. Finally, from liberal feminism, a stream flows down to a swamp located just on the margins of the lake of ecofeminism, entitled "liberal ecofeminism." Meanwhile the voiceover discusses the need for short-term "stop-gap" measures against environmental destruction, though stressing the point that liberal ecofeminism is not willing to undertake the radical economic and social transformation that is deemed necessary.

The next section of the video takes up varieties of ecofeminist activism. Gaard's typology differs from others I've just discussed in its willingness to recognize the centrality of activism to ecofeminist theory (perhaps explaining her inclusion of "womanism" and "anarchism" as categories of feminist theory?). She is unwilling to place activism in any one category of ecofeminism and thus reject it (except, perhaps, the "stop-gap" measures of liberal ecofeminism, which makes our swamp more pleasant without eliminating it—though one might speculate on the ecological necessity of swamps to lakes!). Her listed examples include antitoxics, labor, environmental justice, antibiotechnology, and indigenous rights activism. The representatives of this activism are Cathleen McGuire (part of a "guerrilla" activist group gathered around the newsletter entitled *EVE: Ecofeminist Visions Emerging*), Carol Adams (representing Feminists for Animal Rights), Judi Bari (who tells the story about women's action in the Northern California logging communities which I've recounted in chapter 1), Vandana Shiva (who comments on her work against the bioengineering of native seeds as well as mentioning Chipko), and Erica Briemer Kniepp (who discusses her work against breast cancer in the women's health movement). Finally, the camera focusses on the terms "labor/queer/environmental justice/anti-toxics" while the narrator emphasizes the need for coalitions with others struggling for social justice and environmental quality. Gaard's typology is framed by activism, beginning and ending with it, making it central to rather than separated from feminist theories.

Though clearly conflicted about the place of women of color in ecofeminism, the typologizing practice in this video (perhaps because, as a visual mode, it generates representations unavailable to the written mode) keeps the question about what constitutes the "best" ecofeminist theory up in the air, and highlights the necessity for activism when and where possible, emphasizing the urgent need for coalitions rather than generating a "correct" approach owned by one variation of ecofeminism. This creates possibilities in ways not found in typologies built around the goal of distinguishing essentialist and nonessentialist forms of ecofeminism; perhaps *because* of its focus on the activist imperative, Gaard's typology cannot afford to rule out any version for its theoretical insufficiencies.

In arguing that typologies create exclusions through their distinctions between kinds of feminist theories, I don't want to be seen as eliminating the necessary and useful task of creating unified categories of feminisms in order to make discriminations between ways of conceiving and acting against sexism. I am arguing not against analysis, critique, or debate; nor am I claiming that there are no useful distinctions to be made. I am arguing against a certain pattern of exclusion, embedded in early efforts of feminist typologizing that arose out of a particular historical moment in second-wave feminism. This pattern, overlaid on a dynamic and changing movement, has continued to exclude the overlapping categories of feminist activists, women of color, and working-class women from the arena of "feminist theory," which has become the provenance of academic feminism. Without claiming they are the same, I find typologies like Gaard's and Sandoval's to be more useful, for their making activism and the need to continually strategize against power central to their terms, In particular, Sandoval's "topography," which sees distinct ways of understanding domination as tools—rather than as fixed, competitive, and exclusive locations—seems a more descriptive, hopeful, and powerful way of understanding the crucial tasks before us as feminist theorists and activists.[73]

IS ECOFEMINISM FEMINIST?
OR IS FEMINISM ECOFEMINIST?

Other typologies of ecofeminism concentrate on whether or not ecofeminism is *feminist*. This is the move made by Seager, Agarwal, and Alaimo, provocatively included in my chart of ecofeminist typologizers above. All three, in different ways, support the project of connecting feminism with environmentalism but reject a reductively portrayed ecofeminism as "essentialist," and hence present themselves as "outside" ecofeminism and "inside" feminism.

Both Seager and Alaimo critique forms of "essentialism per se" or biologistic arguments, and "universalism," or positing one experience as universally applicable, which they find in a very selectively depicted "ecofeminism." Given the widespread effort by many ecofeminists themselves to argue against "essentialism per se," all three typologies engage in some rather peculiar acts of naming and renaming in order to conduct their arguments. Seager, for instance, uses Ynestra King (in my account, the person who coined the term "ecofeminism" in the U.S. context) to argue against "ecofeminism's" supposed positive revaluation of the woman/nature equation.[74]

Alaimo's article is a brilliant and lively analysis of "essentialist ecofeminism," but her reductive definition of ecofeminism as essentialist is curious, especially since she relies at crucial points on critiques of such essentialism by other ecofeminists (notably Ariel Salleh,[75] Stephanie Lahar, and Carolyn Merchant). She also characterizes Donna Haraway's work as an outsider's critique of "ecofeminism": "The writings of Donna Haraway and the texts of ecofeminism offer radically different approaches to negotiating a feminist environmentalism."[76] While Haraway has certainly been critical of essentialism (including all three versions Ferguson identifies), her critiques of essentialist moves have not been limited to nor applied to a reductive characterization of "ecofeminism," and she has at a number of points placed herself inside "ecofeminism." Indeed, Haraway has been explicitly interested in expanding the purview of ecofeminism from within. Alaimo's characterization of one of Haraway's arguments against "holism, appreciation of intuitive method, presence of matriarchal myth systems and histories of women's cultural innovation," as an explicit critique of "ecofeminism"[77] is misleading, since Haraway, in the piece referenced, is writing more broadly about a number of elements within "western feminism" that turn toward the "organic" in order to critique western patriarchy. Haraway's citation for this point includes only one "ecofeminist," Carolyn Merchant,[78] whom Haraway does not identify as such and whom Alaimo herself wants to exclude from "ecofeminism" because she cannot characterize her as an essentialist. Some have taken Haraway's last sentence from "The Cyborg Manifesto" as a specific repudiation of ecofeminism: "Though both are bound in the spiral dance, I would rather be a cyborg than a goddess."[79] This is only true if one believes, à la Janet Biehl, that ecofeminism is no more than Goddess worship. As I have been demonstrating, the diversity of ecofeminism belies this reduction. Further, I understand Haraway's position, in binding together the cyborg and the goddess in the "spiral dance," as an argument that both have their uses, while her personal commitment is to an anti-essentialist, nonprimitivist ecofeminism. In "Situated Knowledges," Haraway suggests this reading of her position—once again, significantly, in the last sentence of the article: "Perhaps our hopes for accountability, for politics, for ecofeminism, turn on revisioning the world as coding trickster with whom we must learn to converse."[80] In later work,

Haraway continues to both claim the position of ecofeminist and to considerably expand its meanings.[81]

Agarwal, though in some ways less reductive than Seager and Alaimo in her portrayal of ecofeminism, also wants to define a feminist environmentalism outside of ecofeminism. Her analysis of ecofeminism provides a perfect example of Ferguson's point that critiques of "essentialism" slide too easily between different and incommensurable categories. Agarwal's complaints about ecofeminism are not initially centered on claims that it is "essentialist per se," nor, relying on Merchant, does she find it intrinsically "universalist." But when Agarwal summarizes the problems with ecofeminism, she moves from a complaint about the construction of "unitary categories" (Ferguson's third category of "essentialism," a critique of which she finds "untenable") through a complaint about universalism, to a complaint about essentialism per se.[82] This generates the result that ecofeminism, which up to this point Agarwal has not characterized (through her appreciation of Merchant) as inherently unable to overcome its universalistic tendencies, is now produced as "essentialist," unlike Agarwal's version of an appropriate "ecofeminist" theory, which she calls "feminist environmentalism."

Much of Agarwal's critique of ecofeminism parallels others that we have encountered before, critiques that can be answered by pointing to the variety of ecofeminist arguments as a demonstration that ecofeminism is not innately incapable of addressing questions of diversity, or producing historically specific arguments (positions which Agarwal herself allows at different points in her article). Other points of her critique, such as "the ecofeminist argument does not take into account women's lived material relationship with nature,"[83] sound hollow in the face of an ecofeminism that frequently bases its arguments on women's roles in agricultural production, health care, household work, child care, and consumer activity. Even when presented in problematically universalist terms (which I would not defend) that obscure their origins in white, middle-class, U.S. culture, ecofeminist accounts of women's rock climbing, women's relation to wilderness, women's gardening, and women's experiences with animals are all attempts to account for, describe, and theorize "women's lived material relationship with nature (though a very particular and unacknowledged raced and classed relationship)."[84]

Agarwal's questionable contention that ecofeminist accounts do not address the "materiality" of women's lives is related to her stronger claim, that ecofeminism "locates the domination of women and of nature almost solely in ideology, neglecting the (interrelated) material sources of this dominance (based on economic advantage and political power)."[85] The latter point is provocative, for if, as we have seen, typologists of ecofeminism have consistently organized out the activism of women engaged in issues affecting their communities and the materiality of their daily lives, what would be left would be a critique of ideology. What Agarwal does not consider here are the many ecofeminist writings not engaged in typologizing, that do in fact look at on the "materiality of women's lives." Indeed, this focus may lead them into claims about "women's experience," which Agarwal would reject for their universalism.

The remainder of Agarwal's article demonstrates the strength of an analysis that does pay attention to material questions and their interaction with various relations of power, and she is right that it is a kind of analysis that ecofeminists could engage in more frequently, an analysis that could considerably enrich ecofeminism as a political and theoretical position. But, shorn of her other critiques of ecofeminism, nothing in her "materialist" analysis could not be accomplished within ecofeminism as a feminist theoretical location.

Indeed, the same comment could be applied to Seager and Alaimo as well as to Agarwal. All three of these authors provide insightful, interesting, and wide-ranging arguments for the effectiveness and importance of engaging in both a feminist and environmentalist theoretical endeavor. Why insist on another name for an analysis that combines and connects feminism and environmentalism? Essentialisms of various kinds, as Ferguson has so carefully pointed out, are not avoided by changing the names of your theoretical positions. They are avoided by paying close attention to the exclusionary effects generated by the (inevitable, or at least very difficult to avoid) construction of unitary categories for the purposes of analysis. Or does avoiding "ecofeminism" have to do with the U.S. genesis of the term within activism, which displayed "essentialist" rhetoric in the course of political mobilization and actions? If so, anti-essentialist feminist theory will find itself continually cut off from activist efforts.

The effort represented here by these three articles, to portray ecofeminism as ultimately nonfeminist, is turned on its head by Karen Warren, whose typology's goal is to show that a feminism without an ecofeminist analysis is not adequately *feminist*. Here, Warren examines the four standard categories of feminism found in Jaggar's typology: liberal, Marxist, radical, and socialist. To these she adds a fifth category, "transformative feminism," which, reminiscent of Sandoval's "differential consciousness," operates *through* the other categories of feminism to

> expand on the traditional conception of feminism as "the movement to end women's oppression" by recognizing and making explicit the interconnections between all systems of oppression. In this regard, a transformative feminism would be informed by the conception of feminism which has been advanced by many black feminists and women in development. . . . A transformative feminism would acknowledge the social construction of knowledge and a conception of epistemology that takes seriously the felt experiences of women as a subordinate group—however different those experiences may be. . . . In this respect, it would reflect a commitment to what Iris Young calls "a politics of dif-

ference," viz., one that asserts the value and specificity of group difference in political theory and practice."[86]

Additionally, like Haraway's notion of the cyborg, Warren argues that a "transformative feminism would involve a rethinking of what it is to be human, especially as the conception of human nature becomes informed by a nonpatriarchal conception of the interconnection between human and nonhuman
nature."[87]

Warren makes these claims audaciously, suggesting that a "transformative
feminism" is one that "makes an eco-feminist perspective central to feminist
theory and practice."[88] Here is a typological move that intends to produce
"ecofeminism" as the "best" feminist theory. She bases this argument on the
claim that ecofeminism, with its "central project the unpacking of the connections between the twin oppressions of women and nature" and "by understanding how a patriarchal conceptual framework sanctions the oppression of
both women and nature," is in a position to show why 'naturism' (i.e., the
domination of nature) ought to be included among the systems of oppression
maintained by patriarchy. This opens the door for showing how, in Sheila
Collins' words, 'Racism, sexism, class exploitation, and ecological destruction
are four interlocking pillars upon which the structure of patriarchy rests.'"[89]

This is a bold move, and, as Warren says, "the stakes are high."[90] This is the
environmentalist intervention into feminism, the reverse of the process that
we investigated in chapter 1. Warren is arguing that environmentalism is not
just an important issue that feminists may be concerned with as it impacts
their lives, but that an environmentalist perspective is *theoretically* necessary
to feminism. By critiquing the culture/nature divide that upholds the "patriarchal logic of domination" from the side of nature—that is, accounting for
"naturism" as well as other forms of interlocking oppressions—Warren argues
that ecofeminism addresses "the conceptual and structural interconnections
between *all* forms of domination."[91]

Though I think Warren's argument persuasive on many points, Agarwal's
complaint about the emphasis in ecofeminism on ideological forms of generating oppression, rather than material means of domination, applies to
Warren's analysis here. For instance, Warren states: "Eco-feminism, therefore, encourages us to think ourselves out of 'patriarchal conceptual traps' by
reconceptualizing ourselves and our relation to the nonhuman natural world
in nonpatriarchal ways."[92] While "freeing the mind" is an important function
for radical politics, for which category of women (or men for that matter) is it
sufficient? Warren does make further arguments for the necessity of "making
connections with 'the revolution of insurgent people,'"[93] but this residue of a
certain idealism sits uncomfortably with the radical claims she makes here for
"transformative ecofeminism." Further, she does not qualify a "patriarchal
conceptual framework" as the particular Western, white, capitalistic ideology

which it in fact is. This critique is not meant to vitiate Warren's important contribution to ecofeminist theory, but rather to point to the effects of the way her argument is framed so that it can accomplish an environmentalist intervention into feminism.

Val Plumwood makes claims superficially similar to Warren's as to the explanatory and liberatory value of an ecofeminist theory dedicated to overcoming the culture/nature dualism residing at the heart of Western capitalist patriarchy, but she is more precise about that dualism's cultural, racial, and historical location. She also explicitly refuses the idea that ecofeminism should replace or subsume feminism, or that any form of oppression should be seen as foundational or primary.[94] Like Warren, she also argues that ecofeminism is the "third wave" in feminist theory, because, in its critical versions, it interrogates not only sexism, not only racism, classism, and heterosexism, but also the Western dualism of human/nature that constructs ideologies that justify the cross-cutting hierarchies of male/female, white/black, civilized/savage. However, Plumwood objects to arguments that "the alignment of women to nature [is] the entire basis and source of women's oppression . . . since women often stand in relatively powerless positions even in cultures which have not made the connection of women to nature or which have a different set of genderised dichotomies." Hence, she destabilizes the notion that the culture/nature dualism is foundational to sexism. "Nevertheless," she argues, "the association of women with nature and men with culture and reason can still be seen as providing much of the basis of the cultural elaboration of women's oppression *in the west.*"[95] One could still ask for more clarity, since the "west" (which, with it's "w" in lower case, seems to designate a region rather than a dominant ideology—however, this is more likely a copyeditor's doing than it is Plumwood's) contains within it many cultures and historical residues of cultures that did and do not partake of the dualisms Plumwood identifies and the forms of domination which she argues flows from them.[96] But certainly we would not want to argue against the notion that the contours of the racist, classist, imperialist, sexist forms of power that generate oppression and domination worldwide are deeply shaped by the dualistic Western classical and Enlightenment notions Plumwood is critiquing, especially in her examination of how the culture/nature dualism is also, importantly, a reason/nature dualism. Plumwood is also careful to show the ways in which the culture/nature dualism operates not primarily in terms of hierarchical value dualisms of male/female but instead is implicated across a range of kinds of domination: "The gulf between the rational and the non-rational, and the inferiority of the latter, can be used to support the supposed inferiority not just of women, but also slaves, people of other races and cultures ('barbarians') and those who perform manual as opposed to intellectual work."[97]

Both Warren and Plumwood's very differently inflected claims that ecofeminism is important to feminism, as I have indicated above, do important work in specifying the culture/nature dualism at the heart of white Western capitalist patriarchy as well as including crucial questions of environmental quality, sustainable economic practices, and the exploitation of nonhuman species within a feminist purview. The environmentalist intervention into feminism insists that essentializing nature and exploiting nature are as problematic in our world as "naturalizing" women, people of color, or working-class people.

But the emphasis on critiquing the culture/nature dualism can sometimes retain a static, ironically dualistic framework for theory. This is most clearly seen in Warren's argument, which moves easily from the statement that "there are important connections between the oppression of women and the oppression of nature"[98] to the assertion that "the twin oppressions of women and nature"[99] underlie the "patriarchal conceptual framework" that produces all varieties of domination (she specifically includes racism, classism, and imperialism along with sexism and naturism; she does not mention heterosexism or speciesism). Though she sees her goal as tying "the liberation of women to the elimination of all systems of oppression,"[100] her analysis privileges sexism and naturism as the foundational forms of domination, from which all the others flow. This assumption is common in ecofeminism, focused as it is on the related concepts and practices that produce sexism and environmental degradation. But it does not provide a flexible enough framework for understanding the shifting and complex connections between all forms of domination, particularly racism, classism, and heterosexism. With a residue of the search for a "root cause," Warren's "transformative" feminism, or ecofeminism, generates explanations of domination in which racism, classism, and heterosexism are *derivative* of the interaction between sexism and naturism. Rather, racism, classism or heterosexism could be analyzed as having complicated interrelationships with naturism on their own; or, even more in tune with the kinds of theories of simultaneous oppressions created by feminists of color, these various kinds of domination could be explored as having levels and layers of interrelation with incredible variations historically, economically, and cross-culturally. For instance, in what ways does a "patriarchal, naturist, racist, classist, heterosexist conceptual framework" produce notions of nature that are simultaneously raced and gendered, or in which mobile forms of capital require the naturalization of heterosexuality? How are some people culturally and politically situated in ways that confound the idea that domination always functions along a dual axis, with one group "up" and the other "down," as Warren puts it? What about those that are "up" in some cases at the same time that they are "down" in others? Beyond these theoretical questions, more attention could be paid to the mechanics of activist coalitions. At the moment, radical political theories of all kinds—feminist, antiracist, economic, queer, environmentalist—share an (unevenly theorized) agreement that all the forms of domination on which they reflect are interconnected. While theoretical and scholarly work will always be needed to articulate the nature of these interconnections, we need to put as much emphasis on the details of forming working, activist coalitions around them.

Both Warren and Plumwood, as well as a number of other ecofeminists, social ecofeminists, conceptual ecofeminists, critical ecological feminists, ecological feminists, feminist green socialists, environmental feminists, feminist environmentalists, feminist political ecologists, etc., agree that because the culture/nature dualism has done so much damage to humans, animals, and the earth, radical political theories must attempt to deconstruct this dualism. With Ynestra King, they argue the need for a "third direction," one that neither refuses the equation between women and nature nor celebrates it, but rather that refuses separation both from culture and from nature, and engages in political projects that dissolve and interrogate the boundaries between the two.[101]

These kinds of questions are also brought into view in Donna Haraway's work, which centrally engages the problems involved with the culture/nature divide, but through consistent attention to the boundary-constructing practices and transgressions, rather than through the fixed relations between two objects, which are the ongoing task of both power and resistance to it. Most usefully, her work persistently questions categories on both sides of operative dualisms, nature as much as culture, and brings in a focus on the human/machine dualism. This focus is crucially important to ecofeminism, especially in order to provide a balance between the often counterposed areas of wilderness and animals as against urban life and technology. This is a perspective that is much needed in an ecofeminism which frequently essentializes nature. For Haraway,

> nature is not a physical place to which one can go, nor a treasure to fence in or bank, nor as essence to be saved or violated. Nature is not hidden and so does not need to be unveiled. Nature is not a text to be read in the codes of mathematics and biomedicine. It is not the "other" who offers origin, replenishment, and service. Neither mother, nurse, nor slave, nature is not matrix, resource, or tool for the reproduction of man. Nature is, however, a *topos*, a place, in the sense of a rhetorician's place or topic for consideration of common themes; nature is, strictly, a commonplace. . . . Nature is also a *trópos*, a trope. It is figure, construction, artifact, movement, displacement. Nature cannot pre-exist its construction. This construction is based on a particular kind of move—a *trópos*, or "turn." . . . Nature is a topic of public discourse upon which much turns, even the earth."[102]

Haraway thus insists on a social constructionist perspective that resolutely interrogates the category "nature" while paying attention to nature conceived in Elizabeth Bird's terms as a "social actor."[103] Thus, Haraway's perspective should not be mistaken for an argument that "nature" is entirely constructed by human beings. Rather than supporting such a notion, which she claims is a "violent and reproductive artifactualism, in the form of a hyper-production-ism actually practiced widely throughout the planet,"[104] she argues that

> The actors are not all "us." If the world exists for us as "nature," this designates a kind of relationship, an achievement among many actors, not all of them human, not all of them organic, not all of them technological. In its scientific embodiments as well as other forms, nature is made, but not entirely by humans; it is a construction among humans and non-humans.[105]

This feminist and environmentalist perspective, which refuses to reinstati-ate the culture/nature split, might be playfully named "cyborg ecofeminism." This variant of ecofeminism would include Haraway's work as well as a number of other theorists of the relation between science, sexism, racism, and naturism. "Cyborg ecofeminism" is consciously built on Chela Sandoval's "cyborg feminism," but enacts an environmentalist intervention into her neologism that does not, I think, substantially alter its basic characteristics.[106] This is a renaming which does not have as its project policing the divides between essentialism and anti-essentialism, activism and theory, and that self-consciously does not desire to start its own school nor to install Haraway as the pre-eminent ecofeminist theorist. Rather I take up renaming as serious play, reversing the strategy of typologizing practices which create a divide between antiessentialist feminist environmentalism and essentialist ecofeminism by incorporating antiessentialist positions *within* ecofeminism. "Cyborg ecofeminism" is the variant that informed the theorizing of the affinity group "Surrogate Others," whose story began this book. It has as its motto: "Cyborgs for Earthly Survival!"[107] In Alaimo's words, it would envision "women and nature as political allies [emphasizing] the importance of women as political activists and [stressing] the agency of nature."[108] By challenging the perverse denial of the use of technologies as a masculinist mode of reproduction, cyborg ecofeminism intends to hold the military-industrial complex responsible for their "non-biological children," in Zoë Sofia's words, warning "the Pac-Men, those radiant incorporating heads who have our futures all scoped and scooped out for us, that if they don't start cleaning up all that waste they'd like to pretend they haven't created, we Earthlings will teach them some home truths about the role of recycling in the uroboric economy."[109]

BEYOND NAMING, TOWARD ACTION

"Cyborg ecofeminism," if it were to be created as another form of ecofeminism, would produce its own exclusions, contain its own theoretical insuffeciencies, just as all ecofeminist variants have done. For example, a "cyborg ecofeminism" would have to manage the problems encountered by the figure of the cyborg, which, given its strong articulation to masculinist uses in popular culture, science, and militarism, is a problematic feminist metaphor. But my argument throughout the book has been that we do not need to produce a new and more perfect ecofeminism, but rather to recognize as necessary the dance of critique and consolidation that is part of theorizing and political action; the dialectic of creating, deconstructing, and reforming political identities, new alliances, complex analyses, and creative oppositional strategies. Every theory aimed towards political change contains historically contingent arguments; each solution to political and theoretical problems will be historically transient. We should not cease our search for the most effective political strategies, theories, and practices; so, we should not cease our penchant for critique. But I think we must also recognize the dynamism of social change, and the necessity for strategic calculation in particular political circumstances. We must offer criticism in the spirit of constructive debate, not with the aim of destroying or trashing those who are our allies but keeping in sight the ways in which their intentions are similar to ours. Our most trenchant critiques should be aimed at concrete, material power relations, hegemonic discourses and practices, not at damaging already fragile and internally contested modes of opposition. This doesn't mean that we should avoid debate or disagreement within social movements (as if we could, as long as they are democratically structured!). But if we wait to have the perfect theory before joining popular oppositional movements, we shall surely fail. In my understanding, the most vital radical political theories develop in tandem with radical movement practice; one does not preceed the other.

So in the spirit of offering an agenda for ecofeminist theorizing in this particular historical conjuncture, I close with a series of suggestions which I construct explicitly as the wish list that is the real nature of the supposedly "best" theories in various typologies: the desired political theory and practice whose realization is always deferred toward the future because of the way in which actual policial theory and practice is (thankfully) a messy, imperfect, contested, and dynamic actuality. I focus on strategies, not goals, and concentrate primarly on those issues I've discussed in this book. I make suggestions for an unspecified "we," meaning those who want to work in alliance against sexism, racism, classism, heterosexism, neo-colonialism, transnational capitalism, ableism, naturism, and speciesism. And since it is a "wish list" (as I am reminded by watching my seven-year-old son, Hart, construct such lists) it does not pretend at all to completeness, but allows for the inevitability of future desires arising in the dynamism of historical time and from within the layers of the divisions that separate us.

We should recognize the stress on antiessentialism within feminist scholarship as a particular strategy for scholarship, both in terms of its production of useful feminist knowledges, but also in terms of its primary location in universities, where publication and teaching are two kinds of political action that may not require the production of collective identities in the same way community organizing does, but rather precisely the kind of deconstruction of identity politics that antiessentialist theories are good at.

We should use the insights of antiessentialist feminist theorizing to create more inclusive political coalitions, but not to prevent us from acting collectively as we urgently need to do in the present moment.

We should cultivate difference in our political organizations, but only or especially multiple kinds of difference that exceed or complicate the hegemonic binary differences created by racism, sexism, heterosexism, and classism.

We should bring radical activists and radical scholars together more frequently and in more places, working against the structures of academic knowledge production that maintain barriers between activism and scholarship (and force academic feminists to give up activism in order to get tenure!).

We should hone our tools of critique to a fine point, but also our ability to envision and articulate a practical, constructive radical politics.

We should use environmentalist politics as a fertile location for imagining the deployment of a new strategic and embodied politics, since the environment is not a political location closely tied to one embodied identity constructed by axes of naturalized hierarchies of value, like race, gender, class, or sexuality but it *is* an arena in which we can counter racism, sexism, classism, and heterosexism.

We should make it a priority to create active, ongoing coalitions between all kinds of ecofeminists with environmental justice movements, locally, globally and transnationally. This would require us to deal seriously with, as Haraway puts it, "the terrible political demands of understanding the deep specificities of local situations, [while] understanding the global not as just an additive collection of local points."[110]

Finally, we should fully engage in the interweaving of humor, irony, grace, resistance, struggle, and transformation that constitutes the best of political action.

Notes

INTRODUCTION

1. Elizabeth Bird, "The Social Construction of Nature: Theoretical Approaches to the History of Environmental Problems," *Environmental Review* 11(4) (Winter 1987): 255–64.

2. Deena Hurwitz, ed., *Walking the Red Line: Israelis in Search of Justice for Palestine* (Philadephia: New Society Publishers, 1992).

3. From Donna Haraway, "A Cyborg Manifesto: Science, Technology and Socialist-Feminism in the Late Twentieth Century," in *Simians, Cyborgs and Women: The Reinvention of Nature* (New York: Routledge, 1991), n. 6, p. 245. Haraway also recounts the story of the Surrogate Others and their worm in "The Promises of Monsters: A Regenerated Politics for Inappropriate/d Others," in Lawrence Grossberg, Cary Nelson, and Paula Treichler, with Linda Baughman and John Wise, eds., *Cultural Studies* (New York: Routledge, 1992), pp. 295–337.

4. From Cecile Jackson, "Women/Nature or Gender History? A Critique of Ecofeminist 'Development'," *Journal of Peasant Studies* 20(3) (April 1993); 398.

5. Here, of course, I am following Foucault's notion of "genealogy." For an explication of Foucault's use of the term, see David Shumway, *Michel Foucault* (Charlottesville: University Press of Virginia, 1989), especially pp. 107–113.

6. For an overview of resource mobilization (RM) theory see, Craig Jenkins, "Resource Mobilization Theory and the Study of Social Movements," *Annual Review of Sociology* 9 (1983): 527–53. Recent rethinkings of RM theory can be found in Aldon Morris and Carol Mueller, eds., *Frontiers of New Social Movement Theory* (New Haven: Yale University Press, 1992).

7. Some of the range of new social movement theory could be represented by Alain Touraine, *The Voice and the Eye* (Cambridge: Cambridge University Press, 1981); Alberto Melucci, *Nomads of the Present* (Philadelphia: Temple University Press, 1989); and various essays in Dieter Rucht, ed., *Research on Social Movements: The State of the Art* (Frankfurt, Germany/ Boulder, CO: Campus/Westview Press, 1991). See also Margit Mayer and Roland Roth, "New Social Movements and the Transformation to Post-Fordist Society," in Marcy Darnovsky, Barbara Epstein, and Richard Flacks, eds., *Cultural Politics and Social Movements* (Philadelphia: Temple University, 1995), pp. 299–319.

8. See Noël Sturgeon, "Theorizing Movements: Direct Action and Direct Theory," in Darnovsky et al., *Cultural Politics*; and Sturgeon's "Direct Theory and Political Action: The U.S. Nonviolent Direct Action Movement," Ph.D. dissertation, University of California, Santa Cruz, March 1991.

9. I thank Katie King for suggesting this "mystery story" trope.

10. I have learned a lot about the idea of the "outsider within" from Audre Lorde. See, for example, *Sister Outsider: Essays and Speeches* (Trumansburg, NY: Crossing Press, 1984).

11. See Katie King, *Theory in Its Feminist Travels: Conversations in U.S. Women's Movements* (Bloomington, IN: Indiana University Press, 1994).

12. I thank T. V. Reed for conversations that helped me clarify this point.

13. Especially in its treatment of "radical" or "cultural" feminism, a point to which I will return in chapter 6. For a brilliant discussion of these kinds of distortions of the history of feminisms in the U.S., see Katie King, *Theory in Its Feminist Travels*.

14. Trinh T. Minh-ha, *Woman, Native, Other: Writing Postcoloniality and Feminism* (Bloomington: Indiana University, 1989).

15. The term "oppositional consciousness" is first used in Chéla Sandoval, *Women Respond to Racism: A Report on the National Women's Studies Association Conference* (Oakland, CA: Center for Third World Organizing, n.d.), revised as "Feminism and Racism: A Report on the 1981 National Women's Studies Association Conference," in Gloria Anzaldua, ed., *Making Face, Making Soul: Haciendo Caras* (San Francisco: Aunt Lute, 1990), pp. 55–71.

16. The term is Judith Butler's, "Contingent Foundations: Feminism and the Question of 'Postmodernism'," in Judith Butler and Joan W. Scott, eds., *Feminists Theorize the Political* (New York: Routledge, 1992), pp. 3–21.

17. Teresa de Lauretis, "Upping the Anti (sic) in Feminist Theory," in Marianne Hirsch and Evelyn Fox Keller, *Conflicts in Feminism* (London and New York: Routledge, 1990), pp. 254–70.

18. For a discussion of the way in which "lesbian separatists" were characterized and dismissed as essentialist, see Katie King, "The Situation of Lesbianism as Feminism's Magical Sign: Contests for Meaning and the U.S. Women's Movement, 1968–1972," *Communication* 9 (1986): 65–91. For one recent criticism of the essentialism of feminist antimilitarism and ecofeminism, see Kathy Ferguson, *The Man Question: Visions of Subjectivity in Feminist Theory* (Berkeley: University of California Press, 1993), especially her section on "cosmic feminism," pp. 97–120. The conflation of activist politics, essentialist formulations of female identity, and "radical" or "cultural" feminism is apparent in many typologies of feminism and is addressed specifically in chapter 6.

19. See Elizabeth V. Spelman, *Inessential Woman: Problems of Exclusion in Feminist Thought* (Boston: Beacon, 1988).

20. Adrienne Rich, "Compulsory Heterosexuality and Lesbian Existence," *SIGNS* 5 (1980): 631–60; Angela Y. Davis, "Racism, Birth Control and Reproductive Rights," in *Women, Race and Class* (New York: Random House, 1981); Cherrie Moraga and Gloria Anzaldua, eds., *This Bridge Called My Back* (Watertown, MA: Persephone Press, 1981); Audre Lorde, "The Master's Tools Will Never Dismantle the Master's House," presented at the Second Sex Conference at Barnard in 1979, then printed in *This Bridge Called My Back*, pp. 98–101; Combahee River Collective, "A Black Feminist Statement," in Gloria T. Hull, Patricia Smith, and Barbara Smith, eds., *But Some of Us Were Brave: Black Women's Studies* (New York, Feminist Press, 1982), pp. 13–22; Carol S. Vance, ed., *Pleasure and Danger: Explorations of Female Sexuality* (Boston: Routledge and Kegan Paul, 1984). The Mohanty essay was originally read at a conference in 1983 (see King, *Theory in Its Feminist Travels*, p. 35); it can be found in Chandra Mohanty, Ann Russo, and Lourdes Torres, eds., *Third World Women and the Politics of Feminism* (Bloomington: Indiana University Press, 1991), pp. 51–80. Of course, many other books and articles could be cited to show different moments of a critique of Western, white, heterosexist, middle-class feminism; here I am just providing a few important touchstones.

21. For a rich discussion of this problem, see Elizabeth Spelman, *Inessential Woman*.

22. bell hooks, "Feminism: A Transformational Politic," in Deborah L. Rhodes, ed., *Theoretical Perspectives on Sexual Difference* (New Haven: Yale University Press, 1990), pp. 185–93, p. 188.

23. Judith Butler points out that there is much confusion over the terms "poststructuralism" and "postmodernism," as well as over who gets included within them. She finds the term "post-

modernism" to be particularly problematic, and prefers "poststructuralism." She remarks that the effort to lump several very different theorists within one or the other of these terms usually has as its object the dismissal of these theories and the various critiques of power that they enact. In contrast, she notes the usefulness of these kinds of theories, in similar ways as I summarize them above, for feminist theory, particularly the critique of foundationalism. Butler, "Contingent Foundations." An example of such a problematically reductionist critique of "poststructuralism" can be found in Barbara Epstein, "Why Poststructuralism is a Dead End for Progressive Thought," *Socialist Review* 25(2) (1995): 83–120. While Epstein and I share a concern that there is presently a divide between radical academics and movements, I don't share her assessment of "postmodernism" and I would not want my arguments here mistaken for hers.

24. Joan Scott, "Deconstructing Equality-Versus-Difference: Or, the Uses of Poststructuralist Theory for Feminism," in Hirsch and Keller, *Conflicts in Feminism*, pp. 134–48, esp. pp. 135–38.

25. Chandra Mohanty, "Under Western Eyes," p. 74.

26. Diana Fuss, *Essentially Speaking* (London and New York: Routledge, 1989), p. 21; her emphasis.

27. Fuss, pp. 19–20.

28. Fuss, p. 119.

29. Fuss, p. 6.

30. Cristina Crosby, "Dealing with Differences," in Judith Butler and Joan W. Scott, eds., *Feminists Theorize the Political* (New York: Routledge, 1992), pp. 130–47, p. 137.

31. Crosby, "Dealing with Differences," p. 140.

32. Joan Scott, "Experience," in Butler and Scott, *Feminists Theorize the Political*, pp. 22–40.

33. Jane Roland Martin, "Methodological Essentialism, False Difference, and Other Dangerous Traps," *SIGNS* 19(3) (Spring 1994); 637.

34. Martin, "Methodological Essentialism," p. 654.

35. Fuss, *Essentially Speaking*, p. 6; her emphasis.

36. bell hooks, "Feminism: A Transformational Politic," p. 190.

37. de Lauretis, "The Essence of the Triangle, or, Taking the Risk of Essentialism Seriously: Feminist Theory in Italy, the U.S., and Britain," *differences* 1 (Summer 1989): 3.

38. The quote in this sentence is from Teresa de Lauretis, "The Essence of the Triangle," p. 10. I deal extensively with the problems of certain typologies of feminism and ecofeminism in chapter 6.

39. Linda Alcoff, "Cultural Feminism versus Post-Structuralism: The Identity Crisis in Feminist Theory," *SIGNS* 13 (Spring 1988): 420. Katie King points out that Alcoff "assumes that one must stand in the place of 'woman' to make feminist politics" (King, personal communication, March 1996).

40. Rosi Braidotti, *Nomadic Subjects: Embodiment and Sexual Difference in Contemporary Feminist Theory* (New York: Columbia University, 1994), p. 34.

41. Butler, "Contingent Foundations," p. 7.

42. Alcoff's term.

43. Haraway's term.

44. Gayatri Spivak's term.

45. Ferguson's term. See Kathy Ferguson, *The Man Question: Visions of Subjectivity in Feminist Theory* (Berkeley: University of California, 1993).

46. Braidotti's term.

47. Chéla Sandoval's term. See Sandoval's "U.S. Third World Feminism: The Theory and Method of Oppositional Consciousness in the Postmodern World," *Genders* 10 (Spring 1991): 1–24; and her "New Sciences: Cyborg Feminism and the Methodology of the Oppressed," in Chris Hables Gray, with Heidi J. Figueroa-Sarriera and Steven Mentor, *The Cyborg Handbook* (New York: Routledge, 1995), pp. 407–422.

48. Chéla Sandoval, "Feminism and Racism."

49. hooks refers to the necessity of consciousness-raising groups in numerous places in her work, especially in the essay I have cited above, "Feminism: A Transformational Politic." See also

Marilyn Frye, "The Possibility of Feminist Theory," in Rhodes, *Theoretical Perspectives on Sexual Difference*, pp. 174. Chéla Sandoval also places the practice of consciousness-raising at the center of her description of the construction of feminist theory and political identities.

50. Val Plumwood, "Ecosocial Feminism as a General Theory of Oppression," in Carolyn Merchant, ed., *Ecology: Key Concepts in Critical Theory* (Atlantic Highlands, NJ: Humanities Press International, 1994): 207–219, P. 215.

51. Plumwood, "Ecosocial Feminism," p. 215–216.

52. Though I argue that certain movement structures are useful in that they destabilize essentialism and provide opportunities for alliances, I will not deal here with the question of other strategic consequences of these structures for radical movements. The disadvantages of these structures for the nonviolent direct-action movement have been sympathetically presented and critically evaluated by Barbara Epstein, *Political Protest and Cultural Revolution: Nonviolent Direct Action in the 1970s and 1980s* (Berkeley: University of California Press, 1991). In my study of the nonviolent antimilitarist direct-action movement, I deal at greater length with the question of the effectiveness of such movement structures and the way in which a form of "direct theory" (the construction of meaning through the use of particular organizational structures and political practices) intervenes in hegemonic processes. See Sturgeon, "Direct Theory and Political Action." In important ways, my argument in this study challenges many of the assumptions of Epstein's critique in *Political Protest*.

53. The term "public happiness" is Hannah Arendt's, which she uses to describe the intense feelings of delight, joy, and community found in collective political action, particularly during revolutions. See *On Revolution* (New York: Viking, 1965).

CHAPTER ONE

1. Ynestra King, personal communication, May 1990, repeated in several public speeches. The concept of ecofeminism as a "third wave" is echoed by Val Plumwood, who usefully qualifies the claim by stating: "It is not a tsunami, or freak tidal wave which has appeared out of nowhere sweeping all before it. Rather, it is prefigured in and builds on work not only in ecofeminism but in radical feminism, cultural feminism, and socialist feminism over the last decade and a half." *Feminism and the Mastery of Nature* (London and New York: Routledge, 1993), p. 39.

2. As I have mentioned in the Introduction, I do not see ecofeminism as a "social movement" in most traditional senses, i.e., a particular mobilization around a specific grievance that acquires organizational form. Neither do I see it purely as an "intellectual movement," the other way the term is often used—that is, a set of ideas elaborated by a school of thinkers and writers.

3. This definition paraphrases Greta Gaard, "Living Interconnections with Animals and Nature," in *Ecofeminism: Women, Animals, Nature* (Philadelphia: Temple University Press, 1993), pp. 1–12, p. 1.

4. Donna Haraway, a white socialist feminist deeply influenced by poststructuralism, explicitly aligns herself with ecofeminism in "Situated Knowledges: The Science Question in Feminism and the Privilege of Partial Perspective," in *Simians, Cyborgs, and Women: The Reinvention of Nature* (New York: Routledge, 1991), p. 201, and in Haraway's interview with Marcy Darnovsky entitled, "Overhauling the Meaning Machines," *Socialist Review* 21:2 (1991): 65–84, esp. 69–70, 78. Mary Daly's radical feminist classic, *Gyn/Ecology* (Boston: Beacon Press, 1978; 1990) is now considered by many to be one foundation for ecofeminist theory. Alice Walker, a prominent best-selling African American writer, has contributed explicitly to ecofeminist antimilitarist and animal liberationist concerns, most clearly through her pieces, "Only Justice Can Stop a Curse," in *In Search of Our Mother's Gardens* (San Diego: Harcourt Brace Jovanovich, 1983), pp. 338–42, and "Am I Blue?" in *Living By The Word* (San Diego: Harcourt Brace Jovanovich, 1988), pp. 3–8. Rachel Carson, a natural scientist who was not an explicit feminist, is claimed as an ecofeminist foremother because of her book, *Silent Spring*, which arguably intitiated the first nonconservationist environmental movement in America (see Grace Paley's dedication to

Rachel Carson in Irene Diamond and Gloria Feman Orenstein, eds., *Reweaving the World: The Emergence of Ecofeminism* [San Francisco: Sierra Club Books, 1990], p. ii). Starhawk, a pagan, witch, activist in the nonviolent antimilitarist direct-action movement, writer, and theorist, has been an important influence on ecofeminism; see her *Dreaming the Dark* (Boston: Beacon Press, 1982), *The Spiral Dance: A Rebirth of the Ancient Religion of the Great Goddess* (San Francisco: Harper & Row, 1988), and *Truth or Dare* (San Francisco: Harper & Row, 1985). Vandana Shiva is a theoretical physicist who is also the director of an environmental research institute in Dehra Dun, India; her book *Staying Alive: Women, Ecology and Development in India* (London: Zed Press, 1988) is an important ecofeminist text.

5. However, my description is not simply an arbitrary construction. Both my own participation in the ecofeminist movement as an activist and theorist since 1984, and my experience as the editor of *The Ecofeminist Newsletter* (published annually from 1990–1996), gives me a broad and immediate sense of the movement and ongoing personal contact with a wide variety of people who call themselves "ecofeminists." In the following section of this chapter, I deliberately avoid the typologizing of ecofeminisms as radical, cultural, Marxist, socialist, and poststructuralist for reasons I will address in chapter 6. Here, I will just say that such typologies would work against the genealogical method I employ in this chapter.

6. The term "genealogy" in its current usage is derived from Nietzsche via Michel Foucault in the latter's essay, "Nietzsche, Genealogy, History," in D. F. Bouchard ed., *Language, Counter-Memory, Practice*, trans. by D. F. Bouchard (Ithaca, NY: Cornell University Press, 1977), pp. 139–64.

7. The last few years have seen a rapid increase in the literature on ecofeminism, in the context of a growing body of environmental literature. An analysis of the publication history of ecofeminist literature indicates a trend from more marginal "movement-oriented" publications to more scholarly journals and university presses. Journals that have devoted special issues to the topic are: *Heresies* 13 (1981); *New Catalyst* 10 (Winter 1987–88); *Woman of Power* (Spring 1988); *Studies in the Humanities* 15(2) (1988); *Hypatia: Journal of Women and Philosophy* 6(1) (1991); *American Philosophical Assocation Newsletter on Feminism and Philosophy* 2 (Fall 1991); and *Society and Nature* 2(1) (1993). Besides those listed above, journals that have published numerous articles on ecofeminism include *Capitalism, Nature, Socialism; Environmental Ethics; Environmental Review; The Trumpeter; Women and Environments; Women's International Network News*; and *Women's Studies International Forum*. A partial, chronological listing of books on ecofeminism would include Rosemary Radforth Ruether, *New Woman/New Earth: Sexist Ideologies and Human Liberation* (New York, Seabury Press, 1975); Susan Griffin, *Women and Nature: The Roaring Inside Her* (San Francisco: Harper & Row, 1978); Elizabeth Dodson Gray, *Green Paradise Lost* (Wellesley, MA: Roundtable Press, 1979); Carolyn Merchant, *The Death of Nature: Women, Ecology and the Scientific Revolution* (San Francisco: Harper & Row, 1980); Brian Easlea, *Science and Sexual Oppression: Patriarchy's Confrontation with Women and Nature* (London: Weidenfeld and Nicholson, 1981); Leonie Caldecott and Stephanie Leland, eds., *Reclaim the Earth: Women Speak Out for Life on Earth* (London: The Women's Press, 1983); Andreé Collard with Joyce Contrucci, *Rape of the Wild: Man's Violence Against Animals and the Earth* (Bloomington: Indiana University Press, 1988); Vandana Shiva, *Staying Alive: Women, Ecology and Development in India* (London: Zed Books, 1988); Irene Dankelman and Joan Davidson, *Women and Environment in the Third World* (London: Earthscan Publications, 1988); Judith Plant, ed., *Healing the Wounds: The Promise of Ecofeminism* (Philadelphia: New Society Publishers, 1989); Carolyn Merchant, *Ecological Revolutions: Nature, Gender and Science in New England* (Chapel Hill: University of North Carolina Press, 1989); Irene Diamond and Gloria Feman Orenstein, eds., *Reweaving the World: The Emergence of Ecofeminism* (San Francisco: Sierra Club Books, 1990); Janet Biehl, *Finding Our Way: Rethinking Ecofeminism Politics* (Boston: South End Press, 1991); Carol Adams, *The Sexual Politics of Meat: A Feminist-Vegetarian Critical Theory* (New York: Continuum Press, 1991); Rosemary Radford Ruether, *Gaia and God: An Ecofeminist Theology of Earth Healing* (San Francisco: Harper & Row, 1992); Mary Mellors, *Breaking the Boundaries: Toward a Feminist Green Socialism* (London: Virago

Press, 1992); Greta Gaard, ed., *Ecofeminism: Women, Animals, Nature* (Philadelphia: Temple University Press, 1993); Carol Adams, ed., *Ecofeminism and the Sacred* (New York: Continuum Press, 1993); Val Plumwood, *Feminism and the Mastery of Nature* (New York: Routledge, 1993); Maria Mies and Vandana Shiva, *Ecofeminism* (London and Atlantic Highlands, NJ: Zed Press, 1993); Vera Norwood, *Made From This Earth: American Women and Nature* (Chapel Hill: University of North Carolina Press, 1993); Karen Warren, ed., *Ecological Feminism* (New York: Routledge, 1994); Irene Diamond, *Fertile Ground: Women, Earth, and the Limits of Control* (Boston: Beacon Press, 1994); Vandana Shiva, ed., *Close to Home: Women Reconnect Ecology, Health and Development Worldwide* (Philadelphia: New Society Publishers, 1994); Rosi Braidotti, Ewa Charkiewicz, Sabine Häusler, Saskia Wieringa, *Women, the Environment and Sustainable Development* (London: Zed Books, 1994); Carol Adams, *Neither Man nor Beast: Feminism and the Defense of Animals* (New York: Continuum Press, 1994); Vandana Shiva and Inguna Moser, eds., *Biopolitics: A Feminist and Ecological Reader on Biotechnoology* (London: Zed Books, 1995); Carol Adams and Josephine Donovan, eds., *Animals and Women: Feminist Theoretical Explorations* (Durham, NC and London: Duke University Press, 1995); Carolyn Merchant, *Earthcare: Women and the Environment* (London and New York: Routledge, 1996); Karen Warren, ed., *Ecological Feminist Philosophies* (Indianapolis: Indiana University Press/Hypatia, 1996), and Karen Warren, ed., *Ecofeminism: Women, Culture, Nature* (Bloomington: Indiana University Press, 1997). A number of books on ecofeminism are forthcoming at this writing, including Ynestra King, *Ecofeminism: The Reenchantment of Nature* (Boston: Beacon Press); Chaia Heller, *The Revolution That Dances: From a Politics of Desire to a Desirable Politics* (Littleton, CO: Aigis Publications). Manuscripts in process that I know of are those by Greta Gaard, *Ecological Politics: Ecofeminists and the Greens* (Philadelphia: Temple University Press, forthcoming); and Christine Cuomo (on ecofeminist ethics). For a sampling of the periodical literature on ecofeminism, see Carol Adams and Karen Warren, "Feminism and the Environment: A Selected Bibliography," *American Philosophical Association Newsletter on Feminism and Philosophy* 90(3) (Fall 1991): 148–57. A popular interest in ecofeminism is indicated by special issues of *The Utne Reader* 36 (November/December 1989) and *Ms.* 2(2) (1991); the sporadic, uneven column on ecofeminism in *Ms.*; as well as the growing interest in ecofeminism evinced by trade publishers (Beacon, Harper & Row, Vintage, etc.). The word "ecofeminism" became a Library of Congress subject heading around 1992.

8. The most thorough historian of ecofeminism to date is Carolyn Merchant. See her section entitled "Ecofeminism," in *Radical Ecology: The Search for A Livable World* (New York: Routledge, 1992), pp. 183–210, and *Earthcare: Women and the Environment* (New York: Routledge, 1995), especially the chapters "Earthcare: Women and the American Environmental Movement" (pp. 139–166) and "Conclusion: Partnership Ethics: Earthcare for a New Millennium" (pp. 209–224). Other accounts of ecofeminism's beginnings and development can be found in Ynestra King, "The Eco-Feminist Imperative," in Caldecott and Leland, eds., *Reclaim the Earth*, pp. 12–16, and "Ecological Feminism" *Z Magazine* 1(7/8) (1988): 124–27; Charlene Spretnak, "Ecofeminism: Our Roots and Flowering," in Diamond and Orenstein, *Reweaving the World*, pp. 3–14; Braidotti et al., "Ecofeminism: Challenges and Contradictions," in *Women, the Environment and Sustainable Development*, pp. 161–168; and Greta Gaard and Lori Gruen, "Ecofeminism: Toward Global Justice and Planetary Health," *Society and Nature*, 2(1) (1993): 1–35. Many of these accounts (except for King's) start with the coining of the word "ecofeminism" in 1974 by Françoise d'Eaubonne and cite her *Le Féminisme ou la Mort* (Paris: Pierre Horay, 1974), though Braidotti cites "Feminism or Death?" in Elaine Marks and Isabelle de Courtivron, eds., *New French Feminisms: An Anthology* (Amherst: University of Massachusetts Press, 1980), pp. 64–67. Aside from the 1980 essay cited above, which does not explicitly mention ecofeminism, d'Eaubonne's work was not available in English translation until 1994, in an essay translated by Ruth Hottel as "The Time for Ecofeminism," in Carolyn Merchant, ed., *Key Concepts in Critical Theory: Ecology* (Atlantic Highlands, NJ: Humanities Press, 1994), pp. 174–97. Though undoubtedly d'Eaubonne's 1974 formulation was an early use of the term, since her work was not available in English translation until 1994, the notion of her authorship of the term appears to

have been introduced by Karen Warren in "Toward an Ecofeminist Ethic," *Studies in the Humanities* 15 (1988): 140–56; after that, D'Eaubonne appears as the coiner of the word in most accounts. Since d'Eaubonne's formulation enters histories of U.S. ecofeminism well after the word comes to signify a set of interlocking concerns about the status of women and degradation of the environment articulated by feminist antimilitarist activists in 1980, I am inclined to give Ynestra King the credit for the invention of the word in its U.S. context. Ariel Salleh comments that the delay in translating d'Eaubonne to English signifies the U.S. imperialist context of the production of feminist knowledge, while centering d'Eaubonne as the founder of ecofeminism in turn closes off possible nonWestern origins for the word. She states that "the term 'ecofeminism' (was) spontaneously appearing across several continents in the 1970s" but for "politico-economic reasons . . . , ecofeminists working from more visible niches in the dominant English-speaking culture have tended to get their views broadcast first." See Salleh's book review of Vandana Shiva's *Staying Alive, Hypatia* 6(1) (1991): 206.

9. My thanks to Ann Megisikwe (Ann Filemyr) (who, along with Marjaree Chimera, edited *W.E.B*) for telling me about the newsletter and providing me with copies. Another important ecofeminist newsletter was *E. V. E.* (Ecofeminist Visions Emerging) published in NYC by Cathleen and Colleen McGuire from 1991–1993. The newsletter I edit, *The Ecofeminist Newsletter*, was a similar effort. Back issues (1990, 1991, 1992, 1993, 1994, and 1996), are available from Noël Sturgeon, Women's Studies, Washington State University, Pullman, WA, 99164-4007, USA. Because of the widespread, grassroots, and decentralized nature of the early period of ecofeminism's development, it is extremely difficult to track down materials documenting the movement. It is very likely that there were many more groups and publications than I name in this section.

10. See Spretnak, "Our Roots and Flowering," for a fuller list of organizers; also see Barbara Epstein, *Political Protest and Cultural Revolution: Nonviolent Direct Action in the 1970s and 1980s* (Berkeley: University of California Press, 1991), p. 161.

11. Ynestra King, "Where the Spiritual and Political Come Together," *Women For Life on Earth* (Winter 1984): 4. King has given different figures in "What Is Ecofeminism?" *The Nation* (December 12, 1987): 730, claiming 800 attendees and 200 workshops. I am inclined to stick to the description dated closer to the conference itself.

12. CCHW is presently an important group in the environmental justice movement.

13. Other speakers were Ynestra King and Catherine Carlotti. I am citing speakers whose speeches I have copies of, but there were many more. I thank Riley Dunlap for lending me his archive on Women and Life on Earth.

14. *Tidings* (May 1981): 1–16.

15. Anna Gyorgy, "Evaluating Eco-Feminism West Coast," *Tidings* (May 1981): 14.

16. *Women for Life on Earth* (Winter 1984): 58–59.

17. The Unity Statement, including its original illustrations depicting women of all races and ages, has been reprinted in Lynne Jones, ed., *Keeping the Peace* (London: Women's Press, 1983), pp. 42–43. For descriptions of the action, see Ynestra King. "All is Connectedness," in *Keeping the Peace*, pp. 40–63, and Rhoda Linton and Michele Whitham, "With Mourning, Rage, Empowerment and Defiance: The 1981 Women's Pentagon Action," *Socialist Review* 12(3/4) (1982): 11–36

18. For a discussion of the complex political agenda of the WPA, see T. V. Reed, "Dramatic Ecofeminism: The Women's Pentagon Action as Theater and Theory," in *Fifteen Jugglers, Five Believers: Literary Politics and the Poetics of American Social Movements* (Berkeley: University of California Press, 1992), pp. 120–141. In particular, the WPA actions were criticized for the "essentialism" of their rhetoric connecting women and nature. See Ellen Willis's columns in *The Village Voice* 25(25) (June 18–24, 1980): 28 and 25(29) (July 16–22, 1980): 34. Additionally, and more relevant to my argument in chapter 3, many feminist activists of color identified the feminist antimilitarist movement as a white-dominated movement.

19. Particularly Griffin's *Women and Nature: The Roaring Inside Her* (New York: Harper & Row, 1978).

20. Especially as the editor of *The Politics of Women's Spirituality: Essays on the Rise of Spiritual Power Within the Feminist Movement* (New York: Anchor Books, 1982).

21. An important ecofeminist theorist, King has usefully collected many of her classic essays in *What is Ecofeminism?* (New York: Ecofeminist Resources, 1990), available from Ecofeminist Resources, c/o Women's Studies Program, Antioch College, Yellow Springs, OH 45387 for U.S. $3.50.

22. See Judith McDaniel, ed., *Reweaving the Web of Life: Feminism and Nonviolence* (Philadelphia: New Society Publishers, 1982), for several early formulations of the connections between feminism and environmentalism stemming from feminist antimilitarism. Note the reworking of this title in Diamond and Orenstein's explicitly ecofeminist anthology, *Reweaving the World*.

23. Anonymous, *Tidings* (May 1981): 14.

24. See Irene Diamond and Gloria Feman Orenstein's description of the conference and its importance; "Ecofeminism: Weaving the Worlds Together," *Feminist Studies* 14 (Summer 1988): 368–70. There have been a number of important ecofeminist conferences since.

25. Greta Gaard's essay, "Toward a Queer Ecofeminism," thus promises to break new and exciting ground when it is published (*Hypatia*, forthcoming). In this essay, she notes that "the May 1994 special issue of the Canadian journal *UnderCurrents* is the first to address the topic of 'Queer Nature.'" Gaard goes on (in n. 1) to note that though several of the essays in this special issue initiate an exploration of a "queer ecofeminism," none of them specifically develop connections between queer theory and ecofeminism, which is the purpose of her essay.

26. This position is especially common in the ecofeminist analyses that operate within the political and academic arena called "Women, Environment, and Development."

27. For a detailed description of the different theories useful to ecofeminism, see Greta Gaard and Lori Gruen, "Global Justice and Planet Health," *Society and Nature*, 2(1) (1993): 1–35.

28. Gwyn Kirk, "Blood, Bones, and Connective Tissue: Grassroots Women Resist Ecological Destruction," paper presented at the National Women Studies Association, Austin, June 1992; Giovanna Di Chiro, "Defining Environmental Justice: Women's Voices and Grassroots Politics," *Socialist Review* 22(4) (October–December 1992): 93–130.

29. I am thinking here especially of feminist analyses that were not explicitly ecofeminist in that they were oriented toward arguments that the nature/culture split produced social injustices, but without being concerned about environmental problems. See Sherry Ortner, "Is Female to Male as Nature is to Culture?" in Michelle Z. Rosaldo and Louise Lamphere, *Woman, Culture and Society* (Palo Alto, CA: Stanford, 1974), pp. 7–88. Ortner's article is often used as a basis for ecofeminist arguments or lumped together with ecofeminists by critics of ecofeminism. An especially useful analysis of the way in which a nature/culture dualism operates to produce sexism in Marxist and pyschoanalytic theories is Hilary Klein, "Marxism, Pyschoanalysis and Mother Nature," in *Feminist Studies* 15(2) (1989): 255–78.

30. Greta Gaard's forthcoming book on ecofeminism and the U.S. Greens will do some of this work. If I were to tell this story, I would focus on the intervention of the Ecofeminist Caucus at the Green Gathering at Eugene, Oregon, in 1989. For ecofeminist interventions into animal liberation, see the work of Marti Kheel, Carol Adams, and Deborah Slicer. Complex relations between ecofeminism and the animal rights movement are also suggested by Carol Adams's story in the introduction to *Ecofeminism and the Sacred*, in which she expresses her initial doubts about the word "ecofeminist," as well as the debate within the journal *Feminists for Animal Rights* about whether to change the name of the journal to *Ecofeminists for Animal Rights*.

31. Murray Bookchin, "Looking for Common Ground," in Steve Chase, ed., *Defending the Earth: A Dialogue Between Murray Bookchin and Dave Foreman* (Boston: South End Press, 1991), p. 27.

32. Murray Bookchin, "Open Letter to the Ecology Movement," in *Toward an Ecological Society* (Montreal: Black Rose Books, 1980), reprinted in Andrew Dobson, ed., *The Green Reader* (San Francisco: Mercury Books, 1991), p. 60.

33. Epstein, *Political Protest and Cultural Revolution*, pp. 58–91; and Noël Sturgeon, "Direct

Theory and Political Action: The Political Theory of the U.S. Nonviolent Direct Action Movement," Ph.D. dissertation, History of Consciousness Program, University of California, Santa Cruz, March 1991, passim.

34. Murray Bookchin, "Ecology and Revolutionary Thought," in *Post-Scarcity Anarchism* (San Francisco: Ramparts Press, 1971), p. 63.

35. Frederick Engels, *The Origin of the Family, Private Property, and the State*, trans. Eleanor Leacock (New York: International Publishers, 1972).

36. Murray Bookchin, "The Concept of Social Ecology," originally published in *CoEvolution Quarterly* (Winter 1981): 15–22; reprinted in Merchant, *Key Concepts in Critical Theory: Ecology*: 152–162. The first quote here is p. 153, the footnote is p. 162, n. 1.

37. Published in 1982 by Cheshire Books, the first four chapters of *Ecology and Freedom* were written in 1972. A revised edition with a substantial new introduction was published in 1991 by Black Rose Books in Montreal (all references here will be to this revised edition). The reworking and, even more, the amount of nonreworking of this text marks it as the most important statement of Bookchin's views, though he is a prolific writer. That he has returned to this text as a place both to reissue his early formulations and to qualify some of their implications indicates the importance he places on the book.

38. Bookchin, *Ecology of Freedom*, p. 75–77.

39. Bookchin, *Ecology of Freedom*, p. 79.

40. Bookchin, *Ecology of Freedom*, p. 83.

41. Bookchin, *Ecology of Freedom*, p. 83.

42. Bookchin, *Ecology of Freedom*, p. 120–121.

43. Bookchin, *Ecology of Freedom*, p. 305.

44. See on this point Plumwood, *Feminism and the Mastery of Nature*, p. 15.

45. See Epstein, *Political Protest and Cultural Revolution*; and Margot Adler, *Drawing Down the Moon* (New York: Beacon Press, 1986).

46. My account of the conflict within ISE over feminism, feminist spirituality, ecofeminism, and social ecology is based on interviews with Ynestra King and Chaia Heller in June 1995, as well as the published pieces I cite throughout this section.

47 King, Starhawk, and Adler's accounts of feminist spirituality's role in radical political action will be dealt with in more detail in chapter 4.

48. See Chaia Heller, "Down to the Body, Down to Earth: Toward a Social Ecofeminism," in Andrew Light, *The Environmental Materialist Reader* (Minneapolis: University of Minnesota, forthcoming).

49. Heller, rather than rejecting spiritually, reframes it in terms of the 'erotic.' As she has said: "I prefer to use the term 'eros' rather than the term 'spirituality,' which is derived from the latin term 'espiritus,' implying an external, non-physical activating principle such as the breath, which was thought to be required to animate an otherwise passive, inert body. The term 'eros,' in contrast, transcends a binary opposition between spirit and matter by referring to the attraction and connection between bodies. If 'spirituality' indicates a connection among people and to the earth, and the meaning that derives from those connections, then 'eros,' in its sexual and non-sexual form, might be a more integrative and dialectical term." Personal communication from Chaia Heller, November 1996. See Chaia Heller, *The Revolution That Dances: From a Politics of Desire Toward a Desirable Politics* (Littleton, CO: Aigis Press, forthcoming).

50. *Kick It Over* (special supplement) (Winter 1987): 2A–4A.

51. *Green Perspectives* 11 (October 1988): 1–8.

52. Janet Biehl, *Rethinking Ecofeminist Politics* (Boston: South End Press, 1991): 5.

53. Greta Gaard, in a review of Biehl's book in the Spring 1992 issue of *Women and Environments*, (pp. 20–21), credits Biehl with bringing up important concerns, notably the romanticization of "prehistory and the Neolithic Goddess," the biologistic rationale for the woman-nature connection, and the emphasis on personal transformation rather than social transformation in works by Riane Eisler and Charlene Spretnak. But she faults Biehl for ignoring important ecofeminists, her "unprofessional tone and . . . occasional lapses in scholarship," her definition of

patriarchy as "limited to sexism alone," and her "return to appeals for 'objectivity' and 'rationalism',"(p. 21).

54. A claim made by Charlene Spretnak in a letter criticizing Biehl that was circulated among radical environmentalist circles. Spretnak also emphatically denies valuing personal transformation above collective political action (contrary to Gaard's opinion cited above), and cites her activity in the U.S. Greens as proof of her commitment to social and political change rather than personal change alone. I published this letter in *The Ecofeminist Newsletter* 4(1) (Summer 1993): 3–4 (available from the Women's Studies Program, Washington State University, Pullman, WA, 99164–4007).

55. Douglas Buege, "Rethinking Again," in Karen J. Warren, ed., *Ecological Feminism* (London and New York: Routledge, 1994), p. 60.

56. It remains a contradiction that Bookchin could seem so open to many parts of a feminist analysis and that he could remain so supportive of ecofeminists like Heller, at the same time that he engages in such public, often vitrolic, attacks on an ecofeminism defined only as essentialist feminist spirituality. I will speculate here that one motivation may be his wish to distinguish his reliance on the notion of nonhierarchical "organic" societies as a model for the utopian "ecological" society from the romanticized prehistoric, Neolithic, and purportedly matricentric societies that function as ideals for some versions of feminist spirituality. Much of what Biehl says about the dangers of such idealization could be applied to Bookchin's use of the organic society, particularly given the universalistic, generalized portrayal which he constructs. Shelagh Young, in a relatively positive review of Biehl's book, also notes "an unnerving similarity between Biehl's enthusiastic espousal of Bookchin's theory and the work of ecofeminist writers," in the depiction of "organic" societies. Shelagh Young, in *Feminist Review* 48 (Autumn 1994): 130.

57. For a number of recent examinations of the connection, see Carol Adams, ed., *Ecofeminism and the Sacred* (New York: Continuum Press, 1993). Two theorists who have consistently connected ecofeminism and feminist spirituality, in ways that avoid many of the problems Biehl focusses on, are Elizabeth Dodson Gray, *Green Paradise Lost*; and Rosemary Radford Ruether, from her *New Woman, New Earth: Sexist Ideologies and Human Liberation* to her recent *Gaia and God: Toward an Ecofeminist Theology of Earth Healing*.

58. Karen Warren "A Feminist Philosophical Perspective on Ecofeminist Spiritualities," in Adams, ed., *Ecofeminism and the Sacred*, pp. 119–32, comes closest to acknowledging the tension between the two. She starts her essay: "Ecofeminists disagree about the nature and place of spirituality in ecofeminist politics and practice" (p. 119). But she is wary of taking up this debate directly. "My goal is modest," she writes. "I do not discuss the particular positions which have been advanced in the ecofeminist debate over spirituality . . . consequently I do not resolve that debate. . . . I simply attempt to offer a feminist philosophical perspective on how one might think about ecofeminist spiritualities such that one captures and extends important ecofeminist insights about the twin dominations of women and nature in ecofeminist philosophy" (p. 121). Ecofeminists have felt more comfortable criticizing the connection between ecofeminism and feminist spirituality, especially Goddess worship, when it is made by men. See Ynestra King's critique of Kirkpatrick Sale in *The Nation* (December 12, 1987): 702, 730–31; and Deborah Slicer's critique of Michael Zimmerman in "Is There an Ecofeminism-Deep Ecology 'Debate'?" *Environmental Ethics* 17 (Summer 1995): 151–69.

59. Plumwood, *Feminism and the Mastery of Nature*, pp. 15–16.

60. An exception to this would be Joni Seager, who, although she prefers the designation feminist environmentalist over ecofeminist, is centrally concerned with the connections between bureaucracy, government, corporations, sexism, and environmental degradation. However, this critique does not lead Seager to explicitly advocate anarchism. See Seager, *Earth Follies: Coming to Feminist Terms With the Global Environmental Crisis* (New York: Routledge, 1993).

61. Warwick Fox distinguished the two and argues for the use of "ecocentric" rather than "biocentric" in "The Deep Ecology-Ecofeminism Debate and Its Parallels," *Environmental Ethics* 11 (Spring 1989): 5–25, pg. 7–8.

62. But see the debate between Kirkpatrick Sale, Murray Bookchin, and Ynestra King in *The*

Nation in late 1987 and early 1988, as an example of the triangulation becoming manifest.

63. Val Plumwood is an exception to these characterizations. She has paid a great deal of attention to the conflict between all three positions, treating them all as worthy of consideration. See Plumwood, "The Ecopolitics Debate and the Politics of Nature, " in Warren, ed., *Ecological Feminism* pp. 64–87; and some of the same material in Plumwood, *Feminism and the Mastery of Nature*, pp. 13–18 and chapters 6 and 7.

64. The following articles concern themselves *primarily* with conflicts between deep ecology and ecofeminism. There are others not in this list that, in the context of arguments about other subjects, mention or briefly join in this debate. Ariel Kay Salleh, "Deeper Than Deep Ecology: The Eco-Feminist Connection," *Environmental Ethics* 6 (Winter 1984): 340–45; Marti Kheel, "The Liberation of Nature: A Circular Affair," *Environmental Ethics* (Summer 1985): 135–49; Donald Davis, "Ecosophy: The Seduction of Sophia," *Environmental Ethics* 8 (1986): 151–62; Alan Wittbecker, "Deep Anthropology, Ecology, and Human Order," *Environmental Ethics* 8 (1986): 268–70; Michael E. Zimmerman, "Feminism, Deep Ecology, and Environmental Ethics," *Environmental Ethics* 9 (Spring 1987): 21–44; Jim Cheney, "Ecofeminism and Deep Ecology," *Environmental Ethics* 9 (Summer 1987): 115–45; Ynestra King, "What is Ecofeminism?" *The Nation* (December 12, 1987): 702, 730–31; Warwick Fox, "The Deep Ecology-Ecofeminism Debate and Its Parallels,"; Jim Cheney, "The Neo-Stoicism of Radical Environmentalism," *Environmental Ethics* 11 (Winter 1989): 293–325; Marti Kheel, "Ecofeminism and Deep Ecology: Reflections on Identity and Difference," in Diamond and Orenstein, eds., *Reweaving the World*, pp. 127–37; Michael E. Zimmerman, "Deep Ecology and Ecofeminism: The Emerging Dialogue," in Diamond and Orenstein, eds., *Reweaving the World*, pp. 138–54; Val Plumwood, "Nature, Self, and Gender: Feminism, Environmental Philosophy and the Critique of Rationalism," *Hypatia* 6 (Spring 1991): 3–27; Robert Sessions, "Deep Ecology versus Ecofeminism: Healthy Differences or Incompatible Philosophies?" *Hypatia* 6 (Spring 1991): 90–107; Ariel Salleh, "The Ecofeminism/Deep Ecology Debate: A Reply to Patriarchal Reason," *Environmental Ethics* 14 (Fall 1992): 195–216; Ariel Salleh, "Class, Race, and Gender Discourse in the Ecofeminism/Deep Ecology Debate," *Environmental Ethics* 15 (Fall 1993): 225–44; Val Plumwood, "The EcoPolitics Debate," in Warren, ed. *Ecological Feminism*, pp. 64–87; Christine J. Cuomo, "Ecofeminism, Deep Ecology, and Human Population," in Warren, ed., *Ecological Feminism*, pp. 88–105; Deane Curtin, "Dogen, Deep Ecology, and the Ecological Self," *Environmental Ethics* 16 (Summer 1994): 195–213; and Deborah Slicer, "Is There an Ecofeminism-Deep Ecology 'Debate'?" *Environmental Ethics* 17 (Summer 1995): 151–69.

65. Arne Naess, "The Shallow and the Deep, Long-Range Ecology Movement: A Summary," in Alan Drengson and Yuichi Inoue, eds., *The Deep Ecology Movement: An Introductory Anthology* (Berkeley, CA: North Atlantic Books, 1995): 3–10, p. 3.

66. George Sessions, "Preface," in *Deep Ecology for the 21st Century: Readings on the Philosophy and Practice of the New Environmentalism* (Boston: Shambala, 1995), p. ix. Since the two anthologies I've just cited are both recent and intended as comprehensive introductions, I will rely on them as portrayals of deep ecology as a movement. As such, it is interesting to note the way in which Sessions's title claims deep ecology as "the new environmentalism," excluding other environmentalist positions from legitimate consideration. I will discuss this tendency of deep ecology to subsume other environmentalisms at several points in this section.

67. Drengson and Inoue, *The Deep Ecology Movement*, p. xx.

68. Drengson and Inoue, *The Deep Ecology Movement*, p. xxiv.

69. Note the imperative exclamation mark that Naess uses to indicate a normative statement containing a moral imperative to act; this form is copied by Earth First!, which always used the exclamation point in its name. I have not been able to establish whether this was an explicit mirroring of Naess.

70. All quotes in the paragraph from Naess, "The Deep Ecological Movement," p. 80.

71. Warwick Fox, "Transpersonal Ecology and the Varieties of Identification," in Drengson and Inoue, *The Deep Ecology Movement*, pp. 136–154.

72. Salleh, "Deeper Than Deep Ecology," p. 341.

73. See Christine J. Cuomo, "Ecofeminism, Deep Ecology, and Human Population," for a complex articulation of the ecofeminist critique of deep ecology's stand on population reduction.

74. Salleh, "Deeper Than Deep Ecology," p. 344.

75. Salleh, "Deeper Than Deep Ecology," p. 342.

76. Salleh, "Deeper Than Deep Ecology," p. 340.

77. Salleh, "The Ecofeminism/Deep Ecology Debate," p. 203.

78. Salleh, "The Ecofeminism/Deep Ecology Debate," pp. 208–209.

79. Salleh, "The Ecofeminism/Deep Ecology Debate," pp. 213–14.

80. Marti Kheel, "The Liberation of Nature," p. 138. It is important to note that Kheel's work is specifically a feminist intervention into the construction of a political and philosophical position called "animal liberation." If I had space, I would examine Kheel's work and the work of Carol Adams and Deborah Slicer as important variants of ecofeminism developed to critique the masculinist tendencies in animal liberation. As such, their work exhibits particular identifying qualities in the same way that ecofeminism within social ecology, deep ecology, and Earth First! may be seen to develop its own brand of feminist argument.

81. Kheel, "Ecofeminism and Deep Ecology," p. 129.

82. Ynestra King, "What is Ecofeminism," *The Nation* (December 12, 1987): 702.

83. King, "What is Ecofeminism," p. 730.

84. Cheney, "Eco-Feminism and Deep Ecology," p. 116.

85. Cheney, "Eco-Feminism and Deep Ecology," p. 121.

86. Cheney, "Eco-Feminism and Deep Ecology," pp. 126–27.

87. Cheney, "Eco-Feminism and Deep Ecology," p. 122.

88. Cheney, "Eco-Feminism and Deep Ecology," pp. 123–24.

89. Warren, "Feminism and Ecology: Making Connections," pp. 4–5.

90. Fox, "The Deep Ecology and Ecofeminism Debate and Its Parallels."

91. Warren, "The Power and the Promise of Ecological Feminism," p. 145, n. 37.

92. Warren, "Feminism and Ecology," pp. 18–20.

93. See her account of the relationship between Western colonialist ideas of the human and the rational, the near extinction of aboriginal Tasmanians, and the decimation of the Australian and New Zealand populations of fur seals and right whales in "The Ecopolitics Debate and the Politics of Nature," in Warren, *Ecological Feminism*, pp. 75–77.

94. Plumwood, *Feminism and the Mastery of Nature* p. 173.

95. See both "Nature, Self and Gender," and "Deep Ecology and the Denial of Difference," in Plumwood, *Feminism and the Mastery of Nature*, pp. 165–89.

96. Plumwood, *Feminism and the Mastery of Nature*, p. 178.

97. Plumwood, *Feminism and the Mastery of Nature*, p. 196.

98. Slicer, "Is There An Ecofeminism-Deep Ecology 'Debate'?" p. 151.

99. Slicer, "Is There An Ecofeminism-Deep Ecology 'Debate'?" p. 153. Since I have this experience with Fox's essay as well, I heartily concur with Slicer's statement.

100. Slicer, "Is There An Ecofeminism-Deep Ecology 'Debate'?" p. 163.

101. Slicer, "Is There An Ecofeminism-Deep Ecology 'Debate'?" p. 154, n. 7.

102. I am not impugning the individuals who were positioned here as outside interrogators, but those who set up the debate without ecofeminist participation.

103. I have heard that there was a sixth member of the party, a woman who has been involved in mainstream Arizona politics and thus has wished to go unacknowledged as a founder of Earth First!, or at least as being present at the founding of the radical organization. I have been unable to verify this information, but none of the histories of Earth First! refer to the presence of this woman. If she was there, it is interesting that her presence is excluded, leaving intact the mythology of the Earth First! founders as men alone in the desert. If she was not, it is interesting that this rumor circulates, a surreptitious undermining of the masculinist birth of Earth First! Thanks to Paul Hirt for bringing this story to my attention.

104. Edward Abbey, *The Monkey-Wrench Gang* (New York: Avon, 1975).

105. For accounts of Earth First!'s founding and subsequent development, I am relying pri-

marily on Rik Scarce, *EcoWarriors: Understanding the Radical Environmental Movement* (Chicago: Noble Press, 1990); and Christopher Manes, *Green Rage: Radical Environmentalism and the Unmaking of Civilization* (Boston: Little, Brown, 1990). I thank Rik Scarce for many illuminating conversations about Earth First! and the debates within the movement.

106. From "Earth Night Action," by Mike Roselle and Darryl Cherney, copyright 1990, from the tape *Timber* by Darryl Cherney with George Shook and Judi Bari. The song counterposes Earth First! Earth Night Actions to the 1990 Earth Day celebrations, widely seen by radical environmentalists as representing the sellout of environmentalism to corporate "green" capitalism. As the first verse goes: "Now Earth Day 1990 was Dennis Hayes's vision/But instead of keeping us together it only caused division/He said turn down your thermostat and recycle toilet paper/And as long as they contribute don't confront the corporate rapers." From the liner notes to *Timber*.

107. Drawn by Canyon Frog in June 1987, this image appeared as the *The Earth First! Journal* cover on August 1, 1988, entitled "The Compleet Radical Environmentalist." It is reprinted in Joni Seager, *Earth Follies: Coming to Feminist Terms with the Global Environmental Crisis* (New York: Routledge, 1993), p. 228.

108. Seager, *Earth Follies*, p. 227.

109. Scarce, *Eco-Warriors*, p. 90. Seager could have easily made this point herself, given her acute analysis of the production of sexism within patriarchal institutional structures such as the media.

110. Scarce, *Eco-Warriors*, p. 81.

111. Judi Bari, "The Feminization of Earth First!" *Ms.* (May/June 1992): 84.

112. According to Bari, "three-quarters of the leadership" was made up of women. Bari, "The Feminization of Earth First!," p. 85.

113. See Sturgeon, "Direct Theory and Political Action: The Nonviolent Direct Action Movement, 1976–1987"; and Epstein, *Political Protest and Cultural Revolution*.

114. *The Earth First! Journal* (November 1, 1988): 5.

115. See letter from Sher Pierson, *Earth First! Journal*, (December 21, 1988): 9, and letter from Sequoia, *Earth First! Journal* (February 2, 1989): 5.

116. Howie Wolke, "The Grizzly Den," *Earth First! Journal* (November 1, 1988): 28. This editorial was not in direct response to Bari's report on the California Rendezvous, but in reaction to previous comments made by Earth First!ers arguing for connections to be made between racism, sexism, and classism to environmental destruction.

117. Dolores La Chappelle, "No, I'm Not an Eco-Feminist: A Few Words in Defense of Men," *The Earth First! Journal* (March 21, 1989): 31.

118. Loose Hip Circles, "Riotous Rendezvous Remembered," *The Earth First! Journal* (August 1, 1989): 19.

119. Miss Ann Thropy, "Population and AIDs," *The Earth First! Journal* (May 1, 1987): 32, and "Miss Ann Thropy Responds to 'Alien-Nation'," *The Earth First! Journal* (December 22, 1987): 17.

120. Dave Foreman and Nancy Morton, "Good Luck Darlin'. It's Been Great," *The Earth First! Journal* (September 22, 1990): 5.

121. Howie Wolke, "FOCUS On Wilderness," *The Earth First! Journal* (September 22, 1990): 7.

122. Bill Devall, "Maybe the Movement Is Leaving Me," *The Earth First! Journal* (September 22, 1990): 6.

123. Judi Bari, "Expand Earth First!," in *The Earth First! Journal* (September 22, 1990): 5. Reprinted as "Breaking Up is Hard to Do," in Judi Bari, *Timber Wars* (Monroe, ME: Common Courage Press, 1994), pp. 55–59.

124. The Industrial Workers of the World (IWW, or Wobblies) is a very old anarchist labor organization, mostly defunct. But a small chapter of IWW worked in coalition with Redwood Summer organizers. Seeds of Peace was an affinity group formed out of the nonviolent direct-action movement that became expert at feeding large numbers of people in an action, and maintained an organization available for this service to many different radical political groups.

125. Accounts of the bombing and the letter from The Lord's Avenger can be found in *The Earth First! Journal EXTRA* (circa June 1990), as well as Bari, *Timber Wars*, and Bari, "The Feminization of Earth First!" pp. 84–85.

126. A civil rights lawsuit against the FBI and the Oakland Police was filed in 1991. Those wishing to contribute to legal costs can make tax-deductible donations to Redwood Summer Justice Fund, P.O. Box 14720, Santa Rosa, CA, 95402, USA.

127. A useful overview of the diversity and commonalities of ecofeminists, Gaard's video will also be discussed in chapter 6. Greta Gaard, *Ecofeminism Now!* (Medusa Productions, 1996), VHS, 37 minutes, available for $15 plus shipping from Dr. Greta Gaard, Department of English, 420 Humanities Building, University of Minnesota, Duluth, MN, 55812. Note the reappearance of the exclamatory imperative!

128. Bari, in Gaard, *Ecofeminism Now!*

129. Simon "De Beaulivar" Zapotes, "Fucking With Mother Nature: A Critique of Humor, Art, and Eco-Pornography," *The Earth First! Journal* (May 1, 1991): 32–33.

130. Greta Gaard is, at this writing, finishing her book *Ecological Politics: Ecofeminists and the Greens* (Philadelphia: Temple University Press, forthcoming), which will deal more closely than I have with ecofeminism in both the U.S. Greens and in the animal liberation movement. See also her video, *Thinking Green: Ecofeminists and The Greens* (Medusa Productions 1994), VHS, 35 minutes, available for $15 plus shipping from Dr. Greta Gaard, Department of English, 420 Humanities Building, University of Minnesota, Duluth, MN, 55812.

CHAPTER TWO

1. Parts of this chapter are based on research I did for my dissertation. See Noël Sturgeon, "Direct Theory and Political Action: The U.S. Nonviolent Direct Action Movement," Ph.D. dissertation, University of California, Santa Cruz, March 1991.

2. While there is a wealth of scattered materials published on various aspects of the antimilitarist direct action movement, there is very little that treats it as a whole movement. See Barbara Epstein, *Political Protest and Cultural Revolution: Nonviolent Direct Action in the 1970s and 1980s* (Berkeley: University of California Press, 1991); and Sturgeon, "Theorizing Movements: Direct Action and Direct Theory," in Marcy Darnovsky, Barbara Epstein, and Richard Flacks, eds., *Cultural Politics and Social Movements* (Philadelphia: Temple University, 1994), pp. 35–51.

3. "I have met scores of young feminists drawn to actions like the Women's Peace Encampment and to groups like Women for a Non-Nuclear Future by their belief that the maternal love women have for their children can unlock the gates of imperialist oppression. I have great respect for the self-affirming pride of these women, but I also . . . fear that their effect is to reflect and reproduce dominant cultural assumptions about women, which not only fail to represent the variety in women's lives but promote unrealistic expectations about 'normal' female behavior that most of us cannot satisfy." Linda Alcoff, "Cultural Feminism versus Post-Structuralism: The Identity Crisis in Feminist Theory," *SIGNS* 13 (Spring 1988): 413. Important articles examining the essentialism of peace movement women are Micaela di Leonardo, "Morals, Mothers, and Militarism: Antimilitarism and Feminist Theory," *Feminist Studies* 11 (Fall 1985): 599–617; and Johanna Brenner, "Beyond Essentialism: Feminist Theory and Strategy in the Peace Movement," in Mike Davis and Michael Sprinker, eds., *Reshaping the U.S. Left: Popular Struggles in the 1980s* (New York: Verso, 1988), pp. 93–113. Brenner, who has some direct experience with peace movement actions, is far less reductive than di Leonardo, whose critique I examine in detail later in this essay. See also Kathy E. Ferguson, *The Man Question: Visions of Subjectivity in Feminist Theory* (Berkeley: University of California Press, 1993); and Epstein, *Political Protest*.

4. I have found that the particular characterization of this movement as antiracist has very often surprised people who are not familiar with the internal structure and analysis of the movement, since it most participants tended to be white. Nevertheless, the movement's discourse and practice has been consciously antiracist both analytically (for example, in making connections

between the exploitation of Native American uranium miners and nuclear power, or between the rise of our military budget and the racial composition of our poor who depend on social services) and in practice (for instance, the handbooks almost all carry sections on racism and ways to combat it in organizing and in decision-making processes). Further, most of the practices and organizational structures of the movement were pioneered by people of color in this country; there is nothing inherently white about civil disobedience, for example, even if people of color have more to fear from police than do white people. In certain actions, working coalitions were set up between the direct action movement and antimiliarist movements of people of color, for instance in the South Pacific (the action at Vandenberg Air Force Base in 1983) and with Native American activists (for example, at the Nevada Test Site, where the Western Shoshone issue permits to activists "trespassing" onto the Test Site). Much more of this kind of coalition building could have been attempted by the movement, in my view. This does not mean that there wasn't racism within the movement; anywhere there are white people, there is racism to contend with, and the culture of the movement was at times oppressively white. But it is a measure of progress, I think, that a movement be considered, or consider itself, antiracist without first requiring the presence of large numbers of people of color. It seems appropriate, to me, for white people to take responsibility for analyzing the connections between racism and militarism, and not to leave this task up to the many peace activists of color.

5. King's published articles on ecofeminism include: "All is Connectedness: Scenes from the Women's Pentagon Action USA," in Lynne Jones, ed., *Keeping the Peace*, (London: Women's Press Limited, 1983), pp. 40–63; "Feminism and the Revolt of Nature," *Heresies* 13 (1981): 12–15; "Toward an Ecological Feminism and a Feminist Ecology," in Joan Rothschild, ed., *Machina Ex Dea: Feminist Perspectives on Technology*, (New York: Pergamon, 1983), pp. 118–129; "What is Ecofeminism?" *The Nation* (December 12, 1987): 702, 730–31; "Ecological Feminism," *Z Magazine* 1(7/8) (1988): 124–27; "The Ecology of Feminism and the Feminism of Ecology," in Judith Plant, ed., *Healing the Wounds*, (Santa Cruz, CA: New Society Publishers, 1989), pp. 18–28 ; and "Healing the Wounds: Feminism, Ecology, and the Nature/Culture Dualism," in Irene Diamond and Gloria Feman Ornstein eds., *Reweaving the World: The Emergence of Ecofeminism*, (San Francisco: Sierra Club Books, 1990), pp. 106–21.

6. King, "All is Connectedness," pp. 40–41.

7. Interestingly, in the quote above King describes "male technocrats" using masculinist language to define the nuke at Three Mile Island as "female." In this case, it seems, it is the nuclear technology that is represented as a female, rather than male, force, akin to uncontrollable nature. On the masculinist discourse of "defense intellectuals," which may describe nuclear technologies as phallic objects as well as babies, see Carol Cohn's excellent article, "Sex and Death in the Rational World of Defense Intellectuals," *Signs* 12 (Summer 1987): 687–718; and H. Bruce Franklin, "Domesticating the Bomb: Nuclear Weapons in *Testament* and the Fiction of Judith Merrill, Helen Clarkson, Kate Wilhelm and Carol Amen," paper given in the Gender and Nuclear Weapons panel at the American Studies Association Conference, Miami Beach, October 1988.

8. King, "All is Connectedness," p. 44.

9. Ellen Willis, *Village Voice* 25(25) (June 18–24, 1980): 28. A second part to this article appeared in the *Voice* 25(29) (July 16–22, 1980): 34.

10. I owe this point to T. V. Reed.

11. Donna Warnock, "Mobilizing Emotions: Organizing the Women's Pentagon Action," *Socialist Review* 63–64 (May–August 1982): 37–47, p. 37.

12. Warnock, "Mobilizing Emotions," p. 38. Indeed, the largest direct action mobilizations that preceded the Women's Pentagon Actions in the Northeast (where most of the organizers of the WPA were from) were the Seabrook actions, in which feminism was a contested term, though accorded a certain legitimacy from the beginning. See Anna Gyorgy et al., *No Nukes*, (Boston: South End Press, 1979), p. 388. Indications of a controversy over feminism in the Seabrook actions appear in accounts of the October 6, 1979, and May 24, 1980, actions (personal interviews with Seabrook participants crystal and jackrabbit; undated leaflet distributed by the Wandering Star affinity group, personal possession). Yet the decentralized affinity group structures in

these actions also allowed a certain autonomy to feminist participants. Thus, Donna Warnock also says that "the groundwork for autonomous feminist organizing had already been laid [before the WPA], especially by the anti-nuclear movement." "Mobilizing Emotions," p. 38.

13. See Rosalind Petchesky, "Antiabortion, Antifeminism, and the Rise of the New Right," *Signs* 7 (Summer 1981): 206–46; and Zillah Eisenstein, "The Sexual Politics of the New Right: Understanding the 'Crisis of Liberalism' for the 1980s," *Signs* 7 (Summer 1982): 567–88.

14. The "Unity Statement" is reprinted in King, "All is Connectedness," pp. 42–43, including the original graphics, which depict women of different ages and races. A retyped version without graphics can be found in *Fight Back! Feminist Resistance to Male Violence* (Minneapolis: Cleis Press, 1981): 280.

15. Grace Paley, personal communication, February 1987. I am indebted throughout my discussion of the WPA and the "Unity Statement" to the incisive analysis by T. V. Reed in "Dramatic Ecofeminism: The Women's Pentagon Action as Theater and Theory," in *Fifteen Jugglers, Five Believers: Literary Politics and the Poetics of American Social Movements* (Berkeley: University of California, 1992).

16. King, "Feminism and the Revolt of Nature," p. 13.

17. Ibid., p. 14.

18. Ibid.; King's emphasis.

19. King, "Toward an Ecological Feminism and a Feminist Ecology."

20. Ibid., p. 128, n 4.

21. Ibid., p. 123, King's emphasis. This section, especially this first sentence, is possibly the most quoted statement of King's and plays a special part in various efforts to produce a nonessentialist ecofeminism. I'll return to this point in chapter 6.

22. Ibid., p. 127; my emphases.

23. *The Nation* (December 12, 1987): 702.

24. Ibid., p. 731.

25. Ibid., p. 730.

26. King's understanding of ecofeminism as resting on these elements is shared by a second letter critiquing Sale's article in this same issue of *The Nation*, which agrees that ecofeminists share a "radical left-libertarian and direct action-oriented approach." Sharon Helsel and John Ely, pp. 731–32. Helsel and Ely add a further characteristic: that ecofeminists share a "dedicated opposition to the proliferation of nuclear weapons," a conclusion with which Ynestra King would undoubtedly agree. This is the same Sharon Helsel that was a member of the Surrogate Others.

27. Micaela di Leonardo, "Morals, Mothers, and Militarism," p. 602.

28. Participants of the Puget Sound Women's Peace Camp, *We Are Ordinary Women: A Chronicle of the Puget Sound Women's Peace Camp* (Seattle: Seal Press, 1985).

29. *We Are Ordinary Women*, p. 78.

30. A version of this story is recounted by Donna Haraway in "The Promises of Monsters: A Regenerative Politics for Inappropriate/d Others," in Lawrence Grossberg, Cary Nelson, and Paula Treichler, eds., *Cultural Studies* (New York: Routledge, 1992), pp. 295–337. My version of the story predates Haraway's, originating from my dissertation and my essay, "Post-structuralism Feminism, Ecofeminism, and Radical Feminism Revisited," presented to the National Women's Studies Association Meeting in 1989; she drew on her memory of my work as well as her own experience in the action in relating her typically rich rendition (personal communication, Donna Haraway, March 1991).

31. The term is Janice Radway's. Her definition is "those points of intersection between the discourse and practices that together constitute individual subjects . . . in particular ways." From "Identifying Ideological Seams: Mass Culture, Analytical Method, and Political Practice," *Communications* 9 (1986): 110.

32. For an excellent discussion of the complicity of women in the construction of militarism, see Cynthia Enloe, *Does Khaki Become You? The Militarization of Women's Lives* (Boston: South End Press, 1983).

33. Donna Haraway, "A Cyborg Manifesto: Science, Technology and Socialist-Feminism in the Late Twentieth Century," in *Simians, Cyborgs and Women: The Reinvention of Nature* (New York: Routledge, 1991), pp. 149–81.

34. See Judith McDaniel, "One Summer at Seneca," *Heresies* 5 (1985): 6–10; and Louise Krasniewicz, *Nuclear Summer: The Clash of Communities at the Seneca Women's Peace Encampment* (Ithaca, NY: Cornell University Press, 1992). A fascinating analysis of the media's construction of women at Greenham Common as "deviant" can be found in Alison Young, *Femininity in Dissent* (New York: Routledge, 1990).

CHAPTER THREE

1. The term is Michael Omi and Howard Winant's, *Racial Formations in the United States* (New York: Routledge, 1988).

2. The term "double jeopardy" used to describe the intersection of racism and sexism for black women is Frances Beale's, in "Double Jeopardy: To Be Black and Female," in Robin Morgan ed., *Sisterhood is Powerful*, (New York: Vintage, 1970), pp. 340–53.

3. The representative figure here is Barbara Deming, a lesbian-feminist whose career as a nonviolent activist spanned the civil rights movement through feminist antimilitarism to early ecofeminism. Indeed, as will be discussed shortly, Deming had a direct influence on the shape of WomanEarth. Interview with Ynestra King, November 1993.

4. My information about WomanEarth comes from literature I received from the group during 1987–1989: two articles, Rachel Bagby, "A Power of Numbers" from Judith Plant, ed., *Healing the Wounds: The Promise of Ecofeminism* (Philadelphia: New Society Publishers, 1989), 91–95, and Lindsy Van Gelder, "It's Not Nice to Mess With Mother Nature," *Ms.* (January–February 1989): 60–63; papers shared with me through the generosity of Margie Mayman, Starhawk, and Margo Adair; and interviews with Margo Adair, Rachel Bagby, Ynestra King, Gwyn Kirk, Margie Mayman, Papusa Molina, Rachel Sierra, Starhawk, and Luisah Teish from 1991–1995. Margo Adair is a white leftist feminist activist and the author of *Working Inside Out: Tools for Change* (n.p.: Wingbow, 1984). Her involvement with WomanEarth was relatively peripheral, coming only at its last moments. Rachel Bagby is an African American educator, lawyer, and feminist. She has been the coordinator of African American Studies as well as the associate director of the Martin Luther King Papers at Stanford. She is a performance artist and singer with a history of ecological activism. Besides the piece cited above, see her "Daughters of Growing Things," in Irene Diamond and Gloria Orenstein, eds., *Reweaving the World: The Emergence of Ecofeminism* (San Francisco: Sierra Club Books, 1990), pp. 231–48. Also see the interview with her in Penny Rosenwasser, *Visionary Voices: Women on Power* (San Francisco: Aunt Lute, 1992), pp. 71–82. Ynestra King's work and activism I've described in the last chapter; she is a white southern feminist based in New York. Gwyn Kirk is a white British feminist activist and scholar trained in sociology. She was involved in the feminist antimilitarist action at Greenham Common, particularly in developing connections between the Greenham women and women's antinuclear activism in the South Pacific. During the period of WomanEarth's formation she lived in New York, and then moved out to the West Coast for a summer to "co-hub" WomanEarth with Rachel Bagby. Kirk has taught Women's Studies at Rutgers and Antioch University, and her present scholarship is on grassroots urban movements. Margie Mayman is a white New Zealand feminist and an ordained Presbyterian minister who at the time of our interview was doing further theological studies at Union Theological Seminary. Papusa Molina is a Mexican feminist who has lived and worked in the United States since 1981. She was a founder of the Women Against Racism Committee in Iowa City, about which she writes in "Recognizing, Accepting and Celebrating Our Differences," in Gloria Anzaldúa ed., *Haciendo Caras: Making Face, Making Soul* (San Francisco: Aunt Lute, 1990), pp. 326–31. She has also been the director of the Women's Center at the University of Iowa. At the time of our interview, she was teaching Women's Studies at Hamilton

College. See her interview in Penny Rosenwasser, *Visionary Voices*, pp. 1–10. Rachel Sierra is a Chicana feminist based in the San Francisco Bay Area who has been a long-time organizer in grassroots movements of poor urban residents, especially those of color. Starhawk's work as an antinuclear activist, political theorist, and witch I've described in chapter 1; a white Jewish woman, she is also based in the Bay Area. Luisah Teish is an African American feminist, dancer, storyteller, and activist, who teaches and practices African-based spiritualities as an Oshun priestess. She lives in the San Francisco Bay Area, and has written about the connections between African, especially Yoruba, spiritual practices and politics in *Jambalaya* (San Francisco: Harper Collins, 1985).

5. Most of the interviews were conducted face-to-face, some over the phone. In every case but one, the interviewee signed a consent form, agreeing to the following process. After the interview, I transcribed it and indicated the portions of the interview I might quote (except for Starhawk, whose interview did not come out on tape—for her input, I relied on my notes of the interview and large amounts of archival material she kindly lent me). I then sent the transcription back to the interviewee. Within an agreed-upon time, the interviewee could withhold permission for quoting specific material, or edit or contextualize the material as she wished. If I received no response within the time period, the agreement was that I could assume permission to use the material as transcribed. The exception to this process is Gywn Kirk, with whom I've had several informal conversations as well as two approximately formal interviews; one with both Kirk and King together at the Women, Environment, and Grassroots Conference at Barnard in April 1991, and the other with Kirk alone at the National Women's Studies Association Conference in June 1992. However, none of these interviews was transcribed in order to be read by Kirk. Thus my attributions of information to Kirk must be seen as more tentative than information attributed to others. Nevertheless, Kirk's viewpoints on WomanEarth have been very influential to my thinking about the organization. I started from her remarks, and her care in thinking about the successes and failures of the organization provided me with a model of a feminist researcher.

6. Interview with Ynestra King, November 9, 1993. All information and quotes attributed to King in this chapter are from this interview unless otherwise identified.

7. This sentence is attributed to King at several places in the WomanEarth papers I have.

8. According to Margie Mayman, who was hired to manage the WomanEarth office in New York, the amount was well over $40,000 (from interview with Margie Mayman, November 10, 1993; all information and quotes attributed to Mayman in this chapter are from this interview unless otherwise identified). This was a very large amount of money for a small radical political organization, especially one with no previous existence and thus no track record. I've decided to keep the identity of this donor anonymous, calling her "Camille Daney," since her contributions to radical causes are ongoing and since I have not interviewed her directly for this project. I have, however, identified her racial location since it is important to understanding the events that followed.

9. The detail in this summary comes from a report made to Daney by Kirk and King on December 12, 1985. From papers provided to me by Starhawk.

10. Letter from King to Ani Mander, Director of Women's Studies at Antioch West. From papers provided to me by Starhawk.

11. In saying this, I am not implying that King and Starhawk deliberately obscured the fact that they had begun work on the organization. Early meetings often began with a rendition of the history of their efforts, and late material produced by WomanEarth invoked their status as the initiators of the organization. But as I will discuss later, it is also true that several of the women of color did not seem aware until the period around the August 1986 conference that the conception of the institute was tied so closely to the kind of feminist peace politics that King and Starhawk had been involved in—in other words, ecofeminism.

12. Chandra Talpade Mohanty is an Indian feminist scholar who has taught in the United States for many years; she is the editor, along with Ann Russo and Lourdes Torres, of *Third World*

Women and the Politics of Feminism (Bloomington and Indianapolis: Indiana University Press, 1991) and the author of two important essays in that book, "Cartographies of Struggle: Third World Women and the Politics of Feminism" (pp. 1–50) and "Under Western Eyes: Feminist Scholarship and Colonial Discourses (pp. 51–81).

13. Marta Benavides is a Salvadoran feminist activist who at the time was living in Mexico.

14. It seems likely that there at least were two initial New York meetings with Barbara Smith, one at King's apartment and one at Grace Paley's house on March 8, 1986. I have the minutes of that meeting, from the papers provided to me by Starhawk. Given the amount of time that had elapsed between these meetings and my interviews, memories of these meetings were unclear. King's account refers to more than one meeting but doesn't clearly differentiate the two. Molina only refers to one meeting, but her account in terms of participants and subject matter is very different from King's. In Molina's account, Rachel Bagby is absent, though she clearly attended the March 8 meeting. Smith, in the minutes of the March 8 meeting, refers to a meeting at which she was the only woman of color. Mayman, who was at the March 8th meeting and was hired in mid-February, remembers not being able to attend one meeting because of parity imbalance. As a result of this uncertainty, I don't try to distinguish between meetings in this early period.

15. Details from the minutes of the March 8, 1986, meeting that were sent out to all participants. From papers provided to me by Starhawk.

16. If these four were the only women of color involved, this meeting was either not the March 8 meeting, or Marta Benavides was not counted as a "woman of color."

17. Interview with Papusa Molina, February 26, 1995. All information or quotes attributed to Molina in this chapter are from this interview unless otherwise specified.

18. From the minutes of the April 17–20 meeting, from papers provided to me by Starhawk and Mayman. There was apparently an earlier meeting at the funder's home in the Southwest, which was more loosely structured around the idea of WomanEarth. This meeting was attended by about twenty or so women, including at least King, Teish, and Kirk from the Circle One group, but also a number of other women, many of whom were "international" feminist activists who were invited by the funder. Teish remembers Paula Gunn Allen, Elena Featherstone, Asoka Banderage, Merlin Stone, Jacqui Alexander, Marta Benavides, and Uzuri Amini. I have no minutes of that meeting and none of my interviewees have clear recollections of it. I concentrate here on the April 17–20 meeting.

19. Mayman expresses her skepticism about the use of "unconventional spirituality" in her interview in ways that will be referred to later in the chapter. Her sense of herself as "hired help" (in my words, not hers) is also indicated several times in the interview, as well as corroborated by other interviewees who sometimes hesitated about including her in Circle One. On the other hand, her participation definitely counted in terms of assessing racial parity; she was always seen as one of the four white participants balanced by the four women of color. As I discuss later, this indicates the lack of a class analysis in the group. The idea that the language in the minutes reflected her ambivalent feelings, however, is entirely my speculation.

20. It is interesting that, according to all of the interviewees, the question of male participation in WomanEarth was never brought up, except in the context of talking about who would be students in the year-long Antioch program. That the women-only nature of the core group in WomanEarth was not even an issue, was a taken for granted mode of operation, is an artifact of the period. The separatism of many early white women's movement's group was felt to be a barrier to women of color who wanted to address sexism in ways that did not isolate them from men of color and their mutual struggle against racism. But WomanEarth's formation took place after feminists of color had identified a need to work together in all-women's groups as well. For instance, the Combahee River Collective, whose "manifesto" is immensely influential, argues for the necessity of women of color organizing without male involvement in certain situations. Barbara Smith's involvement in both Combahee and WomanEarth is symbolic of the elimination of this barrier. But there still may have been different nuances in the attitude toward female separatist organization among members of Circle One. The minutes of the March 1986 meeting

record a comment by Barbara Smith about the problem of "some feminists never talking about family"; Bagby also comments in her interview about her need to work in both mixed and single-sex groups.

21. From the minutes of the April 17–20 meeting.

22. From the flyer "Reconsituting Feminist Peace Politics," which went out with the invitational letter describing the August gathering on June 21, 1986. From papers provided to me by Starhawk and Mayman.

23. Interview with Gwyn Kirk, June 1992. I did not take complete notes during this interview and thus cannot directly quote Kirk.

24. Molina, in "On the Cutting Edge," interview with Penny Rosenwasser, in *Visionary Voices*, p. 2.

25. Interview with Rachel Sierra, October 12, 1993. All information or quotes attributed to Sierra in this chapter come from this interview unless otherwise specified.

26 Interview with Luisah Teish, October 9, 1993. All information or quotes attributed to Teish in this chapter come from this interview unless otherwise specified.

27. From the minutes of the meeting of May 26–30, 1986, Litchfield, Connecticut; from the papers of Starhawk.

28. Invitational letter from WomanEarth, dated June 27, 1986, apparently written primarily by King; from the papers of Starhawk and Mayman. Spirituality is the only issue identified in this letter as a possible source of conflict stemming from cultural or political difference, other than the overarching concern with racial difference. As will be discussed shortly, this did turn out to be the only area of conflict. That it was the only one identified by the WomanEarth members at this point is interesting.

29. I asked all of the interviewees about what kind of process was used in WomanEarth and whether there was conflict over this issue.

30. From minutes of the May 26–30 meeting in Connecticut.

31. In this section, I am paraphrasing Molina, Teish, and King's already paraphrased words from the minutes of the May meeting.

32. Bagby, in "A Power of Numbers," p. 93.

33. The above quotes are from Sierra's letter to the other members of Circle One, dated July 11, 1986; from papers provided to me by Starhawk.

34. From the roster of the August gathering; from papers provided to me by Margie Mayman. The roster records names, addresses, phone numbers, racial/ethnic identification, areas of interest defined in terms of the five theme areas of the conference, and skill/profession of each participant. As far as I can ascertain, the roster is a fairly accurate rendering of those in attendance, but according to the accounts of the conference in the interviews, it is not absolutely complete. Some women perhaps attended at the last minute, and their names were not recorded on this roster. This did not upset the parity balance, however.

35. Some participants were put in two issue areas, some did not have any marked.

36. Some participants were listed in more than one of these categories.

37. Bagby, in "A Power of Numbers," p. 93. Her emphasis.

38. In Plant, *Healing the Wounds*.

39. As opposed to numerous feminist gatherings that have been wracked by racial conflict. To name just two examples, the National Women's Studies Association meetings in 1981 and 1990, the latter almost bringing about the end of the organization. (Interestingly, the walk-out of many of the women of color during the 1990 NWSA conference was instigated by Papusa Molina, among others.)

40. These details on the evaluation during the last day and the quote from Kirk come from "Reports From the Color Clans on FPI [Feminist Peace Institute]" from Starhawk's papers, and "Report of the Lesbian Caucus" from Mayman's papers.

41. See Van Gelder, "It's Not Nice to Mess."

42. These quotes are from "From Earth to the World: Voices of Ecofeminism, A Think-Tank

Proposal Submitted by WomanEarth Institute [sic]," most likely written by Bagby and Kirk sometime in 1988 to raise money for a meeting to reconstitute Circle One. From Starhawk's papers.
Because of its fund-raising purpose, the figures on the inquiries may be somewhat inflated.

43. I have not been able to ascertain if it is the same proposal I cite above.

44. From a WomanEarth flyer which was distributed at the 1989 Greens Conference in
Eugene, Oregon, most likely written by Irene Diamond.

45. Interview with Margo Adair, October 6, 1993. All quotes and information attributed to
Adair in this chapter are from this interview unless otherwise specified.

46. A sense expressed by King, Kirk, Sierra, Molina, and Bagby.

47. Bernice Johnson Reagon, "Coalition Politics: Turning the Century," in Barbara Smith,
ed., *Home Girls: A Black Feminist Anthology* (New York: Kitchen Table: Women of Color Press,
1983), pp. 356–69.

48. See Chéla Sandoval, "Feminism and Racism: A Report on the 1981 National Women's
Studies Association Conference," in Gloria Anzaldúa, ed., *Haciendo Caras*, pp. 55–71, and "U.S.
Third World Feminism: The Theory and Method of Oppositional Consciousness in the Post-
modern World," *Genders* 10 (Spring 1991): 1–24.

49. For two useful examples of analyses of the construction of "whiteness" which question the
unity of the category, see Biddy Martin and Chandra Talpade Mohanty's discussion of Minnie
Bruce Pratt's autobiographical essay in "Feminist Politics: What's Home Got to Do With It?" in
Teresa de Lauretis, ed., *Feminist Studies/Critical Studies* (Bloomington: Indiana University Press,
1986), pp. 191–212; and Ruth Frankenberg, *White Women, Race Matters: The Social Construction of Whiteness* (Minneapolis: University of Minnesota Press, 1993).

50. For a few examples of this theorization of the politics of racial identity, see Combahee
River Collective, "The Combahee River Collective Statement," in Smith, ed., *Home Girls*,
pp. 272–82; Gloria Anzaldúa, *Borderlands/La Frontera: The New Metiza* (San Francisco: Spin-
sters/Aunt Lute, 1987) (which, by the way, is considered by some to be an ecofeminist text); and
Sandra Harding, "Reinventing Ourselves as Other: More New Agents of History and Knowledge," in Linda S. Kaufmann, ed., *American Feminist Thought at Century's End* (Cambridge,
MA: Basil Blackwell, 1993).

51. One of my interview questions was "Do you identify yourself as an ecofeminist?" Bagby,
Teish, Sierra, and Molina all refused this identification, in most cases explicitly mentioning as a
reason their sense of ecofeminism as a white-identified movement. Adair sees the white-identified tradition of ecofeminism as one reason for Sierra's reluctance to continue "hubbing" the
organization, though Sierra herself does not include this in her reasons. Of the white members of
Circle One, only King and Starhawk answered this question positively and immediately, both
providing me instantly with complex definitions of ecofeminism. Kirk had a qualified sense of
herself as an ecofeminist, wanting to distinguish herself from essentialist and nonactivist elements
of ecofeminism. Mayman saw herself as a feminist, not specifically an ecofeminist.

52. For examples of analyses arising from the movement against environmental racism, see
Benjamin F. Chavis and Charles Lee, *Toxic Wastes and Race in the United States* (New York:
United Church of Christ Commission for Racial Justice, 1987); Robert D. Bullard, *Dumping in
Dixie: Race, Class and Environmental Quality* (San Francisco: Westview, 1990); Robert D.
Bullard, ed., *Confronting Environmental Racism: Voices from the Grassroots* (Boston: South End
Press, 1993); Al Gedick, ed., *The New Resource Wars: Native and Environmental Struggles
Against Multinational Corporations* (Boston: South End Press, 1993); Richard Hofrichter, ed.,
Toxic Struggles: The Theory and Practice of Environmental Justice (Philadelphia: New Society
Publishers, 1993); Andrew Szasz, *Ecopopulism: Toxic Waste and the Movement for Environmen-
tal Justice* (Minneapolis: University of Minnesota Press, 1994); Robert Higgins, "Race, Pollution,
and the Mastery of Nature," *Environmental Ethics* 16:3 (Fall 1994): 251–64; Laura Pulido, *Environmentalism and Economic Justice: Two Chicano Struggles in the Southwest* (Tucson, AZ: University of Arizona, 1996); and the journal *Race, Poverty and the Environment*.

CHAPTER FOUR

1. The construction of a category of "indigeniety" is not only politically useful within a U.S. national context. On the creation of new forms of the "indigenous" as a political strategy within transnational political arenas, see Dorothy Hodgson, "The Politics of Gender, Ethnicity, and 'Development': Images, Interventions, and the Reconfiguration of Maasai Identities, 1916–1993," Ph.D. dissertation, Department of Anthropology, University of Michigan, 1995; and "Critical Interventions: The Politics of Studying 'Indigenous Development'," conference paper presented at the American Anthropological Association meeting in Washington, D.C. (November 1995).

2. Huey-li Li, "A Cross-Cultural Critique of Ecofeminism," in Greta Gaard ed., *Ecofeminism: Women, Animals, Nature* (Philadelphia: Temple University Press, 1993), pp. 272–94.

3. Donna Haraway, *Primate Visions: Gender, Race, and Nature in the World of Modern Science* (New York: Routledge, 1989), p. 257. I was reminded of this section of Haraway's book by Stacy Alaimo, "Cyborg and Ecofeminist Interventions: Challenges for an Environmental Feminism," *Feminist Studies* 20(1) (Spring 1994): 133–52, esp. p. 135.

4. Janet Biehl, as discussed in chapter 1, critiques not only the assumption that nature-based spiritualities are more feminist, but the assumption that ancient Goddess religions were even "nature-based," let alone that they promoted more ecological ways of living. Biehl, *Finding Our Way: Rethinking Ecofeminism Politics* (Boston: South End Press, 1991).

5. I am thinking of Greta Gaard, ed., *Ecofeminism: Women, Animals, Nature* (Philadelphia: Temple University Press, 1993); Carol Adams, ed. *Ecofeminism and the Sacred* (New York: Continuum Press, 1993); Karen Warren, ed., *Ecological Feminism* (New York: Routledge, 1994), and Karen Warren, ed., *Ecofeminism: Women, Culture, Nature* (Bloomington: Indiana University Press, 1997). I am not saying that these anthologies are completely free of the problematic rhetorical and theoretical moves I examine in this chapter, but they are far less prone to them, an indication of the changing and self-critiquing characteristics of U.S. ecofeminism. My focus on these two early anthologies is part of my construction of a particular genealogical narrative about U.S. ecofeminism.

6. I am indebted to Ilene Rose Feinman for helping me think through the differences between these two books.

7. Judith Plant, "Toward a New World: Introduction," *Healing the Wounds: The Promise of Ecofeminism* (Philadelphia: New Society, 1989) (hereafter *Healing*), p. 3–4. Karen Warren once corrected my own use of the term "unity in diversity," saying that she preferred "solidarity in diversity," because it avoided the problem of reducing difference to sameness and pointed to the active and contested construction of political coalitions which must be engaged in previous to any sense of political solidarity, let alone "unity." Warren, personal communication, fall 1994.

8. Plant, "Toward a New World," p. 4.

9. Portions of this section, together with portions of the chapter on WomanEarth, are published together as "The Nature of Race: Discourses of Racial Difference in Ecofeminism," in Karen J. Warren, ed., *Ecofeminism: Women, Nature Culture*. I thank Karen Warren and anonymous readers for Indiana University Press for their insightful comments.

10. A number of feminist environmentalists have refused the term "ecofeminism" because of its essentialist practitioners. I'll discuss this issue in chapter 6.

11. An example is Paula Gunn Allen, whose essay is included in *Reweaving the World*.

12. Twice during presentations of this portion of my work, audience members asked why I was arguing that Native American women *should* identify themselves as ecofeminists. This is not my goal, and I thank those questioners for pointing out my need to clarify this point. One of those questioners was Ilene Feinman; the other was an anonymous woman at the 1993 American Studies Association meeting.

13. It must be noted that I've established the racial/ethnic identities of these authors in a very unsystematic way: through paying attention to self-identifications and comparing other writings of these authors. I fully expect to have made several errors in this process, and I apologize in

advance for them. I thank Elizabeth Carlassare for pointing out the necessity of specifying European Canadian authors and not simply European American, which I had used ethnocentrically in an earlier version of this chapter.

14. There is a debate over whether Native American tribal cultures are all more egalitarian in their gender relations than white American cultures. The debate is complicated by the effort to show, in some cases, not egalitarian relations as much as matriarchal relations. In any case, it seems clear that different tribes have different kinds of gender relations, and that in all cases they have been affected by the imposition of white U.S. gender roles, in different ways, at different historical periods.

15. This characterization of Native American culture, generalized across tribal difference, is not entirely a creation of ecofeminist discourse but, as a multitude of examples could show, is sometimes a self-presentation of Native Americans themselves. This brings up an important question about the automatic quality of the present critique of essentialist discourse: When is a racial essentialism not racist? When it is a self-presentation designed to intervene in racist political and economic structures; then, it may be an "oppositional consciousness." For this reason, white critics of racial essentialism frequently direct their critiques at white purveyors of the discourse, very rarely at people of color, though there may be plenty of internal critiques of racial essentialisms by theorists of color. I've made a similar point about the strategic nature of some essentialisms in chapter 2, in discussing gender essentialism in ecofeminist discourse as an "oppositional consciousness."

16. Winona LaDuke, personal communication, during a question-and-answer period for her lecture, "The Legacy of Columbus: What It Means for Women and the Environment," Washington State University, 1992. The tendency for women environmental activists of color to identify their politics as stemming from community membership rather than their gender and the implications of this for a redefinition of "motherist" or "maternalist" politics is discussed by Giovanna Di Chiro in "Defining Environmental Justice: Women's Voices and Grassroots Politics," in *Socialist Review* 22(4) (October–December 1992): 93–130.

17. Marie Wilson, "Wings of the Eagle: A Conversation with Marie Wilson," in Plant, *Healing*, p. 212.

18. Of course, there are other reasons for a reluctance to identify as a feminist in the late 1980s to early 1990s that have more to do with a backlash against feminism than with anything feminists themselves did (see Susan Faludi, *Backlash* [New York: Crown Books, 1991]). But here I am concentrating on the effect of a certain gender essentialism imbedded in early radical and liberal feminist arguments about the oppression of "women" by "men" that, without a concomitant analysis of race and class oppression, alienated those women who could not afford, in their struggles against racism and classism, to entertain the notions of essentialized difference or separation between women and men that sometimes accompanied such feminist analyses. Another factor in the reluctance to identify with feminism for some women of color is the racial essentialism involved in various racial liberation movements in this country (black nationalisms, Brown Power and Red Power movements, etc.). This is an issue that I must, for interests of space, leave out of my analysis. But it is an important background for the argument I make in this book.

19. For instance, in Andreé Collard with Joyce Contrucci, *Rape of the Wild: Man's Violence Against Animals and the Earth* (Bloomington: Indiana University Press, 1988).

20. Andy Smith, "For All Those Who Were Indian in a Former Life," *Ms.* (November–December 1991): 44–45; reprinted in Carol Adams, ed., *Ecofeminism and the Sacred* (New York: Continuum Press, 1993).

21. Smith, p. 44. Greta Gaard also argues that using portions of Native American philosophy, spirituality, and culture outside of the context of Native American life is a form of imperialism on the part of ecofeminists. See Gaard, "Ecofeminism and Native American Cultures: Pushing the Limits of Cultural Imperialism?" in Gaard, *Ecofeminism*, pp. 295–314.

22. Right before an account of an Indian offering Plant's nonnative community the experience of a sweat lodge, Plant states: "It would be very typical of the 'taking' attitude of western society to think that Indian ways, traditions and rituals could simply be transferred to non-native

people. But this would be stealing, once again. . . . Indian people can, if they are willing, act as guides, as teachers, as wise elders, for people who are trying to make a home for themselves beyond the suburban bungalow." See "The Circle is Gathering," in *Healing*, p. 245. Plant also questions Marie Wilson a number of times on this topic, especially when and where white people can become students of Native Americans. See "Wings of the Eagle," esp., pp. 216–18. But her inclusion of the story "The Give and the Take," an account of a vision-quest by a white student of a Native American woman shaman, as well as numerous internal references to Native American cultures in other articles in the anthology, works against her own warnings. *Reweaving* is far better on this issue. It is interesting that the strongest statements against this form of cultural imperialism come from Ynestra King, and her reference to Luisah Teish to demonstrate the necessity of honoring the integrity of particular traditions points to the possibility that this lesson, or at least a strong reinforcement of it, was learned from King's WomanEarth experience.

23. For two interesting treatments of the problems that inhere in this characterization of Native Americans, see Calvin Martin, "The American Indian as Miscast Ecologist," in Robert C. Schultz and T. Donald Hughes, eds., *Ecological Consciousness* (University Press of America, 1981): 136–148; and Tom Regan, "Environmental Ethics and the Ambiguity of the Native American's Relationship with Nature," in *All That Dwell Therein: Animal Rights and Environmental Ethics* (Berkeley: University of California Press, 1982), pp. 206–239. I thank Jude Todd for bringing these articles to my attention.

24. See Ramachandra Guha, "Radical American Environmentalism and Wilderness Preservation: A Third World Critique," in *Environmental Ethics* 11(1) (Spring 1989): 71–83. Though Guha is concerned mostly about the use of Eastern, rather than Native American, traditions within Western environmentalism, he points out the prevalence of the idea that "at the level of material and spiritual practice 'primal' peoples subordinated themselves to the integrity of the biotic universe they inhabited" (p. 76). More pertinent to my point above, he argues that these tendencies within radical environmentalism (here he means deep ecology) are characteristic of the entire tradition of U.S. environmentalism.

25. Dolores LaChapelle, "Sacred Land, Sacred Sex," in Plant, *Healing*, pp. 155–67.

26. Gaard, "Ecofeminism and Native American Cultures," pp. 295–314.

27. Plant, "The Circle is Gathering," p. 250.

28. Plant, "The Circle is Gathering," p. 245.

29. Marie Wilson, "The Wings of the Eagle," in *Healing*, p. 217. I'll give one example here of the kind of conflict that can arise between Native American struggles for cultural survival and ecofeminist tenets. During the Ecofeminist Colloquium at the Institute for Social Ecology in July 1994, Greta Gaard told a story about being torn between her support of Native American fishing rights in the upper Michigan peninsula and being opposed to the slaughter of fish. Though she did support the Native American struggle financially, she did not otherwise actively support it. She did not reconcile her difficulties with the situation, but accepted it as a cultural contradiction. In this case, Gaard shows an awareness of the problem identified by Wilson and an understanding of the irreconcilability of political positions in a context of cultural difference operating within unequal power relations.

30. Chandra Mohanty, "Under Western Eyes: Feminist Scholarship and Colonial Discourses," in Chandra Mohanty, Ann Russo, and Lourdes Torres eds., *Third World Women and the Politics of Feminism* (Bloomington: Indiana University Press, 1991): pp. 51–80.

31. In a similar vein, the make-up of participants in the World Women's Congress for a Healthy Planet in Miami, 1992 (organized primarily by white U.S. women and discussed in the next chapter) can be analyzed to show the far greater numbers of "international" (i.e., non-U.S.) women compared to U.S. women of color. I'll examine the this conference in more detail in the next chapter.

32.Pamela Philipose, "Women Act: Women and Environmental Protection in India," in Plant, *Healing*, pp. 67–75.

33. Rhada Bhatt, "Lakshmi Ashram: A Gandhian Perspective in the Himalayan Foothills," in Plant, *Healing*, pp. 168–73.

34. Corrine Kumar D'Souza, "A New Movement, a New Hope: East Wind, West Wind, and the Wind from the South," in Plant, *Healing*, p. 36.

35. I will stick to the two anthologies I am examining in this chapter, but evidence of this talismanic quality of the Chipko movement could be found in numerous other ecofeminist writings, particularly in this time period of the late 1980s and early 1990s. See for example, Irene Diamond, *Fertile Ground: Women, Earth, and the Limits of Control* (Boston: Beacon Press, 1994), which, in the context of a complex, provocative, and important critique of mainstream feminism, relies extensively on a discourse of "indigeneity" that presents Third World women as "ultimate ecofeminists."

36. See Aubrey Wallace, "Sowing Seeds of Hope: Wangari Maathai, Kenya," in David Gancher, ed., *Eco-Heroes: Twelve Tales of Environmental Victory* (San Francisco: Mercury House, 1993), pp. 1–22.

37. Joanna Macy, "Awakening to the Ecological Self," in Plant, *Healing*, p. 201.

38. Petra Kelly, "Foreword: Linking Arms, Dear Sisters, Brings Hope!" in Plant, *Healing the Wounds*, p. ix.

39. Irene Diamond and Gloria Orenstein, "Introduction," in *Reweaving the World: The Emergence of Ecofeminism* (San Francisco: Sierra Books, 1990), p. xi.

40. King, "Healing the Wounds: Feminism, Ecology, and the Nature/Culture Dualism," in Diamond and Orenstein, *Reweaving*, p. 118. Note the way the title of King's essay refers back to the earlier anthology, in which she also had an essay.

41. Vandana Shiva's article in *Healing* is entitled "Development, Ecology, and Women," pp. 80–95; her article in *Reweaving* is entitled "Development as a Project of Western Patriarchy," pp. 189–200. The changes between the two texts are minor.

42. Judith Plant, "Recommended Reading," in *Healing*, p. 256.

43. Brinda Rao, "Dominant Constructions of Women and Nature in Social Science Literature," *Capitalism, Nature, Socialism*, Pamphlet 2 (New York: Guilford Publications, 1991); Bina Agarwal, "The Gender and Environment Debate: Lessons from India," *Feminist Studies* 18(1) (Spring 1992): 119–58; Cecile Jackson, "Women/Nature or Gender/History? A Critique of Ecofeminist 'Development'," *Journal of Peasant Studies* 20(3) (April 1993): 389–419. I thank Donna Haraway for providing me with a copy of Rao's essay and Bruce Robbins for pointing me to Jackson's essay.

44. Rao, "Dominant Constructions," p. 2. In almost exactly the same language, Agarwal writes: "poor peasant and tribal women have typically been responsible for fetching fuel and fodder and in hill and tribal communities have also been the main cultivators. They are thus likely to be affected adversely in quite specific ways by environmental degradation" (p. 126).

45. Jackson, "Women/Nature or Gender/History?" p. 412.

46. Jackson, "Women/Nature or Gender/History?" p. 413.

47. Agarwal, "The Gender and Environment Debate," p. 153

48. An incomplete list of the important scholarship on the roots of white feminist paganism, Wicca, and Goddess-worship, would include Merlin Stone, *When God Was a Woman* (New York: Dial Press, 1976); Carol Christ and Judith Plaskow, eds., *Womanspirit Rising: A Feminist Reader in Religion* (New York: Harper & Row, 1979); Elizabeth Dodson Gray, *Green Paradise Lost* (Wellesley, MA: Roundtable Press, 1979); Starhawk, *The Spiral Dance: A Rebirth of the Ancient Religions of the Great Goddess* (San Francisco: Harper & Row, 1979); Charlene Spretnak, ed., *The Politics of Women's Spirituality* (New York: Doubleday, 1982); Carol Christ, *Laughter of Aphrodite: Reflections on a Journey to the Goddess* (San Francisco: Harper & Row, 1987); Raine Eisler, *The Chalice and the Blade* (San Francisco: Harper & Row, 1988); Marie Gimbutas, *The Language of the Goddess* (San Francisco: Harper & Row, 1989); Rosemary Radford Reuther, *Gaia and God: Towards an Ecofeminist Theology of Earth Healing* (San Francisco: Harper & Row, 1992). This list draws attention to the close involvement of many of these scholars of feminist spirituality with ecofeminism, given the connection I've identified between paganism and the ecofeminist critique of the patriarchal Western culture/nature split. Another thing to note is the widespread popular draw of this literature indicated by the investment made by a large trade publisher like Harper & Row in

the subject. The popular attraction of feminist pagan spirituality coupled with the deep suspicion of this literature among feminist academics is another example of the kind of split between academia and activism that I've traced in this book. Indeed, as I've indicated earlier, academic feminist critiques of ecofeminism are often generated by feminism spirituality's connection to it. Since I do not see this connection as automatic or uncontested within ecofeminism, I have in this book tended to downplay it. Yet another tactic could be taken, which evaluates the popular response to feminist spirituality in the more sympathetic terms that I have used in evaluating ecofeminism as strategically deployed. I thank Greta Gaard for pushing me to clarify many of the points I make in this section on "White Indians, Celtic Goddesses and White Identity."

49. Anne Cameron, "First Mother and the Rainbow Children," in Plants, *Healing*, pp. 54–66.

50. Deena Metzger, "Invoking the Grove," in Plant, *Healing*, pp. 118–126.

51. Charlene Spretnak, "Toward an Ecofeminist Spirituality," in Plant, *Healing*, p. 127.

52. Margot Adler, "The Juice and the Mystery," in Plant, *Healing*, p. 152.

53. Starhawk, "Feminist, Earth-based Spirituality and Ecofeminism," in Plant, *Healing*, p. 175.

54. Joanna Macy, "Awakening to the Ecological Self," in Plant, *Healing*, pp. 201–211.

55. Charlene Spretnak, "Ecofeminism: Our Roots and Flowering," in Diamond and Orenstein, *Reweaving*, p. 5.

56. Riane Eisler, "The Gaia Tradition and the Partnership Future: An Ecofeminist Manifesto," in Diamond and Orenstein, *Reweaving*, pp. 23–34.

57. Mara Lynn Keller, "The Elusinian Mysteries: Ancient Nature Religion of Demeter and Persephone," in Diamond and Orenstein, *Reweaving*, pp. 41–52.

58. Starhawk, "Power, Authority and Mystery: Earth-based Spirituality and Ecofeminism," in Diamond and Orenstein, *Reweaving*, p. 74. This essay is a significantly different piece, though with some of the same elements, from her similarly titled essay in *Healing*.

59. Michael Zimmerman, "Deep Ecology and Ecofeminism: The Emerging Dialogue," in Diamond and Orenstein, *Reweaving*, pp. 138–154. The inclusion of the essay and Zimmerman's description of ecofeminism is controversial. See Deborah Slicer, "Is There an Ecofeminism-Deep Ecology 'Debate'?" *Environmental Ethics* 17 (Summer 1995): 151–69.

60. Arisika Razak, "Toward a Womanist Analysis of Birth," in Diamond and Orenstein, *Reweaving*, pp. 172.

61. Irene Javors, "The Goddess in the Metropolis: Reflections on the Sacred in an Urban Setting," in Diamond and Orenstein, *Reweaving*, pp. 211–14. Lest readers think my quick summary of this essay is inaccurate, a further quote from this essay may be more persuasive: "In urban centers, Hecate/Kali teaches us that we heal ourselves and become whole when we reunite with the cycles of nature. She show us that what we most fear in external reality—isolation, poverty, disease, loss of control, ugliness, death—are but the shadows and demons of those aspects of our inner worlds that are ruled by ego" (p. 214). This is near the end of an essay where Javors finds a mentally ill man eating a donut on the subway, a homeless man asking for money, and a homeless woman who hangs out on a streetcorner to be "holy ones." The idea that poverty, homelessness, and social isolation are part of "the cycles of nature" is a particularly egregious example of the way essentialist feminist spirituality can be used to mask white middle-class privilege.

62. Rosemary Radford Ruether, "Toward an Ecological-Feminist Theology of Nature," in Plant, *Healing*, pp. 145–50 and Carol P. Christ, "Rethinking Theology and Nature," in Diamond and Orenstein, *Reweaving*, pp. 58–69.

63. Judith Plant warns against the appropriation of Native American culture in "The Circle is Gathering" in *Healing*, mentioned above. The other essay, also mentioned above in this context, is Ynestra King's "Healing the Wounds" in *Reweaving*. King's critique of certain forms of feminist spirituality is more complex, dealing with issues beyond the exploitation of Native American culture.

64. Carol Adams, "Introduction," in Carol Adams, ed. *Ecofeminism and the Sacred* (New York: Continuum Press, 1993), p. 4.

65. Carol Adams uses the word "Tribal," capitalized, to designate Native American spiritual traditions. See Adams, "Introduction," *Ecofeminism and the Sacred*, pp. 1–9.

66. Catherine Keller, "Women Against Wasting the World: Notes on Eschatology and Ecology," p. 258.

67. One way of judging the prevalence of this critique by 1991 is its mainstreaming. Andy Smith's important article on the subject was circulated in unpublished form at the 1990 National Women Studies Association meeting (see Gaard, "Ecofeminism and Native American Cultures") and then was published in *Ms.* in 1991. But the critique becomes even more mainstream with Sherman Alexie's "White Men Can't Drum," in the *New York Times Magazine*, October 4, 1992, pp. 30–31, which critiqued the men's movement for its exploitation of Native American religious rituals. For another mainstream example, see George Synder, "Indians Protest Rip-off Spirituality," in the *San Francisco Chronicle*, December 25, 1995, pp. A1, A10.

68. Marie Wilson, "Wings of the Eagle," in Plant, *Healing*, quotes taken from pp. 216, 218. A number of other Native Americans have had this response to white desire to use their traditions. An especially thoughtful and revealing response to this problem is Lakota Harden's "Wiconi/Survival," in Penny Rossenwasser, ed., *Visionary Voices: Women on Power* (San Francisco: Aunt Lute, 1991), pp. 217–32, esp. pp. 228–31.

69. Margot Adler, "The Juice and the Mystery," in Plant, *Healing*, p. 151.

70. Starhawk, "Feminist, Earth-based Spirituality and Ecofeminism," pp. 175–76.

71. Vera Norwood, *Made From This Earth: American Women and Nature* (Chapel Hill: University of North Carolina, 1993).

72. Using the "cyborg" as a useful and implicitly ecofeminist identity is advocated by Donna Haraway. See "A Cyborg Manifesto: Science, Technology and Socialist-Feminism in the Late Twentieth Century," in *Simians, Cyborgs, and Women: The Reinvention of Nature* (New York: Routledge, 1991), pp. 149–81. I will have more to say about "cyborg ecofeminism" in chapter 6.

73. Rao, "Dominant Constructions," p. 18. By "well-informed studies," Rao is referring not specifically to ecofeminist writings, but to women, environment, and development studies. As I show in the next chapter, she includes Shiva's work among these, and through this connection identifies these studies with "eco-feminism."

74. Jackson, "Women/Nature," pp. 396–97.

75. Elly Haney, "Towards a White Feminist Ecological Ethic," *Journal of Feminist Studies in Religion* 9 (1–2) (Spring/Fall 1993): 75–93, p. 86.

76. Haney, "Towards a White Feminist Ecological Ethic," p. 87.

77. See Haraway, "The Promises of Monsters: A Regenerated Politics for Inappropriate/d Others," in Lawrence Grossberg, Cary Nelson, and Paula Treichler, with Linda Baughman and John Wise, eds., *Cultural Studies* (New York: Routledge, 1992), pp. 295–337; and Elizabeth Bird, "The Social Construction of Nature: Theoretical Approaches to the History of Environmental Problems," *Environmental Review* 11(4) (Winter 1987): 255–64.

78. *The Fifth Sacred Thing* (New York: Bantam, 1993) explores a multiracial, ecofeminist future culture. Haraway finds comparable resources in some feminist science fiction, among which Starhawk's novel could be placed.

79. See Robert Gottlieb, "Reconstructing Environmentalism: Complex Movements, Diverse Roots," *Environmental History Review* (Winter 1993): 1–19.

80. See Monika Maendler, "The Conception of the Environment in the Environmental Justice Movement," M.A. thesis, American Studies Program, Washington State University, (Spring 1997), and Laura Pulido, *Environmentalism and Economic Justice* (Tuscon, AZ: University of Arizona, 1996).

81. For instance, the environmental justice movement may be another locale for a feminist intervention into a male-dominated environmentalism. Though the environmental justice movement is a place where many women environmentalists are active and are leaders, as the movement context congeals and gains public notice, it may be experiencing a turn toward increasing male dominance, in a process Joni Seager identifies as involving the patriarchal nature of professionalization. See her chapter on "The Ecology Establishment," in *Earth Follies:*

Coming to Feminist Terms with the Global Environmental Crisis (New York: Routledge, 1993), pp. 167–221.

CHAPTER FIVE

1. Brinda Rao, "Dominant Constructions of Women and Nature in Social Science Literature," *Capitalism, Nature, Socialism,* Pamphlet 2 (New York: Guilford Publications, 1991), argues especially against the "victimization" paradigm and the idea that "poor women and marginals enjoyed a harmonious relationship with nature" (p. 18). Also see Bina Agarwal, "The Gender and Environment Debate: Lessons from India," *Feminist Studies* 18(1) (Spring 1992): 119–58; Cecile Jackson, "Women/Nature or Gender/History? A Critique of Ecofeminist 'Development'," *Journal of Peasant Studies* 20(3) (April 1993): 389–419.

2. Jackson, "Women/Nature," p. 399.

3. Rao, "Dominant Constructions," p. 12.

4. Rao, "Dominant Constructions," p. 17.

5. As they are whenever a specific location in power relationships is made to produce an automatic political consciousness and a world-historical figure who is the carrier of the revolution (i.e., for class in Marxist discourse, for race in black nationalist and other racially based "revolutionary" discourses, for gender in "standpoint" feminist discourses).

6. Rao, "Dominant Constructions," p. 18.

7. Rao, "Dominant Constructions," p. 17, p. 17, n. 11.

8. Melissa Leach, *Rainforest Relations: Gender and Resource Use Among the Mende of Gola, Sierra Leone* (Washington, DC: Smithsonian Institution Press, 1994), p. 23. Leach's clearer and fairer identification of ecofeminism, than, say Rao's, may in part be a reflection of the clearer definition of ecofeminism as a location within development discourse generated by the World Women's Congress for a Healthy Planet in November 1991. I will discuss this event below.

9. Leach, *Rainforest Relations,* p. 30.

10. Agarwal, "The Gender and Environment Debate," p. 122.

11. Ortner's essay can be found in M. Z. Rosaldo and L. Lamphere, eds., *Women, Culture, and Society* (Stanford, CA: Stanford University Press, 1974), pp. 7–88.

12. I will take up this distinction, between "political practice" and "theoretical tools," more directly in the next chapter.

13. Leach, *Rainforest Relations,* p. 30.

14. I will take as examples here, in order of their publication: Irene Dankelman and Joan Davidson, *Women and Environment in the Third World* (London: Earthscan Publications, 1988); Heleen van den Hombergh, *Gender, Environment and Development: A Guide to the Literature* (Utrecht: International Books, 1993); Maria Mies and Vandana Shiva, *Ecofeminism* (London and New Jersey: Zed Books, 1993); Rosi Braidotti, Ewa Charkiewicz, Sabine Haüsler, and Saski Wieringa, *Women, the Environment and Sustainable Development: Towards a Theoretical Synthesis* (London and Atlantic Highlands, New Jersey: Zed Books, 1994); and Vandana Shiva, ed., *Close To Home: Women Reconnect Ecology, Health and Development Worldwide* (Philadelphia: New Society Publishers, 1994).

15. The history that follows is deeply indebted to Braidotti et al., *Women, the Environment, and Sustainable Development;* and van den Hombergh, *Gender, Environment and Development.*

16. Braidotti, et al., *Women, the Environment, and Sustainable Development,* p. 78. The chapter I will reference in this section was written by Sabine Häusler.

17. For a description of one effort to harness women's work to produce a successful development project benefiting men, see Richard Schroeder, "Shady Practice: Gender and the Political Ecology of Resource Stabilization in Gambian Garden/Orchards," *Economic Geography* 69(4) (1993): 349–65.

18. Leach, *Rainforest Relations,* p. 25.

19. As Richard Schroeder writes: "Judging from the inflow of capital directed at gender equity

oriented projects . . . it is clear that ideologically motivated gender programming is highly lucrative turf in The Gambia. The enactment of WID strategies in The Gambia translated directly into hundreds of grants to women's garden groups for barbed wire, tools, hybrid seed and well-digging costs." Schroeder, "Co-opted Critiques: Gender, Environment and Development Discourse," conference paper presented at the American Anthropological Association meeting in Washington, DC (November 1995), pp. 6–7.

20. Häusler, "Women, the Environment, and Sustainable Development: Emergence of the Theme and Different Views," in Braidotti, et al,. *Women, the Environment, and Sustainable Development*, p. 80.

21. Häusler, "Women, the Environment, and Sustainable Development," in Braidotti, et al., *Women, the Environment, and Sustainable Development*, p. 80.

22. See van den Hombergh's discussion in *Gender, Environment, and Development*, pp. 58–60.

23. Häusler, "Women, the Environment, and Sustainable Development," in Braidotti, et al., *Women, the Environment, and Sustainable Development*, p. 81.

24. This was also the arena for the Women's Peace Tent, mentioned in chapter 3, in which Ynestra King, Starhawk, and the funder of WomanEarth participated.

25. "The WID approach is associated with a concern to increase women's participation and benefits, thereby making development more effective. Gender and Development represents a transition to 'not only integrate women into development, but look for the potential in development initiatives to transform unequal social/gender relations and to empower women'." Häusler, "Women, the Environment, and Sustainable Development," quoting the Canadian Council for International Cooperation in 1991, p. 82. Interestingly, this tension between "women" and "gender" in the international context is the reverse of the tension between the two terms in the context of U.S. women's studies, in which the prefix "women" signals a feminist intent, while the prefix "gender" is controversial, feared by some as signalling a dilution of feminist attention to women.

26. Häusler, "Women, the Environment, and Sustainable Development," p. 84.

27. Häusler, "Women, the Environment, and Sustainable Development," p. 85.

28. Richard Schroeder, "Shady Practice."

29. The notion of theories operating as "two-way" streets for communication between subordinate groups or as new tools for resistance to power, even when those theories may be part of a dominating force, is complexly argued by Anna Tsing in "Environmentalisms: Transitions as Translations," in Joan Scott, Cora Kaplan, and Debra Keates, eds., *Transitions, Translations, Environments: International Feminism in Contemporary Politics* (New York, Routledge, forthcoming).

30. This ability of environmental problems to challenge notions of "owned" and limited space, whether defined by national boundaries or private property relations, has long been an object of analytic interest.

31. Ramachanda Guha, "Radical Environmentalism and Preservation of Wilderness: A Third World Critique," *Environmental Ethics* 11(1) (1989): 71–83.

32. Peter J. Taylor and Frederick H. Buttell, "How Do We Know We Have Global Environmental Problems: Science and the Globalization of Environmental Discourse," *Geoforum* 23(3) (1992): 405–16, p. 408.

33. Taylor and Buttel, "How Do We Know," p. 409.

34. Taylor and Buttel, "How Do We Know," p. 411–12.

35. Gaile McGregor, "Re constructing environment: A cross-cultural perspective," in *Canadian Review of Sociology and Anthropology* 31(3) (1994): 268–88, p. 269. She says: "Judging from the recent literature, environmental thinking these days is so thoroughly transnationalized that it makes communication studies look parochial" (p. 270). Given McGregor's interest in producing a "Canadian difference," it's important to retain the Canadian form of the noncapitalization of her article title. Americanized into all caps, the title would lose the double entendre of "re constructing."

36. Anna Tsing, "Environmentalism," p. 11. I am quoting from the conference paper of the

same title, presented at the Transitions, Environments, Translations: The Meanings of Feminism in Contemporary Politics conference at the Institute for Research on Women, Rutgers University and the Institute for Advanced Study, Princeton University, April 1995, and forthcoming in Joan Scott, Cora Kaplan, and Debra Keates, eds., *Transitions, Translations, Environments: International Feminism in Contemporary Politics* (New York: Routledge).

37. Tsing, "Environmentalism," pp. 12–13. Ilene Rose Feinman's "Brutal Responsibilities and Second Class Citizens: Women Soldiers, Martial Citizenship, and Feminist Antimilitarism" (Ph.D. dissertation, History of Consciousness Program, University of California, Santa Cruz, Spring 1997) is a complex treatment of shifting feminist antimilitarist discourses within a post-Cold War context that illuminates many issues I touch on here.

38. Steven Greenhouse, "The Greening of American Diplomacy," *New York Times* (October 9, 1995), p. A4. I thank Marion Sturgeon for bringing this article and the one following to my attention.

39. "American Spy Satellites Will Turn More Attention to Nature With End of Cold War," *New York Times* (November 27, 1995): A1, 6. See also Richard Dreyfuss, "James Bond, Meet Captain Planet! The CIA is Aiming at Environmental Command and Control," *Environmental Magazine* 6(1) (January 1995): 28.

40. Robert D. Kaplan, "The Coming Anarchy," *Atlantic Monthly* 273 (February 1994): 44–76, was an article that gained a great deal of attention in U.S. policy-making circles.

41. Tsing's story in this same article about the development of southern environmentalism as both a strategy to resist Western neocolonialism and as a tool in horizontal (Third World country versus Third World country) political positionings is also important here.

42. Shiva's term; see Vandana Shiva, *Staying Alive: Women, Ecology and Development in India* (London: Zed Books, 1988).

43. Joni Seager, *Earth Follies: Coming to Feminist Terms with the Global Environmental Crisis* (New York: Routledge, 1993).

44. Tsing, "Environmentalism," p. 17.

45. My information about WEDO comes from Mim Kelber, "The Women's Environment and Development Organization," *Environment* 36(8) (October 1994): 43–45; Carolyn Merchant, "Partnership Ethics: Earthcare for a New Millennium," in *Earthcare: Women and the Environment* (New York: Routledge, 1996), pp. 209–24; various WEDO documents; interviews with Mim Kelber (March 1995) and Bella Abzug (May 1995); and participant observation of WEDO's activities in New York City at the March 1995 UN Preparatory Meetings for the Fourth World Women's Conference to be held in Beijing. I am deeply grateful to Mim Kelber and Bella Abzug for their time and frankness, and the WEDO staff for their assistance in facilitating my participation in the PrepCom meetings and helping me collect WEDO publications and documents.

46. The Women's USA Fund, Inc., was founded by Bella Abzug, Mim Kelber, Gloria Steinem, Patsy Mink, and Maxine Waters. Kelber, "The Women's Environment and Development Organization," p. 43.

47. Mim Kelber interview, March 1995. All quotes attributed to Kelber in what follows are from this interview unless otherwise specified.

48. See "Meet the Women Who Steer WEDO's Course, Our Co-Chairs," in WEDO's newsletter, *News and Views* 6(2) (September 1993), pp. 2–4.

49. Kelber, "The Women's Environment and Development Organization," p. 43.

50. "Findings of the Tribunal," in *Official Report: World Women's Congress for a Healthy Planet* (New York: WEDO, 1991), p. 2.

51. Michele Landsberg, "Overview," in *Official Report*, pp. 2–3.

52. "Findings of the Tribunal," in *Official Report*, pp. 8–9.

53. This conclusion is based on conversations with participants to the conference, especially Amber Sverdrup, a reporter for *The Ecofeminist Newsletter*, and Greta Gaard. See the special issue on the World Women's Congress for a Healthy Planet, *The Ecofeminism Newsletter* 3(1)

(Winter 1992), especially Amber Sverdrup, "Inspirational Messages, Inconsistent Practices" (p. 6) and Greta Gaard, "Finding a Home in the World" (p. 7). Available from Noël Sturgeon, Women's Studies, Washington State University, Pullman, WA, 99163, USA.

54. Though she was interviewed as part of Greta Gaard's video, "Ecofeminism Now!"

55. Interestingly, the one funder who gave money to WEDO to bring U.S. women of color to the Congress was the funder who had earlier supported WomanEarth Feminist Peace Institute, and who left because U.S. racial diversity was stressed over international diversity. She also funded the only project of WEDO's that focused on U.S. women, especially women of color: the Breast Cancer Project. Was this a lesson learned from WomanEarth? Or simply an independent initiative of the funder?

56. "Regional Caucus Reports," in *Official Report*, pp. 26–35 (with inserted unnumbered page). The caucuses were: African, European, International Indigenous, Las Mujeres de América Latina y el Caribe, Middle East, Asian, Pacific Region, Women of the South, and Women of Color of North America.

57. "International Indigenous Women's Caucus," in *Official Report*, p. 30.

58. Mim Kelber interview, March 1995; Bella Abzug interview, May 1995.

59. "Women's Action Agenda 21," in *Official Report*, pp. 17–23.

60. For a description of "Planeta Fêmea," see Carolyn Merchant, "Partnership Ethics: Earthcare for a New Millennium," in *Earthcare*. See also the book published by organizers of Planeta Fêmea, Rosiska Darcy de Oliveira and Thais Corral, *Terra Femina* (Rio de Janeiro: A Joint Publication of Institute for Cultural Action [IDAC] and The Network in Defense of Human Species [REDEH], 1992). This book contains articles by Carolyn Merchant, Corrine Kumar D'Souza, Maia Mies, Rosiska Darcy de Oliveira, Teresa Santa Clara Gomes, Thai Corral, and Vandana Shiva, and is closely identified with "ecofeminism."

61. See *Agenda 21: An Easy Reference to the Specific Recommendations on Women*, (New York: UNIFEM, undated). Available from UNIFEM, 304 East 45th Street, 6th Floor, New York, NY, 10017.

62. Preamble of "Women's Action Agenda 21" in *Official Report*, p. 16.

63. Greta Gaard, personal communication, letter dated March 12, 1996, p. 6.

64. Bella Abzug interview, May 1995. All quotes from Abzug are from this interview unless otherwise specified.

65. Poster available from WEDO, 845 Third Avenue, 15 Floor, New York, NY, 10022. "It's Time for Women to Mother Earth" was also the title of Margarita Arias's keynote speech at the "Congress for a Healthy Planet." From the initial "Program" for the Congress.

66. It is pertinent to note here that many ecofeminists have criticized and/or complicated both the use of the image of the earth-seen-from-space (the Whole Earth image) and the use of the idea of Mother Earth in environmentalist rhetoric. See Yaakov Garb, "Perspective or Escape? Ecofeminist Musings on Contemporary Earth Imagery," in Irene Diamond and Gloria Orenstein, eds., *Reweaving the World: The Emergence of Ecofeminism* (San Francisco: Sierra Club, 1990), pp. 264–78; Greta Gaard, "Ecofeminism and Native American Cultures," in Greta Gaard, ed., *Ecofeminism: Women, Animals, Nature*, pp. 295–314, esp. 301–305; and Marcy Darnovsky/Donna Haraway, "Overhauling the Meaning Machines: An Interview with Donna Haraway," *Socialist Review* 21(2) (1991): 65–84, pp. 69–70.

67. From "Community Report Card," available from WEDO, 845 Third Avenue, 15th Floor, New York, NY, 10022; phone number: (212) 759–7982; fax: 759–8647.

68. María Fernanda Espinosa, "Indigenous Women on Stage: New Agendas and Political Processes Among Indigenous Women in the Ecuadorian Amazon," paper presented at the Feminist Generations Conference, Bowling Green State University, February 1996.

69. Espinosa, "Indigenous Women on Stage," p. 3.

70. Espinosa, "Indigenous Women on Stage," p. 4.

71. Espinosa, "Indigenous Women on Stage," p. 6.

72. Espinosa, "Indigenous Women on Stage," p. 8.

73. Espinosa, "Indigenous Women on Stage," p. 10, n. 9.

74. I am paraphrasing the story Espinosa told as part of her presentation of the paper to the Feminist Generations conference. This story is not in the text of her paper.

75. Both preceding quotes from Espinosa, "Indigenous Women on Stage," p. 9.

76. Espinosa, "Indigenous Women on Stage," p. 10. Another example of the usefulness of "gender-sensitive NGOs" for local women in sometimes surprising ways can be found in Bina Agarwal, "Gender, Environment and Collective Action," paper presented at the Transitions, Environments, Translations: The Meanings of Feminism in Contemporary Politics conference at the Institute for Research on Women, Rutgers University, and the Institute for Advanced Study, Princeton University, April 1995, and forthcoming in Joan Scott, Cora Kaplan, and Debra Keates, eds., *Transitions, Translations, Environments: International Feminism in Contemporary Politics* (New York: Routledge).

77. Michael Peter Smith, "Can You Imagine? Transnational Migration and the Globalization of Grassroots Politics," *Social Text* 39 (Summer 1994): 15–33, p. 15.

78. Jane Jacobs, "Earth Honoring: Western Desires and Indigenous Knowledges," in Alison Blunt and Gilliam Rose, eds., *Writing Women and Space: Colonial and Postcolonial Geographies* (New York: Guilford, 1994), pp. 169–96, p. 169.

CHAPTER SIX

1. At a meeting of prominent ecofeminists attending the "Ecofeminist Perspectives" conference in Dayton in March 1995, one topic of discussion was the "feminist backlash against ecofeminism," as well as the creation of an ecofeminist journal, fostering ecofeminist activism, and connecting ecofeminism more concretely to the environmental justice movement.

2. Greta Gaard, "Misunderstanding Ecofeminism," *Z Magazine* 3(1) (1994): 22.

3. I thank Virginia Scharff for pushing me to clarify this point,

4. Indeed, the uncertainty built into this dynamic process has historically made many leftists uncomfortable.

5. Katie King, *Theory in Its Feminist Travels: Conversations in U.S. Women's Movements* (Bloomington: Indiana University, 1994), p. 69. To grasp the complexity of King's argument on this point, see especially her chapter, "Writing Conversations in Feminist Theory: Investments in Producing Identities and Struggling With Time," pp. 55–91.

6. For an excellent discussion of the difficulty of separating the terms "theory" and "practice" within feminism and ecofeminism, see Christine Cuomo, "Toward Thoughtful Ecofeminist Action," in Karen J. Warren, ed., *Ecological Feminist Philosophies* (Bloomington: Indiana University, 1996), pp. 42–51. Also see Stephanie Lahar, "Ecofeminist Theory and Grassroots Politics," in Warren, *Ecological Feminist Philosophies*, pp. 1–18.

7. The texts that I will be referring to in this section, which generate various typologies, are Barbara Deckard, *The Women's Movement*, 3d ed. (New York: Harper & Row, 1983); and Alison Jaggar, *Feminist Politics and Human Nature* (Totowa, NJ: Rowman & Allanheld, 1983); Josephine Donovan, *Feminist Theory: The Intellectual Traditions of American Feminism* (New York: Frederick Ungar, 1985); Myra Marx Ferree and Beth B. Hess, *Controversy and Coalition: The New Feminist Movement* (Boston: Twayne Publishers, 1985); Alison M. Jaggar and Paula S. Rothenberg, *Feminist Frameworks: Alternative Theoretical Accounts of the Relations Between Women and Men* (New York: McGraw-Hill, 1978, 1984, 1993).

8. As its usefulness to the argument in this chapter demonstrates, Katie King's book, *Theory in Its Feminist Travels*, provides a great deal of the kind of history of feminism and feminist theory which I call for here.

9. Jo Freeman, "The Women's Liberation Movement: Its Origins, Organizations, Activities, and Ideas," in *Women: A Feminist Perspective* (Palo Alto, CA: Mayfield, 1979), p. 568.

10. Ferree and Hess, in *Controversy and Coalition*, add "career feminism" (a basically conser-

vative, individualistic feminist position) to the categories liberal, radical, and socialist.

11. Donovan, *Feminist Theory*, p. 31.

12. Alice Echols, "The New Feminism of Yin and Yang," in Christine Stansell, Ann Snitow, and Sharon Thompson, eds., *Powers of Desire: The Politics of Sexuality* (New York: Monthly Review Press, 1983), pp. 439–59.

13. Ellen Willis, "Radical Feminism and Feminist Radicalism," in Sohnya Sayres, Anders Stephanson, Stanley Aronowitz, and Fredric Jameson, eds., *The Sixties Without Apology* (Minneapolis: University of Minnesota, 1984), pp. 91–118, p. 107.

14. The story of the construction and various uses of the term "cultural feminism" is complex, and I cannot tell it fully here. In important ways, Willis's and Echols's use of the term are stimulated by the way in which "radical feminism" had been tagged earlier with the essentialist label, complete with accusations of racism and classism, thus engaging them in an effort to distinguish a nonessentialist variant of early feminism, which they called "radical feminism," as well as an essentialist variant of early feminism, which they called "cultural feminism." Though Echols's book received significant attention, it has not changed the conflation between the two early kinds of feminism she wanted to distinguish, as much as it has resulted in the substitution "cultural feminism" for "radical feminism."

15. For instance, in Chris Weedon, *Feminist Practice and Poststructuralist Theory* (Oxford: Basil Blackwell, 1987), and Sandra Harding, *The Science Question in Feminism* (Ithaca, NY: Cornell University Press, 1986).

16. Alice Echols, *Daring to Be Bad* (Minneapolis: University of Minnesota Press, 1989), p. 6.

17. And of course the irony here is that Willis, who objected so strongly to the reductive characterization of "radical feminism" as essentialist, and who was one of the main supporters of Echols's book project, was also one of the most vociferous proponents of the idea that ecofeminism was "cultural feminism" and therefore "essentialist." Echols echoes this judgment; see *Daring to Be Bad*, p. 288.

18. For examples of feminist theorizing by women of color in the early period of the second wave, see Cellestine Ware, *Woman Power: The Movement for Women's Liberation* (New York: Tower, 1970); Pauli Murray, "The Liberation of Black Women," in Mary Lou Thompson, ed., *Voices of the New Feminism* (Boston: Beacon Press, 1970), pp. 87–102; Maryanne Weathers, "An Argument for Black Women's Liberation as a Revolutionary Force," pp 161–64, and Patricia M. Robinson, "A Historical and Critical Essay for Black Women," pp. 274–83, both in Sookie Stambler, ed., *Women's Liberation: A Blueprint for the Future* (New York: Ace, 1970); Frances M. Beale, "'Double Jeopardy,' To Be Black and Female," pp. 340–52, Eleanor Homes Norton, "For Sadie and Maude," pp. 352–59, Black Women's Liberation Group, "Statement on Birth Control," pp. 360–61, Elizabeth Sutherland, "Introduction (to Colonized Women: The Chicana)," pp. 376–78, and Enriqueta Longauex y Vasquez, "The Mexican-American Woman," pp. 379–84, all in Robin Morgan, ed., *Sisterhood is Powerful* (New York: Vintage, 1970); Michele Wallace, "Black Macho and the Myth of the Superwoman," *Ms.* (January 1979); *conditions five: the black women's issue* (1979); Audre Lorde, "The Master's Tools Will Never Dismantle the Master's House," in Cherrie Moraga and Gloria Anzaldua, eds., *This Bridge Called My Back* (Watertown, MA: Persephone Press, 1981), pp. 98–101; Combahee River Collective, "A Black Feminist Statement," in Gloria T. Hull, Patricia Smith, and Barbara Smith, eds., *But Some of Us Were Brave: Black Women's Studies* (New York: Feminist Press, 1982), pp. 13–22; Angela Davis, *Violence Against Women and the Ongoing Challenge to Racism* (Freedom Organizing Series #5), (Latham, NY: Kitchen Table, 1985).

19. Katie King has accomplished an incisive analysis of *Feminist Frameworks*, to which I owe a great deal. She does not discuss the later editions. See King, *Theory in Its Feminist Travels*, pp. 67–70.

20. King, *Theory in Its Feminist Travels*, p. 84.

21. Chela Sandoval, "U.S. Third World Feminism: The Theory and Method of Oppositional Consciousness in the Postmodern World," *Genders* 10 (Spring 1991): 1–24, p. 9.

22. Sandoval, "U.S. Third World Feminism," p. 11.

23. Sandoval, "U.S. Third World Feminism," pp. 12–13.

24. Sandoval, "U.S. Third World Feminism," p. 14.

25. Sandoval, "U.S. Third World Feminism," p. 14.

26. "Interesting to certain third world scholars is the coalescing relationship between these theories of postmodernism (especially between those which celebrate the fragmentations of consciousness postmodernism demands) and the form of differential oppositional consciousness I am outlining here. The juncture I am analyzing in this essay is that which connects the disoriented first world subject, who longs for the postmodern cultural aesthetic as a key to a new sense of identity and redemption, and the form of differential oppositional consciousness developed by subordinated and marginalized Western or colonized subjects, who have been forced to experience the aesthetics of a 'postmodernism' as a requisite for survival. It is this constituency who are most familiar with what citizenship in this realm requires and makes possible." Sandoval, "U.S. Third World Feminism," pp. 21–22, n. 50.

27. Sandoval, "U.S. Third World Feminism," p. 15.

28. I am roughly following Jaggar's assignation of various "politics" to different categories, but the point applies to all of the typologies I've cited above.

29. Jaggar, *Feminist Politics*, p. 123.

30. Ferree and Hess, *Controversy and Coalition*, pp. 154–159.

31. Ferree and Hess, *Controversy and Coalition*, p. 89.

32. Weedon, *Feminist Practice and Poststructuralist Theory*, p. 174.

33. Though she does not focus on the practice of typologizing as I do here, Elizabeth Carlassare has produced an excellent analysis of the essentialism/constructionist debate's effect on conceptualizing ecofeminism. See Carlassare, "Essentialism in Ecofeminist Discourse," in Carolyn Merchant, ed., *Ecology: Key Concepts in Critical Theory* (Atlantic Highlands, NJ: Humanities Press, 1994), pp. 220–34.

34. Janet Biehl, "What is Social Ecofeminism?" *Green Perspectives* 11 (October 1988): 1–8.

35. Carolyn Merchant, "Ecofeminism and Feminist Theory," in Irene Diamond and Gloria Orenstein, eds., *Reweaving the World: The Emergence of Ecofeminism* (San Francisco: New Society Publishers, 1990), pp. 100–105; Merchant, "Ecofeminism," in *Radical Ecology: The Search for a Livable World* (New York: Routledge, 1992), pp. 183–210; and "Gaia: Ecofeminism and the Earth" in *Earthcare: Women and the Environment* (New York: Routledge, 1996).

36. Karen Warren, "Feminism and Ecology: Making Connections," *Environmental Ethics* 9(1) (Spring 1987): 3–20.

37. See Val Plumwood, *Feminism and the Mastery of Nature* (New York: Routledge, 1994), especially "Feminism and Ecofeminism," pp. 119–40.

38. Roger J.H. King, "Caring About Nature: Feminist Ethics and the Environment," in Karen J. Warren, ed., *Ecological Feminist Philosophies* (Bloomington: Indiana University, 1996), pp. 82–96.

39. Victoria Davion, "Is Ecofeminism Feminist?" in Karen J. Warren, ed., *Ecological Feminism* (New York: Routledge, 1994), pp. 8–28.

40. Catherine Roach, "Loving Your Mother: On the Woman-Nature Relation," in Warren, *Ecological Feminist Philosophies*, pp. 52–65.

41. Chaia Heller, *The Revolution That Dances: From a Politics of Desire Toward a Desirable Politics* (Littleton, CO: Aigis Press, forthcoming).

42. Mary Mellors, *Breaking the Boundaries: Toward a Feminist Green Socialism* (London: Virago Press, 1992).

43. Bina Agarwal, "The Gender and Environmental Debate: Lessons From India," *Feminist Studies* 18(1) (Spring 1992): 119–58; and Joni Seager, *Earth Folllies: Coming to Feminist Terms with the Global Environmental Crisis* (New York: Routledge, 1993), especially pp. 9–12, and 236–52.

44. Stacy Alaimo, "Cyborg and Ecofeminist Interventions: Challenges for an Environmental Feminism," *Feminist Studies* 20(1) (Spring 1994): 133–52.

45. Diane Rocheleau, Barbara Thomas-Slayter, and Esther Wangari, eds., *Feminist Political Ecologies: Global Issues and Local Experiences* (New York: Routledge, 1996). This book was brought to my attention by Chaia Heller just as *Ecofeminist Natures* was going to press. Thus, I was unfortunately unable to obtain it in time to consider it in light of the arguments I make here and in chapter 5.

46. Kathy Ferguson, *The Man Question: Visions of Subjectivity in Feminist Theory* (Berkeley: University of California, 1993), p. 81.

47. Ferguson, *The Man Question*, p. 82.

48. This is true even for "cosmic feminism," which is the category of feminist theory in which Ferguson places most ecofeminists. She notes that "essentialism per se is sometimes detected in the writings of cosmic feminism, although it is also contested there; at any rate, the cosmic side of feminism carries so little academic legitimacy that it is accorded scant attention within feminist theory." I'll return to Ferguson's method of typologizing later in this chapter. Ferguson, *The Man Question*, p. 81.

49. Ferguson, *The Man Question*, p. 81.

50. Ferguson, *The Man Question*, pp. 82–83.

51. Ferguson, *The Man Question*, p. 83.

52. Ferguson, *The Man Question*, p. 87.

53. Hopefully, the examples I have provided throughout this book will be evidence enough for this point. T.V. Reed has made a similar argument: "The deployment, for example, of a collective identity (woman, gay, African-American, native) is *most* likely to be recognized as strategic from inside that collective where intimate knowledge of internal differences is greatest; it is on the outside that such gestures are most likely to be mistaken as essentialist." And he continues: "Seemingly essentialist gestures are a necessary, recurring epistemological moment in organizing, one that is never wholly superseded by the equally necessary moments when internal diversity is stressed." Reed, *Fifteen Jugglers, Five Believers: Literary Politics and the Poetics of Social Movements* (Berkeley: University of California, 1991), p. 149.

54. Merchant, "Ecofeminism and Feminist Theory," in Diamond and Orenstein, *Reweaving the World*, p. 102.

55. Merchant, "Ecofeminism and Feminist Theory," p. 103.

56. Merchant, "Ecofeminism," in *Radical Ecology*, pp. 183–210.

57. Merchant, "Ecofeminism," p. 194.

58. Merchant, "Ecofeminism," p. 195.

59. There is a location called "socialist ecofeminism" that could have been characterized in this book as a feminist intervention into the environmentalist category "socialist ecology," represented by James O'Connor's work and the journal *Capitalism, Nature, and Society*, edited by O'Connor. This is a very small grouping, and ecofeminists who have identified themselves as socialist feminists besides Merchant have been few. Mary Mellors uses the label "feminist green socialism." Maria Mies and Val Plumwood both call themselves socialist ecofeminist. As we shall see in a minute, Greta Gaard locates Vandana Shiva as a socialist ecofeminist, as well. See Maria Mies, *Patriarchy and Accumulation on a World Scale* (London: Zed Books, 1986); Maria Mies and Vandana Shiva, *Ecofeminism* (London: Zed Books, 1993); Mary Mellors, *Breaking the Boundaries*; and Gaard, *Ecofeminism Now!* (Medusa Productions, 1996), VHS, 37 minutes, available for $15 plus shipping from Dr. Greta Gaard, Department of English, 420 Humanities Building, University of Minnesota, Duluth, MN 55812.

60. Merchant, "Ecofeminism," p. 195.

61. Merchant, "Ecofeminism," p. 192.

62. Merchant, "Ecofeminism," p. 193.

63. Merchant, "Ecofeminism," p. 201.

64. Merchant, "Ecofeminism," p. 205.

65. Merchant, "Ecofeminism," p. 208.

66. See Noël Sturgeon, "Theorizing Movements: Direct Action and Direct Theory," in Marcy Darnovsky, Barbara Epstein, and Richard Flacks, eds., *Cultural Politics and Social Move-*

ments (Philadelphia: Temple University, 1995), pp. 35–51; and "Direct Theory and Political Action: The U.S. Nonviolent Direct Action Movement," Ph.D. Dissertation, University of California, Santa Cruz, March 1991.

67. This phrase was suggested to me by Ednie Garrison.

68. King, "Caring About Nature," p. 88.

69. King, "Caring About Nature," p. 89.

70. Giovanna di Chiro, "Defining Environmental Justice: Women's Voices and Grassroots Politics," *Socialist Review* 22(4) (October–December 1992): 93–130, p. 115. For similar arguments depicting women's activism arising out of "community," see Joni Seager, "Hysterical Housewives, Treehuggers, and Other Mad Women," in *Earth Follies*, pp. 253–79; Celene Kraus, "Blue-Collar Women and Toxic-Waste Protests: The Process of Politicization," pp. 107–17), and Vernice D. Miller, "Building on Our Past, Planning for Our Future: Communities of Color and the Quest for Environmental Justice," pp. 128–37), both in Richard Hofrichter, ed., *Toxic Struggles* (Philadelphia: New Society Publishers, 1993); and Maria Cuevas, "Community Work as Family Work: Chicana Community Empowerment Strategies in Los Angeles," paper presented at American Movement Cultures: Boundaries, Borders, Bodies conference at Washington State University, June 1996.

71. Di Chiro, "Defining Environmental Justice," p. 118.

72. Greta Gaard, *Ecofeminism Now!*

73. Sandoval's schema of reformulating liberal, Marxist, radical/cultural, and socialist feminisms is especially useful for understanding the process of consciousness-raising that is part of teaching Women's Studies in a university context. In my experience, my primarily white and middle class students come into my Introduction to Women Studies course with the (liberal) assumption that "women are the same as men." In the course of exposure to the analysis of the social construction of gender and the various forms of sexism, they go (rapidly and unevenly) through the stages "women are different from men" and "women are superior to men" (the stages that create the most consternation among conservative and feminist critics of Women Studies alike). My task is to get them to the "women are a racially divided class" moment before they leave the Intro course. In that mode, they come into the upper-level "theory" classes, which, oriented as those classes are around the material and skills appropriate for preparation into professional academic careers, concentrate on the critical, textually based practice known as "poststructuralist feminism" (which Sandoval does not add to her reformulation but which might be recast as "women and men are not unified categories"). This curriculum-based "stage" metaphor (common in conversations around ways of formulating a Women's Studies program) recapitulates the idea that a move from (essentialist) cultural feminisms to (anti-essentialist) poststructural feminisms is a matter of "development," in which the last stage is the best. I have always been uncomfortable with how this process of professionalization is obscured for what it is and how it reappears as the "maturity" phase for a young feminist (an obfuscation, by the way, that many students in "theory" classes furiously resist). This is particularly troublesome, as the "earlier" stages of "women are different than men," "women are superior to men," and "women are a racially divided class" are moments in which the feminist solidarity is created that pushes young feminists to understand the interconnections between racism, classism, sexism, and heterosexism. Furthermore, that solidarity provides the material basis for feminist activism. Am I saying that poststructuralist feminism can't be used for generating feminist activism? Not unless we discount academic political practice as activism, which I (personally!) would not want to do. But we must also not privilege this as the "best" kind of feminist activism. Ongoing studies of third-wave feminism will be the place to look for some of the answers to these questions; see, for instance, Ednie Garrison, "The Third Wave and Postmodern Cultural Conditions: Feminist Consciousness in the 1990s," Kerri Dyan Gentine, "Earth Mothers and Riot Grrrls: Why My Mother May Never Be My Sister," and Crystal Kile, "Hello Kitty Explains Kinderwhore to You: Third Wave Feminism and Riot Grrrl Style," all papers presented at the Feminist Generations conference, Bowling Green University, February 1996. I am especially indebted to Ednie Garrison for her helpful comments on this chapter.

74. Joni Seager, *Earth Follies*, p. 12.

75. The use of Salleh as a critic of essentialism is especially peculiar since we have seen, in chapter 1, that one of Salleh's early articles made a quite explicitly biologistic argument for "ecofeminism," though her later work rejected "essentialism per se" strongly. Perhaps Alaimo only read this later work. See Ariel Kay Salleh, "Deeper Than Deep Ecology: The Eco-Feminist Connection," *Environmental Ethics* 6 (Winter 1984): 340–45; "The Ecofeminism/Deep Ecology Debate: A Reply to Patriarchal Reason," *Environmental Ethics* 14 (Fall 1992): 195–216; and "Class, Race, and Gender Discourse in the Ecofeminism/Deep Ecology Debate," *Environmental Ethics* 15 (Fall 1993): 225–44.

76. Alaimo, "Cyborg and Ecofeminist Interventions," p. 133.

77. Alaimo introduces these quotes from Haraway by saying: "Haraway critiques the ecofeminist positions on nature and science by analyzing them in a non-Western context." Alaimo, "Cyborg and Ecofeminist Interventions," p. 135. All of the material from Haraway that I cite in what follows was available to Alaimo at the time of her writing.

78. Donna Haraway, *Primate Visions: Gender, Race and Nature in the World of Modern Science* (New York: Routledge, 1989), p. 412, n.30.

79. Donna Haraway, "A Cyborg Manifesto: Science, Technology, and Socialist Feminism in the 1980s," in *Simians, Cyborgs, and Women* (New York: Routledge, 1991), pp. 149–81, p. 181.

80. Donna Haraway, "Situated Knowledges: The Science Question in Feminism and the Privilege of Partial Perspective," in *Simians, Cyborgs, and Women*, pp. 183–201, p. 201.

81. See especially her interview with Marcy Darnovsky entitled, "Overhauling the Meaning Machines," in *Socialist Review* 21(2) (1991): 65–84, especially p. 69–70, 78.

82. The relevant section is as follows: "At the same time [as ecofeminism makes useful connections between feminism and environmentalism] the ecofeminist argument fails on several counts. First, it posits 'woman' as a unitary category and fails to differentiate among women by class, race, ethnicity, and so on. It thus ignores forms of domination other than gender which also impinge critically on women's position. Second, it locates the domination of women and of nature almost solely in ideology, neglecting the (interrelated) material sources of this dominance (based on economic advantage and political power). Third, even in the realm of ideological constructs, it says little (with the exception of Merchant's analysis) about the social, economic, and political structures within which these constructs are produced and transformed. Nor does it address the central issue of the means by which certain dominant groups (predicated on gender, class, etc.) are able to bring about ideological shifts in their own favor and how such shifts get entrenched. Fourth, the ecofeminist argument does not take into account women's lived material relationship with nature, as opposed to what others or they themselves might conceive that relationship to be. Fifth, those strands of ecofeminism that trace the connection between women and nature to biology may be seen as adhering to a form of essentialism (some notion of a female 'essence' which is unchangeable and irreducible). Such a formulation flies in the face of wide-ranging evidence that concepts of nature, culture, gender, and so on, are historically and socially constructed and vary across and within cultures and time periods." For her example of the "biologistic" ecofeminist argument, Agarwal uses Ortner's famous essay, "Is Male to Female as Nature is to Culture?" which, as I have noted before, is not explicitly ecofeminist and indeed predates U.S. ecofeminism. Agarwal, "The Gender and Environment Debate," pp. 122–23.

83. Agarwal, "The Gender and Environment Debate," p. 123.

84. Agarwal would not count these explorations as "materialist" because she is working with a Marxist definition of "materialist," which retains an implicit reliance on the economic, dualistic, hierarchical "base/superstructure" model of orthodox Marxism in which "nature" is primarily a resource for production. Also, I want to be clear I am not saying that all accounts of the "nature-engaging" activities I list above necessarily *have to be* in terms of universalizing white, U.S., or middle-class experience uncritically, nor that these experiences are always only undertaken by white, middle-class, U.S. women. See, for an account of women's "lived material relationship" with gardening and animals, which is quite sensitive to historical, class, and race questions, Vera Norwood, *Made From This Earth: American Women and Nature* (Chapel Hill and London: Uni-

versity of North Carolina Press, 1993). See, for an account of African American women's relation to gardening and to animals, Alice Walker, "In My Mother's Garden," *In Search of Our Mother's Gardens* (San Diego: Harcourt Brace Jovanovich, 1983), and "Am I Blue?" in *Living By The Word* (San Diego: Harcourt Brace Jovanovich, 1988), pp. 3–8. See, for a complex account of women of color's relationship with "nature" figured in various ways, Gloria Anzaldúa, *Borderlands/La Frontera* (San Francisco: Spinsters/Aunt Lute, 1987). Elly Haney suggests that, given her own raced, classed, gendered, and historicized subject location, "nature was a sphere of activity free from the various constraints of being female. It was freedom, not nurturance and fertility/creativity, that shaped my relationship with the out-of-doors." Haney, "Towards a White Feminist Ecological Ethic," *Journal of Feminist Studies in Religion* 9(1–2) (Spring/Fall 1993): 75–93, p. 91. A complex, breath-takingly materialist race- and class-specific narrative of encountering nature can be found in Val Plumwood's "Human Vulnerability and the Experience of Being Prey," *Quadrant* (March 1995): 2, 30–33.

85. Agarwal, "The Gender and Environment Debate," p. 122.

86. Karen Warren, "Feminism and Ecology," pp. 18–19.

87. Warren, "Feminism and Ecology," p. 19.

88. Warren, "Feminism and Ecology," p. 5.

89. Warren, "Feminism and Ecology," p. 7.

90. Warren, "Feminism and Ecology," p. 8.

91. Warren, "Feminism and Ecology," p. 17; my emphasis.

92. Warren, "Feminism and Ecology," p. 7.

93. Warren, "Feminism and Ecology," p. 19.

94. Plumwood, "Ecosocial Feminism as a General Theory of Oppression," in Carolyn Merchant, ed., *Ecology*, pp. 207–19.

95. Plumwood, *Feminism and the Mastery of Nature*, p. 11.

96. I thank Julie Graham for this point.

97. Plumwood, *Feminism and the Mastery of Nature*, p. 47.

98. Warren, "Feminism and Ecology," p. 4, and repeated on p. 7.

99. Warren, "Feminism and Ecology," p. 6.

100. Warren, "Feminism and Ecology," p. 7.

101. Ynestra King, "The Ecology of Feminism and the Feminism of Ecology," in Judith Plant, ed., *Healing the Wounds: The Promise of Ecofeminism* (Philadephia: New Society, 1989), pp. 18–28, p. 23.

102. Haraway, "The Promises of Monsters: A Regenerative Politics for Inappropriate/d Others," in Lawrence Grossberg, Gary Nelson, and Paula Treichler, eds., *Cultural Studies* (New York: Routledge, 1991), pp. 295–337, p. 296.

103. See Elizabeth Bird, "Nature As A Social Actor: Conversations in Biotechnology," Ph.D. dissertation, University of California, Santa Cruz, March 1993.

104. Haraway, "The Promises of Monsters," in Grossberg, et al., *Cultural Studies*, p. 297.

105. Haraway, "The Promises of Monsters," in Grossberg, et al., *Cultural Studies*, p. 297.

106. Chela Sandoval, "New Sciences: Cyborg Feminism and the Methodology of the Oppressed," in Chris Hables Gray with Heidi J. Figueroa-Sarriera and Steven Mentor, eds., *The Cyborg Handbook* (New York: Routledge, 1995), pp. 407–22.

107. Imperative exclamation point intended and necessary. Coined by Elizabeth Bird during the Mothers and Others Day Action at the Nevada Test Site, May 1987.

108. Stacy Alaimo, "Cyborg and Ecofeminist Interventions," p. 150.

109. Zoë Sofia, "Exterminating Fetuses: Abortion, Disarmament, and the Sexo-Semiotics of Extraterrestrialism," *Diacritics* 14 (Summer 1984): 47–59, p. 58.

110. Haraway, interviewed by Marcy Darnovsky, in "Overhauling the Meaning Machines," p. 69.

Bibliography

Abbey, Edward. 1975. *The Monkey-Wrench Gang*. New York: Avon.

Adair, Margo. 1984. *Working Inside Out: Tools for Change*. Wingbow.

Adams, Carol. 1991. *The Sexual Politics of Meat: A Feminist-Vegetarian Critical Theory*. New York: Continuum Press.

——. 1994. *Neither Man nor Beast: Feminism and the Defense of Animals*. New York: Continuum Press.

Adams Carol, ed. 1993. *Ecofeminism and the Sacred*. New York: Continuum Press.

Adams, Carol and Josephine Donovan, eds. 1995. *Animals and Women: Feminist Theoretical Explorations*. Durham, NC and London: Duke University Press.

Adams, Carol and Karen Warren. 1991. "Feminism and the Environment: A Selected Bibliography." *American Philosophical Association Newsletter on Feminism and Philosophy* 90(3): 148–57.

Adler, Margot. 1986. *Drawing Down the Moon*. New York: Beacon Press.

Agarwal, Bina. 1992. "The Gender and Environment Debate: Lessons from India." *Feminist Studies* 18(1): 119–58.

——. 1995. "Gender, Environment and Collective Action." Paper presented at the Transitions, Environments, Translations: The Meanings of Feminism in Contemporary Politics Conference at the Institute for Research on Women, Rutgers University, and the Institute for Advanced Study, Princeton University, April.

Alaimo, Stacy. 1994. "Cyborg and Ecofeminist Interventions: Challenges for an Environmental Feminism." *Feminist Studies* 20(1): 133–52.

Alcoff, Linda. 1988. "Cultural Feminism versus Post-Structuralism: The Identity Crisis in Feminist Theory," *SIGNS* 13: 405–436.

Alexie, Sherman. 1992. "White Men Can't Drum." *The New York Times Magazine*. (October 4): 30–31.

Anzaldúa, Gloria. 1987. *Borderlands/La Frontera: The New Metiza*. San Francisco: Spinsters/Aunt Lute.

Arendt, Hannah. 1965. *On Revolution*. New York: Viking.

Bagby, Rachel. 1989. "A Power of Numbers." In *Healing the Wounds: The Promise of Ecofeminism*, edited by Judith Plant. Philadelphia: New Society Publishers, 91–95.

——. 1990. "Daughters of Growing Things." In *Reweaving the World: The Emer-*

gence of Ecofeminism, edited by Irene Diamond and Gloria Orenstein. San Francisco: Sierra Club Books, 231–48.

Bari, Judi. 1988. "Report from the California Rendezvous." *The Earth First! Journal* (November 1): 5.

— — —. 1990. "Expand Earth First!," in *The Earth First Journal* (September 22): 5.

— — —. 1992. "The Feminization of Earth First!" *Ms.* (May/June): 84.

— — —. 1994. "Breaking Up is Hard to Do." In *Timber Wars*. Monroe, ME: Common Courage Press, 55–59.

— — —. 1994. *Timber Wars*. Monroe, ME: Common Courage Press.

Beale, Frances. 1970. "Double Jeopardy: To Be Black and Female." In *Sisterhood is Powerful*, edited by Robin Morgan. New York: Vintage, 340–53.

Biehl, Janet. 1987. "It's Deep, But Is It Broad? An Ecofeminist Looks at Deep Ecology." *Kick It Over* (special supplement): 2A–4A.

— — —. 1988. "What Is Social Ecofeminism?" *Green Perspectives*. 11:1–8.

— — —. 1991. *Finding Our Way: Rethinking Ecofeminism Politics*. Boston: South End Press.

Bird, Elizabeth. 1987. "The Social Construction of Nature: Theoretical Approaches to the History of Environmental Problems." *Environmental Review* 11(4): 255–64.

— — —. 1993. "Nature As A Social Actor: Conversations in Biotechnology." Ph.D. Dissertation, History of Consciousness Program, University of California, Santa Cruz.

Black Women's Liberation Group. 1970. "Statement on Birth Control." In *Sisterhood is Powerful*, edited by Robin Morgan. New York: Vintage 360–61.

Bookchin, Murray. 1971. *Post-Scarcity Anarchism*. San Francisco: Ramparts Press.

— — —. 1980. "Open Letter to the Ecology Movement." In *Toward an Ecological Society*. Montreal: Black Rose Books.

— — —. 1981. "The Concept of Social Ecology." *CoEvolution Quarterly* : 15–22.

— — —. 1991. *The Ecology of Freedom*. Montreal: Black Rose Books.

— — —. 1991. "Looking for Common Ground." In *Defending the Earth: A Dialogue Between Murray Bookchin and Dave Foreman*, edited by Steve Chase. Boston: South End Press.

Braidotti, Rosi. 1994. *Nomadic Subjects: Embodiment and Sexual Difference in Contemporary Feminist Theory*. New York: Columbia University.

Braidotti, Rosi, Ewa Charkiewicz, Sabine Häusler, Saskia Wieringa. 1994. *Women, the Environment and Sustainable Development*. London: Zed Books.

Brenner, Johanna. 1988. "Beyond Essentialism: Feminist Theory and Strategy in the Peace Movement." In *Reshaping the U.S. Left: Popular Struggles in the 1980s*, edited by Mike Davis and Michael Sprinker. New York: Verso, 93–113.

Buege, Douglas. 1994. "Rethinking Again," In *Ecological Feminism*, edited by Karen J. Warren. London and New York: Routledge, 42–63.

Bullard, Robert D. 1990. *Dumping in Dixie: Race, Class and Environmental Quality*. San Francisco: Westview.

Bullard, Robert D., ed. 1993. *Confronting Environmental Racism: Voices from the Grassroots*. Boston: South End Press.

Butler, Judith. 1992. "Contingent Foundations: Feminism and the Question of 'Postmodernism'." In *Feminists Theorize the Political*, edited by Judith Butler and Joan W. Scott. New York: Routledge, 3–21.

Caldecott, Leonie and Stephanie Leland, eds. 1983. *Reclaim the Earth: Women Speak Out for Life on Earth*. London: The Women's Press.

Carlassare, Elizabeth. 1994. "Essentialism in Ecofeminist Discourse." In *Ecology: Key Concepts in Critical Theory*, edited by Carolyn Merchant. Atlantic Highlands, NJ: Humanities Press, 220–34.

Charkiewicz, Ewa. 1994. "Ecofeminism: Challenges and Contradictions." In *Women, the Environment and Sustainable Development*, edited by Rosi Braidotti, Ewa Charkiewicz, Sabine Häusler, Saskia Wieringa. London: Zed Books, 161–168.

Chavis, Benjamin and Charles Lee. 1987. *Toxic Wastes and Race in the United States.* New York: United Church of Christ Commission for Racial Justice.

Cheney, Jim. 1987. "Ecofeminism and Deep Ecology." *Environmental Ethics* 9: 115–45.

———. 1989. "The Neo-Stoicism of Radical Environmentalism." *Environmental Ethics* 11: 293–325.

Christ, Carol. 1987. *Laughter of Aphrodite: Reflections on a Journey to the Goddess.* San Francisco: Harper & Row.

Christ, Carol and Judith Plaskow, eds. 1979. *Womanspirit Rising: A Feminist Reader in Religion.* New York: Harper & Row.

Circles, Loose Hip. 1989. "Riotous Rendezvous Remembered." *The Earth First! Journal* (August 1): 19.

Cohn, Carol. 1987. "Sex and Death in the Rational World of Defense Intellectuals." *Signs* 12: 687–718.

Collard, Andreé with Joyce Contrucci. 1988. *Rape of the Wild: Man's Violence Against Animals and the Earth.* Bloomington: Indiana University Press.

Combahee River Collective, 1982. "A Black Feminist Statement." In *But Some of Us Were Brave: Black Women's Studies*, edited by Gloria T. Hull, Patricia Smith, and Barbara Smith. New York, Feminist Press, pp. 13–22.

Crosby, Cristina. 1992. "Dealing with Differences." in Judith Butler and Joan W. Scott, eds., *Feminists Theorize the Political*. New York: Routledge, 130–47.

Cuevas, Maria. 1996. "Community Work as Family Work: Chicana Community Empowerment Strategies in Los Angeles." Paper presented at American Movement Cultures: Boundaries, Borders, Bodies conference at Washington State University, June.

Cuomo, Christine J. 1994. "Ecofeminism, Deep Ecology, and Human Population." In *Ecological Feminism*, edited by Karen J. Warren. New York: Routledge, 88–105.

———. 1996. "Toward Thoughtful Ecofeminist Action." In *Ecological Feminist Philosophies*, edited by Karen J. Warren. Bloomington: Indiana University, 42–51.

Curtin, Deane. 1994. "Dogen, Deep Ecology, and the Ecological Self." *Environmental Ethics* 16: 195–213.

d'Eaubonne, Françoise. 1974. *Le Féminisme ou la Mort*. Paris: Pierre Horay.

———. 1980. "Feminism or Death?" In *New French Feminisms: An Anthology* , edited by Elaine Marks and Isabelle de Courtivron. Amherst: University of Massachusetts Press, 64–67.

———. 1994. "The Time for Ecofeminism." In *Ecology: Key Concepts in Critical Theory*, edited by Carolyn Merchant, translated by Ruth Hottel. Atlantic Highlands, NJ: Humanities Press,174–97.

Daly, Mary. 1978. *Gyn/Ecology* . Boston: Beacon Press, 1978.

Dankelman, Irene and Joan Davidson. 1988. *Women and Environment in the Third World*. London: Earthscan Publications.

Darnovsky, Marcy, Barbara Epstein and Richard Flacks, eds. *Cultural Politics and Social Movements*. Philadelphia: Temple University

Davion, Victoria. 1994. "Is Ecofeminism Feminist?" In *Ecological Feminism*, edited by Karen J. Warren. New York: Routledge, 8–28.

Davis, Angela. 1981. *Women, Race and Class*. New York: Random House.

———. 1985. *Violence Against Women and the Ongoing Challenge to Racism* (Freedom Organizing Series 5). Latham, NY: Kitchen Table.

Davis, Donald. 1986. "Ecosophy: The Seduction of Sophia." *Environmental Ethics* 8: 151–62.

de Lauretis, Teresa. 1989. "The Essence of the Triangle, or, Taking the Risk of Essentialism Seriously: Feminist Theory in Italy, the U.S., and Britain." *differences* 1: 3–37.

———. 1990. "Upping the Anti (sic) in Feminist Theory." In *Conflicts in Feminism*, edited by Marianne Hirsch and Evelyn Fox Keller. London and New York: Routledge, 254–70.

de Oliveira, Rosiska Darcy and Thais Corral, *Terra Femina*. Rio de Janeiro: A Joint Publication of Institute for Cultural Action [IDAC] and The Network in Defense of Human Species [REDEH].

Deckard, Barbara. 1983. *The Women's Movement*. New York: Harper & Row.

Devall, Bill. 1990. "Maybe the Movement Is Leaving Me." *The Earth First! Journal* (September 22): 6.

di Leonardo, Micaela. 1985. "Morals, Mothers, and Militarism: Antimilitarism and Feminist Theory." *Feminist Studies* 11: 599–617.

Di Chiro, Giovanna. 1992. "Defining Environmental Justice: Women's Voices and Grassroots Politics." *Socialist Review* 22(4): 93–130.

Diamond, Irene. 1994. *Fertile Ground: Women, Earth, and the Limits of Control*. Boston: Beacon Press.

Diamond, Irene and Gloria Feman Orenstein. 1988. "Ecofeminism: Weaving the Worlds Together." *Feminist Studies* 14: 368–70.

Diamond, Irene and Gloria Feman Orenstein, eds. 1990. *Reweaving the World: The Emergence of Ecofeminism*. San Francisco: Sierra Club Books.

Dobson, Andrew, ed. 1991. *The Green Reader*. San Francisco: Mercury Books.

Donovan, Josephine. 1985. *Feminist Theory: The Intellectual Traditions of American Feminism*. New York: Frederick Ungar.

Drengson, Alan and Yuichi Inoue, eds. *The Deep Ecology Movement: An Introductory Anthology*. Berkeley, CA: North Atlantic Books.

Dreyfuss, Richard. 1995. "James Bond, Meet Captain Planet! The CIA is Aiming at Environmental Command and Control." *Environmental Magazine* 6(1) (January): 28.

Easlea, Brian. 1981. *Science and Sexual Oppression: Patriarchy's Confrontation with Women and Nature*. London: Weidenfeld and Nicholson.

Echols, Alice. 1983. "The New Feminism of Yin and Yang." In *Powers of Desire: The Politics of Sexuality*, edited by Christine Stansell, Ann Snitow, and Sharon Thompson. New York: Monthly Review Press, 439–59.

———. 1986. *Daring to Be Bad*. Minneapolis: University of Minnesota Press.

Eisenstein, Zillah. 1982. "The Sexual Politics of the New Right: Understanding the 'Crisis of Liberalism' for the 1980s." *Signs* 7: 567–88.

Eisler, Riane. 1988. *The Chalice and the Blade*. San Francisco: Harper & Row.

Engels, Frederich. 1972. *The Origin of the Family, Private Property, and the State*, translated by Eleanor Leacock. New York: International Publishers.

Enloe, Cynthia. 1983. *Does Khaki Become You? The Militarization of Women's Lives*. Boston: South End Press.

Epstein, Barbara. 1991. *Political Protest and Cultural Revolution: Nonviolent Direct Action in the 1970s and 1980s*. Berkeley: University of California Press.

———. 1995. "Why Poststructuralism is a Dead End for Progressive Thought," *Socialist Review* 25(2): 83–120.

Espinosa, Maria Fernanda, 1996. "Indigenous Women on Stage: New Agendas and Political Processes Among Indigenous Women in the Ecuadorian Amazon." Paper presented at the Feminist Generations Conference, Bowling Green State University, February. Revised for "Intersections of Environmentalism and Feminism." Special issue edited by Noël Sturgeon. *Frontiers: A Journal of Women Studies* 18(2), Forthcoming 1997.

Faludi, Susan. 1991. *Backlash*. New York: Crown Books.

Ferguson, Kathy. 1993. *The Man Question: Visions of Subjectivity in Feminist Theory*. Berkeley: University of California Press.

Feinman, Ilene Rose. 1997. "Brutal Responsibilities and Second Class Citizens: Women Soldiers, Martial Citizenship, and Feminist Antimilitarism." Ph.D. Dissertation, History of Consciousness Program, University of California, Santa Cruz.

Ferree, Myra Marx and Beth B. Hess, *Controversy and Coalition: The New Feminist Movement*. Boston: Twayne Publishers.

Foreman, Dave and Nancy Morton. 1990. "Good Luck Darlin'. It's Been Great." *The Earth First! Journal* (September 22): 5.

Foucault, Michel. 1977. "Nietzsche, Genealogy, History" In *Language, Counter-Memory, Practice*, edited and translated by D. F. Bouchard. Ithaca, NY: Cornell University Press, 139–64.

Fox, Warwick. 1989. "The Deep Ecology-Ecofeminism Debate and Its Parallels." *Environmental Ethics* 11: 5–25.

———. 1995. "Transpersonal Ecology and the Varieties of Identification." In *The Deep Ecology Movement: An Introductory Anthology*, edited by Alan Drengson and Yuichi Inoue. Berkeley, CA: North Atlantic Books, 136–154.

Frankenberg, Ruth. 1993. *White Women, Race Matters: The Social Construction of Whiteness*. Minneapolis: University of Minnesota Press.

Franklin, H. Bruce. 1988. "Domesticating the Bomb: Nuclear Weapons in *Testament* and the Fiction of Judith Merrill, Helen Clarkson, Kate Wilhelm and Carol Amen." Paper presented at the American Studies Association Conference, Miami Beach, October 1988.

Freeman, Jo. 1979. "The Women's Liberation Movement: Its Origins, Organizations, Activities, and Ideas." In *Women: A Feminist Perspective*. Palo Alto, CA: Mayfield, 448–460.

Frye, Marilyn. "The Possibility of Feminist Theory." In *Theoretical Perspectives on Sexual Difference*, edited by Deborah Rhodes. New Haven: Yale University Press, 174–184.

Fuss, Diana. 1989. *Essentially Speaking*. London and New York.

Gaard, Greta. 1992. Review of Janet Biehl's *Rethinking Ecofeminist Politics*. *Women and Environments*: 20–21.

———. 1992. "Finding a Home in the World" *The Ecofeminist Newsletter* 3(1):7. Available from Women's Studies, Washington State University, Pullman, WA, 99164-4007, USA.

———. 1993. "Living Interconnections with Animals and Nature." In *Ecofeminism: Women, Animals, Nature*, edited by Greta Gaard. Philadelphia: Temple University Press, 1–12.

———. 1993. "Ecofeminism and Native American Cultures: Pushing the Limits of Cultural Imperialism?" in Gaard, *Ecofeminism*, pp. 295–314.

———. ed. 1993. *Ecofeminism: Women, Animals, Nature*. Philadelphia: Temple University Press.

———. 1994. *Thinking Green: Ecofeminists and The Greens*. Medusa Productions. VHS, 35 minutes. Available for $15 plus shipping from Dr. Greta Gaard, Department of English, 420 Humanities Building, University of Minnesota, Duluth, MN, 55812.

———. 1994. "Misunderstanding Ecofeminism," *Z Magazine* 3(1): 22.

———. 1996. *Ecofeminism Now!* Medusa Productions, VHS, 37 minutes. Available for $15 plus shipping from Dr. Greta Gaard, Department of English, 420 Humanities Building, University of Minnesota, Duluth, MN, 55812.

———. Forthcoming. "Toward a Queer Ecofeminism." *Hypatia*.

———. Forthcoming. *Ecological Politics: Ecofeminists and the Greens*. Philadelphia: Temple University Press.

Gaard, Greta and Lori Gruen. 1993. "Ecofeminism: Toward Global Justice and Planetary Health," *Society and Nature*, 2(1) : 1–35.

Gaard, Greta and Patrick Murphy, eds. Forthcoming. "Ecofeminist Literary Criticism." Special Issue. *ISLE*.

Garb, Yaakov. 1990. "Perspective or Escape? Ecofeminist Musings on Contemporary Earth Imagery." In *Reweaving the World: The Emergence of Ecofeminism*, edited by Irene Diamond and Gloria Orenstein. San Francisco: Sierra Club, 264–78.

Garrison, Ednie. 1996. "The Third Wave and Postmodern Cultural Conditions: Feminist Consciousness in the 1990s." Paper presented at the Feminist Generations Conference, Bowling Green State University, February.

Gedick, Al, ed. 1993. *The New Resource Wars: Native and Environmental Struggles Against Multinational Corporations*. Boston: South End Press, 1993.

Gentine, Kerri Dyan. 1996. "Earth Mothers and Riot Grrrls: Why My Mother May Never Be My Sister." Paper presented at the Feminist Generations Conference, Bowling Green State University, February.

Gimbutas, Marie. 1989. *The Language of the Goddess*. San Francisco: Harper & Row.

Gottlieb, Robert. 1993. "Reconstructing Environmentalism: Complex Movements, Diverse Roots." *Environmental History Review*: 1–19.

Gray, Elizabeth Dodson. 1979. *Green Paradise Lost*. Wellesley, MA: Roundtable Press.

Greenhouse, Steven. 1995. "The Greening of American Diplomacy," *New York Times* (October 9): A4.

Griffin, Susan. 1978. *Women and Nature: The Roaring Inside Her*. San Francisco: Harper & Row.

Guha, Ramachandra. 1989. "Radical American Environmentalism and Wilderness Preservation: A Third World Critique." *Environmental Ethics* 11(1): 71–83.

Gyorgy, Anna and Friends. 1979. *No Nukes*. Boston: South End Press, 1979.

Gyorgy, Anna. 1981. "Evaluating Eco-Feminism West Coast." *Tidings* (May 1981): 14.

Haney, Elly. 1993. "Towards a White Feminist Ecological Ethic." *Journal of Feminist Studies in Religion* 9(1–2): 75–93.

Haraway, Donna. 1989. *Primate Visions: Gender, Race, and Nature in the World of Modern Science*. New York: Routledge.

— — —. 1991. "A Cyborg Manifesto: Science, Technology and Socialist-Feminism in the Late Twentieth Century." In *Simians, Cyborgs and Women: The Reinvention of Nature*. New York: Routledge, 149–82.

— — —. 1991. "Situated Knowledges: The Science Question in Feminism and the Privilege of Partial Perspective." in *Simians, Cyborgs, and Women: The Reinvention of Nature*. New York: Routledge, 183–202.

— — —. 1991. "Overhauling the Meaning Machines." Interview with Marcy Darnovsky. *Socialist Review* 21:2 (1991): 65–84.

— — —. 1992. "The Promises of Monsters: A Regenerated Politics for Inappropriate/d Others." In *Cultural Studies*, edited by Lawrence Grossberg, Cary Nelson, and Paula Treichler, with Linda Baughman and John Wise. New York: Routledge, 295–337.

Harden, Lakota. 1991. "Wiconi/Survival." In *Visionary Voices: Women on Power*, edited by Penny Rossenwasser. San Francisco: Aunt Lute, 217–32.

Harding, Sandra. 1986. *The Science Question in Feminism*. Ithaca, NY: Cornell University Press.

— — —. 1993. "Reinventing Ourselves as Other: More New Agents of History and Knowledge." In *American Feminist Thought at Century's End*, edited by Linda S. Kaufmann. Cambridge, MA: Basil Blackwell, 140–64.

Häusler, Sabine. 1994. "Women, the Environment, and Sustainable Development: Emergence of the Theme and Different Views." In *Women, the Environment, and Sustainable Development*, edited by Rosi Braidotti, Ewa Charkiewicz, Sabine Häusler, and Saksi Wieringa. London and Atlantic Highlands, New Jersey: Zed Books, 77–106.

Heller, Chaia. Forthcoming. "Down to the Body, Down to Earth: Toward a Social Ecofeminism." In *The Environmental Materialist Reader*, edited by Andrew Light. Minneapolis: University of Minnesota.

Heller, Chaia. Forthcoming. *The Revolution That Dances: From a Politics of Desire to a Desirable Politics*. Littleton, Colorado: Aigis Publications.

Higgins, Robert. 1994. "Race, Pollution, and the Mastery of Nature." *Environmental Ethics* 16:3: 251–64

Hodgson, Dorothy. 1995. "The Politics of Gender, Ethnicity, and 'Development': Images, Interventions, and the Reconfiguration of Maasai Identities, 1916–1993." Ph.D. Dissertation, Department of Anthropology, University of Michigan, 1995.

— — —. 1995. "Critical Interventions: The Politics of Studying 'Indigenous Development'." Paper presented at the American Anthropological Association meeting in Washington, D.C., November.

Hofrichter, Richard, ed. 1993. *Toxic Struggles: The Theory and Practice of Environmental Justice*. Philadelphia: New Society Publishers.

hooks, bell. 1990. "Feminism: A Transformational Politic." In *Theoretical Perspectives on Sexual Difference*, edited by Deborah L. Rhodes. New Haven: Yale University Press, 185–93.

Hurwitz, Deena, ed. 1992. *Walking the Red Line: Israelis in Search of Justice for Palestine*. Philadephia: New Society Publishers.

Jackson, Cecile. 1993. "Women/Nature or Gender History? A Critique of Ecofeminist 'Development'." *Journal of Peasant Studies* 20(3): 389–419.

Jacobs, Jane. 1994. "Earth Honoring: Western Desires and Indigenous Knowledges." In *Writing Women and Space: Colonial and Postcolonial Geographies*, edited by Alison Blunt and Gilliam Rose. New York: Guilford, 169–96.

Jaggar, Alison M. 1983. *Feminist Politics and Human Nature*. Totowa, NJ: Rowman & Allanheld.

Jaggar, Alison M. and Paula S. Rothenberg. 1978, 1984, 1993. *Feminist Frameworks: Alternative Theoretical Accounts of the Relations Between Women and Men*. New York: McGraw-Hill.

Jenkins, Craig. 1983. "Resource Mobilization Theory and the Study of Social Movements." *Annual Review of Sociology* 9: 527–53

Jones, Lynne, ed. 1983. *Keeping the Peace*. London: Women's Press.

Kaplan, Robert D. 1994. "The Coming Anarchy," *Atlantic Monthly* 273 (February): 44–76.

Kelber, Mim. 1994. "The Women's Environment and Development Organization." *Environment* 36(8): 43–45.

Kheel, Marti. 1985. "The Liberation of Nature: A Circular Affair." *Environmental Ethics*: 135–49.

———. 1990. "Ecofeminism and Deep Ecology: Reflections on Identity and Difference." In *Reweaving the World: The Emergence of Ecofeminism*, edited by Irene Diamond and Gloria Orenstein. San Francisco: Sierra Club Books, 127–37.

Kile, Crystal. 1996. "Hello Kitty Explains Kinderwhore to You: Third Wave Feminism and Riot Grrrl Style." Paper presented at the Feminist Generations Conference, Bowling Green State University, February.

King, Katie. 1986. "The Situation of Lesbianism as Feminism's Magical Sign: Contests for Meaning and the U.S. Women's Movement, 1968–1972." *Communication* 9: 65–91.

———. 1994. *Theory in Its Feminist Travels: Conversations in U.S. Women's Movements*. Bloomington, IN: Indiana University Press.

King, Roger J. H. 1996. "Caring About Nature: Feminist Ethics and the Environment." In *Ecological Feminist Philosophies*, edited by Karen J. Warren. Bloomington: Indiana University, 82–96.

King, Ynestra. 1981. "Feminism and the Revolt of Nature." *Heresies* 13: 12–15.

———. 1983. "All is Connectedness." In *Keeping the Peace*, edited by Lynne Jones. London: Women's Press, 40–63.

———. 1983. "The Eco-Feminist Imperative." In *Reclaim the Earth: Women Speak Out for Life on Earth*, edited by Leonie Caldecott and Stephanie Leland. London: The Women's Press, 12–16.

———. 1983. "Toward an Ecological Feminism and a Feminist Ecology." In *Machina Ex Dea: Feminist Perspectives on Technology*, edited by Joan Rothschild. New York: Pergamon, 118–129.

———. 1984. "Where the Spiritual and Political Come Together." *Women For Life on Earth*: 4.

———. 1987. "What Is Ecofeminism?" *The Nation* (December 12): 702, 730–731.

———. 1988. "Ecological Feminism." *Z Magazine* 1(7/8): 124–27.

———. 1989. "The Ecology of Feminism and the Feminism of Ecology." In *Healing the Wounds*, edited by Judith Plant. Santa Cruz, CA: New Society Publishers, 18–28.

———. 1990. "Healing the Wounds: Feminism, Ecology, and the Nature/Culture

Dualism." In *Reweaving the World: The Emergence of Ecofeminism,* edited by Irene Diamond and Gloria Feman Orenstein. San Francisco: Sierra Club Books, 106–21.

———. 1990. *What is Ecofeminism?* New York: Ecofeminist Resources. Available from Ecofeminist Resources, c/o Women's Studies Program, Antioch College, Yellow Springs, OH 45387 for U.S. $3.50.

———. Forthcoming. *Ecofeminism: The Reenchantment of Nature.* Boston: Beacon Press.

Kirk, Gwyn. 1992. "Blood, Bones, and Connective Tissue: Grassroots Women Resist Ecological Destruction." Paper presented at the National Women Studies Association, Austin, June.

Klein, Hilary. 1989. "Marxism, Pyschoanalysis and Mother Nature," in *Feminist Studies* 15(2): 255–78.

Krasniewicz, Louise. 1992. *Nuclear Summer: The Clash of Communities at the Seneca Women's Peace Encampment.* Ithaca, NY: Cornell University Press.

Kraus, Celene. 1993. "Blue-Collar Women and Toxic-Waste Protests: The Process of Politicization." In *Toxic Struggles: The Theory and Practice of Environmental Justice,* edited by Richard Hofrichter. Philadelphia: New Society Publishers, 107–17.

La Chappelle, Dolores. 1989. "No, I'm Not an Eco-Feminist: A Few Words in Defense of Men." *The Earth First! Journal* (March 21): 31.

LaDuke, Winona. 1992. "The Legacy of Columbus: What It Means for Women and the Environment." Talk delivered at Washington State University, September 1992.

Lahar, Stephanie. 1996. "Ecofeminist Theory and Grassroots Politics." In *Ecological Feminist Philosophies,* edited by Karen J. Warren. Bloomington: Indiana University, 1–18.

Landsberg, Michele. 1991. "Overview," In *Official Report: World Women's Congress for a Healthy Planet.* New York: WEDO, 2–3.

Leach, Melissa. 1994. *Rainforest Relations: Gender and Resource Use Among the Mende of Gola, Sierra Leone.* Washington, DC: Smithsonian Institution Press.

Li, Huey-li. 1993. "A Cross-Cultural Critique of Ecofeminism." In *Ecofeminism: Women, Animals, Nature,* edited by Greta Gaard. Philadelphia: Temple University Press, 272–94.

Linton, Rhoda and Michele Whitham. 1982. "With Mourning, Rage, Empowerment and Defiance: The 1981 Women's Pentagon Action." *Socialist Review* 12(3/4): 11–36.

Longauex y Vasquez, Enriqueta. 1970. "The Mexican-American Woman." In *Sisterhood is Powerful,* edited by Robin Morgan. New York: Vintage, 379–84.

Lorde, Audre. 1981. "The Master's Tools Will Never Dismantle the Master's House." In *This Bridge Called My Back,* edited by Cherrie Moraga and Gloria Anzaldua. Watertown, MA: Persephone Press, 98–101.

———. 1984. *Sister Outsider: Essays and Speeches.* Trumansburg, NY: Crossing Press.

Maendler, Monika. 1997. "An Analysis of the Environmental Justice Movement in the United States: Environmentalism Redefined in Terms of the Disadvantaged." M.A. Thesis, American Studies Program, Washington State University.

Manes, Christopher. 1990. *Green Rage: Radical Environmentalism and the Unmaking of Civilization.* Boston: Little, Brown.

Martin, Biddy and Chandra Talpade Mohanty. 1986. "Feminist Politics: What's Home Got to Do With It?" In *Feminist Studies/Critical Studies*, edited by Teresa de Lauretis. Bloomington: Indiana University Press, 191–212.

Martin, Calvin. 1981. "The American Indian as Miscast Ecologist." In *Ecological Consciousness*, edited by Robert C. Schultz and T. Donald Hughes. University Press of America, 136–148.

Martin, Jane Roland. 1994. "Methodological Essentialism, False Difference, and Other Dangerous Traps." *SIGNS* 19(3):630–657.

Mayer, Margit and Roland Roth. 1995. "New Social Movements and the Transformation to Post-Fordist Society." In *Cultural Politics and Social Movements*, edited by Marcy Darnovsky, Barbara Epstein, and Richard Flacks. Philadelphia: Temple University, 299–319.

McDaniel, Judith, ed. 1982. *Reweaving the Web of Life: Feminism and Nonviolence*. Philadelphia: New Society Publishers.

McGregor, Gaile. 1994. "Re constructing environment: A cross-cultural perspective." *Canadian Review of Sociology and Anthropology* 31(3): 268–88.

Mellors, Mary. 1992. *Breaking the Boundaries: Toward a Feminist Green Socialism*. London: Virago Press.

Melucci, Alberto. 1989. *Nomads of the Present*. Philadelphia: Temple University Press.

Merchant, Carolyn. 1980. *The Death of Nature: Women, Ecology and the Scientific Revolution*. San Francisco: Harper & Row.

———. 1989. *Ecological Revolutions: Nature, Gender and Science in New England*. Chapel Hill: University of North Carolina Press.

———. 1990. "Ecofeminism and Feminist Theory." In *Reweaving the World: The Emergence of Ecofeminism*, Irene Diamond and Gloria Orenstein. San Francisco: New Society Publishers, 100–105.

———. 1992. "Ecofeminism." In *Radical Ecology: The Search for A Livable World*. New York: Routledge, 183–210.

———. ed. 1994. *Ecology: Key Concepts in Critical Theory*. Atlantic Highlands, NJ: Humanities Press.

———. 1996. *Earthcare: Women and the Environment*. London and New York: Routledge.

———. 1996. "Partnership Ethics: Earthcare for a New Millennium," in *Earthcare: Women and the Environment*. New York: Routledge, 209–24.

McDaniel, Judith. 1985. "One Summer at Seneca," *Heresies* 5: 6–10.

Mies, Maria. 1986. *Patriarchy and Accumulation on a World Scale*. London: Zed Books.

Mies, Maria and Vandana Shiva. 1993. *Ecofeminism*. London and Atlantic Highlands, NJ: Zed Press.

Miller, Vernice D. 1993. "Building on Our Past, Planning for Our Future: Communities of Color and the Quest for Environmental Justice." In *Toxic Struggles*, edited by Richard Hofrichter. Philadelphia: New Society Publishers, 128–37.

Minh-ha, Trinh T. 1989. *Woman, Native, Other: Writing Postcoloniality and Feminism*. Bloomington: Indiana University.

Mohanty, Chandra Talpade. 1991. "Cartographies of Struggle: Third World Women and the Politics of Feminism." In *Third World Women and the Politics of Feminism*, edited by Chandra Talpade Mohanty, Ann Russo, and Lourdes Torres. Bloomington and Indianapolis: Indiana University Press, 1–50.

— — —. 1991. "Under Western Eyes: Feminist Scholarship and Colonial Discourses. In *Third World Women and the Politics of Feminism*, edited by Chandra Talpade Mohanty, Ann Russo, and Lourdes Torres. Bloomington and Indianapolis: Indiana University Press, pp. 51–81.

Molina, Papusa. 1990. "Recognizing, Accepting and Celebrating Our Differences." In *Haciendo Caras: Making Face, Making Soul*, edited by Gloria Anzaldua. San Francisco: Aunt Lute, 326–31.

Moraga, Cherrie and Gloria Anzaldua, eds. 1981. *This Bridge Called My Back*. Watertown, MA: Persephone Press.

Morris, Aldon and Carol Mueller, eds. 1992. *Frontiers of New Social Movement Theory*. New Haven: Yale University Press.

Murray, Pauli Murray. 1970. "The Liberation of Black Women." In *Voices of the New Feminism*, edited by Mary Lou Thompson. Boston: Beacon Press, 87–102.

Naess, Arne. 1995. "The Shallow and the Deep, Long-Range Ecology Movement: A Summary." In *The Deep Ecology Movement: An Introductory Anthology*, edited by Alan Drengson and Yuichi Inoue. Berkeley, CA: North Atlantic Books, 3–10.

Norton, Eleanor Holmes. 1970. "For Sadie and Maude." In *Sisterhood is Powerful*, edited by Robin Morgan. New York: Vintage, 352–59.

Norwood, Vera. 1993. *Made From This Earth*. Chapel Hill: University of North Carolina Press.

Omi, Michael and Howard Winant. 1988. *Racial Formations in the United States*. New York: Routledge.

Ortner, Sherry. 1974. "Is Female to Male as Nature is to Culture?" In *Woman, Culture and Society*, edited by Michelle Z. Rosaldo and Louise Lamphere. Palo Alto, CA: Stanford, 7–88.

Participants of the Puget Sound Women's Peace Camp. 1985. *We Are Ordinary Women: A Chronicle of the Puget Sound Women's Peace Camp*. Seattle: Seal Press.

Petchesky, Rosalind. 1981. "Antiabortion, Antifeminism, and the Rise of the New Right." *Signs* 7: 206–46.

Pierson, Sher. 1988. Letter to the Editor. *The Earth First! Journal*, (December 21): 9.

Plant, Judith. 1989. "Toward a New World: Introduction." In *Healing the Wounds: The Promise of Ecofeminism*, edited by Judith Plant. Philadelphia: New Society, 3–4.

— — —. 1989. "The Circle is Gathering," In *Healing the Wounds: The Promise of Ecofeminism*, edited by Judith Plant. Philadelphia: New Society, 242–53.

Plant, Judith, ed. 1989. *Healing the Wounds: The Promise of Ecofeminism*. Philadelphia: New Society Publishers.

Plumwood, Val. 1991. "Nature, Self, and Gender: Feminism, Environmental Philosophy and the Critique of Rationalism." *Hypatia* 6: 3–27.

— — —. 1993. *Feminism and the Mastery of Nature*. London and New York: Routledge.

— — —. 1994. "Ecosocial Feminism as a General Theory of Oppression." In *Ecology: Key Concepts in Critical Theory*, edited by Carolyn Merchant. Atlantic Highlands, NJ: Humanities Press International, 207–219.

— — —. 1994. "The Ecopolitics Debate and the Politics of Nature. " In *Ecological Feminism*, edited by Karen J. Warren. New York: Routledge, 64–87.

— — —. 1995. "Human Vulnerability and the Experience of Being Prey," *Quadrant*: 2, 30–33.

Pulido, Laura. 1996. *Environmentalism and Economic Justice: Two Chicano Struggles in the Southwest*. Tucson, AZ: University of Arizona.

Radway, Janice. 1986. "Identifying Ideological Seams: Mass Culture, Analytical Method, and Political Practice," *Communications* 9: 93–123.

Rao, Brinda. 1991. "Dominant Constructions of Women and Nature in Social Science Literature." *Capitalism, Nature, Socialism,* Pamphlet 2. New York: Guilford Publications.

Reagon, Bernice Johnson. 1983. "Coalition Politics: Turning the Century." In *Home Girls: A Black Feminist Anthology,* edited by Barbara Smith. New York: Kitchen Table: Women of Color Press, 356–69.

Reed, T. V. 1992. "Dramatic Ecofeminism: The Women's Pentagon Action as Theater and Theory." *Fifteen Jugglers, Five Believers: Literary Politics and the Poetics of American Social Movements.* Berkeley: University of California Press, 120–141.

Regan, Tom. 1982. "Environmental Ethics and the Ambiguity of the Native American's Relationship with Nature." In *All That Dwell Therein: Animal Rights and Environmental Ethics.* Berkeley: University of California Press, 206–239.

Rich, Adrienne. 1980. "Compulsory Heterosexuality and Lesbian Existence." *SIGNS* 5: 631–60.

Roach, Catherine. 1996. "Loving Your Mother: On the Woman-Nature Relation." In *Ecological Feminist Philosophies,* edited by Karen J. Warren. Bloomington: Indiana University, 52–65.

Robinson, Patricia M. 1970. "A Historical and Critical Essay for Black Women." In *Women's Liberation: A Blueprint for the Future,* edited by Sookie Stambler. New York: Ace, 274–83.

Rocheleau, Diane, Barbara Thomas-Slayter, and Esther Wangari, eds. 1996. *Feminist Political Ecologies: Global Issues and Local Experiences.* New York: Routledge.

Roselle, Mike and Darryl Cherney. 1990. "Earth Night Action." Song Lyrics from *Timber* by Darryl Cherney with George Shook and Judi Bari.

Rosenwasser, Penny. 1992. *Visionary Voices: Women on Power.* San Francisco: Aunt Lute, 71–82.

Ruether, Rosemary Radford. 1975. *New Woman/New Earth: Sexist Ideologies and Human Liberation* . New York, Seabury Press.

— — —. 1992. *Gaia and God: An Ecofeminist Theology of Earth Healing.* San Francisco: Harper & Row.

Rucht, Dieter, ed. 1991. *Research on Social Movements: The State of the Art.* Frankfurt, Germany/Boulder, CO: Campus/Westview Press.

Salleh, Ariel. 1984. "Deeper Than Deep Ecology: The Eco-Feminist Connection." *Environmental Ethics* 6: 340–45.

— — —. 1991. Book review of Vandana Shiva's *Staying Alive. Hypatia* 6(1): 206.

— — —. 1992. "The Ecofeminism/Deep Ecology Debate: A Reply to Patriarchal Reason." *Environmental Ethics* 14: 195–216.

— — —. 1993. "Class, Race, and Gender Discourse in the Ecofeminism/Deep Ecology Debate." *Environmental Ethics* 15: 225–44.

Sandoval, Chéla. n.d. *Women Respond to Racism: A Report on the National Women's Studies Association Conference.* Oakland, CA: Center for Third World Organizing.

— — —. 1990. "Feminism and Racism: A Report on the 1981 National Women's Studies Association Conference." In *Making Face, Making Soul: Haciendo Caras,* edited by Gloria Anzaldua. San Francisco: Aunt Lute, 55–71.

— — —. 1991. "U.S. Third World Feminism: The Theory and Method of Oppositional Consciousness in the Postmodern World." *Genders* 10: 1–24.

— — —. 1995. "New Sciences: Cyborg Feminism and the Methodology of the

Oppressed." In *The Cyborg Handbook*, edited by Chris Hables Gray, with Heidi J. Figueroa-Sarriera and Steven Mentor. New York: Routledge, 407–422.

Scarce, Rik. 1990. *EcoWarriors: Understanding the Radical Environmental Movement*. Chicago: Noble Press.

Schroeder, Richard. 1993. "Shady Practice: Gender and the Political Ecology of Resource Stabilization in Gambian Garden/Orchards." *Economic Geography* 69(4): 349–65.

— — —. 1995. "Co-opted Critiques: Gender, Environment and Development Discourse." Paper presented at the American Anthropological Association meeting in Washington, D.C., November.

Scott, Joan. 1990. "Deconstructing Equality-Versus-Difference: Or, the Uses of Post-structuralist Theory for Feminism." In *Conflicts in Feminism*, edited by Marianne Hirsch and Evelyn Fox Keller. London and New York: Routledge, 134–48.

— — —. 1992. "Experience," In *Feminists Theorize the Political*, edited by Judith Butler and Joan W. Scott. New York, Routledge, 22–40.

Seager, Joni. 1993. *Earth Follies: Coming to Feminist Terms With the Global Environmental Crisis*. New York: Routledge.

Sequoia. 1989. Letter to the Editor. *Earth First! Journal* (February): 5.

Sessions, Robert. 1991. "Deep Ecology versus Ecofeminism: Healthy Differences or Incompatible Philosophies?" *Hypatia* 6: 90–107.

Sessions, George. 1995. *Deep Ecology for the 21st Century: Readings on the Philosophy and Practice of the New Environmentalism*. Boston: Shambala.

Shiva, Vandana. 1988. *Staying Alive: Women, Ecology and Development in India*. London: Zed Press.

— — —. ed., 1994. *Close to Home: Women Reconnect Ecology, Health and Development Worldwide*. Philadelphia: New Society Publishers.

Shiva, Vandana and Inguna Moser, eds. 1995. *Biopolitics: A Feminist and Ecological Reader on Biotechnoology*. London: Zed Books.

Shumway, David. 1989. *Michel Foucault*. Charlottesville: University Press of Virginia.

Slicer, Deborah. 1995. "Is There an Ecofeminism-Deep Ecology 'Debate'?" *Environmental Ethics* 17: 151–69.

Smith, Andy. 1991. "For All Those Who Were Indian in a Former Life," *Ms.* (November–December): 44–45.

Smith, Michael Peter. 1994. "Can You Imagine? Transnational Migration and the Globalization of Grassroots Politics." *Social Text* 39: 15–33.

Sofia, Zoë. 1984. "Exterminating Fetuses: Abortion, Disarmament, and the Sexo-Semiotics of Extraterrestrialism." *Diacritics* 14: 47–59.

Spelman, Elizabeth V. 1988. *Inessential Woman: Problems of Exclusion in Feminist Thought*. Boston: Beacon.

Spretnak, Charlene. 1982. *The Politics of Women's Spirituality: Essays on the Rise of Spiritual Power Within the Feminist Movement*. New York: Anchor Books.

— — —. 1993. Letter to the Editor. *The Ecofeminist Newsletter* 4(1): 3–4. Available from Women's Studies, Washington State University, Pullman, WA, USA, 99164–4007.

Starhawk. 1982. *Dreaming the Dark*. Boston: Beacon Press

— — —. 1985. *Truth or Dare*. San Francisco: Harper & Row.

— — —. 1988. *The Spiral Dance: A Rebirth of the Ancient Religion of the Great Goddess*. San Francisco: Harper & Row.

— — —. 1993. *The Fifth Sacred Thing*. New York: Bantam.

Stone, Merlin. 1979. *When God Was a Woman*. New York: Dial Press.

Sturgeon, Noël. 1991. "Direct Theory and Political Action: The U.S. Nonviolent Direct Action Movement, 1976–1987." Ph.D. Dissertation, History of Consciousness Board, University of California at Santa Cruz.

———. 1994. "Positional Feminism, Ecofeminism, and Radical Feminism Revisited," *American Philosophical Newsletter of Feminism and Philosophy*, 93(1): 41–47.

———. 1995. "Theorizing Movements: Direct Action and Direct Theory." In *Cultural Politics and Social Movements*, edited by Marcy Darnovsky, Barbara Epstein, and Richard Flacks. Philadelphia: Temple University, 35–51.

———. 1997. "The Nature of Race: Discourses of Racial Difference in Ecofeminism." In *Ecofeminism: Women, Nature and Culture*, edited by Karen J. Warren. Bloomington, Indiana: Indiana University Press, 260–78.

———. Forthcoming. "Ecofeminist Appropriations and Transnational Environmentalisms." *Identities: Global Studies in Culture and Power*. Special issue entitled "Unintended Consequences: On the Practice of Transnational Cultural Critique," edited by Peter Brosius.

———. ed. Forthcoming. "Intersections of Environmentalism and Feminism." Special issue of *Frontiers: A Journal of Women Studies* 18(2).

Sutherland, Elizabeth. 1970. "Introduction." In *Sisterhood is Powerful*, edited by Robin Morgan. New York: Vintage, 376–78.

Sverdrup, Amber. 1992. "Inspirational Messages, Inconsistent Practices." *The Ecofeminist Newsletter* 3(1):6. Available from Women's Studies, Washington State University, Pullman, WA, 99164-4007, USA.

Synder, George. 1995. "Indians Protest Rip-off Spirituality." *San Francisco Chronicle*. (December 25): A1, A10.

Szasz, Andrew. 1994. *Ecopopulism: Toxic Waste and the Movement for Environmental Justice*. Minneapolis: University of Minnesota Press.

Taylor, Peter J. and Frederick H. Buttell. 1992. "How Do We Know We Have Global Environmental Problems? Science and the Globalization of Environmental Discourse." *Geoforum* 23(3): 405–16.

Teish, Luisah. 1985. *Jambalaya*. San Francisco: Harper Collins.

Thropy, Miss Ann. 1987. "Population and AIDs." *The Earth First! Journal* (May 1): 32.

———. 1987. "Miss Ann Thropy Responds to 'Alien-Nation'." *The Earth First! Journal* (December 22): 17.

Touraine, Alain. 1981. *The Voice and the Eye*. Cambridge: Cambridge University Press.

Tsing, Anna. 1997. "Environmentalisms: Transitions as Translations." In *Transitions, Translations, Environments: International Feminism in Contemporary Politics*, edited by Joan Scott, Cora Kaplan, and Debra Keates. New York, Routledge.

UNIFEM. n.d. *Agenda 21: An Easy Reference to the Specific Recommendations on Women*. New York: UNIFEM. Available from UNIFEM, 304 East 45th Street, 6th Floor, New York, NY, 10017.

van den Hombergh, Heleen. 1993. *Gender, Environment and Development: A Guide to the Literature*. Utrecht: International Books.

Van Gelder, Lindsy. 1989. "It's Not Nice to Mess With Mother Nature." *Ms*. (January–February): 60–63

Vance, Carol S. ed. 1984. *Pleasure and Danger: Explorations of Female Sexuality*. Boston: Routledge and Kegan Paul.

Walker, Alice. 1983. "Only Justice Can Stop a Curse." In *In Search of Our Mother's Gardens*. San Diego: Harcourt Brace Jovanovich, 338–42.

———. 1988. "Am I Blue?" In *Living By The Word*. San Diego: Harcourt Brace Jovanovich, 3–8.

Wallace, Aubrey. 1993. "Sowing Seeds of Hope: Wangari Maathai, Kenya." In *Eco-Heroes: Twelve Tales of Environmental Victory*, edited by David Gancher. San Francisco: Mercury House, 1–22.

Wallace, Michele. 1990. *Black Macho and the Myth of the Superwoman*. New York: Verso.

Ware, Cellestine. 1970. *Woman Power: The Movement for Women's Liberation*. New York: Tower.

Warnock, Donna. 1982. "Mobilizing Emotions: Organizing the Women's Pentagon Action." *Socialist Review* 63/64: 37–47.

Warren, Karen. 1987. "Feminism and Ecology: Making Connections." *Environmental Ethics* 9(1): 3–20.

———. 1988. "Toward an Ecofeminist Ethic," *Studies in the Humanities* 15: 140–56.

———. 1993. "A Feminist Philosophical Perspective on Ecofeminist Spiritualities," In *Ecofeminism and the Sacred*, edited by Carol Adams. New York: Continuum Press, 119–32.

———. ed. 1994. *Ecological Feminism*. New York: Routledge.

———. ed. 1996. *Ecological Feminist Philosophies*. Indianapolis: Indiana University Press/Hypatia.

———. ed. 1997. *Ecofeminism: Women, Nature, Culture* (Bloomington: Indiana University Press.

Warren, Karen and Jim Cheney. Forthcoming. *Ecological Feminism: What It Is and Why It Matters*. Boulder, CO: Westview Press.

Weathers, Maryanne. 1970. "An Argument for Black Women's Liberation as a Revolutionary Force." In *Women's Liberation: A Blueprint for the Future*, edited by Sookie Stambler. New York: Ace, 161–64.

Weedon, Chris. 1987. *Feminist Practice and Poststructuralist Theory*. Oxford: Basil Blackwell.

Willis, Ellen. 1980. Column in *The Village Voice* 25(25) (June 18–24): 28.

———. 1980. Column in *The Village Voice* 25(29) (July 16–22): 34.

———. 1984. "Radical Feminism and Feminist Radicalism." In *The Sixties Without Apology*, edited by Sohnya Sayres, Anders Stephanson, Stanley Aronowitz, and Fredric Jameson. Minneapolis: University of Minnesota, 91–118.

Wilson, Marie. 1992. "Wings of the Eagle: A Conversation with Marie Wilson." In *Healing the Wounds: The Promise of Ecofeminism*, edited by Judith Plant. Philadelphia: New Society, 212–18.

Wittbecker, Alan. 1986. "Deep Anthropology, Ecology, and Human Order." *Environmental Ethics* 8: 268–70.

Wolke, Howie. 1988. "The Grizzly Den." *The Earth First! Journal* (November 1): 28.

———. 1990. "FOCUS On Wilderness." *The Earth First! Journal* (September 22): 7.

Women's Environment and Development Organization. 1991. "Findings of the Tribunal." In *Official Report: World Women's Congress for a Healthy Planet*. New York: WEDO, 2.

Young, Alison. 1990. *Femininity in Dissent*. New York: Routledge.

Young, Shelagh. 1994. Review of Janet Biehl's *Rethinking Ecofeminist Politics*. *Feminist Review* 48: 130.

Zapotes, Simon "De Beaulivar." 1991. "Fucking With Mother Nature: A Critique of Humor, Art, and Eco-Pornography." *The Earth First! Journal* (May 1): 32–33.

Zimmerman, Michael E. 1987. "Feminism, Deep Ecology, and Environmental Ethics." *Environmental Ethics* 9: 21–44.

———. 1990. "Deep Ecology and Ecofeminism: The Emerging Dialogue." In *Reweaving the World: The Emergence of Ecofeminism*, edited by Irene Diamond and Gloria Orenstein. San Francisco: Sierra Club Books, 138–54.

Index